Mastering QuickBooks 2025
Sixth Edition

Bookkeeping for small businesses with US QuickBooks® Online

Crystalynn Shelton, CPA

Mastering QuickBooks® 2025
Sixth Edition

Copyright © 2024 Packt Publishing

All rights reserved. No part of this book may be reproduced, stored in a retrieval system, or transmitted in any form or by any means, without the prior written permission of the publisher, except in the case of brief quotations embedded in critical articles or reviews.

Every effort has been made in the preparation of this book to ensure the accuracy of the information presented. However, the information contained in this book is sold without warranty, either express or implied. Neither the author, nor Packt Publishing or its dealers and distributors, will be held liable for any damages caused or alleged to have been caused directly or indirectly by this book.

Packt Publishing has endeavored to provide trademark information about all of the companies and products mentioned in this book by the appropriate use of capitals. However, Packt Publishing cannot guarantee the accuracy of this information.

Senior Publishing Product Manager: Larissa Pinto
Acquisition Editor – Peer Reviews: Swaroop Singh
Project Editor: Janice Gonsalves
Content Development Editor: Tanya D'cruz
Copy Editor: Safis Editor
Technical Editor: Karan Sonawane
Proofreader: Safis Editor
Indexer: Hemangini Bari
Presentation Designer: Pranit Padwal
Developer Relations Marketing Executive: Anamika Singh

First published: December 2019
Second edition: January 2021
Third edition: January 2022
Fourth edition: November 2022
Fifth edition: December 2023
Sixth edition: December 2024

Production reference: 2080125

Published by Packt Publishing Ltd.
Grosvenor House
11 St Paul's Square
Birmingham
B3 1RB, UK.

ISBN 978-1-83664-997-7

www.packt.com

Foreword

Every year, when a new edition of *Mastering QuickBooks* arrives, I feel like a kid on Christmas morning. I've been fortunate to work with Crystalynn Shelton in a professional capacity—as a writer and editor—and have witnessed firsthand her extraordinary ability to take complex accounting concepts and translate them into clear, actionable steps. Whether you're an experienced bookkeeper, a small business owner, or someone just getting started, Crystalynn meets you where you are and helps you navigate QuickBooks with confidence.

As a CPA and QuickBooks ProAdvisor, Crystalynn brings an unmatched depth of expertise. But what truly sets her apart is her ability to think like a business owner. She understands the pressures of managing a company's financials and the need for tools that are both effective and accessible. This book reflects that understanding. It's not just a guide—it's a lifeline.

One of the things I appreciate most about *Mastering QuickBooks 2025* is its practicality. The book feels like a well-organized reference manual that answers questions exactly when you need it. Wondering how to tackle a specific functionality? You'll find step-by-step instructions complete with screenshots that show you exactly what to do. Crystalynn has thought of everything to make this resource as user-friendly as possible. I keep a copy of her book at arm's reach—it's just that valuable.

This sixth edition continues the legacy of excellence established in earlier versions, with updates to ensure you're learning the most current features of the software. Whether you're reconciling accounts, running reports, or troubleshooting an issue, *Mastering QuickBooks 2025* will guide you through it.

If you're picking up this book, you're in good hands. Crystalynn's expertise makes QuickBooks feel manageable, and her warmth and clarity make learning enjoyable. She has created a resource that will serve you for years to come.

Dr. Megan Hanna

Program Director, Business (BSA/ECN), Yavapai College

Contributors

About the author

Crystalynn Shelton has managed accounting teams at Fortune 500 companies such as Texaco and Paramount Pictures, operated her own bookkeeping and payroll practice for three years, and spent another three years at Intuit (QuickBooks) as a senior learning specialist. She is the author of Amazon bestseller series Mastering QuickBooks, now in its Sixth edition. She serves as an adjunct instructor at UCLA Extension, teaching accounting, bookkeeping, and QuickBooks to numerous small business owners and accounting students annually. She holds an accounting degree from the University of Texas, Arlington, and is a licensed CPA and an Advanced Certified QuickBooks ProAdvisor. In 2022, she was recognized as one of the Top 100 ProAdvisors in the United States. For more information on her services and to subscribe to her weekly newsletter featuring QuickBooks tips and tricks, visit her website at https://crystalynnshelton.com/. Connect with her on social media at https://www.instagram.com/crystalynnshelton/.

> *To the small business owners all over the world, you are my inspiration for writing this book. I do what I do so you can do what you love most. I hope this book helps you understand the crucial role that managing your business finances plays in the future success of your business.*

About the reviewer

Dominique Waits is a CPA, a CGMA, and a Top 100 QuickBooks ProAdvisor with 30 years of experience in public and private accounting, and was nominated as one of Ignition's Top 50 Women in Accounting. She received her degree in accounting from Transylvania University in Lexington, KY, where she completed multiple internships in non-profit accounting, the Volunteer Income Tax Assistance program, and public accounting. She has been a small business owner, running a successful restaurant for many years. Currently, Dominique serves as a senior manager in the CAS department at Blue & Co., a regional accounting firm with offices in Indiana, Ohio, Kentucky, and Michigan. She works with individuals and small businesses, providing full outsourced accounting and CFO, financial management and advisory, as well as tax preparation and planning services.

> *I would like to thank my husband, Chris, and daughter, Mackenzie, for always supporting me on my work endeavors, one of which is reviewing this book. I would also like to thank my CAS team, Laura, Rebekah, and Brenda, for holding down the fort, which enabled me to have the time to review this training guide.*

Join our community on Discord

Join our community's Discord space for discussions with the authors and other readers:

https://packt.link/powerusers

Table of Contents

Preface	xv

Part 1: Setting Up Your Company File	**23**

Chapter 1: Getting Started with QuickBooks Online	**3**
What is QuickBooks?	4
Exploring QBO editions	4
Choosing the right QBO edition	7

QBO Simple Start • 8

QBO Essentials • 8

QBO Plus • 8

QBO Advanced • 9

Creating a QBO account	10
Navigating in QBO	21

QBO dashboards and the left navigation menu • 22

QuickBooks Online icons • 29

QuickBooks Online menus • 30

Summary	33

Chapter 2: Company File Setup — 35

Key information and documents 36

Setting up company preferences in QBO 38

    Company settings • 38

    Usage settings • 40

    Payments settings • 43

    QuickBooks Checking settings • 44

    Sales settings • 44

    Expenses settings • 48

    Time settings • 51

    Advanced settings • 52

Summary 55

Chapter 3: Customizing QuickBooks for Your Business — 57

Customizing the chart of accounts list 58

    Adding a new account to the chart of accounts list • 58

    Importing a chart of accounts list • 62

    Editing accounts on the chart of accounts list • 64

    Inactivating an account on the chart of accounts list • 67

    Reactivating an account on the chart of accounts list • 69

    Merging accounts in QBO • 70

Connecting bank accounts to QBO 73

    Importing banking transactions automatically • 73

    Uploading banking transactions from an Excel or CSV file • 77

Connecting credit card accounts to QBO 85

    Importing credit card transactions automatically • 86

    Uploading credit card transactions from an Excel or CSV file • 88

Giving other users access to your QuickBooks data 97

    Standard all access user • 98

    Standard no access user • 100

    Accounts receivable manager • 100

Table of Contents ix

    Accounts payable manager • 101

    Standard limited customers and vendors • 101

    In house accountant • 102

    Company administrator • 102

    Primary administrator • 102

    Reports-only user • 103

    Time tracking user • 103

    Accountant user • 103

    Editing user privileges • 106

Using apps in QBO 107

    Overview of the QuickBooks App Center • 108

    Finding apps for your business • 112

Summary 114

Chapter 4: Managing Customer, Vendor, and Products and Services Lists   117

Managing customer lists in QBO 118

    Manually adding customers in QBO • 118

    Importing customers into QBO • 127

    Making changes to existing customers in QBO • 129

    Inactivating customers in QBO • 131

    Merging customers in QBO • 132

Managing vendor lists in QBO 135

    Manually adding vendors in QBO • 136

    Importing vendors into QBO • 142

    Making changes to existing vendors in QBO • 143

    Inactivating vendors in QBO • 145

    Merging vendors in QBO • 146

Managing products and services lists in QBO 150

    Manually adding products and services in QBO • 150

    Importing products and services in QBO • 157

    Making changes to existing products and services in QBO • 159

Inactivating products and services in QBO • 160

Merging products and services in QBO • 161

Summary 164

Part 2: Recording Transactions in QuickBooks Online   167

Chapter 5: Managing Sales Tax   169

Do you need to charge sales tax? 170
Setting up sales tax in QBO 170
Creating an invoice that includes sales tax 177
Sales tax reports 180
Summary 182

Chapter 6: Recording Sales Transactions in QuickBooks Online   185

Entering sales forms 186
  Recording income using a sales receipt • 186
  Recording income using a deposit • 191
  Recording income using a sales invoice • 194
Customizing sales templates 198
Recording customer payments 203
Managing credit card payments 206
Recording payments to the payments to deposit account 209
Issuing credit memos and refunds to customers 211
Applying a credit memo to an open invoice 214
Summary 215

Chapter 7: Recording Expenses in QuickBooks Online   217

Adding and paying bills 218
  Entering bills into QuickBooks Online • 218
  Uploading bills to QuickBooks • 222

Table of Contents   xi

   Paying bills in QuickBooks Online • 225

   Entering vendor credits into QuickBooks Online • 230

Managing recurring expenses 233

Writing checks 237

Printing checks 240

Editing, voiding, and deleting expenses 242

Capturing and categorizing receipts and bills 243

Summary 246

Part 3: Managing Employees and Contractors   247

Chapter 8: Managing Employees and 1099 Contractors in QuickBooks Online   249

Setting up payroll 250

   Payroll setup checklist and key documents • 251

   Signing up for an Intuit payroll subscription • 254

Generating payroll reports 258

Filing payroll tax forms and payments 261

Managing 1099 contractors in QBO 262

   Setting up 1099 contractors • 262

   Tracking and paying 1099 contractors • 265

   1099 year-end reporting • 268

Introducing QuickBooks Time 275

Summary 277

Part 4: Closing the Books and Handling Special Transactions   279

Chapter 9: Closing the Books in QuickBooks Online   281

Recording journal entries 282

Reviewing a checklist for closing your books 285
1. Reconciling all bank and credit card accounts 285
2. Making year-end accrual adjustments 286
3. Reviewing new fixed asset purchases and adding them to the chart of accounts 286
4. Making depreciation journal entries 289
5. Taking a physical inventory and recording inventory adjustments 290
6. Adjusting retained earnings for owner/partner distributions 292
7. Setting a closing date and password 293
8. Preparing key financial reports 295
Giving your accountant access to your data 300
Summary 303

Chapter 10: Handling Special Transactions in QuickBooks Online　　305

Setting up business loans and lines of credit 306
    Adding a business loan or line of credit to the chart of accounts • 306
    Making payments on a loan or line of credit • 309
Recording bad debt expenses 311
    Creating a bad debt item • 312
    Creating a credit memo • 314
    Applying a credit memo to an outstanding customer invoice • 315
    Issuing a customer refund • 318
Tracking delayed charges and credits 319
Summary 323

Part 5: Integrating E-Commerce Platforms And Advanced Inventory Management　　325

Chapter 11: Integrating E-Commerce Platforms with QuickBooks Online　　327

Reviewing apps before connecting them to QBO 329
Pros of connecting a sales channel to QuickBooks 330

Table of Contents | xiii

Cons of connecting a sales channel to QuickBooks 331
How to connect a sales channel to QuickBooks 332
Summary 339

Chapter 12: Advanced Inventory Management — 341

Turning on inventory tracking in QuickBooks 342
Adding products in QuickBooks Online 345
Recording product sales in QuickBooks Online 350
Ordering products from vendor suppliers in QuickBooks 353
Receiving products into inventory 355
Generating inventory reports 357

   Open Purchase Order List report • 357

   Purchases by Product/Service Detail report • 358

   Inventory Valuation Detail report • 359

   Sales by Product/Service Detail report • 360

   Purchases by Vendor Detail report • 361

   Physical Inventory Worksheet summary • 362

Summary 363

Part 6: Online Bonus Content — 365

Other Books You May Enjoy — 369

Index — 373

Preface

Intuit QuickBooks is an accounting software package that helps small business owners manage all their bookkeeping tasks. Its complete range of accounting capabilities, such as tracking income and expenses, managing payroll, simplifying taxes, and accepting online payments, makes QuickBooks software a must-have for business owners and aspiring bookkeepers.

The goal of this book is to teach small business owners, bookkeepers, and aspiring accountants how to properly use QuickBooks Online. Using a fictitious company, we will demonstrate how to create a QuickBooks Online account; customize key settings for a business; manage customers, vendors, and products and services; enter transactions; generate reports; and close the books at the end of the period.

QuickBooks records debits and credits for you so that you don't have to know accounting. However, we will show you what's happening behind the scenes in QuickBooks so that you understand how your actions in QuickBooks impact financial statements. We will also provide tips, shortcuts, and best practices to help you save time and become a QuickBooks pro.

In this new edition, we've included bonus content that includes not only step-by-step instructions on nine additional topics, such as *Small Business Bookkeeping 101*, but also video tutorials to give you a live demonstration of the concepts taught.

Who this book is for

If you're a small business owner, bookkeeper, or accounting student who wants to learn how to make the most of QuickBooks Online, this book is for you. Business analysts, data analysts, managers, professionals working in bookkeeping, and QuickBooks accountants will also find this guide useful. If you are planning to take the **QuickBooks Certified User (QBCU)** exam, this book is an excellent study guide. We have also provided a list of the topics covered on the QBCU exam and cross-referenced it with the chapters in the book so you can go directly to that content.

The QBCU syllabus can be found at https://packt.link/supplementary-content-9781836649977. No experience with QuickBooks Online is required to get started; however, some bookkeeping knowledge would be helpful.

The US edition of QuickBooks Online was used to create this book. If you are using a version that is outside of the US, results may differ.

What this book covers

Part 1: Setting Up Your Company File

Chapter 1, *Getting Started with QuickBooks Online*, starts off with a brief description of QuickBooks Online, then it outlines the key features in all four editions of the software. We also explain how to choose the right edition for your business. There are step-by-step instructions on how to create a QuickBooks Online account and how to navigate the software.

Chapter 2, *Company File Setup*, shows you how to customize the QuickBooks Online account created in *Chapter 1* to meet your business needs. First, we explain the documents and key information you will need to have handy for the setup. Next, we walk you through all of the available settings in QuickBooks Online and explain the purpose and benefit of utilizing the various options available.

Chapter 3, *Customizing QuickBooks for Your Business*, introduces customization for the chart of accounts and then dives into the different ways of connecting bank accounts and credit cards to your QuickBooks Online account, followed by granting users access to your QuickBooks data. Finally, you will learn how to discover and install apps in QuickBooks Online. Apps are a great way to help you streamline day-to-day business tasks that can otherwise be time-consuming.

Chapter 4, *Managing Customer, Vendor, and Products and Services Lists*, gives you detailed insight into how to manage your customers, vendors, products, and services. This includes importing customer, vendor, and product and service data from an Excel spreadsheet and manually entering it into the software.

Part 2: Recording Transactions in QuickBooks Online

Chapter 5, *Managing Sales Tax*, covers how to set up sales tax for the various tax jurisdictions you are required to collect sales tax for, how to create an invoice with sales tax, and what reports will help you to report and pay the appropriate sales tax amount when it becomes due.

Chapter 6, Recording Sales Transactions in QuickBooks Online, starts by giving detailed information on different forms of sales, followed by information on how the customer can record payments using different methods, and finally teaches you how to initiate refunds for your customers. You will also learn how to customize sales templates with your company branding, such as adding a name and logo.

Chapter 7, Recording Expenses in QuickBooks Online, teaches you how to enter and pay bills for your QuickBooks Online account. Then, we'll start exploring how to manage recurring expenses, followed by writing and printing checks.

Part 3: Managing Employees and Contractors

Chapter 8, Managing Employees and 1099 Contractors in QuickBooks Online, shows you what information and key documents are needed to set up payroll, how to sign up for an Intuit Payroll subscription plan, and how to generate payroll reports. You will also learn how to file payroll tax forms and payments. You will be introduced to 1099 contractors, how to define them, what forms to use, and how to make payments to them.

Part 4: Closing the Books and Handling Special Transactions

Chapter 9, Closing the Books in QuickBooks Online, covers the steps needed to close your books each month or for the year, including, but not limited to, reconciling all bank and credit card accounts, making year-end accrual adjustments (if applicable), recording fixed asset purchases made throughout the year, recording depreciation, taking a physical inventory, adjusting retained earnings, and preparing financial statements.

Chapter 10, Handling Special Transactions in QuickBooks Online, covers some of the more complicated or uncommon transactions that you may need to handle in your business. It covers how to set up business loans and lines of credit, including how to make payments on a loan. You will also learn how to keep track of petty cash and record delayed charges.

Part 5: Integrating E-Commerce Platforms and Advanced Inventory Management

Chapter 11, Integrating E-Commerce Platforms with QuickBooks Online, covers the basics of integrating your online store (e.g., Shopify or Etsy) with QuickBooks Online. We cover how to find your sales channel in the QuickBooks Apps Center, the pros and cons of connecting apps to QuickBooks Online, and how to connect your sales channel to QuickBooks Online.

Chapter 12, Advanced Inventory Management, takes a deeper dive into how to set up and manage the products that you sell to your customers. We begin by showing you how to turn on the inventory tracking feature, and then we show you how to add your products to QuickBooks, how to record product sales, how to create purchase orders to send to vendor suppliers to place orders, how to receive products in the inventory, and finally, how to generate inventory reports.

Part 6: Online Bonus Content

As mentioned previously, we have taken some of the content that was in previous editions and enhanced it by making it available online only. In addition, we have taken it one step further and provided you with video tutorials where we walk you through the steps to demonstrate the concepts taught in these online chapters. Below, we have listed the title and a brief description of the bonus content that is available online at https://packt.link/supplementary-content-9781836649977.

Chapter 13, Small Business Bookkeeping 101, provides you with some basic bookkeeping knowledge that you will need to successfully use QuickBooks Online. We cover money coming in and money going out of your business, inventory and fixed asset purchases, tracking the money you owe (liabilities), how to set up and use the chart of accounts, cash versus accrual accounting, and double-entry bookkeeping.

Chapter 14, Customer Sales Reports in QuickBooks Online, focuses on reports that will give you insight into your customers and sales. We will discuss what information you will find on each report, how to customize the reports, and how to generate each report. Once they are generated, we will observe when to check these reports and what decisions they might encourage us to make.

Chapter 15, Reconciling Uploaded Bank and Credit Card Transactions, gives you an overview of the Banking Center in QuickBooks Online and an understanding of how the bank rules work, followed by how to edit QuickBooks Online transactions and how to reconcile bank accounts. We wrap this chapter up with a few troubleshooting tips for reconciling bank/credit card accounts.

Chapter 16, Report Center Overview, highlights the key reports that you need in order to keep track of your business finances. It takes you through the Report Center, its purpose, and how to navigate it. You will then go through instructions for generating and customizing the main reports that are available, as well as how to export reports and send them via email. You will learn how regularly you need to check these reports, what to look out for, and what actions or decisions these findings might prompt.

Chapter 17, Vendor and Expenses Reports, dives into reports that help you manage your outgoings and have a clearer view of your profitability. The main reports that are covered are the accounts payable aging report, unpaid bills report, expense by vendor summary report, and bill payments report. You will learn how to generate and customize these reports to help you manage your expenses and cash flow.

Chapter 18, Business Overview and Cash Management Tools and Reports, discusses the three primary reports that provide a good overview of your business: the profit and loss statement, balance sheet report, and statement of cash flows. You will learn when to check these reports and how to use them to evaluate your business's performance. It also introduces you to the Cash Flow Center, where you can find important tools like the Cash Flow Planner and audit log.

Chapter 19, Shortcuts and Test Drive, summarizes the keyboard shortcuts you can use in QuickBooks Online to save time, and also provides links to the QuickBooks Online test drive account as well as a QuickBooks Online discount code.

Chapter 20, Intuit QuickBooks Online Certified User Exam Objectives, is where you can find the full list of things you need to know to pass the QBCU exam, along with references to where the relevant content appears in the book – a handy reference.

Chapter 21, QuickBooks Online Advanced, takes a deep dive into the features included in this top-tier QuickBooks Online subscription. We show you how to access the QuickBooks Online Advanced test drive account, use the new fixed asset manager to automatically calculate and record monthly depreciation, add custom fields, and manage customized user permissions, as well as understanding what workflow automation is and how to use it, how to import invoices and budgets, and much more.

To get the most out of this book

This book is ideal for anyone who has accounting/bookkeeping knowledge as well as those that don't. Each chapter builds on the knowledge and information presented in the previous chapters. If you don't have any experience in using QuickBooks Online, we recommend you start with *Chapter 1, Getting Started with QuickBooks Online,* and complete the chapters in the order they are presented. If you have experience in using QuickBooks Online, feel free to advance to the chapters that cover the topics you need to brush up on.

Download additional files

The code bundle for the book is hosted on GitHub at `https://github.com/PacktPublishing/Mastering-QuickBooks-2025-Sixth-Edition`. We also have other code bundles from our rich catalog of books and videos available at `https://github.com/PacktPublishing/`. Check them out!

Download the color images

We also provide a PDF file that has color images of the screenshots/diagrams used in this book. You can download it here: `https://packt.link/gbp/9781836649977`.

Conventions used

Bold: Indicates a new term, an important word, or words that you see on screen. For example, words in menus or dialog boxes appear in the text like this. Here is an example: "Click on the **Accounting** tab located in the left menu bar and select **Chart of Accounts**."

`CodeInText`: Indicates text that the user should type into a field or search bar. For example: "The email address in our example is `George_Jetson@thejetsons.com`."

 Warnings or important notes appear like this.

 Tips and tricks appear like this.

Get in touch

Errata: Although we have taken every care to ensure the accuracy of our content, mistakes do happen. If you have found a mistake in this book we would be grateful if you would report this to us. Please visit `www.packtpub.com/support/errata`, selecting your book, clicking on the **Errata Submission Form** link, and entering the details.

Piracy: If you come across any illegal copies of our works in any form on the Internet, we would be grateful if you would provide us with the location address or website name. Please contact us at `copyright@packtpub.com` with a link to the material.

If you are interested in becoming an author: If there is a topic that you have expertise in and you are interested in either writing or contributing to a book, please visit `http://authors.packtpub.com`.

Share your thoughts

Thank you for purchasing this book from Packt Publishing—we hope you enjoy it! Your feedback is invaluable and helps us improve and grow. Once you've completed reading it, please take a moment to leave an Amazon review; it will only take a minute, but it makes a big difference for readers like you.

https://packt.link/r/1836649975

Download the free PDF and supplementary content

Thanks for purchasing this book!

Do you like to read on the go but are unable to carry your print books everywhere?

Is your eBook purchase not compatible with the device of your choice?

Don't worry, now with every Packt book you get a DRM-free PDF version of that book at no cost.

Read anywhere, any place, on any device. Search, copy, and paste code from your favorite technical books directly into your application.

Additionally, with this book you get access to supplementary/bonus content for you to learn more about QuickBooks. You can use this to add on to your learning journey on top of what you have in the book.

The perks don't stop there, you can get exclusive access to discounts, newsletters, and great free content in your inbox daily.

Follow these simple steps to get the benefits:

1. Scan the QR code or visit the link below:

https://packt.link/supplementary-content-9781836649977

2. Submit your proof of purchase.
3. Submit your book code. You can find the code on page no. 102 of the book.
4. That's it! We'll send your free PDF, supplementary content, and other benefits to your email directly.

Part 1

Setting Up Your Company File

Before diving into QuickBooks Online, it's crucial to get the setup right. In this section, we'll walk you through creating and customizing your company file step by step. From choosing the right QuickBooks edition and understanding the software's features to setting up your chart of accounts and connecting bank accounts, you'll learn everything you need to tailor QuickBooks to your business. You'll also explore how to manage customer, vendor, and product lists and discover powerful apps to make your day-to-day tasks more efficient.

This part comprises the following chapters:

- *Chapter 1, Getting Started with QuickBooks Online*
- *Chapter 2, Company File Setup*
- *Chapter 3, Customizing QuickBooks for Your Business*
- *Chapter 4, Managing Customer, Vendor, and Products and Services Lists*

1
Getting Started with QuickBooks Online

QuickBooks is the most popular accounting software for small businesses. The desktop version has been around for more than 30 years, and the online version for more than 20 years. It is affordable, easily accessible, and ideal for non-accountants. Before diving into the nuts and bolts of setting up QuickBooks for your business, you should understand what QuickBooks is and what your options are when it comes to using it. Once you know what your options are, you will be in a better position to choose the version of QuickBooks that will best suit your business needs. We will then show you how to create a **QuickBooks Online (QBO)** account and how to navigate QBO.

If you don't have previous experience as a bookkeeper, you will need to know a few bookkeeping basics before you get started. In the *Small Business Bookkeeping 101* online chapter, we will cover five key areas in terms of recording transactions in your business: money coming in, money going out, inventory purchases, fixed asset purchases, and liabilities. In this section, we also cover the importance of the chart of accounts and accounting methods, as well as what double-entry bookkeeping is. You can access *Chapter 13, Small Business Bookkeeping 101*, online using this link: https://packt.link/supplementary-content-9781836649977

We will cover the following key concepts in this chapter:

- What is QuickBooks?
- Exploring QBO editions
- Choosing the right QBO edition

- Creating a QBO account
- Navigating in QBO

Once you've got these key concepts under your belt, you will be ready to dive into setting up your business in QBO.

 The US edition of QBO was used to create this book. If you are using a version that is outside of the US, results may differ.

What is QuickBooks?

QuickBooks is an accounting software program that allows you to track your financial transactions such as income and expenses for your business. One of the benefits of using QuickBooks is having access to key financial reports (such as profit and loss reports) so that you can see the overall health of your business at any time. Having access to these reports makes filing your taxes a lot easier. QuickBooks has been around for more than three decades and is the accounting software used by millions of small businesses around the globe.

QuickBooks Online (QBO) is a cloud-based program that is accessible from any mobile device or desktop computer with an internet connection. It is available in four editions and we'll focus on discussing each edition in detail next.

QuickBooks Desktop Enterprise is also available for large businesses requiring more advanced features. It runs on a subscription model and includes advanced inventory management, support for multiple companies, and multi-user functionality. However, since this book is focused on QBO, we won't be covering Enterprise in detail here.

Exploring QBO editions

As described, QBO comes in four editions:

- Simple Start
- Essentials
- Plus
- Advanced

Each edition varies in terms of price, number of users to whom you can give access, and features included.

The following figure gives a summary of the pricing and features for each edition of QBO at the time of writing:

	Simple Start	Essentials	Plus	Advanced
Cost	$35	$65	$99	$235
Maximum number of users	1	3	5	25
Accountant users included	2	2	2	3
Income and expenses tracking	✓	✓	✓	✓
Invoice and payments (known as **accounts receivable (A/R)**)	✓	✓	✓	✓
Maximize tax deductions	✓	✓	✓	✓
Reports included	40+	70+	90+	90+
Capture and organize receipts	✓	✓	✓	✓
Track mileage with a smartphone	✓	✓	✓	✓
Cash flow management	✓	✓	✓	✓
Sales and sales tax tracking	✓	✓	✓	✓
Create and send estimates	✓	✓	✓	✓
Pay 1099 contractors	✓	✓	✓	✓
Connect online sales channels	1	3	Unlimited	Unlimited
Bill management (A/P)		✓	✓	✓
Track billable hours by customer		✓	✓	✓
Inventory tracking			✓	✓

Track project profitability				✓	✓
Data sync with Excel					✓
Track employee expenses					✓
Batch invoices, expenses, bills, and checks					✓
Custom user access by roles					✓
Automate workflows					✓
Back up and restore data					✓
24/7 support and training					✓
Revenue recognition					✓

Table 1.1: QBO edition comparison

As you can see from the preceding table, all four editions of QBO include the following features:

- **Maximum number of users**: Each plan includes a set number of users; Simple Start includes one user, Essentials includes three users, Plus comes with five users, and Advanced includes up to twenty-five users.
- **Accountant users included**: Each plan includes two or more accountant users. Simple Start, Essentials, and Plus include two accountant users and Advanced includes three accountant users. Typically, you would give this level of access to a **Certified Public Accountant (CPA)** or tax preparer who has the authority to make changes to your books.
- **Track income and expenses**: Keep track of all sales to customers and expenses paid to vendors.
- **Invoice and payments (accounts receivable)**: Invoice customers, enter payments, and stay on top of unpaid invoices.
- **Tax deductions**: Keeping track of all expenses will ensure you don't miss out on any tax deductions you may qualify for.

- **Reports**: All plans include pre-set reports so you don't have to create them from scratch. The number of reports available is based on your subscription plan. Simple Start includes the minimum number of reports (40), and Advanced includes unlimited reports.
- **Receipt capture**: All plans allow you to use your phone or mobile device to snap a photo of a receipt and upload it to QuickBooks. You can also link expense receipts to transactions.
- **Mileage tracking**: Automatically track miles with your phone's GPS and categorize them as business or personal trips.
- **Cash flow**: Stay on top of your cash flow by using the cash flow tools available in all QBO plans.
- **Track sales and sales tax**: Keep track of sales tax collected from customers, submit electronic payments to state and local authorities, and complete required sales tax forms and filings.
- **Estimates**: Create a quote or proposal and email it to prospective clients for approval.
- **Pay 1099 contractors**: You can keep track of payments made to independent contractors and generate 1099 forms at the end of the year.
- **Sales channels**: E-commerce businesses can connect QBO to their Amazon, Shopify, or eBay accounts to sync sales with QBO.

We will discuss the features of each plan in more detail, as well as how to choose the right QBO edition for your business, in the next section.

Choosing the right QBO edition

Depending on the edition, QBO can be ideal for anyone from solopreneurs and freelancers all the way to mid-to-large-sized businesses. If you tend to hire 1099 contractors, also known as independent contractors, QBO can help you keep track of payments made to contractors throughout the year. Since contractors are not employees of the business, you must provide a 1099 form at the end of the year to any contractor you have paid $600 or more to in the calendar year. If you have questions about who qualifies as a contractor for 1099 filing purposes or need assistance with selecting the right QBO edition, please reach out to a qualified tax professional. A great resource to locate someone in your geographical area is Intuit's Find An Accountant directory:

`https://quickbooks.intuit.com/find-an-accountant/`

The needs of your business will determine which edition of QBO is ideal for you. The following provides some additional insight into the ideal edition of QBO for different types of businesses.

When you purchase a QBO subscription, you can track business finances for one business entity. If you need to track more than one business, you will need to purchase a QBO subscription for each business entity that you have. In general, any business with a unique tax ID number will need its own set of books.

 Keep in mind that pricing is subject to change and that the pricing reflected in this book is based on what is reflected on the Intuit website at the time of writing.

QBO Simple Start

The Simple Start plan is the most economical, at $35 per month, on sale currently with the first three months at 50% off, costing $17.50 per month. It includes one user and two accountant users. QBO Simple Start is ideal for a freelancer or sole proprietor that sells services only, and no products. You may have employees that you need to pay, or 1099 contractors. The majority of your expenses are paid via online banking or wire transfer, so you don't need to write or print checks to pay bills.

QBO Essentials

The Essentials plan is the next tier and starts at $65 per month, on sale currently with the first three months at 50% off, costing $32.50 per month. It includes three users and two accountant users. Unlike Simple Start, you can manage bills (also known as **accounts payable**, or **A/P**) with the Essentials plan.

QBO Essentials includes all the features found in QBO Simple Start. QBO Essentials is ideal for freelancers and sole proprietors who only sell services and no products (or those who sell "non-inventory" products, such as ebooks, other digital items, or subscription offerings). You have employees and/or contractors whose time you need to keep track of in order to bill back to clients. Unlike QBO Simple Start, you pay most of your bills by writing checks, and you need the ability to keep track of your unpaid bills. QBO Essentials is the next step for small businesses that may need more reporting options.

QBO Plus

The Plus plan is $99 per month, on sale currently with the first three months having 50% off, at $49.50 per month. It includes five users and two accountant users. Unlike the Simple Start and Essentials plans, you can track your inventory and project profitability with the Plus plan.

QBO Plus includes all of the features found in Simple Start and Essentials. Unlike QBO Simple Start and QBO Essentials, QBO Plus is ideal for small businesses that sell products, since it includes inventory tracking. Similar to QBO Simple Start and QBO Essentials, you can pay employees. If you tend to work on a project basis, QBO Plus is ideal because you can track the profitability of all of your projects, as well as creating income and expense budgets.

QBO Advanced

The Advanced plan is the top-tier QBO plan. It starts at $235 per month, currently on sale with 50% off for the first three months, costing $117.50 per month. It includes up to 25 users and three accountant users.

QBO Advanced includes all of the features found in Simple Start, Essentials, and Plus. QBO Advanced is ideal for businesses that have more than five users needing access to their data. QBO Advanced is QBO Plus on steroids; it includes all of the features found in QBO Plus, along with some great bonus features, such as on-demand online training for your entire team, and spreadsheet sync with Excel.

The bonus features you will find in QBO Advanced are as follows:

- **Spreadsheet sync with Excel**: Connect QBO to Excel to gain access to pre-made templates, and the ability to build consolidated reports for multiple companies and easily refresh your data.
- **Employee expenses tracking**: Employees can submit expenses directly to QuickBooks for easy tracking, review, and reimbursement.
- **Batch invoices and expenses**: Enter, edit, and email hundreds of invoices, checks, expenses, and bills instead of entering them one by one.
- **Custom access control**: Provides a deeper level of user permissions that allows you to manage access to sensitive data, such as bank accounts.
- **Exclusive premium apps**: Intuit has more than 700 best-in-class apps to customize QuickBooks for your business needs. For example, Amazon Marketplace Connector is available to automatically sync e-commerce sales to QuickBooks.
- **24/7 support & training**: With QBO Advanced, you get support 24 hours a day, 7 days a week, at no additional cost. In addition, on-demand online training videos are available to help you and your staff get up to speed on how to use QBO. This training has an annual value of $3,000 but is included with your subscription to QBO Advanced at no additional cost.

- **Workflow automation**: This feature helps you save time and minimize risk by implementing automation for repetitive tasks.
- **Data restoration**: This allows you to continuously back up changes to your company file or restore a specific version.
- **Revenue recognition**: This new feature allows you to automatically track and enter deferred revenue into your books so that you can stay compliant with standards that state how and when businesses should recognize their revenue.

We will cover more in-depth information about the features and benefits of QBO Advanced in *Chapter 21, QuickBooks Online Advanced* that can be accessed at `https://packt.link/supplementary-content-9781836649977`. In that chapter, we take a deep dive into the features available in this top-tier QBO plan.

Depending on your business and individual circumstances, you should now be able to determine whether you will need QBO Simple Start, Essentials, Plus, or Advanced. It is important to pick the right version for you so that you have access to the appropriate features you will need. However, you can upgrade or downgrade your QBO plan at any time. Now that you know about the QBO subscription plans, we will show you how to create a QBO account.

Creating a QBO account

The first step to setting up your business in QBO is to create a QBO account. In this section, we will create a QBO account for **Small Business Builders, LLC**, a fictitious business we will use to demonstrate features and explain concepts taught throughout this book. Small Business Builders is owned by a partnership that provides consulting services in business plans, marketing plans, bookkeeping, tax planning, and website development to small businesses. Small Business Builders is in its first year of business and has no employees. However, the partners do hire a few contractors to help meet the demand during the peak months of the year.

To create a QBO account, go to the Intuit website and select a QBO subscription plan.

Follow these steps to create a QBO account:

1. Open your web browser and go to the Intuit website, `www.intuit.com`.

Chapter 1

2. Click on **Products** and select **QuickBooks**, as shown in *Figure 1.1*:

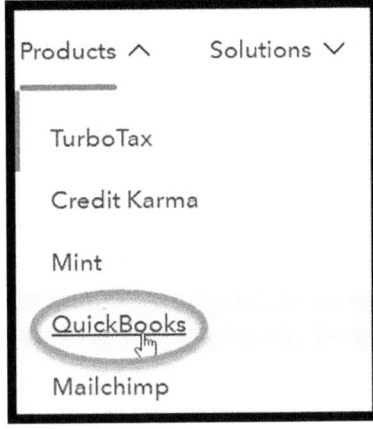

Figure 1.1: Navigating to QuickBooks

3. Click on **Plans & Pricing**, as indicated in *Figure 1.2*:

Figure 1.2: Choosing Plans & Pricing

4. Choose from four pricing plans: **Simple Start**, **Essentials**, **Plus**, or **Advanced**, as indicated in *Figure 1.3*:

Figure 1.3: Choosing a pricing plan

The pricing shown here is correct as of the time of writing this book and is subject to change. To get a special discount on your QBO subscription, use my referral link:

https://quickbooks.grsm.io/crystalynnshelton4264

5. After selecting a plan, you will be asked if you want to continue without payroll. Select this option; in *Chapter 8, Managing Employees and 1099 Contractors in QuickBooks Online*, we will cover payroll in more detail.

 Intuit has a service called QuickBooks Live Bookkeeping that connects you with a bookkeeper, who can assist you in getting things set up properly and managing ongoing tasks.

6. Select **Off** for the QuickBooks **Live Bookkeeping** option.
7. Create an Intuit account by providing your business email address, a secure password, and mobile number, as indicated in *Figure 1.4*:

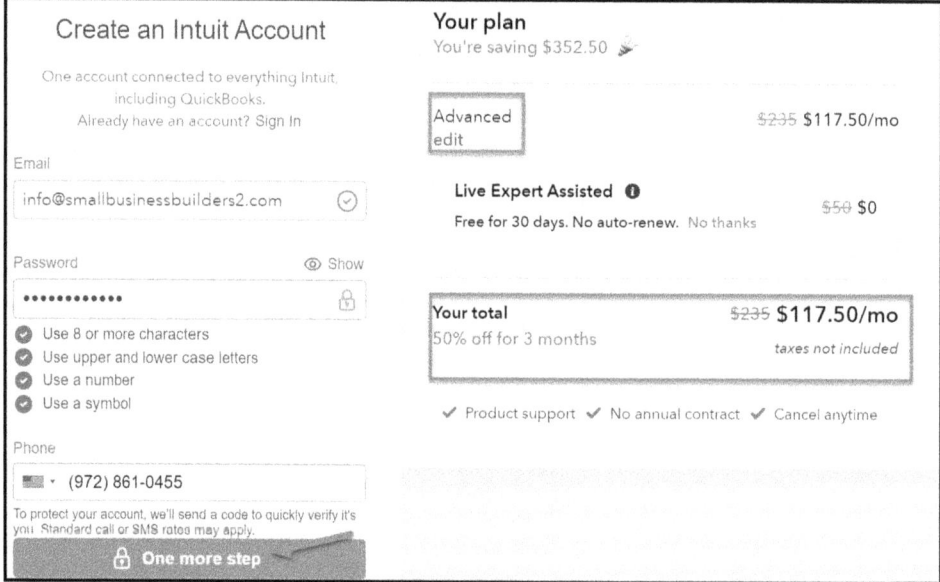

Figure 1.4: Creating an Intuit account

If you need to set up multiple companies, you will be able to use the same email address to set up additional companies.

Chapter 1

8. On the right, you will see the plan you have selected along with the monthly cost. After entering and saving your credit card info, the following welcome screen will appear:

Figure 1.5: Welcome screen after account creation

9. Click **Get started** as indicated in *Figure 1.5*. The following screen will appear:

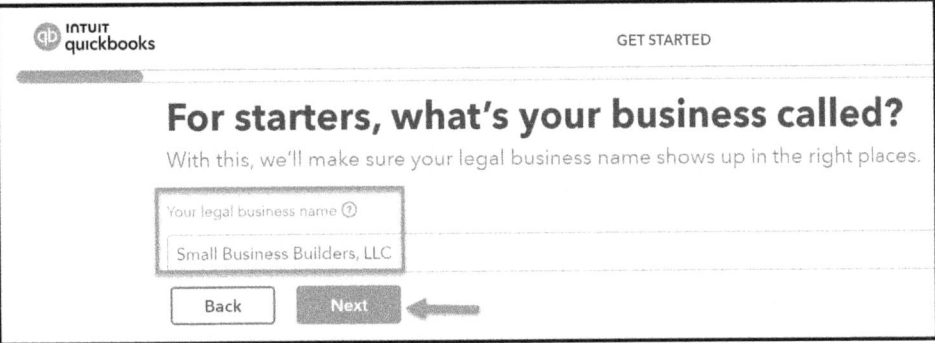

Figure 1.6: Entering your legal business name

10. Type your legal business name, as shown in the screenshot, and click the **Next** button. The following screen will appear:

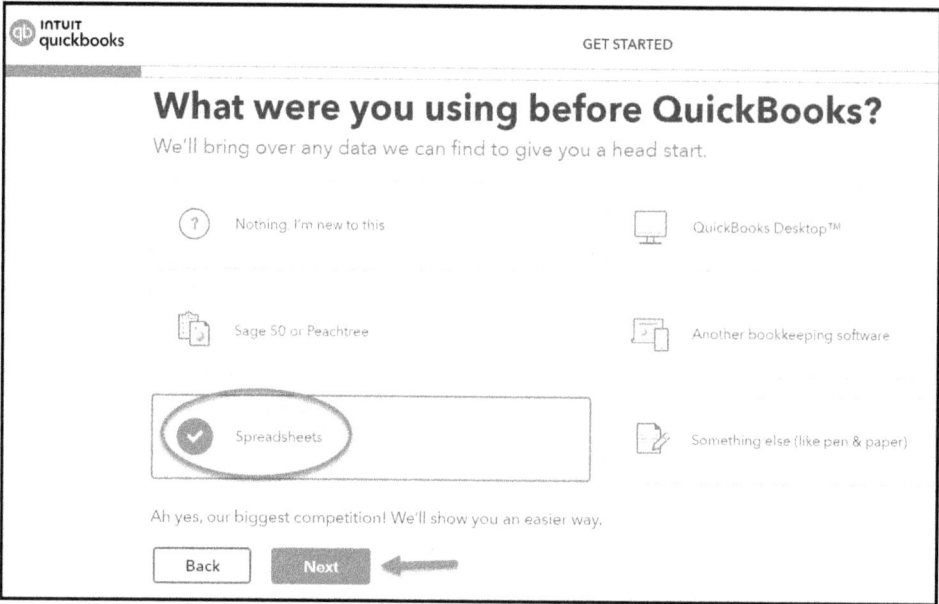

Figure 1.7: Confirm how you have been managing your finances

11. Select how you are currently keeping track of your finances. If you select **QuickBooks Desktop** or **Sage 50 or Peachtree**, instructions for how you can convert that data into QBO will come up. For Small Business Builders, select **Spreadsheets**.

 If you are migrating from another accounting software to QBO, check out this helpful YouTube tutorial by Intuit QuickBooks at `https://www.youtube.com/watch?v=Ddph_qKThYw` for step-by-step instructions.

12. On the next screen, indicate the industry your business falls into. You will see a variety of options start to display as you type in the field. Small Business Builders, LLC falls into the *consulting* industry:

Chapter 1

Figure 1.8: Confirm your industry

Notice, in *Figure 1.8*, an option to select **Can't find an industry that fits?**, which will allow you to use the industry that you have typed in.

13. On the next screen, indicate the structure of your business. Small Business Builders is an LLC with multiple partners that own the business, so select **Partnership** as indicated in *Figure 1.9*:

Figure 1.9: Selecting business type

> QuickBooks uses industry selection to create a chart of accounts. Instead of having to create a chart of accounts list from scratch, QBO will provide you with a preset list of accounts that will include a few customized accounts commonly used by businesses in the industry that you select.

14. Click the **Next** button.

> Most small businesses start out as sole proprietors. If you're not sure what your business structure is, talk to your accountant. You can always select **I'm not sure** and answer this question in the *Company settings* section that we will explore in *Chapter 2, Company File Setup*. However, it's important that you select a business structure to customize QuickBooks for your business.

15. On the next screen, select your role in the business so that QuickBooks can customize your user experience to meet your specific needs.

16. For Small Business Builders, choose **CEO or Owner** and select **Just the owner(s)** in the number of employees field, as shown in *Figure 1.10*:

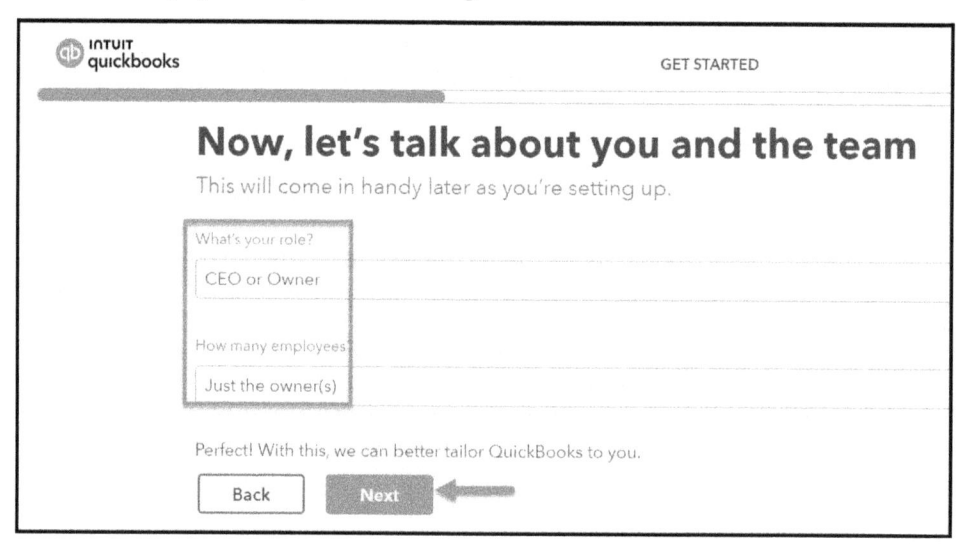

Figure 1.10: Selecting your role in the business

17. Click **Next**. On the next screen, select the type of people that work at the business. Small Business Builders is a partnership with multiple owners who occasionally use contractors. Make the selections indicated in *Figure 1.11*:

Chapter 1

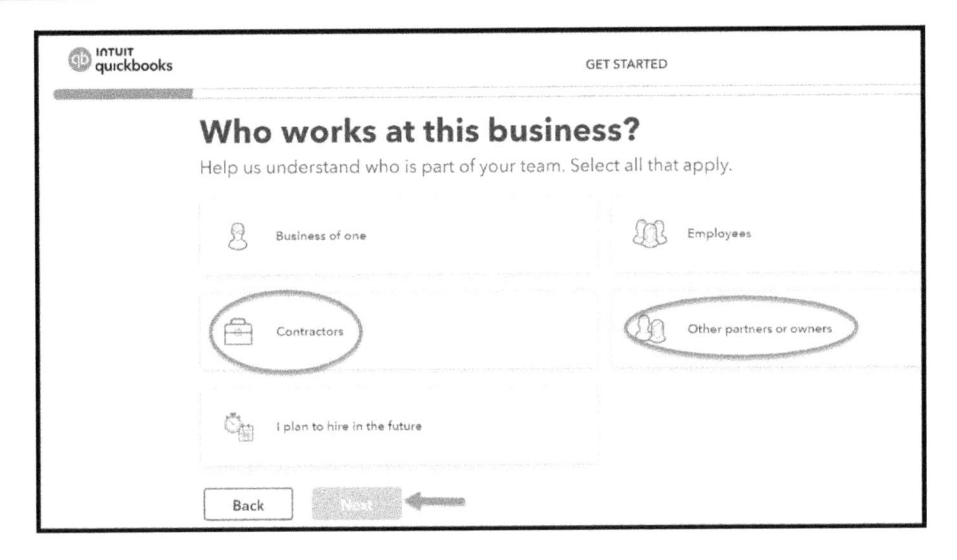

Figure 1.11: Selecting who works at the business

> The purpose of this question is to determine whether you need to use the payroll features for employees or the contractor features for 1099 vendors.

18. Select **Contractors and Other partners or owners**. You can always turn on the payroll features when you are ready to hire employees.
19. Click **Next**. On the next screen, you can schedule a complimentary call with a live bookkeeper who can assist you in getting your books set up properly. Select **Skip for now** for Small Business Builders, LLC:

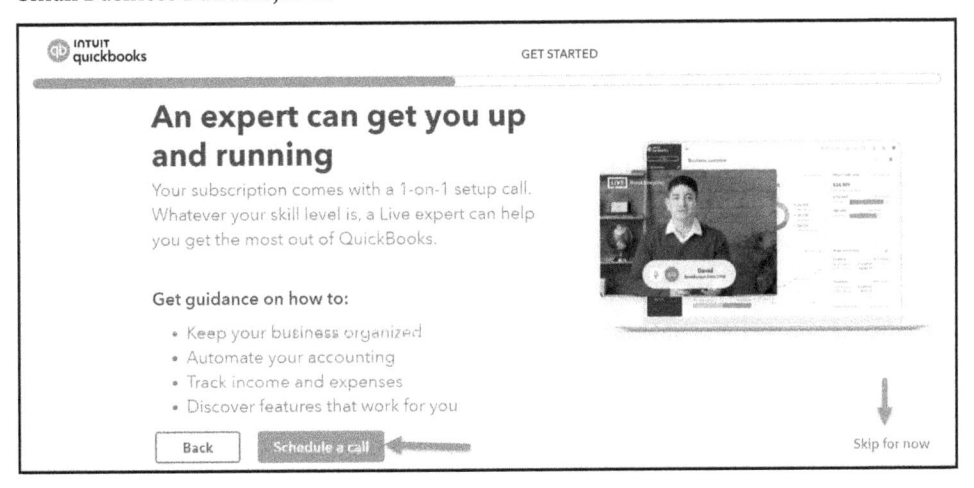

Figure 1.12: Schedule a call with a live expert

20. On the next screen, you can choose to set up invoices to accept online payments from customers or connect your bank and credit card accounts to sync with QBO. Click on **Do this first** below the **Link a bank or credit card to start getting organized** option as indicated in *Figure 1.13*.

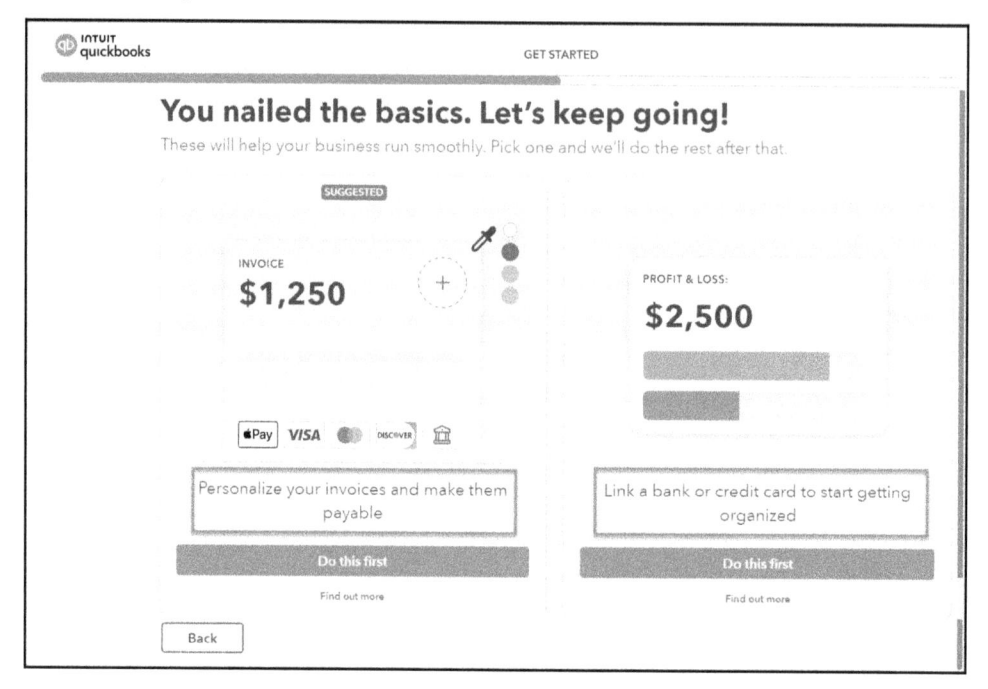

Figure 1.13: Choosing online payments setup or connecting bank/credit card accounts

One of the benefits of using QBO is the ability to allow customers to pay their invoices online using a variety of payment methods such as ApplePay, Venmo, and debit/credit card. The advantage is that when your customers make a payment, the invoice is automatically marked as paid and you receive immediate notification via email that an invoice has been paid.

21. QuickBooks allows you to link your bank and credit card accounts, so transactions are automatically downloaded. We will cover this in *Chapter 3, Customizing QuickBooks for Your Business*, so let's click **Skip for now**.

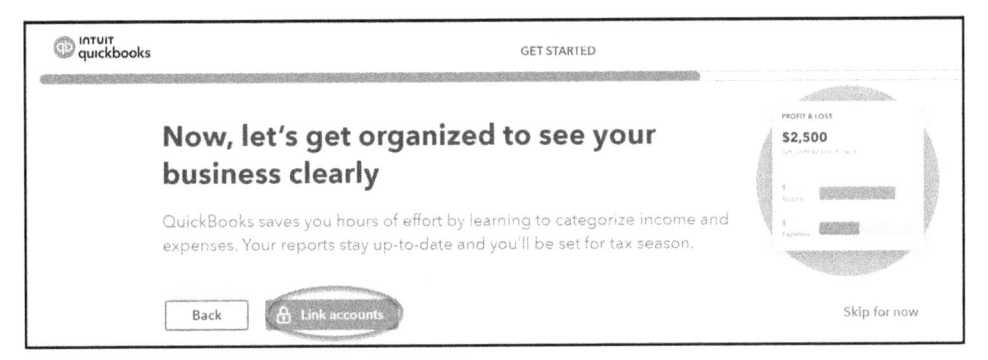

Figure 1.14: Option to link your bank and credit card accounts to QBO

22. On the next screen, indicate how you currently manage paper and digital receipts. Small Business Builders currently saves paper and digital receipts:

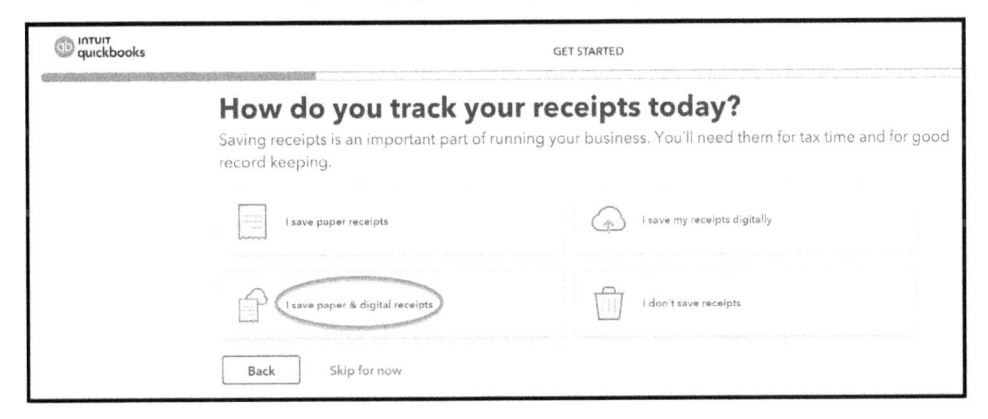

Figure 1.15: Confirm how you currently track your paper receipts (for better visualization, refer to https://packt.link/gbp/9781836649977)

23. On the next screen, you can download the QBO app using your Apple or Android device by scanning the QR code displayed.

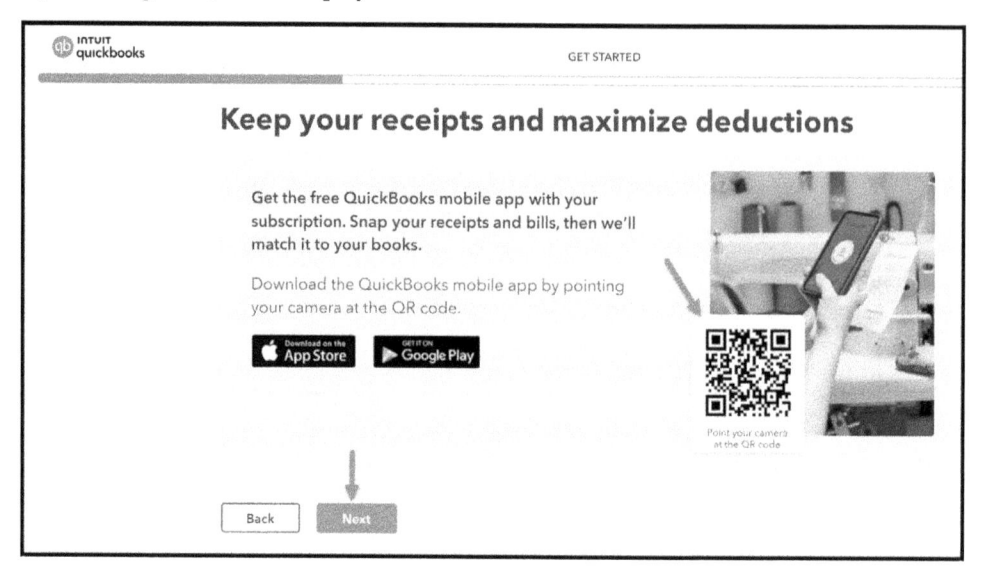

Figure 1.16: Download the QuickBooks mobile app

24. On the next screen, you can select the features you plan to use in QuickBooks. This information will be used to further customize your user interface to meet your needs.

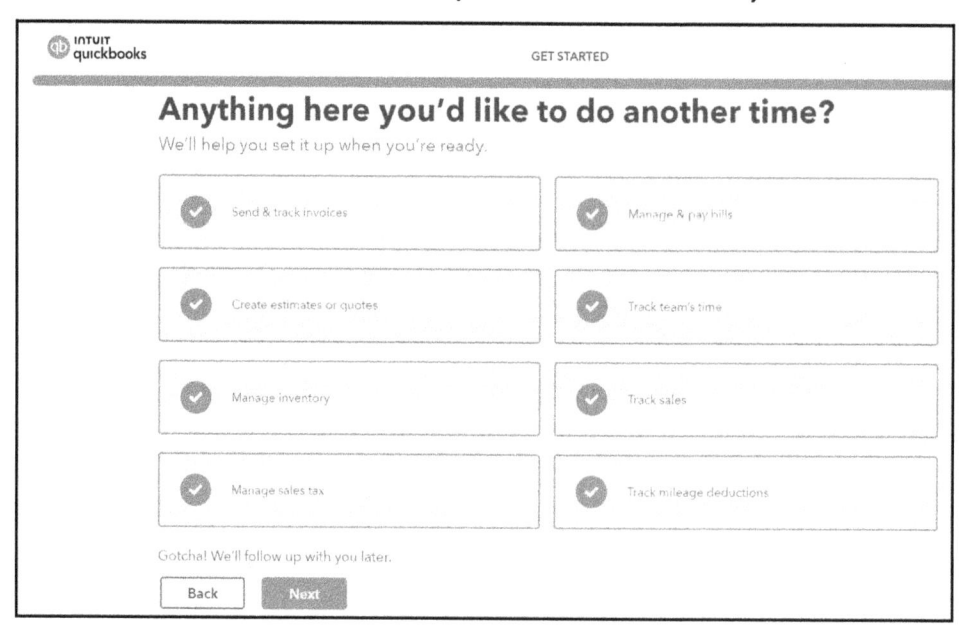

Figure 1.17: Selecting what you want to use QuickBooks for

After making your selections, click **Next** and the following screen will appear:

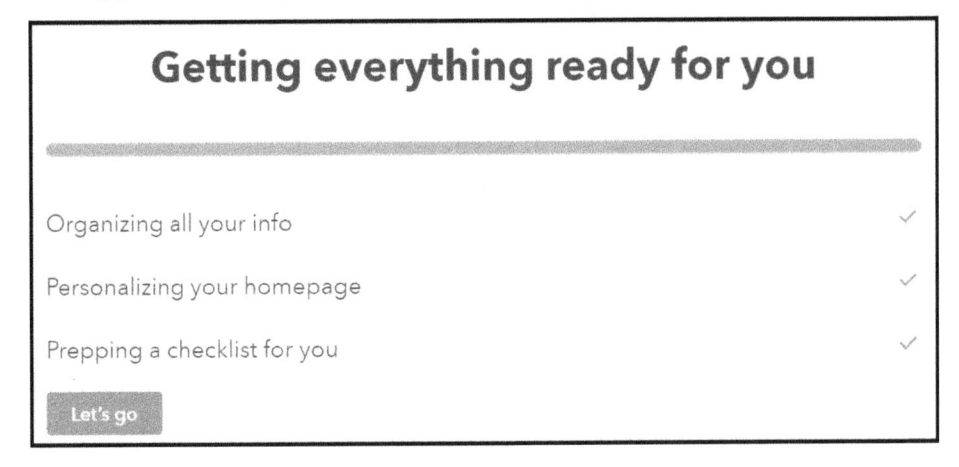

Figure 1.18: Completing the account setup

Congratulations! You have completed the initial QuickBooks setup, taking you one step closer to managing your books. Next, we will show you how to navigate through the program, which will help you locate what you need to complete your business setup.

Navigating in QBO

The QBO user interface is currently undergoing several changes as of the writing of this book. This means that screenshots in this section might vary slightly from what you see when you log in to your QBO account. There are a variety of ways you can navigate within the program, including via the following:

- Dashboards
- Left navigation menu
- The **Shortcut icons** on the **Home** tab
- Gear menu
- **Quick Create** menu

Let's look at the dashboards and left navigation menu first.

QBO dashboards and the left navigation menu

To explore what the QBO dashboards look like, we will use our sample company, Small Business Builders, LLC:

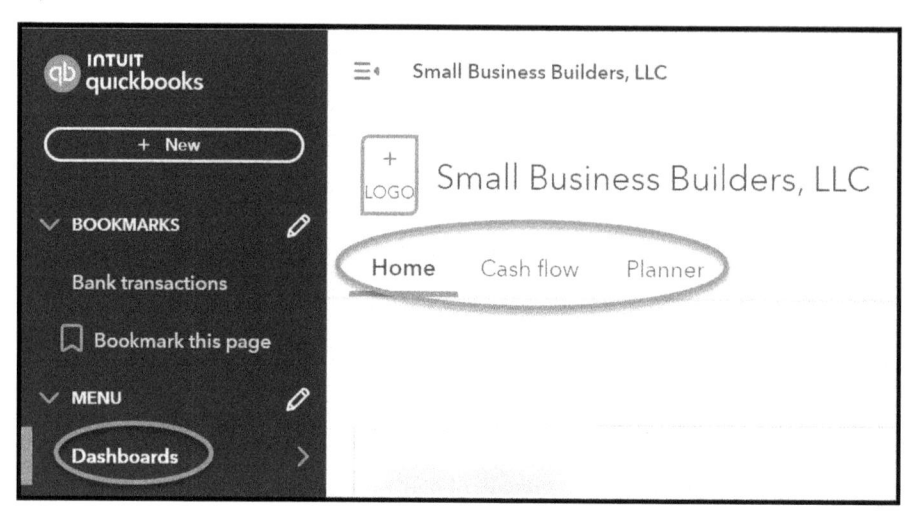

Figure 1.19: QBO dashboards

There are three dashboards that can be accessed from the **Dashboards** tab located on the left menu bar: **Home**, **Cash flow**, and **Planner**. The following is a brief explanation of what you can find on each dashboard along with some snapshots:

- **Home**: When you access QBO for the first time, you will see a **SETUP CHECKLIST**. This checklist is designed to help you complete your QBO setup so that you can start managing your business finances. As you complete each task, it will be marked as completed so that you know what you have left to do.

Chapter 1   23

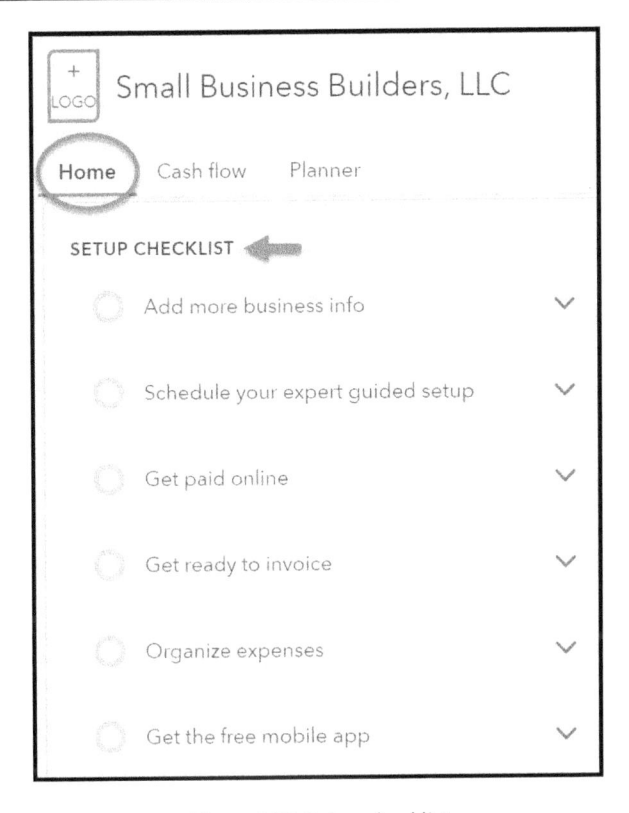

Figure 1.20: Setup checklist

- The **SHORTCUTS** section includes icons that allow you to quickly get paid online, create invoices, record expenses, add bank deposits, and create a check, to name a few. To see all of the shortcuts, click the **Show all** link shown in *Figure 1.21*. You can also add or remove shortcuts using the pencil icon shown:

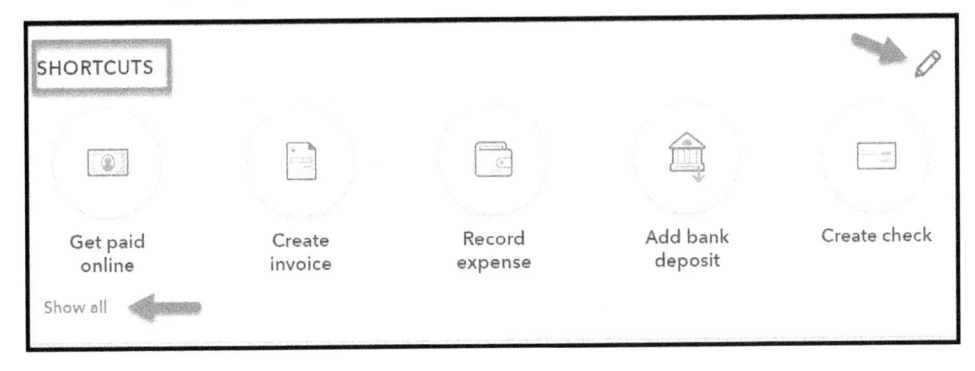

Figure 1.21: Adding/removing shortcuts from the QBO dashboard

- **Key business insights** are also available on the **Home** dashboard. You can find your sales, mileage, bank accounts, profit and loss, accounts receivable, accounts payable, expenses, and outstanding invoices (paid and unpaid), here. Similar to shortcuts, you can customize the insights that appear on this page.

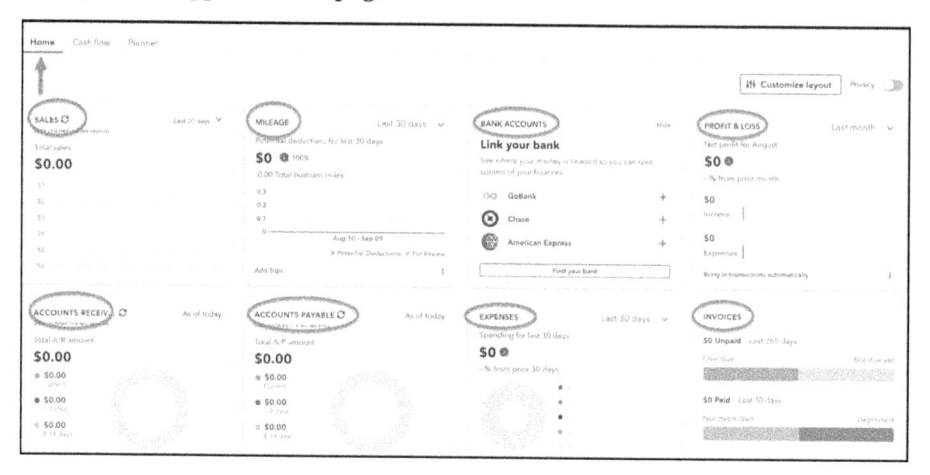

Figure 1.22: Business insights on the Home dashboard (for better visualization, refer to https://packt.link/gbp/9781836649977)

- **Cash flow**: This dashboard provides a way for you to track the money coming into and going out of your business. You can see how the **Money in** activities, such as customer payments, compare to the **Money out** activities, including payments to suppliers and creditors.

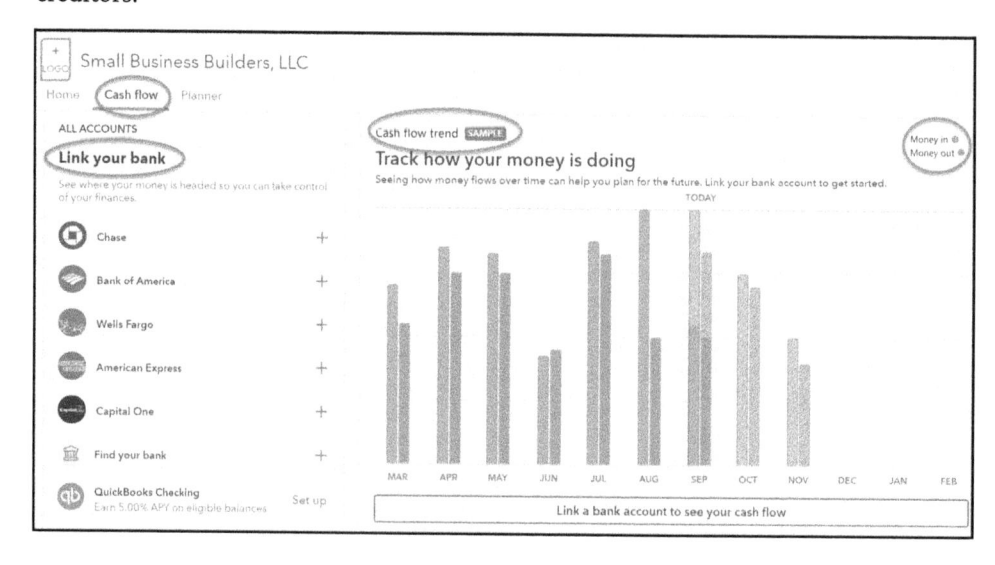

Figure 1.23: Cash flow dashboard

- **Monthly outlook:** This dashboard provides insight into upcoming **MONEY IN** activities such as open or overdue customer invoices and customer payments that are coming up. In addition, you can view the **MONEY OUT** activities, which include unpaid or overdue bills and recent payments. Last but not least, at the very bottom of this screen, you can see an **Insights and ideas** section that includes upcoming invoices and expenses in the next few months, as indicated in *Figure 1.24*:

Figure 1.24: Cash flow outlook

- **Planner**: The cash flow planner pulls in the next three months of QuickBooks transactions for both money coming into and going out of your business. This allows you to see what the overall impact on your cash flow will be. With this information, you can take the necessary steps to plan for any cash shortfalls or decide how you want to invest a cash surplus. To begin, click **Start planning** as indicated in *Figure 1.25*:

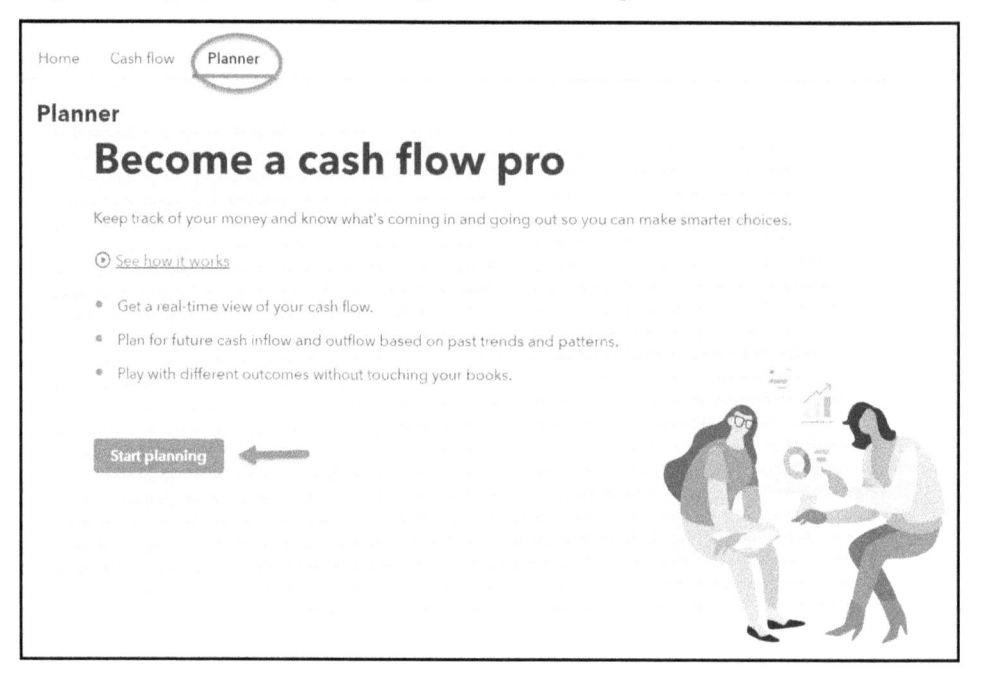

Figure 1.25: Cash flow planner dashboard

The left navigation menu is another way you can maneuver around QuickBooks. In the past, there was a business view and an accountant view that you could switch between. However, as of the writing of this book, both menus have been consolidated into one menu that works best for both accountants and business owners. The following is a snapshot of the new and improved left navigation menu:

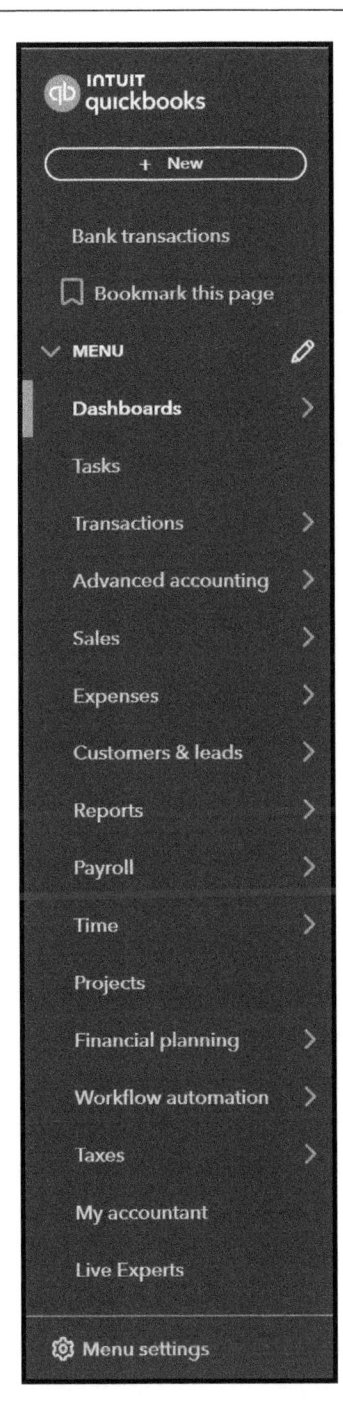

Figure 1.26: Left navigation menu

Within each menu, there are sub-menus. For example, if you hover your mouse over **Transactions**, you will see the following sub-menus:

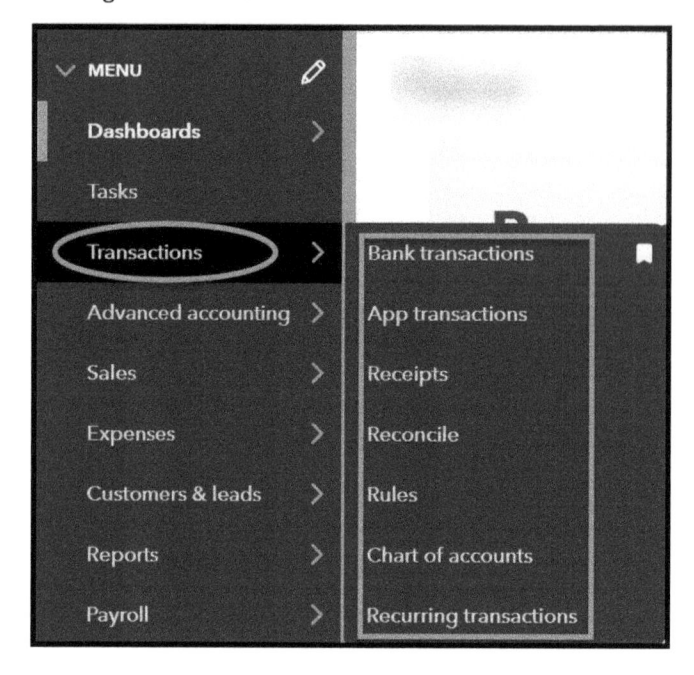

Figure 1.27: QBO sub-menus

Within the **Transactions** menu are **Bank transactions**, **App transactions**, **Receipts**, **Reconcile**, **Rules**, **Chart of accounts**, and **Recurring transactions** options. A brief explanation of each of these follows:

- **Bank transactions**: You can manage all the transactions downloaded into QBO from the bank and credit card accounts you have linked to QuickBooks.
- **App transactions**: This is where you can manage transactions downloaded from the apps you have linked to QBO, such as PayPal, Shopify, Square, and so on.
- **Receipts**: You can find any receipts you have uploaded using the QBO app.
- **Reconcile**: This allows you to match up your bank and credit card statements with what has been recorded in QBO.
- **Rules**: This allows you to create bank rules so that QBO can automatically categorize recurring bank/credit card transactions.
- **Chart of accounts**: This provides a list of categories you can use to organize income and expense transactions.

Chapter 1

- **Recurring transactions**: This allows you to create a template for repeat expenses like rent and telephone expenses.

Now that you have a better understanding of how to navigate QBO from the dashboards and the left navigation menu, along with how to customize it to fit your needs, let's look at the next navigation tool: icons.

QuickBooks Online icons

The following screenshot shows the common icons that can be found at the top of any screen in QBO:

Figure 1.28: Icons on the home page

The following are explanations of the options in the preceding screenshot:

- **Contact experts**: This allows access to a live bookkeeper who can help you get your books set up and is available through this link
- **New Features**: This allows you access to video tutorials that highlight new features as they become available.
- **Help**: If you have a question or need to learn how to do something in QBO, you can click on this icon to launch the **Help** menu. You will find detailed support articles, video tutorials, and access to a sample company file in this section.
- **My apps**: All sales channels and other apps you have connected with QBO will appear here so that you can easily manage them.
- **Search**: If you need to locate an invoice, bill, or any transaction, you can do a global search of the program by typing an account name, the name of a vendor, or any information in this field to search for it.
- **Notifications**: Notifications about changes that have been made to your account or upgrades to your QBO subscription can be found here.
- **Tasks**: This enables you to create a to-do list with a due date to help you prioritize your work.
- **Gear**: This icon will display a menu of tasks that you can perform in QBO. Tasks related to global company settings, lists, and tools such as reconciling and budgeting can be found here.

- **Account info**: This allows you to log out of QuickBooks or manage your Intuit account.

As we mentioned previously, the QBO icons allow you to navigate the program so that you can quickly get to the information you need. In addition to icons, the QBO menus allow you to access your overall company settings, lists, tools, and your company profile. We will cover QBO menus next.

QuickBooks Online menus

In addition to the left navigation menu, there are a couple more menus you can use to navigate QBO.

The first menu is accessible through the gear icon, located in the upper right-hand corner, next to the **Notifications** icon. The following screenshot shows the menu that will display when you click on the gear icon:

YOUR COMPANY	LISTS	TOOLS	PROFILE
Account and settings	All lists	Manage workflows	Subscriptions and billing
Manage users	Products and services	Reclassify transactions	Feedback
Custom form styles	Recurring transactions	Order checks	Privacy
Chart of accounts	Attachments	Import data	
Workers' comp	Custom fields	Import desktop data	
Get the desktop app	Tags	Export data	
Additional info	Rules	Reconcile	
Priority Circle		Budgeting	
		Spreadsheet Sync	
		Audit log	
		Back up company	
		SmartLook	
		Resolution center	

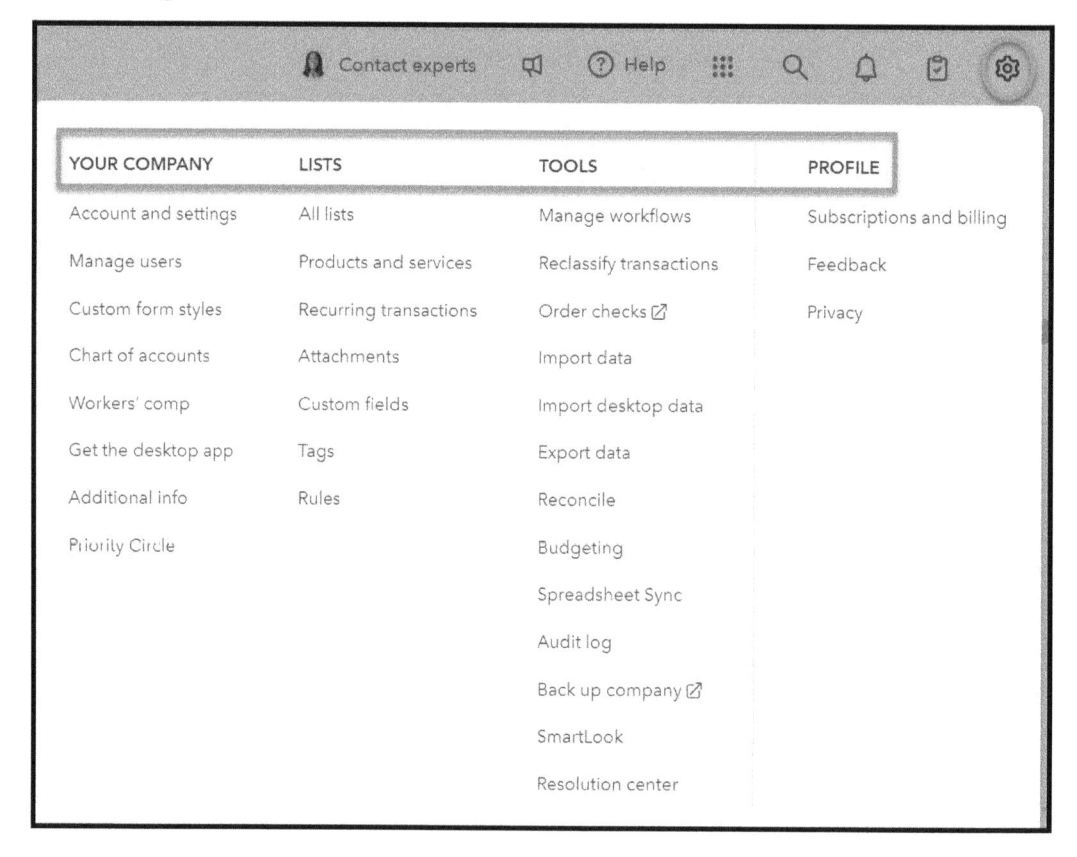

Figure 1.29: Menu options after clicking the gear icon

Chapter 1

A brief description of the areas of QBO that you can access through the gear icon is as follows:

- **YOUR COMPANY:** This menu includes global company accounts and settings, which we will explore in detail in the next chapter. It also allows you to access **Manage users**, which is where you can give other users access to your QuickBooks data. You can customize forms such as invoices and estimates, launch the chart of accounts, and access additional information, which shows you the keyboard shortcuts you can use to navigate QBO more efficiently.

- **LISTS:** The **LISTS** menu includes several QuickBooks lists, such as products and services, recurring transactions, attachments, custom fields, tags, and rules. You can manage recurring transactions such as monthly rent or utility expenses from this menu. In addition, files or images that you have attached to QuickBooks transactions, such as receipts or signed contracts, are accessible in the form of attachments.

- **TOOLS:** If you need to order checks that you can print from QuickBooks, you can do so by selecting the **Order checks** option in this column. If you have customer, vendor, product, or service information that you need to import, you can select **Import data** and follow the on-screen instructions. If you are currently using QuickBooks Desktop, you can use the **Import desktop data** option to migrate your data from desktop to QBO. Also available are the bank and credit card reconciliation tool, the budgeting tool, and the audit log.

- **PROFILE:** You can manage your QBO subscription under the **Subscriptions and billing** section. There is also a **Feedback** section where you can submit recommendations or issues to the Intuit team. The **Privacy** option provides you with information about the built-in privacy features included in QBO.

Another menu that is available in QuickBooks is the **Quick Create** menu. You can access this menu by clicking on the **+ New** button located at the very top of the left navigation menu. The following screenshot shows the menu that you will see when you click on the **+ New** button:

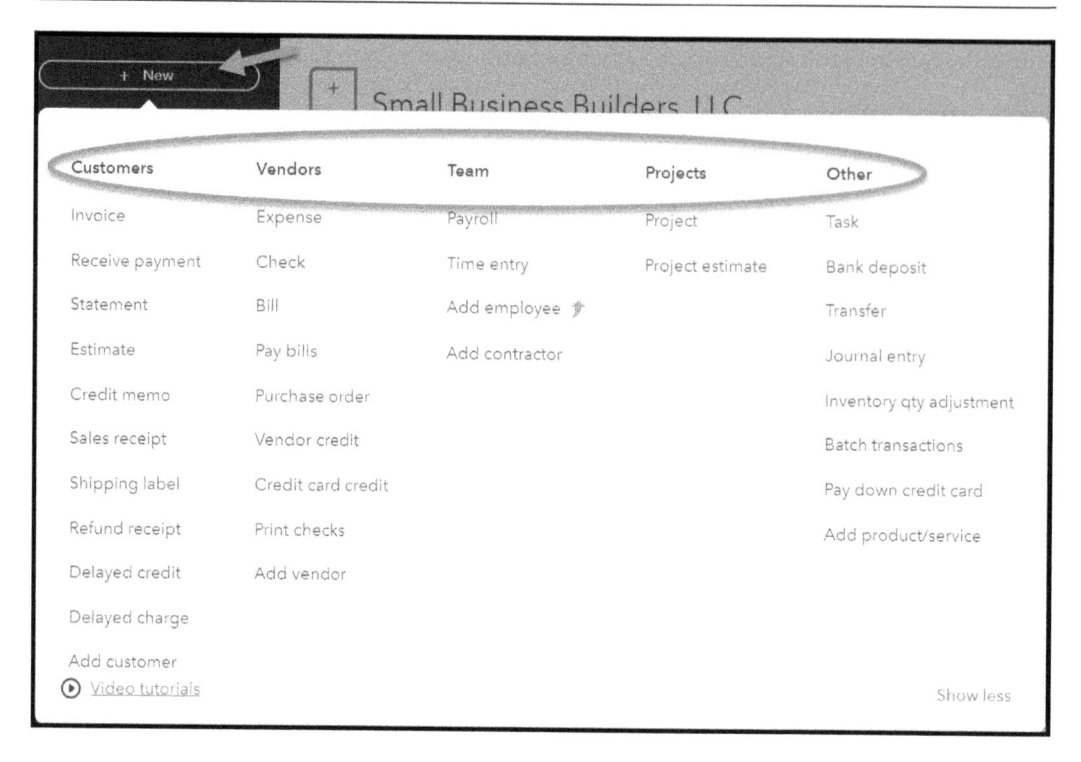

Figure 1.30: The Quick Create menu

The areas of QBO that you can access through the **Quick Create** menu are as follows:

- **Customers**: Most of the transactions that pertain to customers can be found here, from creating invoices and sales receipts to accepting customer payments and adding new customers, to name a few. At the bottom of this column, you should see a **Video tutorials** link. This link will take you to a page that has a library of short step-by-step video tutorials.
- **Vendors**: Tasks related to vendors can be found in this section. This includes recording expenses, writing checks, tracking unpaid bills, creating purchase orders, and adding new vendors.
- **Team**: If you sign up for a QuickBooks Payroll subscription, you can access all payroll-related tasks in this section. This includes adding new employees, setting up employee deductions, running payrolls, and making payroll tax payments.
- **Projects**: If you have QBO Advanced, you will see a **Projects** menu. Within this menu, you can create projects and project estimates, as well as manage all projects.

- **Other:** This section includes creating tasks, making bank deposits and bank transfers, recording journal entries, generating customer statements, making inventory adjustments, paying down credit cards, and adding products and services.

In this section, we learned how to access the menus of QBO, all of which give you access to your company information, lists, tools, and profile. In addition, the **Quick Create** menu allows you to access customers, vendors, employees, and other areas of QuickBooks. From *Chapter 2, Company File Setup*, onward, we will show you how to navigate through these and customize QuickBooks for your business. To conclude this chapter, you may access *Chapter 13, Small Business Bookkeeping 101*, at `https://packt.link/supplementary-content-9781836649977`. In this supplementary section, we will introduce you to a few important bookkeeping concepts to improve your use of QuickBooks.

Summary

In this chapter, we explained what QuickBooks is and introduced you to the QBO product line. We covered setting up your QBO account and basic navigation using dashboards, icons, and online menus in QBO. We also provided tips on how to choose the right software for your business. Having a good understanding of the QuickBooks product line will help you to choose the best product for your business. In addition, having a basic knowledge of bookkeeping helps you understand the accounting that takes place behind the scenes in QuickBooks when you enter an invoice or pay a bill.

In the next chapter, we will show you how to customize QuickBooks for your business. This will include setting up company preferences and other key information you will need in order to tailor QuickBooks to your business needs.

Join our community on Discord

Join our community's Discord space for discussions with the authors and other readers:

`https://packt.link/powerusers`

2
Company File Setup

Picking up where we left off in *Chapter 1, Getting Started with QuickBooks Online*, we will show you how to customize your **QuickBooks Online (QBO)** account using company preferences. Company preferences allow you to establish how sales and expenses are recorded, how payments are handled, and other advanced settings, such as selecting the start of your fiscal year and which accounting method to use.

Before we dive into company preferences, we will spend some time discussing key information and documents that you need to have handy. This will help you to include as much information as possible; otherwise, you will be missing key details that should appear on customer invoices, documents, and forms that can be produced in QuickBooks. In addition, we will show you how easy it is to edit information in this section whenever you need to.

In this chapter, we'll cover the following topics:

- Key information and documents required to complete the company file setup in QBO
- Setting up company preferences in QBO

> The US edition of QBO was used to create this book. If you are using a version that is outside of the United States, results may differ.

Key information and documents

Before we get into the mechanics of creating your company file, you will need to gather some key documents and answer a few questions first. This information is necessary so that you can customize QuickBooks for your business. Plus, having this information at your fingertips will help you complete the company setup a lot faster.

The information you will need to know includes the following:

- **Company name**: This needs to be the legal name or the business name that should appear on all legal documents and payroll forms.
- **Company contact information**: This will include the mailing address, business telephone number, business email address, and website address of the company.
- **Industry**: In QuickBooks, you will select the industry that your business falls into. Using this information, a default chart of accounts list will be created for you. Selecting the correct industry can open up additional reporting for KPIs and other industry-specific information, depending on which version of QBO you are using.
- **Federal tax ID number**: This is a nine-digit number that identifies your business to the IRS. If you don't have a federal tax ID number, you can use your social security number. If you plan to process payroll within QBO, be sure to have your state and local payroll tax account numbers available.
- **Company organization type**: In QuickBooks, you will need to select from one of the following organization types—sole proprietor, partnership or LLC, nonprofit organization, C-Corp, or S-Corp.

> If you are a new business, information on the type of your company organization can be found in the letter from the IRS that includes your **federal employer identification number (FEIN)**. If you are an existing business, this information can be found on your most recently filed tax return for your business.

- **Fiscal year**: In QuickBooks, you will need to enter your company's fiscal year. For example, if you are on a calendar year, it will be January 1 to December 31.

- **List of products you sell**: If you have a lot of products, you should create an Excel or CSV spreadsheet that includes the product name, product description, cost, price, and quantity on hand. If you track inventory, we will show you how to import this information in *Chapter 4, Managing Customer, Vendor, and Products and Services Lists*.

- **List of services you sell**: Similar to products, you should create an Excel or CSV spreadsheet that includes the name of the service you offer, a brief description, and the price. We will show you how to import this information in *Chapter 4, Managing Customer, Vendor, and Products and Services Lists*.

- **List of sales tax rates**: A list of each city, state, or jurisdiction for which you are required to collect sales tax, along with the name of the tax authority that you pay, is required to properly set up sales tax in QuickBooks.

- **List of customers**: Customer contact details, such as an address, email address, telephone number, Facebook handle, or other information you have on file, can be entered into an Excel or CSV file if you wish to import the information into QuickBooks. Like products and services, we will show you how to import this information in *Chapter 4, Managing Customer, Vendor, and Products and Services Lists*.

- **List of vendor suppliers**: Vendor contact details, such as a remit-to address, email address, telephone number, primary contacts, and other information you have on file, can be entered into an Excel or CSV file and imported into QuickBooks. Similar to products, services, and customers, we will show you how to import this information in *Chapter 4, Managing Customer, Vendor, and Products and Services Lists*.

- **Chart of accounts list**: Your current list of accounts can be entered into an Excel spreadsheet if you wish to easily import it into QuickBooks. We show you how to import this information in *Chapter 4, Managing Customer, Vendor, and Products and Services Lists*.

> Be sure to have copies of your most recent bank and credit card statements, along with the last bank reconciliations completed.

By taking the time to gather these documents, you will ensure that you are not missing key information when you create forms such as customer invoices. In addition, your financial statements will be more accurate and reliable.

QuickBooks includes default settings called **preferences**. You can edit preferences to customize them to your specific business needs.

Setting up company preferences in QBO

Before you start entering data into QuickBooks, you should spend some time going through the company preferences, which allow you to activate features that you would like to use and deactivate features that you don't plan on using. If you are not sure of what to select in this section, you can always update the settings later on. Click on the gear icon and select **Account and settings**, located below the **Your Company** column.

The company preferences are made up of eight key areas:

- Company settings
- Usage settings
- Payments settings
- QuickBooks Checking
- Sales settings
- Expenses settings
- Time settings
- Advanced settings

Let's look at each one of these in more detail.

Company settings

In your company preferences, you will provide basic information about your business, such as the contact email and telephone number, where customers can reach you, your company logo, and your mailing address. The contact information that's included in this section will appear on customer invoices and emails that are sent to them, ensuring that they know how to get in contact with you. You will also provide your company name and entity type (sole proprietor, partnership, LLC, C-Corp, or S-Corp). It is also a good idea to enter your **employer identification number** (**EIN**) or social security number in this section. This information will be used to file payroll tax returns and 1099 forms, and it can also be used by your tax preparer when filing your taxes.

A brief explanation of the entity types are as follows:

- **Sole proprietor**: Individuals who own and operate a business alone, known as sole proprietors, generally file a Schedule C to report their business income and expenses, along with IRS Form 1040.
- **Partnership**: Businesses with two or more owners, known as partnerships, generally file IRS Form 1065 to report their business income and expenses to the IRS.

- **Limited Liability Company (LLC):** This refers to a company with one or more owners who are not personally liable for the LLC's debts or lawsuits. Your LLC can also be a partnership or S-Corp. Check your EIN letter or ask your accounting professional which entity type your LLC was set up as.
- **C-Corp:** This refers to a corporation that is taxed separately from its owners. C-Corps typically file IRS Form 1020 to report business income and expenses.
- **S-Corp:** These are closely held corporations that elect to be taxed under IRS Subchapter S. S-Corps typically file IRS Form 1020S to report business income and expenses.

Once you have filled in the **Company** settings, this page should resemble the one for our fictitious company, Small Business Builders, LLC:

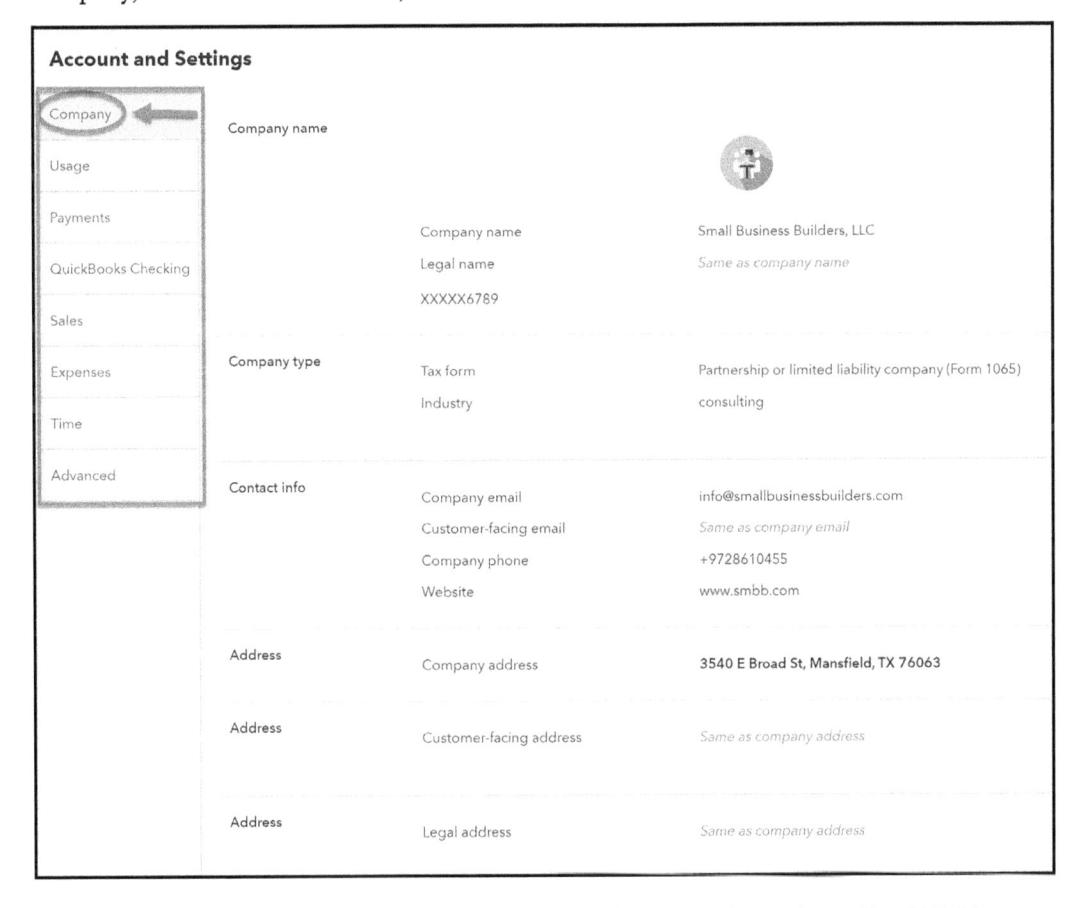

Figure 2.1: Company settings (for better visualization, refer to https://packt.link/gbp/9781836649977)

The information provided in the **Company** preferences can impact several areas of QuickBooks, such as customer invoices, tax forms, and documents. Therefore, it's important to complete this information in its entirety before you begin using QuickBooks to track your business activity. Next, we will explain what information you will find in the **Usage** settings.

Usage settings

A few years ago, Intuit implemented usage limits on all QBO plans. What this means is that each plan will have a maximum number of billable users, classes, locations, and accounts that you can add to the chart of accounts. The following is a brief description of these:

- **Billable users**: This refers to the total number of users you can give access to your QBO account. This includes bookkeepers, accountants, employees, and contractors.

- **Classes**: Depending on your business, a class can represent departments, office locations, or product lines. For example, our business management and consulting business could create a class for each type of service that they offer (for example, business plans, marketing plans, bookkeeping, tax planning, social media, etc.). One of the benefits of using classes is the ability to generate reports you can filter by class.

- **Locations**: If you have multiple locations, you can turn on location tracking in QuickBooks. One of the benefits of using locations is you can generate reports and filter by location.

- **Chart of accounts**: We discussed the chart of accounts in the *Small business bookkeeping 101* section, which you can access online using at https://packt.link/supplementary-content-9781836649977. The chart of accounts is used to classify your day-to-day business transactions. For example, office supplies and telephone expenses are two accounts that appear on the chart of accounts.

- **Tag groups**: Tags are customizable labels that let you track transactions in a variety of ways. You can tag invoices, expenses, and bills. You can also group tags together and run reports to see how specific areas of your business are doing.

Chapter 2

The following is a summary table that includes the usage limits for each QBO plan:

	QBO Simple Start	QBO Essentials	QBO Plus	QBO Advanced
Classes and locations (combined)	0	0	40	Unlimited
Chart of accounts	250	250	250	Unlimited
Tag groups	10	20	40	Unlimited
Billable users	1	3	5	25

Table 2.1: QBO usage limits for each plan

Here is a brief explanation of the usage limits for each QBO plan:

- **QBO Simple Start**: QBO Simple Start does not have the ability to track classes or locations, but you can have up to 250 accounts on the chart of accounts list. One billable user and two accountant users are also included in this plan.
- **QBO Essentials**: Similar to Simple Start, QBO Essentials does not have the ability to track classes or locations, but you can have up to 250 accounts on the chart of accounts list. Three billable users (that is, bookkeepers or employees) and two accountant users are included in this plan.
- **QBO Plus**: QBO Plus allows you to track classes and locations. You can add up to a total of 40 classes and/or locations combined. Five billable users and two accountant users are included in this plan.
- **QBO Advanced**: QBO Advanced allows you to track unlimited classes and locations. In addition, 25 billable users and 3 accountant users are included in this plan.

Your **Usage** settings should resemble the ones for our fictitious company, Small Business Builders, LLC, as shown in *Figure 2.2*:

Account and Settings

Company
Usage ←
Payments
QuickBooks Checking
Sales
Expenses
Time
Advanced

Usage limits

Your usage limits depend on your plan. Your current plan is QuickBooks Online Advanced. Find out more about usage limits

Billable Users ⓘ   1 OF 25

1 user(s)

Chart of accounts ⓘ   0 OF UNLIMITED

0 account(s)

Tag Groups   0 OF UNLIMITED

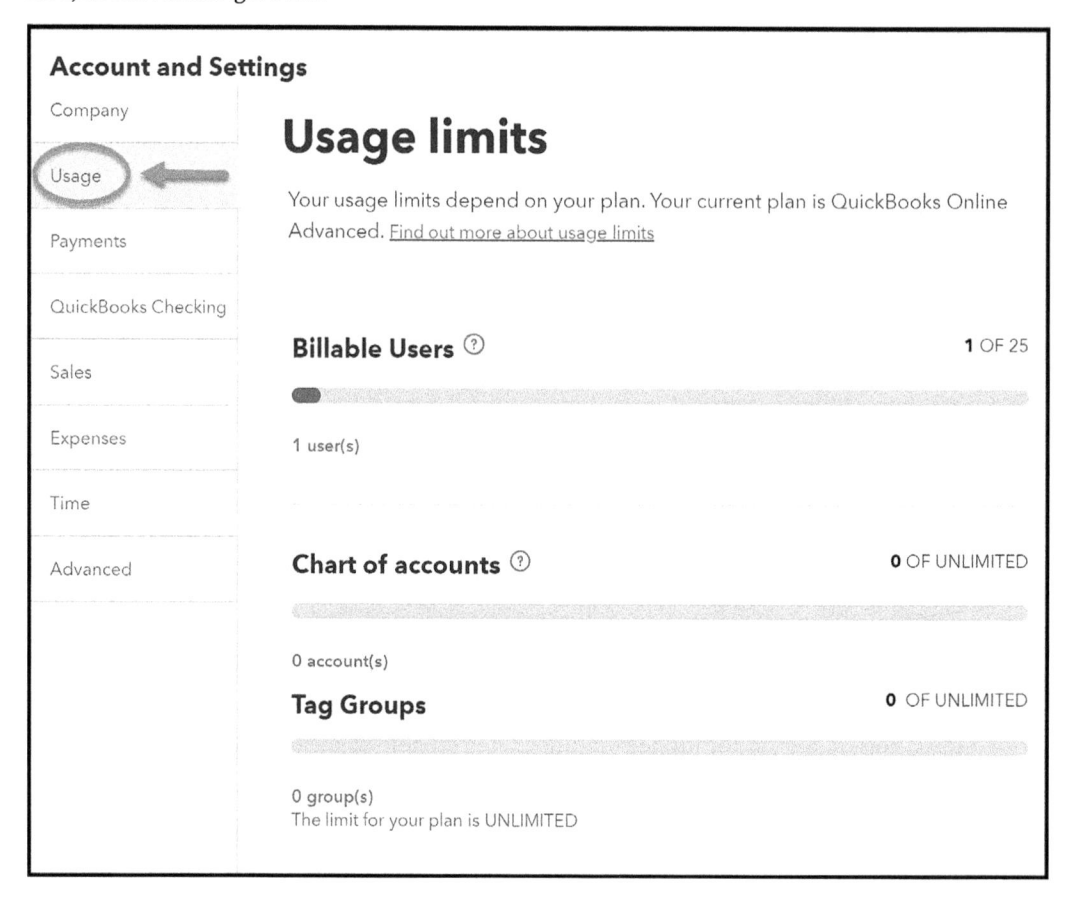

0 group(s)
The limit for your plan is UNLIMITED

Figure 2.2: Usage settings

Usage limits can impact the number of users you can add to QBO and the classes, locations, and accounts you add to the chart of accounts. This can have a significant effect on how much you pay for your QBO subscription if you hit the maximum usage settings and need to upgrade.

Payments settings

QuickBooks **Payments** allows you to accept online payments from customers in the form of bank transfers, debit cards, and credit cards. Once approved, all the invoices that you email to customers (directly from QuickBooks) will include a payment link. Your customers can click on the link, enter their payment details, and submit a payment in just a few minutes.

To apply for a **QuickBooks Payments** account, click on the **Learn more** option and follow the on-screen instructions. Once your account is approved, it will resemble the information shown in *Figure 2.3* below:

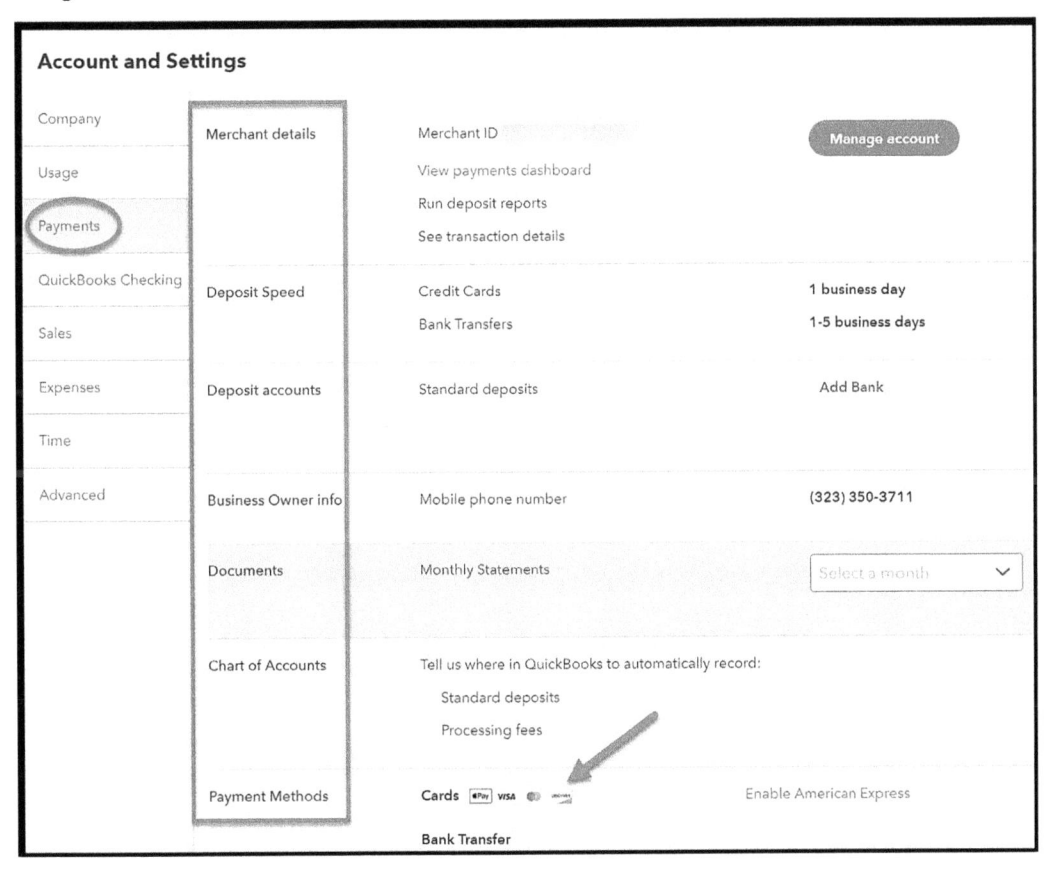

Account and Settings			
Company	Merchant details	Merchant ID	Manage account
Usage		View payments dashboard	
Payments		Run deposit reports	
		See transaction details	
QuickBooks Checking	Deposit Speed	Credit Cards	1 business day
Sales		Bank Transfers	1-5 business days
Expenses	Deposit accounts	Standard deposits	Add Bank
Time			
Advanced	Business Owner info	Mobile phone number	(323) 350-3711
	Documents	Monthly Statements	Select a month
	Chart of Accounts	Tell us where in QuickBooks to automatically record:	
		Standard deposits	
		Processing fees	
	Payment Methods	Cards Pay VISA	Enable American Express
		Bank Transfer	

Figure 2.3: Payments settings

If you have an existing Payments account, you can connect it by clicking the **Connect** button and following the on-screen instructions.

As we mentioned previously, QuickBooks Payments makes it easier to get paid by customers in a timely manner. This will allow you to maintain a positive cash flow, which is important for your business.

QuickBooks Checking settings

QuickBooks Checking is a monthly fee-free checking account where all of your customer payments get deposited. Use your QuickBooks Checking account like you do any bank account. You can save money, or use features like envelopes to save proactively and earn 5% APY (at the time of the writing of this book).

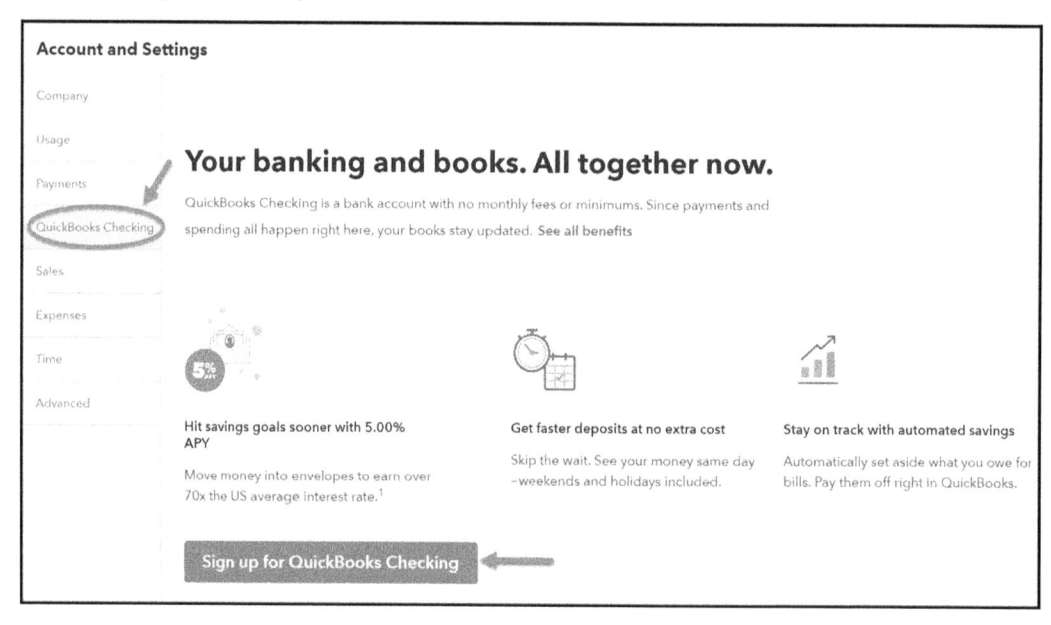

Figure 2.4: Sign up for QuickBooks Checking (for better visualization, refer to https://packt.link/gbp/9781836649977)

Sales settings

The **Sales** settings allow you to select and customize invoices, estimates, and sales receipt templates. In this section, payment terms are set for customers. If you have a few customers whose payment terms differ, you can customize payment terms when you add a new customer. If you offer discounts to customers or require upfront deposits, you can turn these features on here.

The following is a screenshot of the settings for **Sales**:

Chapter 2

Account and Settings

Company	**Sales form content**	Preferred invoice terms	Net 30
Usage		**Preferred delivery method**	None
		Shipping	Off
Payments		**Custom fields**	
QuickBooks Checking		Custom transaction numbers	On
		Service date	On
Sales ←		Discount	Off
		Deposit	Off
Expenses		Accept tips	Off
Time		Tags	Off
Advanced			
	Invoice payments	Accept Credit Cards Pay VISA	On
		Accept ACH BANK	On
		Payment instructions	
		Contact Small Business Builders, LLC to pay.	
	Products and services	Show Product/Service column on sales forms	On
		Show SKU column	Off
		Turn on price rules BETA	Off
		Track quantity and price/rate	On
		Track inventory quantity on hand	On
		Track inventory for sales channels	Off
		Revenue recognition Learn more	Off
	Late fees	Default charge applied to overdue invoices	Off
		Appears as a line under **Product/Service** on the invoice, and applies to all customers.	
	Progress Invoicing	Create multiple partial invoices from a single estimate	Off
	Messages	Default email message sent with sales forms	
	Reminders	Set up invoice reminder emails	

Figure 2.5: Sales settings

Here is a brief explanation of the information you can update/change in the **Sales** settings. You can click within each section or on the pencil icon to make the necessary changes:

1. **Sales form content**: In this section, you can select the default payment terms for most customers. For example, if the invoice due date for most customers is *Net 30* days, you will make that selection in the **Preferred invoice terms** field (shown in *Figure 2.5*). If you have customers that have different payment terms, you can select those terms when you add the customer to QuickBooks.

   If you offer customer discounts, accept deposits, or want to add custom fields, you will also turn these features on in this section. The main reason why you may want to offer customer discounts is to incentivize customers to order more or use them as a way to reward customers who make frequent purchases. If you typically need to include a shipping address on your sales form, you can turn this feature on here. QuickBooks will automatically assign transaction numbers (invoice numbers), but if you prefer to generate custom transaction numbers, you can turn this feature on. Keep in mind that you can always return to the **Sales form content** section to activate any of these settings later on.

2. **Invoice payments**: If you sign up for a QuickBooks Payments account, the payment methods that you accept will appear in this section. We will discuss how to apply for a Payments account in the *Payment settings* section later in this chapter.

3. **Products and services**: The **Products and services** settings allow you to determine what information you would like to appear on the sales form. You can turn on **price rules**, which is a feature that allows you to set up automatic discounts for certain customers or on specific products and services. If you want to track inventory, you will need to turn on both the **Track quantity and price/rate** and **Track inventory quantity on hand** features. Keep in mind that inventory tracking is only available in QBO Plus and Advanced.

4. **Late fees**: Create a default charge that is automatically applied to delinquent invoices. Please note that when you turn this feature on, it applies to all customers. You won't be able to pick and choose which customers you want to apply the feature to. Therefore, I recommend that you leave this feature off and set up reminders. We will cover how to set up reminders in the *Advanced settings* section at the end of this chapter.

5. **Progress Invoicing**: **Progress Invoicing** allows you to bill a customer in installments. For example, imagine you have a job that is going to result in $100,000 in revenue but you are required to complete certain milestones before you can submit an invoice. Progress invoicing allows you to create multiple invoices for one estimate. QuickBooks allows you to run reports that will show you how much you have billed against the estimate and the remaining amount to be billed.

6. **Messages**: When you email invoices, sales receipts, or estimates directly from QuickBooks, you can customize the message that is included in the body of the email. You can also select whether you want the invoice to be attached to the email as a PDF document or whether you prefer the invoice details to be included in the body of the email.

In *Figure 2.6* is a screenshot of the custom email message options you can choose from:

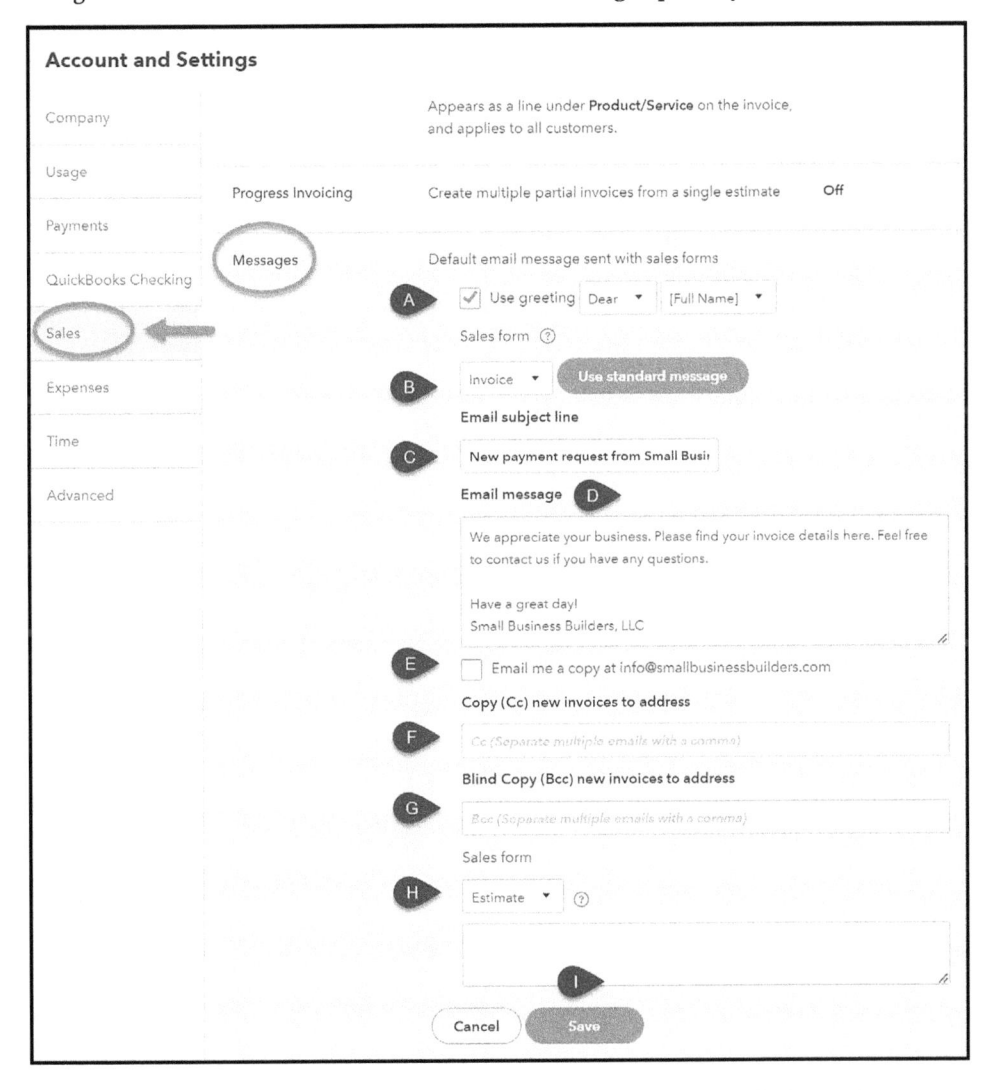

Figure 2.6: Customizing the email message for invoices, estimates, and sales receipts (for better visualization, refer to https://packt.link/gbp/9781836649977)

To customize emails, you can choose to use a greeting (**A**), select the type of form (**B**), customize the email subject line (**C**), customize the email message (**D**), or choose to use the standard message shown. You can have a copy of the email sent to you (**E**), send a carbon copy to someone else (**F**), and **blind-copy** (**Bcc**) new invoices to multiple people (**G**). You can also customize emails for estimates and sales receipts by choosing the preferred option from the drop-down (**H**).

After making your selections, be sure to click the **Save** button (**I**).

> When sending invoices to customers via email, you now have the option to enter their mobile number so that they also receive a text message. This helps make it even easier for your customers to make a payment.

7. **Reminders**: QuickBooks allows you to send payment reminder emails to customers. You can customize the message that goes out to your customers in this section.

Now that you know how to customize sales forms, set payment terms for customers, and turn on discounts and deposits, it's time to learn how to manage expenses using the **Expense** settings next.

Expenses settings

The settings in the **Expenses** section include preferences for managing bills, expenses, and purchase orders. In this section, you will determine what information you want to appear on expense and purchase forms, whether you want to track expenses and items by customer, and default payment terms.

Chapter 2

The following is a screenshot of the **Expenses** settings:

Account and Settings

Company
Usage
Payments
QuickBooks Checking
Sales
Expenses ←
Time
Advanced

Expenses

Bills and expenses	
	Show Items table on expense and purchase forms
	Show Tags field on expense and purchase forms
	Track expenses and items by customer
	Make expenses and items billable
	☐ Markup with a default rate of 0.00 %
	☑ Track billable expenses and items as income
	● In a single account
	○ In multiple accounts
	☐ Charge sales tax
	Default bill payment terms Enter Text
	Cancel Save
Purchase orders	Use purchase orders On
Messages	Default email message sent with purchase orders

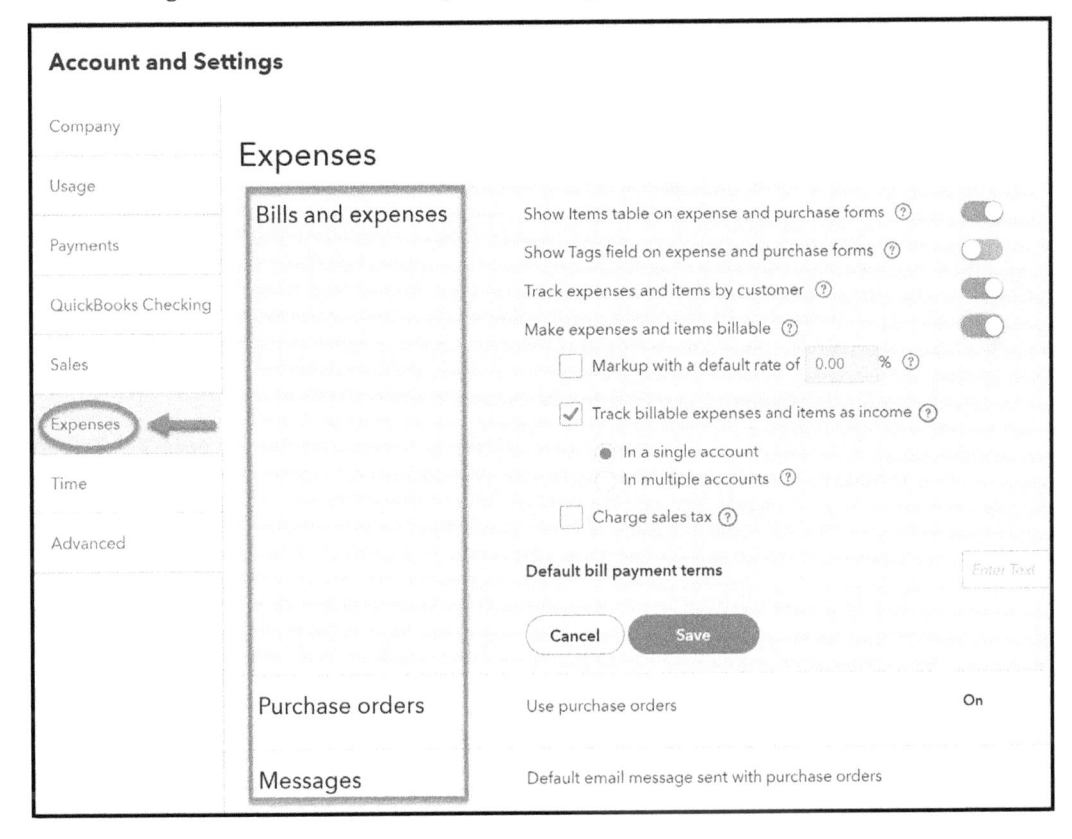

Figure 2.7: Expenses settings

The following is a brief explanation of what you can find in the **Expenses** preferences:

1. **Bills and expenses**: This section includes the following five options for tracking expenses:

    - **Show Items table on expense and purchase forms**: This feature is automatically turned on, and it will add a *products and services* table to your expense and purchase forms so that you can itemize your products and services. You will learn more about products and services lists in *Chapter 4, Managing Customer, Vendor, and Products and Services Lists*.

    - **Show Tags field on expense and purchase forms**: This feature is automatically turned on. If you don't use tags to track expenses, you can turn this feature off.

    - **Track expenses and items by customer**: This feature allows you to track expenses with a specific customer. This is ideal for reporting purposes if you want to keep track of specific items that have been purchased but may or may not be billable to customers. For example, let's say we want to keep track of the hours worked by contractors for each client. If Small Business Builders, LLC bill their customers a flat rate, then there is no need to bill the client back for those hours worked, but they need to keep track of them to ensure the flat rate is accurate.

    - **Make expenses and items billable**: This feature adds a billable column on all expense and purchase forms so that you can bill customers for items you've purchased on their behalf. Using our previous example, if Small Business Builders, LLC did bill their customers by the hour, they could easily select the client and mark the billable column to bill their clients for the hours worked by contactors, as opposed to billing them a flat fee.

    - To see a list of unbilled expenses, you can run the *Unbilled Charges* report, which is located in the **Who Owes You** report group.

    - **Default bill payment terms**: If most of the bills you receive have similar payment terms (for instance, **Net 30**), you can set payment terms for all vendors here and then change the vendor profile for those vendors whose payment terms may differ. In *Chapter 4, Managing Customer, Vendor, and Products and Services Lists*, we cover this in detail.

Chapter 2   51

2. **Purchase orders**: If you plan to create purchase orders, be sure to turn this feature on. If you don't need to create purchase orders, you can leave it turned off.

3. **Messages**: You can email purchase orders directly from QuickBooks to vendor suppliers. This section allows you to customize the email message that your vendor supplier will receive along with the purchase orders.

Now that you are familiar with the **Expenses** settings that affect bills, purchase orders, and expenses, you can set up QuickBooks the way you need in order to track expenses that are incurred by your business. Next, we will discuss a way for you to keep track of the hours worked by employees and contractors.

Time settings

Basic time tracking is included in all QBO subscription plans. Time tracking allows your team to keep track of the hours they work, using a mobile app with GPS. With GPS, you are able to see the location that a worker clocked in from. In addition, workers can keep track of their mileage. As a business owner, you can schedule workers, manage time off, and review reports in real time. To learn more about the time tracking plans available, click on the **See plans** button, as shown in *Figure 2.8*:

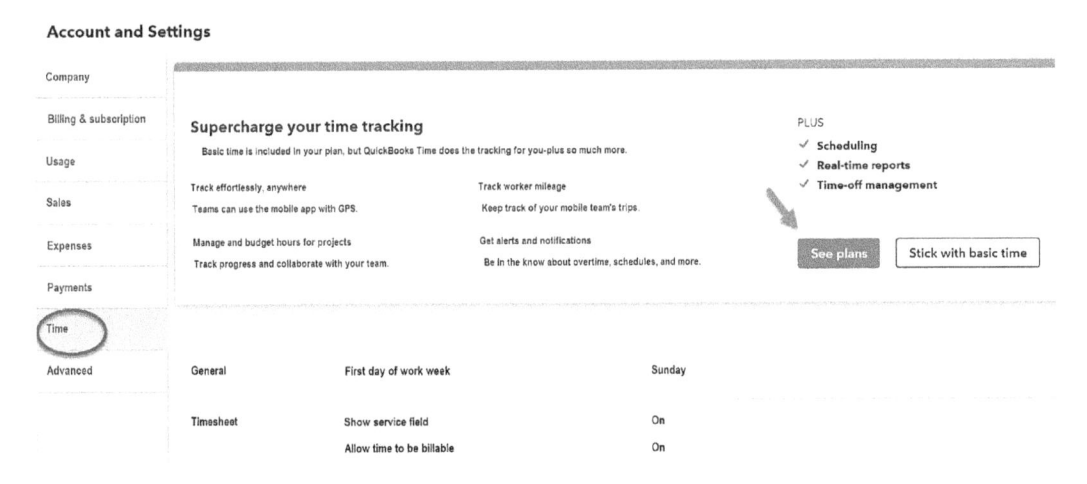

Figure 2.8: See plans button on the Time settings page (for better visualization, refer to https://packt.link/gbp/9781836649977)

Advanced settings

The **Advanced settings** page includes eight key settings: **Accounting, Company type, Chart of accounts, Categories, Automation, Projects, Currency, Business Network**, and **Other preferences**.

The following is a screenshot of the **Advanced** settings section:

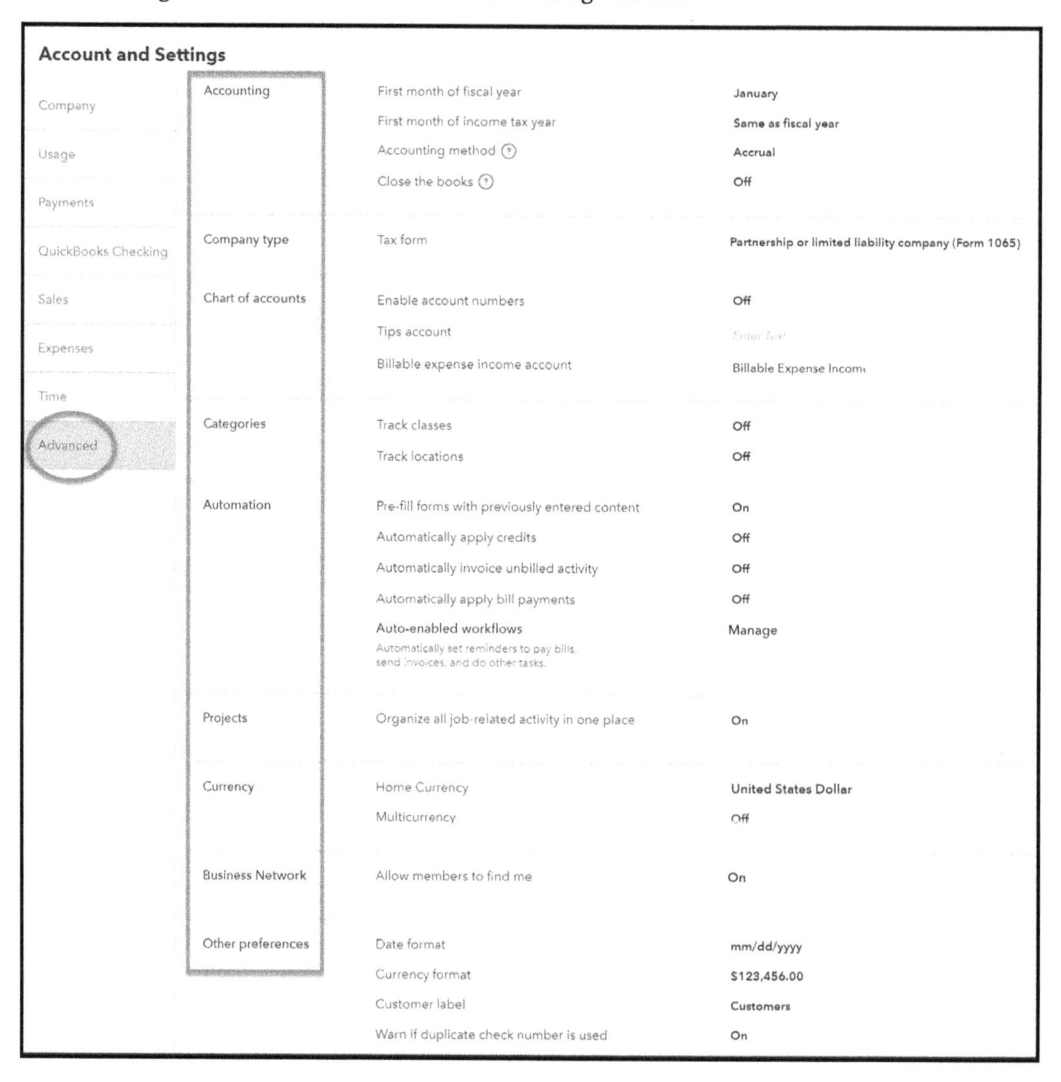

Account and Settings			
Company	Accounting	First month of fiscal year	January
		First month of income tax year	Same as fiscal year
Usage		Accounting method (?)	Accrual
Payments		Close the books (?)	Off
QuickBooks Checking	Company type	Tax form	Partnership or limited liability company (Form 1065)
Sales	Chart of accounts	Enable account numbers	Off
		Tips account	Enter text
Expenses		Billable expense income account	Billable Expense Income
Time	Categories	Track classes	Off
Advanced		Track locations	Off
	Automation	Pre-fill forms with previously entered content	On
		Automatically apply credits	Off
		Automatically invoice unbilled activity	Off
		Automatically apply bill payments	Off
		Auto-enabled workflows Automatically set reminders to pay bills, send invoices, and do other tasks.	Manage
	Projects	Organize all job-related activity in one place	On
	Currency	Home Currency	United States Dollar
		Multicurrency	Off
	Business Network	Allow members to find me	On
	Other preferences	Date format	mm/dd/yyyy
		Currency format	$123,456.00
		Customer label	Customers
		Warn if duplicate check number is used	On

Figure 2.9: Advanced settings

A brief description of what information is included in the **Advanced** settings section is as follows:

- **Accounting**: In the **Accounting** settings, you will select the first month of your fiscal year and income tax year, which may be the same. You will indicate your accounting method (for example, cash or accrual), and there is an option to close the books. Closing the books allows you to prevent any changes from being made to your financial data after a certain date. For example, once you have filed your tax returns for the year, you should enter the last day of the previous year as your closing date (for example, 12/31/2025). This will ensure that information dated 12/31/2025 and prior cannot be changed. A password will be assigned to prevent changes to closed periods.

- **Company type**: In this field, you will select the structure of your business. The common business structures are sole proprietor, partnership, limited liability, C-Corp, and S-Corp. In our example, Small Business Builders is a **limited liability company (LLC)**.

> The company type is helpful in assigning your chart of accounts to specific line items on the tax return. This is beneficial for linking to tax software or for your tax preparer. For example, if you are a sole proprietor, then you will complete *Schedule C* to report your business income and expenses to the IRS. When adding a new account to the chart of accounts list, the field named **Tax form** will list the categories on *Schedule C* so that you can assign an account to the specific line item on the tax form.

- **Chart of accounts**: As we discussed in the previous chapter, the chart of accounts is a way to categorize your day-to-day business transactions. You have the option to assign account numbers to your chart of accounts list by turning on the **Enable account numbers** preference. If your business allows customers to leave tips, you can keep track of these tips in a separate account.

- **Categories**: There are two types of categories in QuickBooks—classes and locations. Classes are generally used to track income and expenses for departments or product lines. Locations are used to track income and expenses for multiple locations of your business. These preferences must be turned on for you to use them.

- **Automation**: You can save time by automating certain tasks. QuickBooks will automatically pre-fill forms based on the information you have provided in a previous transaction for a customer or vendor. You can also allow QuickBooks to automatically apply credit that's been received from vendor suppliers and bill payments. However, setting up your QBO file correctly is important before enabling any of the automated features.

- **Projects**: The **Projects** feature allows you to keep track of all income and expenses for jobs/projects that you are working on. To view all projects, click on the **Projects** tab, which is located on the left navigation bar.
- **Currency**: QuickBooks allows you to create invoices and pay bills in multiple currencies. You can do business with vendor suppliers and customers across the globe by providing invoices in their native currency. All of your financial reports can be generated in your home currency or any currency that you choose.

> Once you turn on the multi-currency feature, it cannot be turned off. This is because several conversion tables are activated in the background once you turn this feature on and start using it.

- **Business Network**: The QuickBooks Business Network lets you connect with your customers and vendors. By connecting, you can send invoices to your customers through the network, and receive bills from your vendors directly in QuickBooks. They're ready to review and pay, which means you don't have to manually enter bills.
- **Other preferences**: The **Other preferences** section involves general formatting preferences for the dates and numbers that appear throughout the program. You can also select the type of label for your customers. For example, if you are a nonprofit organization, you can select **Donors**, and if you are a real estate investor, you can select **Tenants**. This nomenclature will appear throughout the program. This preference also includes a warning if you use a duplicate check number or vendor invoice number.

> You should turn both of these features on to help prevent duplicate payments. A similar warning is also included when recording journal entries. A journal entry is an adjustment made to the books for transactions that are only recorded prior to closing the books, like depreciation. For security reasons, QBO will automatically sign you out after you have been inactive for 1 hour. However, you can change this setting to a maximum of 3 hours.

You now know that accounting settings affect several areas of QuickBooks. You can determine your chart of accounts structure, turn on time tracking, set your home currency, and turn on the multi-currency feature if you do business in other countries. In addition, you can turn on the projects and categories feature for additional tracking of income and expenses.

Summary

In this chapter, we have covered key information and documents required to set up a QBO account. We have also shown you how to customize the company settings, which include billing and subscription, usage limits, QuickBooks checking, sales, expenses, time, and advanced settings. Taking the time to set up your company file will help you save time in the long run because you won't have to do it later on. Plus, you won't have to worry about customer invoices or vendor bills missing key information because your company file wasn't set up properly.

Remember, you can always edit these settings whenever you need to. While it is ideal to complete this setup now so that when you are ready to start recording transactions in QBO, many of the fields on invoices and bills will automatically populate for you, at some point, if your contact information or business entity changes, you can always make any necessary updates.

In the next chapter, we will show you how to customize QuckBooks Online for your business. You will learn how to customize the chart of accounts list, how to connect your bank and credit card accounts to QBO, how to give other users access to your QBO file and how to use apps with QBO.

Join our community on Discord

Join our community's Discord space for discussions with the authors and other readers:

`https://packt.link/powerusers`

3
Customizing QuickBooks for Your Business

Whether you created your **QuickBooks Online (QBO)** account from scratch or transferred your details from another accounting software program, there are some additional areas that you need to set up to further customize QBO for your business.

In this chapter, we will show you how to add, edit, and delete accounts to customize the chart of accounts for your business. We will walk through the process of connecting your bank and credit card accounts to QBO so that transactions will automatically be downloaded. By connecting your bank accounts to QuickBooks, you will reduce, if not eliminate, the need to manually enter these transactions into QuickBooks. Please note that uploading bank and credit card transactions to QBO does not record them in your books. You will need to review and record these transactions after they are uploaded. In *Chapter 15, Reconciling Uploaded Bank and Credit Card Transactions*, accessible online using this link: `https://packt.link/supplementary-content-9781836649977` we will cover this in detail. If you need to give other users access to your QuickBooks data, you can easily do so; we will show you how to give your bookkeeper, accountant, and other users access.

We will wrap this chapter up by showing you how to navigate the QuickBooks App Center. Apps are a great way to help you streamline day-to-day business tasks that can be time-consuming.

The following are the key topics that will be covered in this chapter:

- Customizing the chart of accounts list
- Connecting bank accounts to QBO
- Connecting credit card accounts to QBO
- Giving other users access to your QuickBooks data
- Using apps in QBO

> The US edition of QBO was used to create this book. If you are using a version that is outside of the US, results may differ.

Customizing the chart of accounts list

As we saw in *Chapter 1, Getting Started with QuickBooks Online*, the chart of accounts is a list of accounts that is used to categorize your day-to-day business transactions. It is the backbone of every accounting system, and if it is not set up properly, it can result in inaccurate financial statements.

One of the benefits of using QuickBooks is that you don't have to create a chart of accounts from scratch. Based on the industry that you selected when you created your QBO account, QuickBooks will include a preset chart of accounts list. You can customize the chart of accounts by adding, editing, or deleting accounts to fit your business needs. In this section, we will show you how to add, edit, delete (inactivate), and merge accounts on the chart of accounts list.

Adding a new account to the chart of accounts list

The default chart of accounts list will include a generic list of accounts used by most businesses, with a few custom accounts related to your industry. However, you will most likely need to customize the list based on your accountant's preferences or your own. For example, if you sell products and services, you may want to create an income account for each, as opposed to lumping sales for both into one account.

Chapter 3

Go through the following three steps to add a new account to the chart of accounts list:

1. Click on the **Transactions** tab located on the left menu bar and select **Chart of accounts**, as shown in *Figure 3.1*:

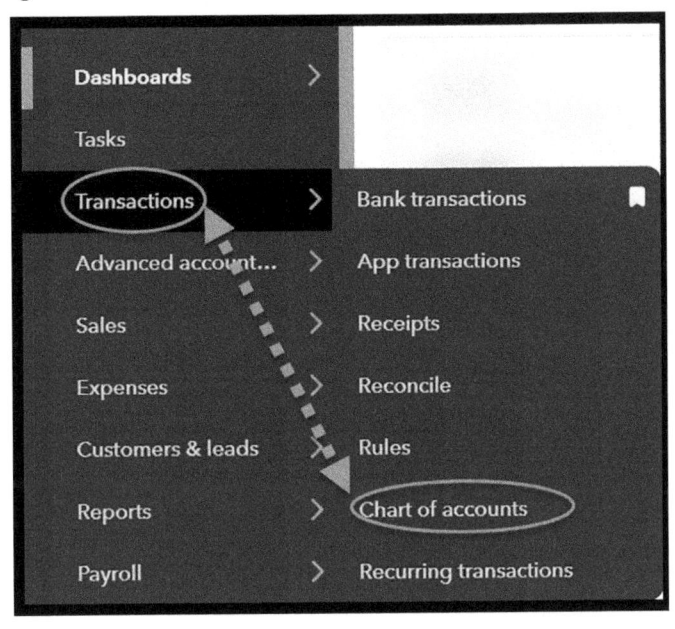

Figure 3.1: Navigating to the Chart of accounts option

2. Click on the **New** button located in the upper-right corner of the screen, directly to the right of the **Run Report** button, as shown in *Figure 3.2*:

Figure 3.2: The New button

3. To create a new account, you will need to provide the account name, account type, detail type, and a description of the account, as shown in *Figure 3.3*:

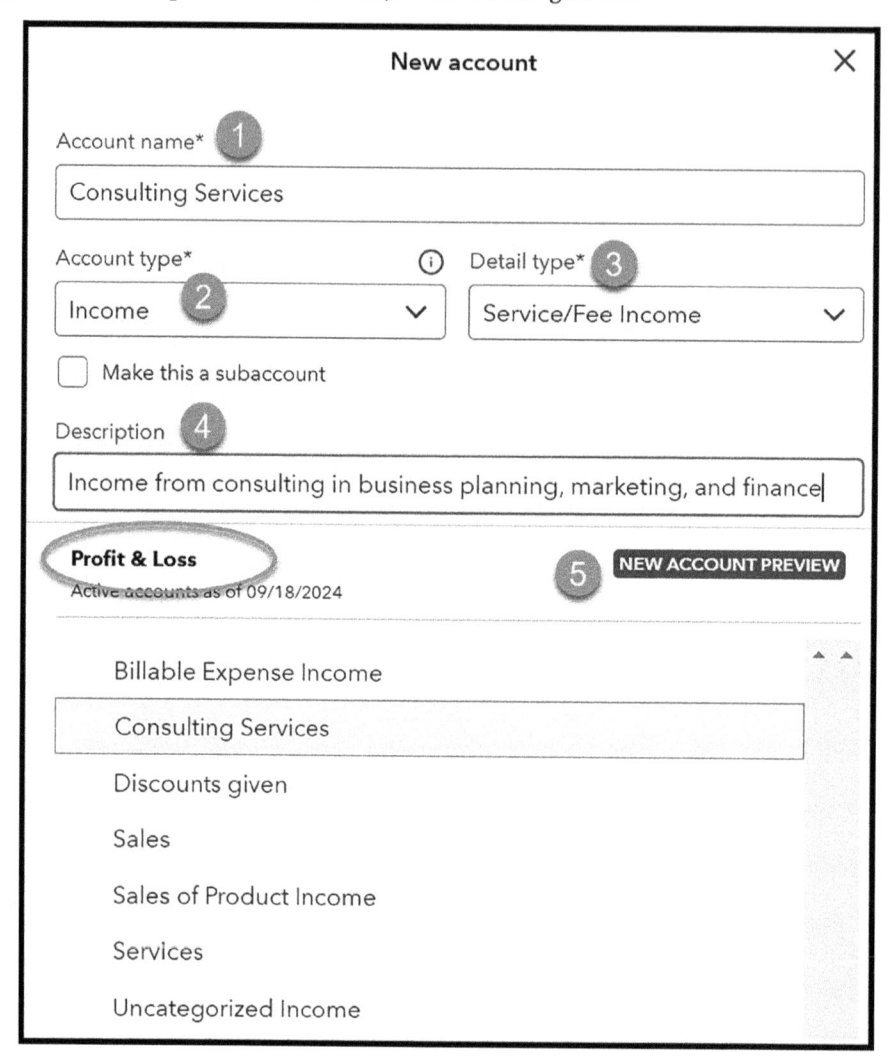

Figure 3.3: New account creation page

The following is a brief description of what information should be included in the fields that are labeled:

- **Account name (1)**: Type the name of the account in this field. In our example, it is **Consulting Services**.

- **Account type (2)**: From the menu, select the account type that the new account should be categorized as. As we saw in *Chapter 1, Getting Started with QuickBooks Online*, the five main account types are assets, liabilities, equity, income, and expenses. You will also find other account types in this list, such as fixed assets, banks, and credit cards, and they should be used when appropriate.
- **Detail type (3)**: From the drop-down, select the description that is the closest match to the account that you are setting up.
- **Description (4)**: This field is self-explanatory, and should include a brief description of the types of transactions that should be posted to this account.

> While you may be tempted to leave the **Description** field blank, we recommend that you don't. It can be useful to include a detailed description so that a bookkeeper or someone you have hired to manage your books will know what type of transactions belong in this account. If you don't think a description is needed, copy and paste the account name into this field. That way, this field will not appear blank on reports. You can also use this field to enter more details about the accounts, such as account numbers or other useful information.

- **NEW ACCOUNT PREVIEW (5)**: This section informs you of the financial report the account will show up on (**Profit & Loss**, in our example). In addition, it shows that **Consulting Services** will be grouped with the **Income** accounts, in alphabetical order on the profit and loss report.

4. Once you have completed all the fields for the new account and saved it, the new account will appear on your chart of accounts list, as shown in *Figure 3.4*:

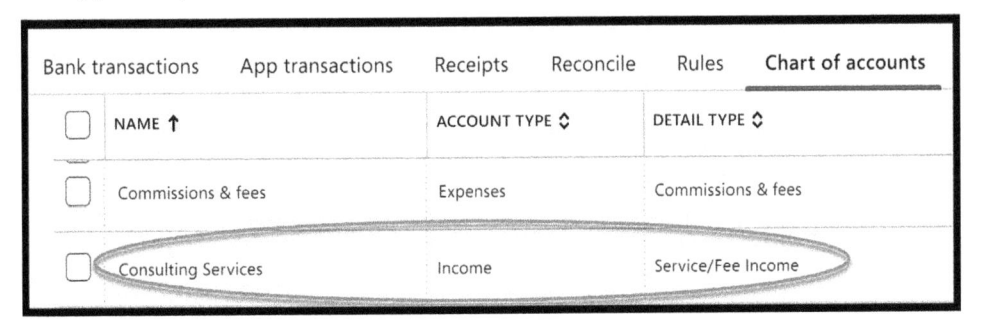

Bank transactions	App transactions	Receipts	Reconcile	Rules	Chart of accounts
NAME ↑		ACCOUNT TYPE ◊		DETAIL TYPE ◊	
Commissions & fees		Expenses		Commissions & fees	
Consulting Services		Income		Service/Fee Income	

Figure 3.4: The Chart of accounts list

As you can see, adding a new account to the chart of accounts list is pretty straightforward. If you need to add more than five accounts, you may want to consider importing new accounts instead of manually entering them. I recommend that you set up accounts that will be useful for you in managing your business.

> **Sub-accounts** are used to provide a more detailed breakdown of an account that is used for multiple types of transactions. For example, it is a good idea to create a main account for car expenses and sub-accounts for repairs, registration, and gasoline. Having a detailed breakdown of each type of expense will allow you to easily run a report to see how much you have spent on each account.

In the next section, we will show you how to import a chart of accounts list from an Excel file.

Importing a chart of accounts list

If your accountant has given you a chart of accounts list that they prefer you to use, you can import that list into QBO. Go through the following steps to import a chart of accounts list. The template can be found at `https://github.com/PacktPublishing/Mastering-QuickBooks-2025-Sixth-Edition/tree/main/Chapter04`.

1. Format your Excel spreadsheet to include the following columns (**Account Number, Account Name, Type,** and **Detail Type**) and save it in `.csv` or `.xls` format:

Account Number	Account Name	Type	Detail Type
112720	Checking Account - Bank of America	Bank	Checking
112721	Money Market - First National Bank	Bank	Money Market
410790	Product Sales Revenue	Income	Sales of Product Income
500780	Cost of materials	Cost of Goods Sold	Supplies & Materials

Figure 3.5: Chart of accounts import template

2. Navigate to **Transactions | Chart of accounts,** as indicated below:

Chapter 3 63

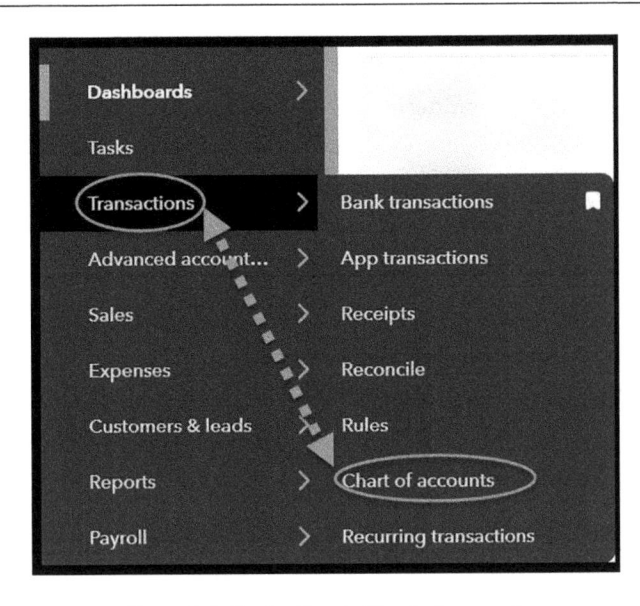

Figure 3.6: Navigating to Chart of accounts

3. Click on the arrow to the right of the **New** button and select **Import**, as shown in *Figure 3.7*:

Figure 3.7: Clicking Import

4. The **Import Accounts** screen is displayed:

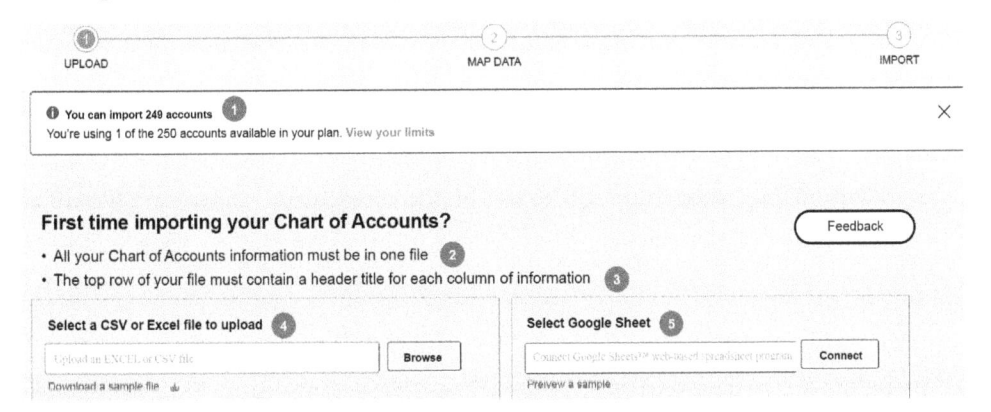

Figure 3.8: Import Accounts screen with highlighted items

A brief description of the highlighted items is as follows:

- **Import limit (1)**: Depending on the QBO plan you have purchased, you will be limited to a certain number of accounts you can import. In our example, the limit is 250, but we can only import 249 accounts after adding the **Consulting Services** account in the previous example. If you have QBO Advanced, you won't see a limit since the number of accounts is *unlimited*.

- **All of your Chart of Accounts information must be in one file (2)**: Be sure to organize all of your accounts in a single spreadsheet.

- **Include header information (3)**: When formatting your spreadsheet, be sure that the first row is a header row that contains a description of the info included in each column. Refer to *Figure 3.5*.

- **CSV or Excel file upload (4)**: You can upload a CSV or Excel (.xls) file format; no other file format is allowed.

- **Google Sheet (5)**: If you have your data in a Google Sheet, it is also compatible with QBO. Simply click the **Connect** button shown above and follow the onscreen instructions.

Follow the onscreen prompts to complete the import. Next, we will show you how to edit the chart of accounts list.

Editing accounts on the chart of accounts list

On occasion, you may want to make changes to an existing account on the chart of accounts list. You can change the account name, description, and account type at any time; however, be careful with making a change to the account type if you have transactions that have already been posted. Changing the account type can impact the financial statements. Therefore, make sure you consult your accountant before doing so.

You can edit accounts on the chart of accounts list by going through the following steps:

1. Click on the **Transactions** tab located on the left menu bar and select **Chart of accounts**, as shown in *Figure 3.9*:

Chapter 3

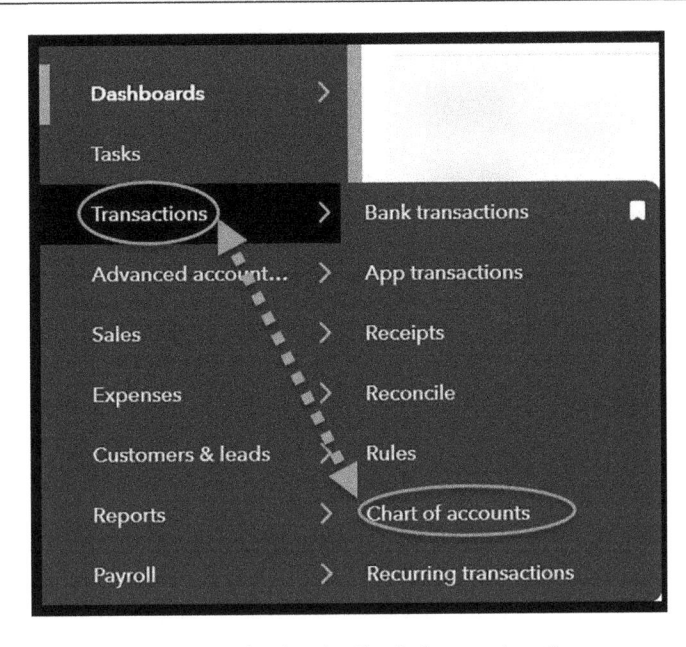

Figure 3.9: Selecting the Chart of accounts option

2. Scroll through the chart of accounts list or use the search bar to find the account you want to edit. *Figure 3.10* shows the **ACTION** column on the far right. Click on the arrow located to the right of **Run Report**:

NAME ▲	TYPE	DETAIL TYPE	ACTION
Advertising & Marketing	Expenses	Advertising/Promotional	Run Report ▼

Figure 3.10: Editing an account

3. On the next screen, you will see two options: **Edit** and **Make inactive**, as shown in *Figure 3.11*:

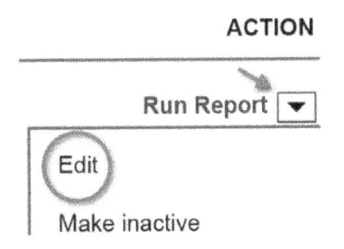

Figure 3.11: Choosing the Edit option

> All accounts that appear on the **Balance Sheet** report will show a **View register** link in the **Action** column. This is because all balance sheet accounts keep a running balance from one period to the next, whereas income and expense accounts do not keep a running balance because they are closed at the end of each fiscal period (i.e., month). Therefore, income and expense accounts will show a **Run Report** link in the **Action** column.

The following is a brief explanation of when you should edit an account and when you should make an account inactive:

- **Edit**: To make changes to the account name, account description, or sub-account, click on the **Edit** button.
- **Make inactive**: Once you have created an account in QuickBooks, there is no way to delete it. Instead, you will need to inactivate the account. When you inactivate an account in QuickBooks, it will still exist, but it will disappear from the chart of accounts list and will not appear in any drop-down lists. The primary reason for this is that if you have recorded transactions to an account that you decide to stop using, your transactions will still remain in QuickBooks. This is very important in order to maintain accurate financial records. If you need to review accounts that have been made inactive or reactivate an account, you can easily do so. We will cover this later, in the *Reactivating an account on the chart of accounts list* section.

4. When you click **Edit**, the current account setup will be displayed. Make the necessary changes, as shown in *Figure 3.12*:

Edit Account

Account name*
Advertising & marketing

Account type*
Expenses

Detail type*
Advertising/Promotional

☐ Make this a subaccount

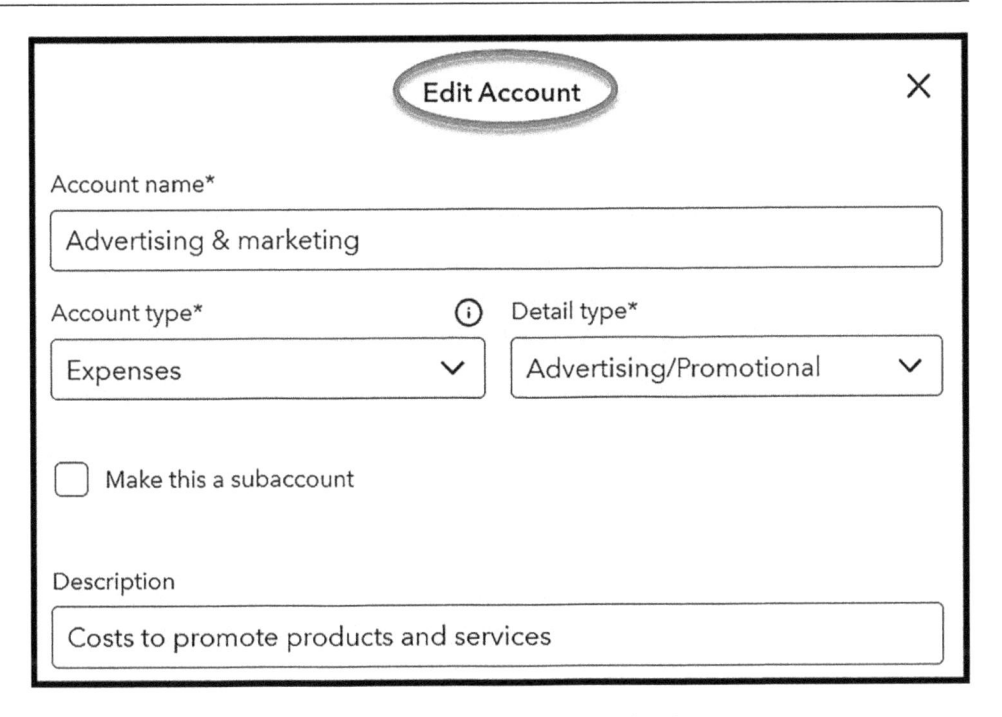

Description
Costs to promote products and services

Figure 3.12: Editing the account details

If you have not used the account in a transaction, the **Account name** and **Account type** fields will be editable.

In this section, we covered how to make changes to an existing account on your chart of accounts list. We also explained the difference between editing an account and making an account inactive. As previously mentioned, you cannot delete an account, but you can make it inactive. In the next section, we will show you how to inactivate an existing account.

Inactivating an account on the chart of accounts list

Once you add an account to the chart of accounts list, you cannot delete it; however, if you decide that you no longer want to use an account, you can inactivate the account. Inactivating an account will remove the account from the chart of accounts list and the drop-down menus, but it will still exist in the program. This will ensure that any transactions that have been recorded will remain intact, which will also ensure that you have accurate financial statements.

To inactivate an account, go through the following steps:

1. Click on the **Transactions** tab located on the left menu bar and select **Chart of accounts**, as shown in *Figure 3.13*:

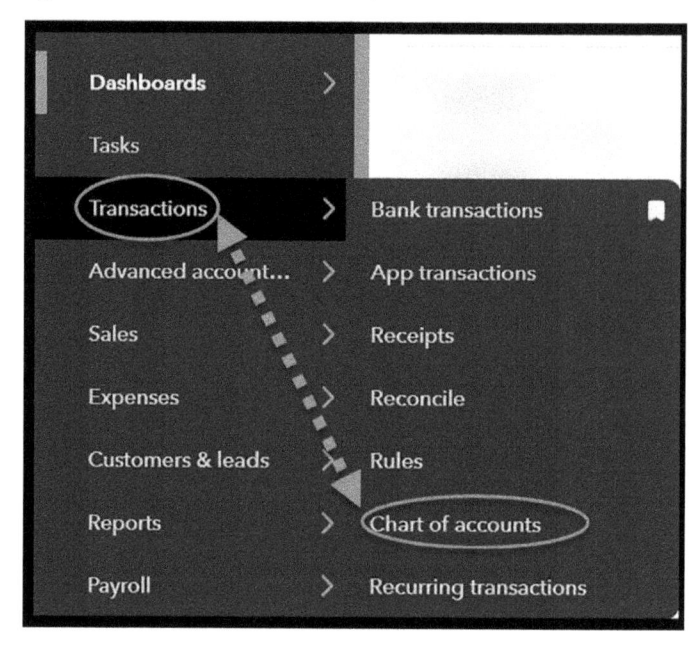

Figure 3.13: Navigating to the Chart of accounts option

2. Scroll through the chart of accounts list to find the account you want to make inactive. In the **ACTION** column on the far right, click on the arrow located to the right of **Run Report**, as shown here:

NAME ▲	TYPE	DETAIL TYPE	ACTION
Advertising & Marketing	Expenses	Advertising/Promotional	Run Report ▼

Figure 3.14: Editing an account

Chapter 3

3. Select **Make inactive** from the drop-down arrow, as shown here:

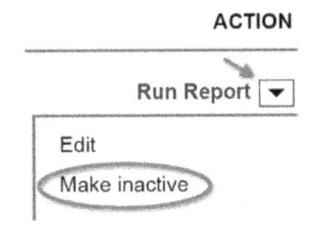

Figure 3.15: Making an account inactive

4. You will then receive a message similar to the one shown in the following screenshot, asking you to confirm that you would like to inactivate the account:

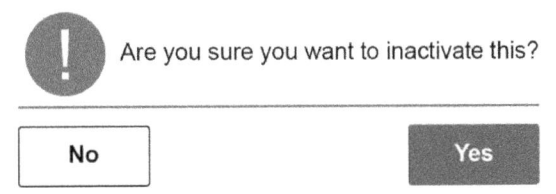

Figure 3.16: Inactivation confirmation message

5. Click **Yes** to proceed with the inactivation or **No** to leave the account active.

Reactivating an account on the chart of accounts list

If you decide to reactivate an account that was previously made inactive, you can easily do this:

1. From the chart of accounts list, click on the gear icon located directly above the **ACTION** column, as indicated below:

Figure 3.17: The gear icon

2. Put a checkmark in the box that says **Include inactive** so that all inactive accounts appear on the chart of accounts list, as indicated below:

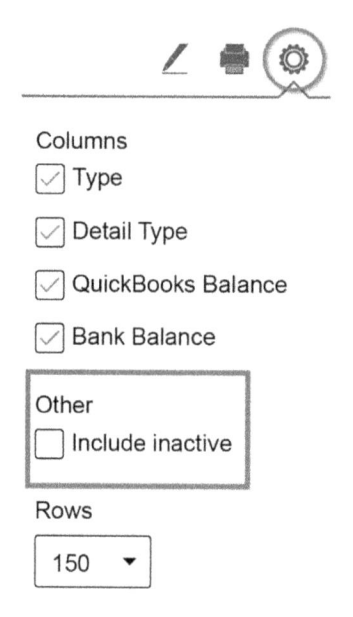

Figure 3.18: The Include inactive option

3. Next to the inactive accounts, click the link that says **Make active** to the right of the account, as shown here:

NAME ▲	TYPE	DETAIL TYPE	ACTION
Advertising & Marketing (deleted)	Expenses	Advertising/Promotional	Make active ▼

Figure 3.19: The Make active option

As mentioned previously, you cannot delete accounts in QBO. However, when an account is made inactive, you will see **deleted** in parentheses next to the account name. This may be confusing, but keep in mind that **deleted** does not mean the account has been deleted; it has actually been inactivated.

Merging accounts in QBO

An issue that you may encounter at some point is duplicate accounts. For example, you may end up having accounts with similar names, like *office supplies* and *office supplies expense*. This can happen if you have more than one person adding accounts to the chart of accounts, or if you have not documented a procedure for creating new accounts. However, you can easily fix this issue by merging the accounts, which will combine all of the data from both accounts into one.

Chapter 3

Follow the steps below to merge accounts:

1. Navigate to the account list and identify the duplicate accounts:

NAME	ACCOUNT TYPE	DETAIL TYPE	ACTION
Supplies & materials - COGS	Cost of Goods Sold	Supplies & Materials - COGS	Run report
Materials & Office Supplies	Expenses	Office/General Administrative Expenses	Run report
Office supplies	Expenses	Office/General Administrative Expenses	Run report

Figure 3.20: Identifying duplicate accounts in the chart of accounts

In the image above, **Materials & Office Supplies** and **Office supplies** are the same accounts.

2. Click once on the account you plan to remove and choose **Edit** from the **Run report** drop-down in the far-right column. In our example, we will remove **Office supplies**.

The following account information will appear:

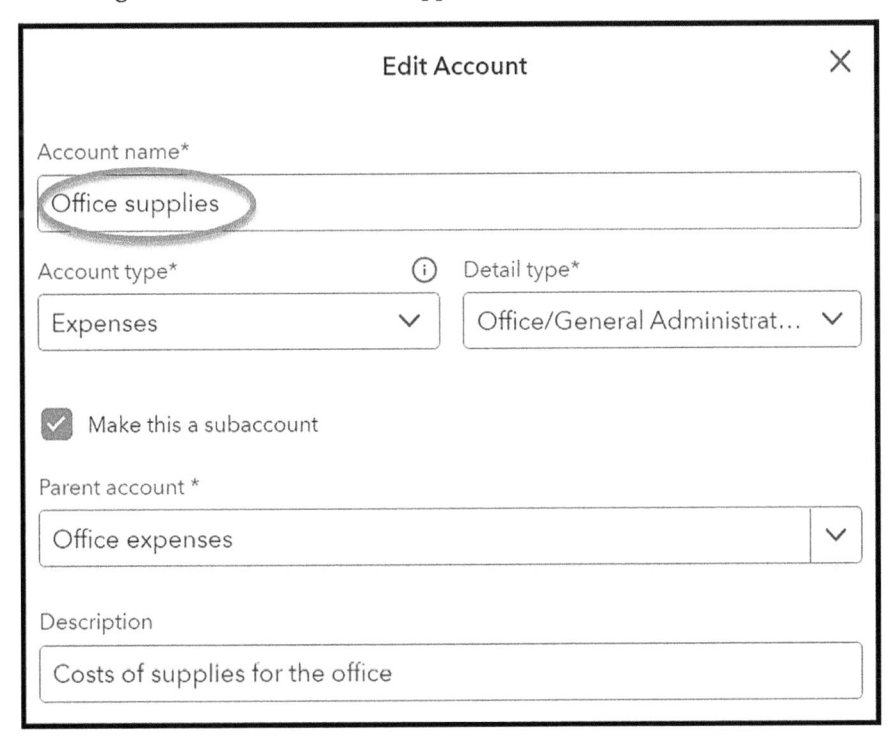

Figure 3.21: Displaying account information

3. Type the name of the account you wish to keep in the **Account name** field. In our example, this would be **Materials & Office Supplies**.
4. Click the **Save** button.

> You must type the name of the account you would like to keep (in our case, **Materials & Office Supplies**) exactly as it appears in QuickBooks. To ensure accuracy, I recommend that you use your keyboard shortcuts to copy (*Ctrl + C*) and paste (*Ctrl + V*) the name so that it is correct. If you are a Mac user, it would be *Command + C* to copy and *Command + V* to paste.
>
> Please note that the account type and detail type must be the same for the accounts that you are merging. If they are not, QBO will not allow you to merge the accounts.

The following message will appear:

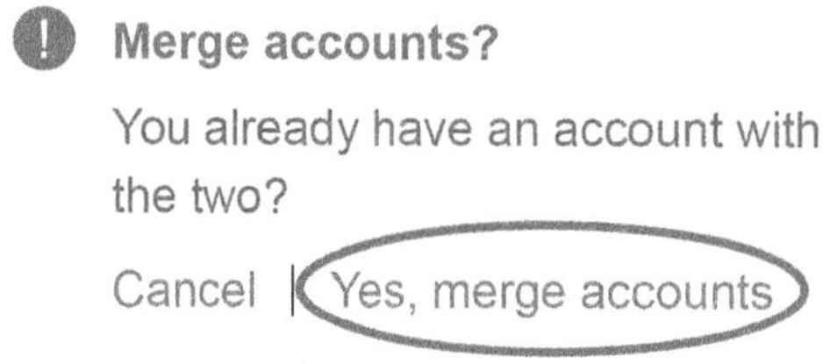

Merge accounts?

You already have an account with that name. Would you like to merge the two?

Cancel | **Yes, merge accounts**

Figure 3.22: Confirm that you would like to merge the duplicate accounts

5. Choose **Yes, merge accounts** and then click the **Save** button, and the two accounts will be consolidated into one:

Materials & Office Supplies	Expenses	Office/General Administrative Expenses
Supplies	Expenses	Supplies & Materials

Figure 3.23: Chart of accounts list with the duplicate account removed

As you can see, the duplicate account (**Office Supplies**) is no longer on the chart of accounts list. All transactions recorded for this account have been transferred to the **Materials & Office Supplies** account.

You now know how to add an account, import a chart of accounts list, edit an account, inactivate and reactivate an account, and merge accounts on the chart of accounts list. The chart of accounts is, therefore, the backbone of the system, and now that you know how to manage your chart of accounts list, you can be confident that your financial statements will be accurate.

In the next section, we will show you how to reduce the number of transactions entered manually by connecting your bank accounts to QuickBooks. In the long run, this will save you a lot of time.

Connecting bank accounts to QBO

One of the best features of using cloud accounting software such as QBO is the ability to connect your bank account to the software so that your books are always up to date with the most recent deposits and withdrawals that have been made to your bank accounts.

There are two ways in which you can update QuickBooks with your banking activity. You can connect your bank account to QuickBooks so that transactions are imported automatically into QuickBooks, or you can upload transactions from an Excel spreadsheet. We will walk you through each of these processes in more detail now.

Importing banking transactions automatically

There are several benefits to importing your banking transactions automatically. First, you will save a ton of time because you won't have to enter transactions manually. Second, QuickBooks will be updated on a *daily* basis with the most recent banking activity on your account. And finally, it will be a breeze to reconcile your bank account on a daily, weekly, or monthly basis.

Go through the following steps to import banking transactions automatically into QBO:

1. Select **Transactions** and then **Bank transactions** from the left menu bar, as shown in *Figure 3.24*:

74   *Customizing QuickBooks for Your Business*

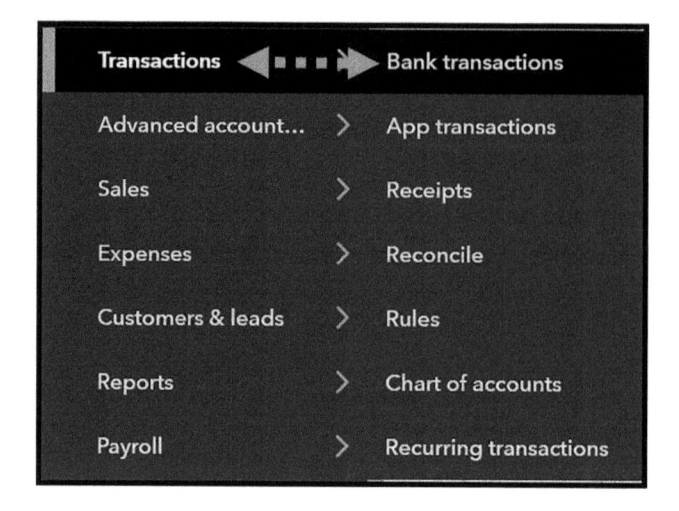

Figure 3.24: Selecting Bank transactions

2. If this is your first time connecting to a bank/credit card account, you will get the following screen. Click on the **Connect account** button, as shown here:

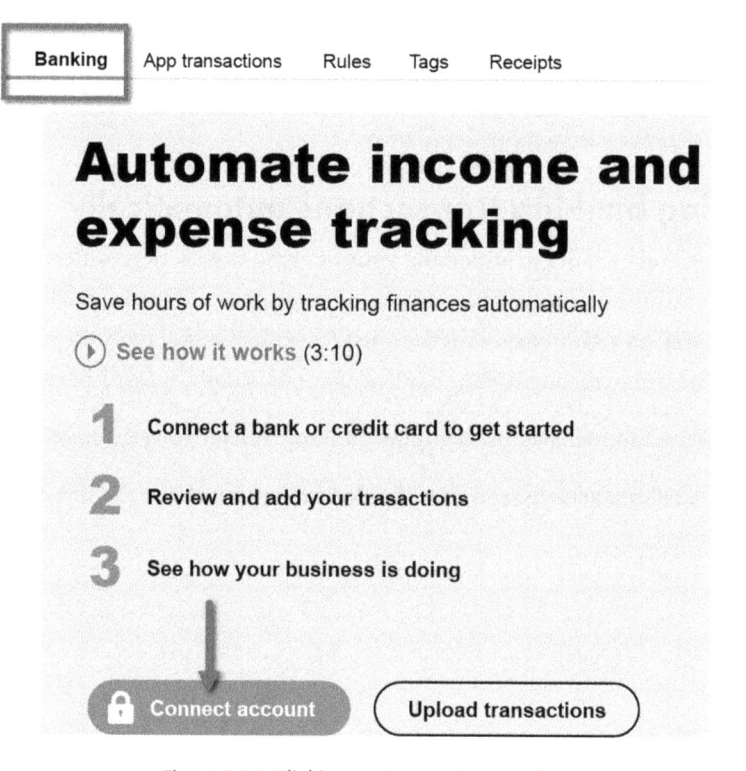

Figure 3.25: Clicking on Connect account

Chapter 3

3. If you have connected to a bank/credit card account previously, you will see the **Link account** option. Click on it:

+ Link account ∨

Figure 3.26: The Link account button

4. To connect your bank account, select your bank by clicking on the icon or typing the name of the bank in the search box, as shown here:

Connect your bank or credit card to bring in your transactions.

Enter your bank name or URL

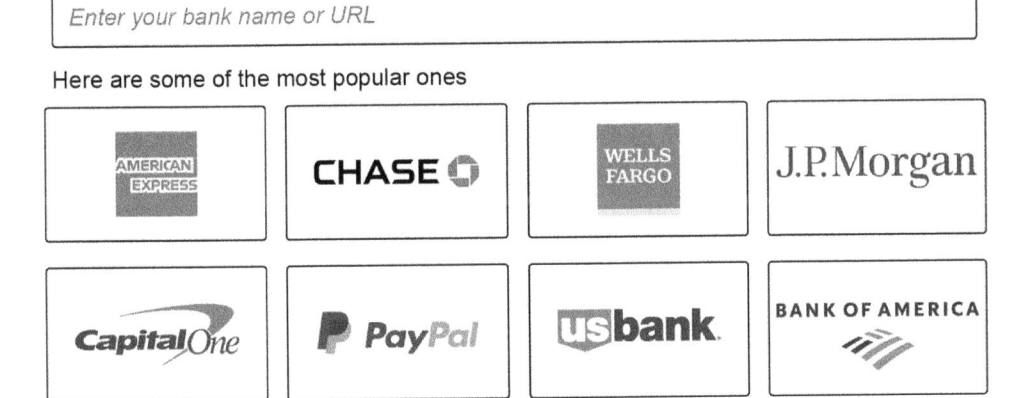

Here are some of the most popular ones

| AMERICAN EXPRESS | CHASE | WELLS FARGO | J.P.Morgan |
| CapitalOne | PayPal | USbank | BANK OF AMERICA |

Figure 3.27: Selecting your bank

If you cannot locate your bank, you will not be able to connect your account to QuickBooks; however, you can still download your banking information into QuickBooks, which we will cover in the next section.

76 | *Customizing QuickBooks for Your Business*

5. Sign in to your bank account using the secure user ID and password issued by your bank:

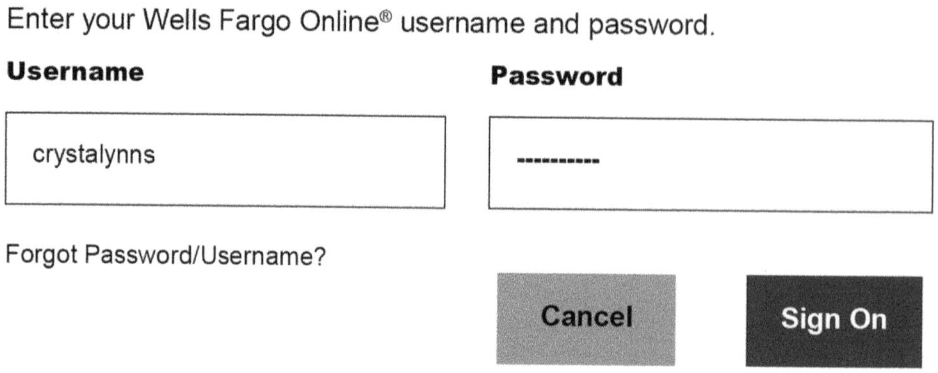

   Enter your Wells Fargo Online® username and password.

   Username

   crystalynns

   Password

   Forgot Password/Username?

   Cancel   Sign On

   Figure 3.28: Signing into your bank account

6. Before connecting your bank account to QBO, you will be required to consent to the terms and conditions set by your bank. This consent confirmation is documentation that proves you agree to share your financial data with QuickBooks:

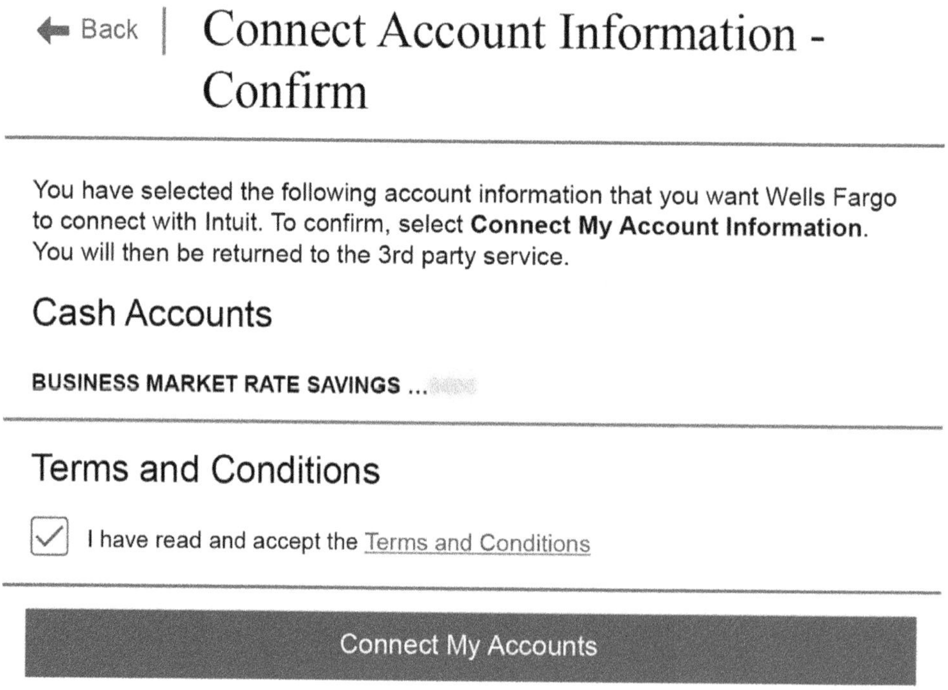

   ← Back | **Connect Account Information - Confirm**

   You have selected the following account information that you want Wells Fargo to connect with Intuit. To confirm, select **Connect My Account Information**. You will then be returned to the 3rd party service.

   ## Cash Accounts

   BUSINESS MARKET RATE SAVINGS ...

   ## Terms and Conditions

   [✓] I have read and accept the Terms and Conditions

   Connect My Accounts

   Figure 3.29: Consenting to your bank's terms and conditions

Chapter 3

7. Follow the remaining onscreen instructions to connect your bank account to QuickBooks. If you have more than one account with the same financial institution, you will have the option to connect all bank accounts or select specific bank accounts to connect with QuickBooks.

> Make sure that you only connect *business* bank accounts to QuickBooks and not personal bank accounts; otherwise, you will have personal banking activity mingled with business transactions, which is not a best practice.
>
> Some financial institutions limit how far back in time you are able to pull data from. Let's say you need to import data for the last 12 months, but your bank only allows you to go back 90 days; go ahead and import those last 90 days. For the data that it did not allow you to access, you can either request a CSV (Excel) file from your online banking department so you can import it or enter the data manually from your bank statement.

You can save yourself a lot of time by connecting your bank account to QuickBooks so that your transactions automatically download. However, if your bank does not allow you to connect your account, you can still save time by obtaining an Excel (.xls) or CSV (.csv) file from your bank so that you can upload the transactions to your QuickBooks file.

Uploading banking transactions from an Excel or CSV file

If your financial institution does not integrate with QuickBooks, then you need to upload your banking transactions as an Excel or CSV file. Most banks allow you to download your transactions as a PDF or CSV file. Log in to your bank account and look for the **Download Transactions** option or other data download options. If you don't see this option, contact your bank and inform them that you need your banking transactions in a CSV file so that you can upload them into QuickBooks.

1. At the beginning of this chapter, we showed you how to add a new account to the chart of accounts list. Follow those step-by-step instructions and add your bank account to QuickBooks.

2. Your bank account setup screen should resemble the one here:

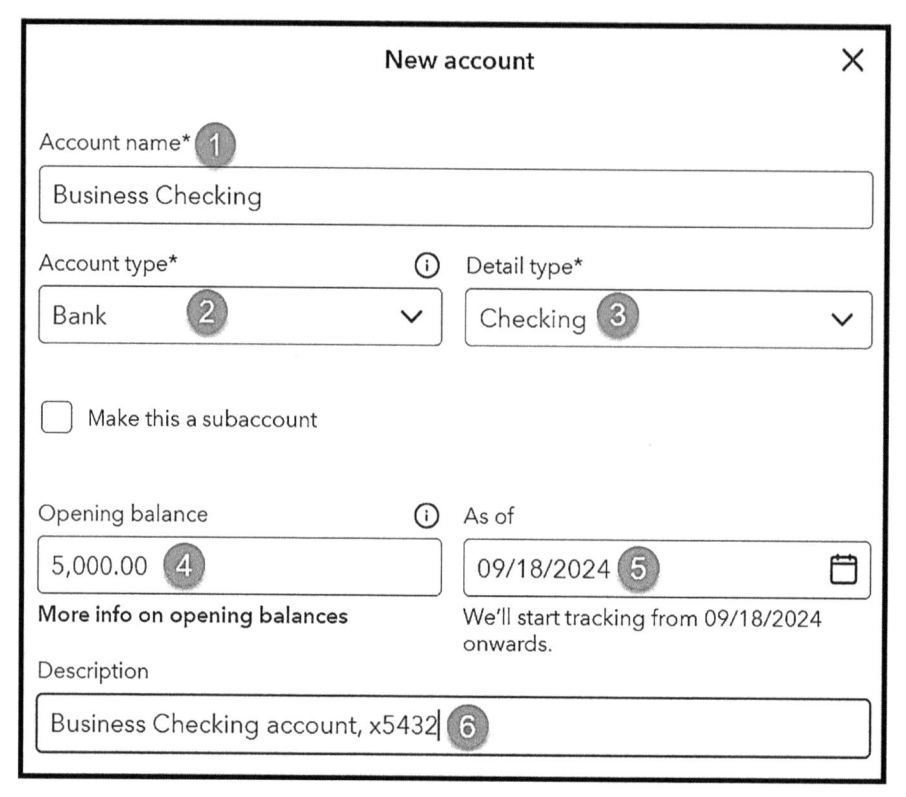

Figure 3.30: Bank account setup screen

3. Here is a brief explanation of how to fill in the new bank account fields:

    - **Account name (1)**: The name of the bank account belongs in this field. In our example, we have created a business checking account and named it accordingly. This will work if all of your bank accounts are at the same financial institution; however, if you have multiple bank accounts set up at different financial institutions, you should include the name of the bank along with the type of account in this field – for example, Wells Fargo Business Checking, Bank of America Business Savings, and so on.

      > If you have several accounts, it might be helpful to include the last four digits of each account number as part of the account name (such as Chase Business Checking, x5432). This will help you to quickly determine which account you are in.

Chapter 3

- **Account type (2)**: Select **Bank** from the drop-down menu.
- **Detail type (3)**: Select the type of bank account you are setting up from the drop-down menu (**Savings, Checking**, etc.).
- **Opening balance (4)**: Enter the current balance in your bank account as of your QuickBooks start date, which is the field next to it. For example, if you are starting to use QuickBooks as of January 1, enter the balance of your bank account as of the last day of the previous period, which would be December 31 of the previous year.
- **As of (5)**: The **As of** date will be the last day of the previous period discussed in **Opening balance (4)** above. In our example, September 18 will be the **As of** date and anything after that date will be tracked directly in QBO.
- **Description (6)**: You can include a brief description of the account that you are adding in this field, such as the name of the bank or financial institution and account number.

> It's important to have your bank statements handy as you are adding bank accounts to QuickBooks. This is to ensure that you enter the correct balance and effective dates. It will also help you to balance later on when you are ready to reconcile the account.

4. From the gear icon, select **Import Data**, which is located in the **Tools** column, as shown here:

Tools

Import Data

Import Desktop Data

Export Data

Reconcile

Figure 3.31: The Import Data option

5. The **Import Data** screen is where you can import bank data, charts of accounts, customers, invoices, journal entries, products and services, and vendors. Select the **Bank Data** option as shown here:

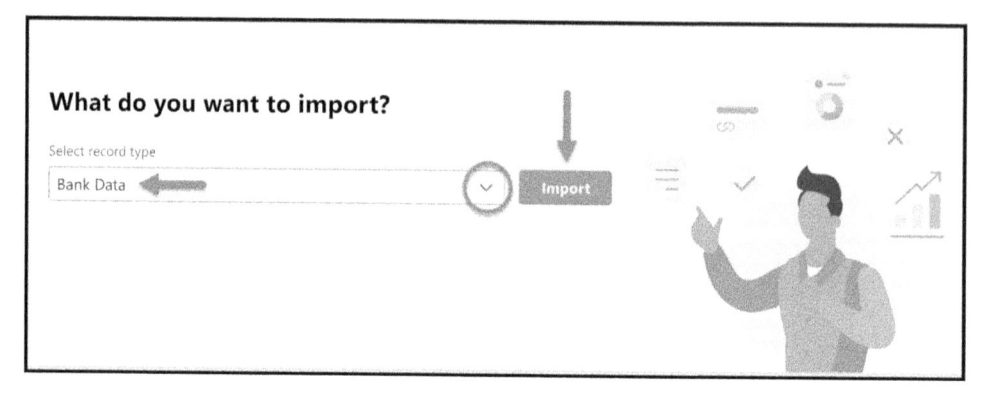

Figure 3.32: The Import Data screen

6. The following screen appears. Click on **select files** to select the file that includes your bank data or make use of the drag-and-drop feature, as indicated below:

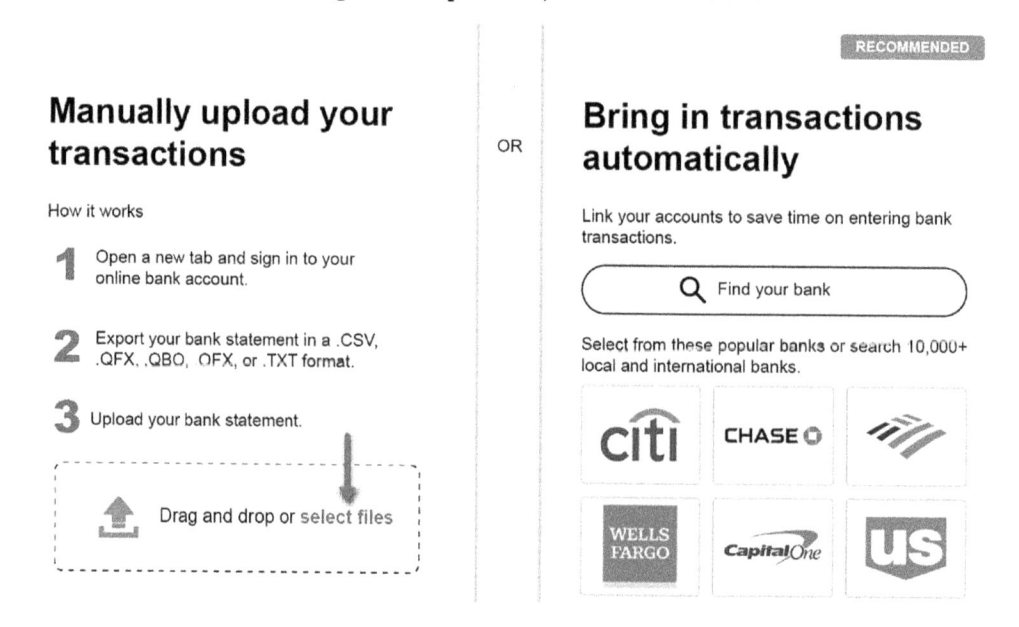

Figure 3.33: Clicking select files

The selected filename will appear in the field, as shown below:

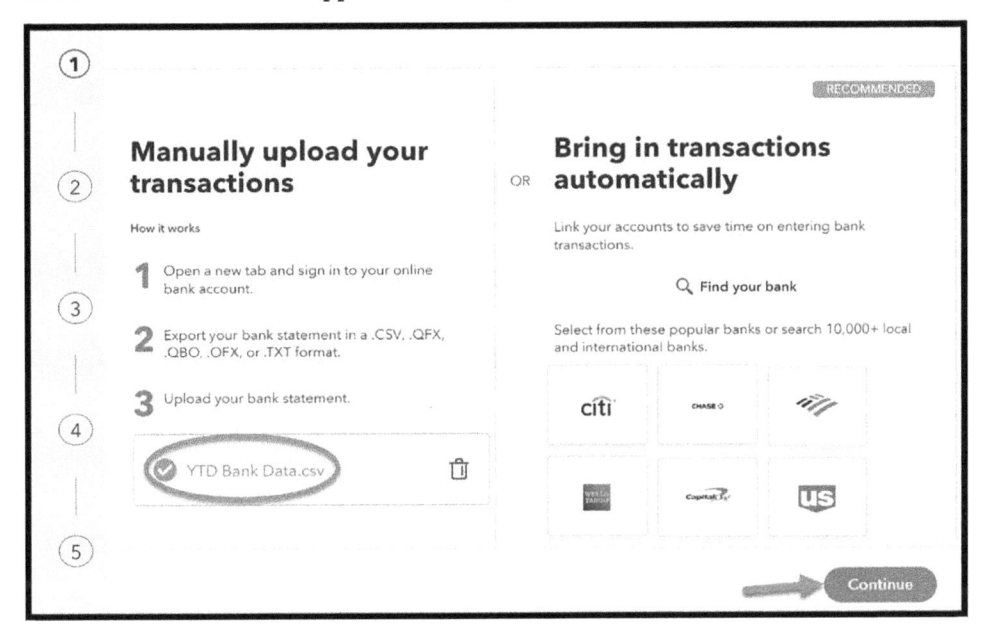

Figure 3.34: Checking the filename

7. Click the **Continue** button to proceed to the next step.
8. In this step, you will select the bank account from which you want the transactions to be uploaded to QuickBooks. Select the **Business Checking** account from the drop-down menu, as shown here:

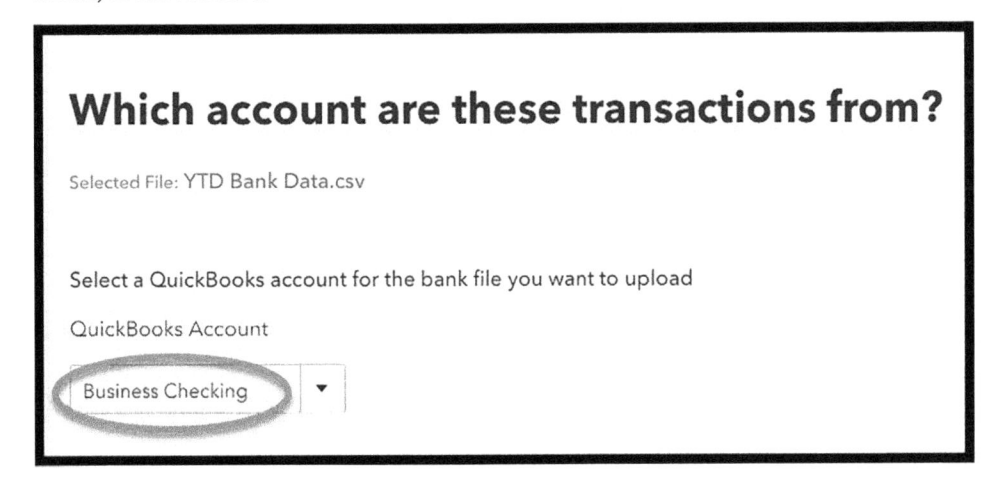

Figure 3.35: Selecting the bank account

9. Click **Continue**.

> If you have more than one bank account, you will need to set up an account on the chart of accounts for each bank account and link them.

The following setup screen will appear:

Let's set up your file in QuickBooks

Step 1: Tell us about the format of your data

Is the first row in your file a header?

Yes

How many columns show amounts?

One column

What's the date format used in your file?

Select a date format

Step 2: Select the fields that correspond to your file

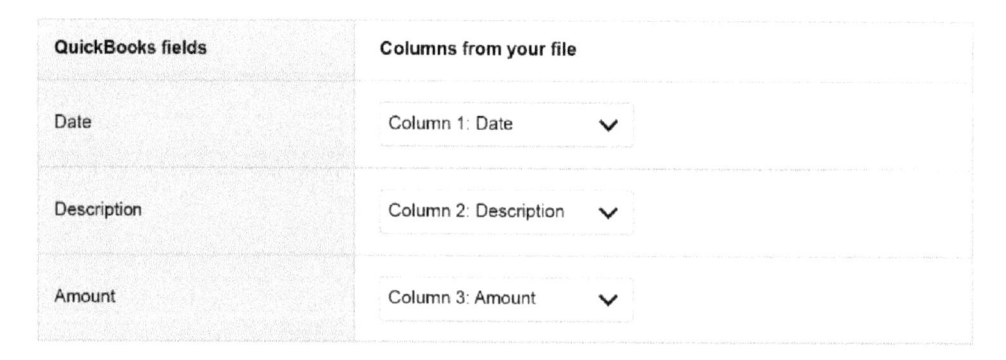

QuickBooks fields	Columns from your file
Date	Column 1: Date
Description	Column 2: Description
Amount	Column 3: Amount

Figure 3.36: Setup screen

On this screen, you will provide responses to the three questions in step 1, and in step 2 you will map the columns in your CSV file to a field in QuickBooks. This is a very important step to ensure that the information is entered into the correct fields in QuickBooks.

For each QBO field located on the left, select the column from your import file that includes the corresponding data, as shown in *Figure 3.36* above. There are three fields that need to be populated in QuickBooks: the transaction date, a brief description, and the transaction amount. You will need to indicate what column in your CSV file includes this information:

- **Date:** From the drop-down, select the column in the CSV file that includes the date of the banking transactions. You can also select the format that the date is in (for example, mm/dd/yyyy).
- **Description:** Select the column in the CSV file that includes descriptions of the transactions.
- **Amount:** From the drop-down, select the column in the CSV file that includes the transaction amounts. Amounts can be formatted into one column that includes both positive and negative numbers, or into two separate columns, one for positive numbers (deposits) and one for negative numbers (withdrawals). In our example, both positive and negative numbers are formatted into one column.

10. Click **Continue**.

A preview of how your data will be uploaded to QuickBooks will appear. It's important to review the data to ensure that the correct fields are populated:

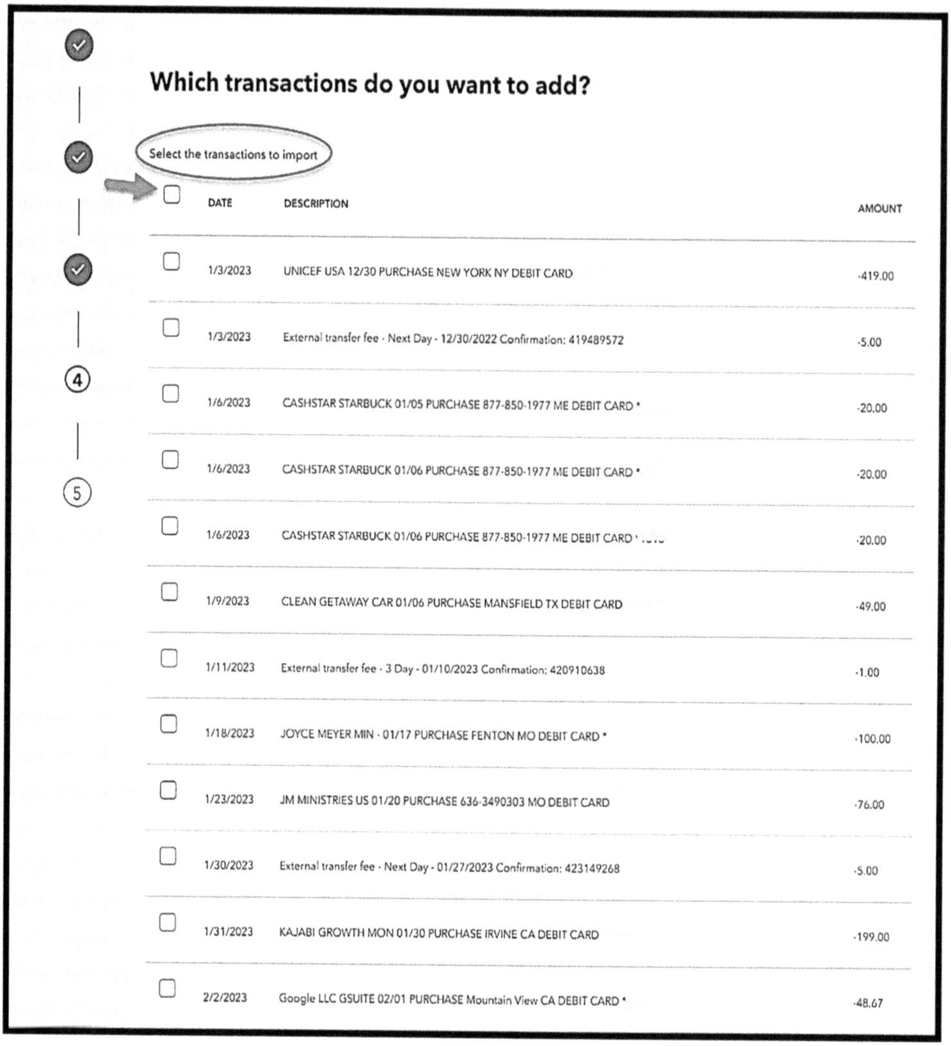

Customizing QuickBooks for Your Business

Which transactions do you want to add?

Select the transactions to import

	DATE	DESCRIPTION	AMOUNT
☐	1/3/2023	UNICEF USA 12/30 PURCHASE NEW YORK NY DEBIT CARD	-419.00
☐	1/3/2023	External transfer fee - Next Day - 12/30/2022 Confirmation: 419489572	-5.00
☐	1/6/2023	CASHSTAR STARBUCK 01/05 PURCHASE 877-850-1977 ME DEBIT CARD *	-20.00
☐	1/6/2023	CASHSTAR STARBUCK 01/06 PURCHASE 877-850-1977 ME DEBIT CARD *	-20.00
☐	1/6/2023	CASHSTAR STARBUCK 01/06 PURCHASE 877-850-1977 ME DEBIT CARD *	-20.00
☐	1/9/2023	CLEAN GETAWAY CAR 01/06 PURCHASE MANSFIELD TX DEBIT CARD	-49.00
☐	1/11/2023	External transfer fee - 3 Day - 01/10/2023 Confirmation: 420910638	-1.00
☐	1/18/2023	JOYCE MEYER MIN - 01/17 PURCHASE FENTON MO DEBIT CARD *	-100.00
☐	1/23/2023	JM MINISTRIES US 01/20 PURCHASE 636-3490303 MO DEBIT CARD	-76.00
☐	1/30/2023	External transfer fee - Next Day - 01/27/2023 Confirmation: 423149268	-5.00
☐	1/31/2023	KAJABI GROWTH MON 01/30 PURCHASE IRVINE CA DEBIT CARD	-199.00
☐	2/2/2023	Google LLC GSUITE 02/01 PURCHASE Mountain View CA DEBIT CARD *	-48.67

Figure 3.37: A preview of your data before importing to QBO

Chapter 3

11. To select all transactions for import, put a checkmark in the box highlighted in the above screenshot. Alternatively, you can put a checkmark next to each individual transaction you wish to import into QBO.
12. Click the **Next** button in the lower-right corner to proceed to the next screen.
13. On the next screen, QuickBooks will provide you with the number of transactions to be uploaded. This is your final opportunity to confirm that the data is correct. Once you confirm this, there will be no option to undo it. To proceed with the upload, click the **Yes** button, as shown here:

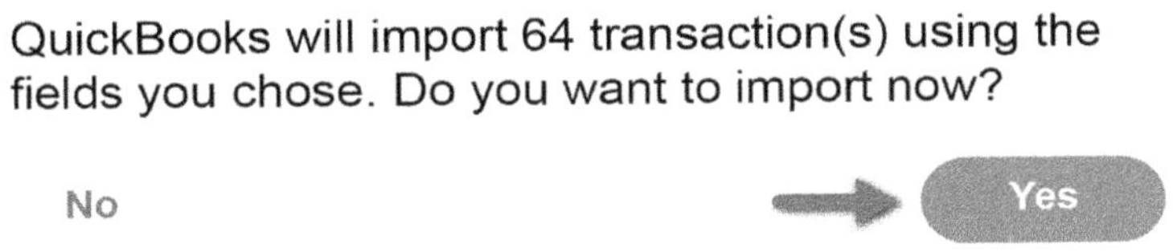

> QuickBooks will import 64 transaction(s) using the fields you chose. Do you want to import now?
>
> No   → Yes

Figure 3.38: Confirming the import

14. After confirming the number of transactions to import, your transactions will be added to QuickBooks. To verify the data was imported correctly, head over to the banking center where you can see the number of transactions that were successfully imported from your CSV file, along with their dates, descriptions, and dollar amounts. In *Chapter 15, Reconciling Uploaded Bank and Credit Card Transactions*, accessible online using this link: `https://packt.link/supplementary-content-9781836649977` we will show you what to do with this data after it has been imported.

Now that we know how to import banking transactions from a CSV or XLS file, let's learn how to connect our credit card accounts in the next section.

Connecting credit card accounts to QBO

Similar to bank accounts, you can connect your credit card accounts to QBO. There are two ways that you can update QuickBooks with your credit card activity. You can connect your credit card account to QuickBooks so that transactions are imported automatically into QuickBooks. The other option is to upload transactions from an Excel spreadsheet. We will walk you through each process in more detail in the following sections.

Importing credit card transactions automatically

There are several benefits to importing your credit card transactions automatically. First, you will save a lot of time because you won't have to manually enter transactions. Second, QuickBooks will be updated on a daily basis with the most recent credit card activity on your account. Third, it will be much easier to reconcile your credit card accounts.

Listed below are the steps required to import credit card transactions automatically into QBO:

1. Select **Transactions** and **Bank transactions** from the left menu bar, as shown here:

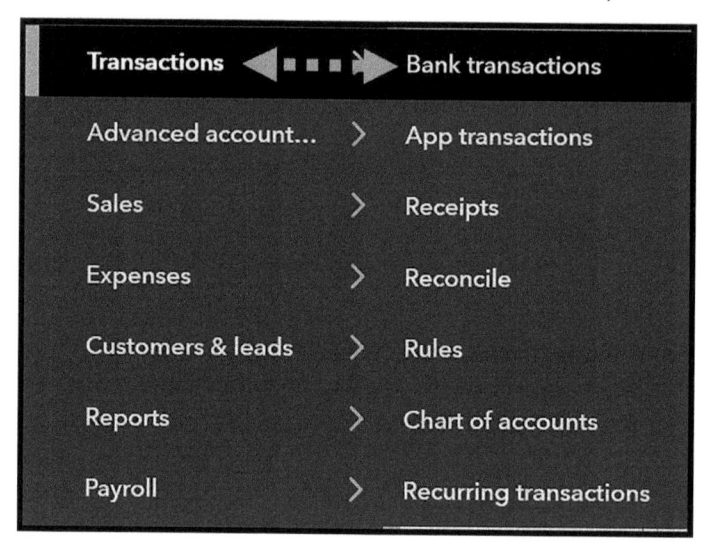

Figure 3.39: The Bank transactions option

2. On the following screen, you will see a link to a short video tutorial (**See how it works**) shown in blue in *Figure 3.40*. This is a demo of how the banking center works. Click on the **Connect account** button, or the **Link account** button if you have previously connected a bank/credit card account:

Chapter 3

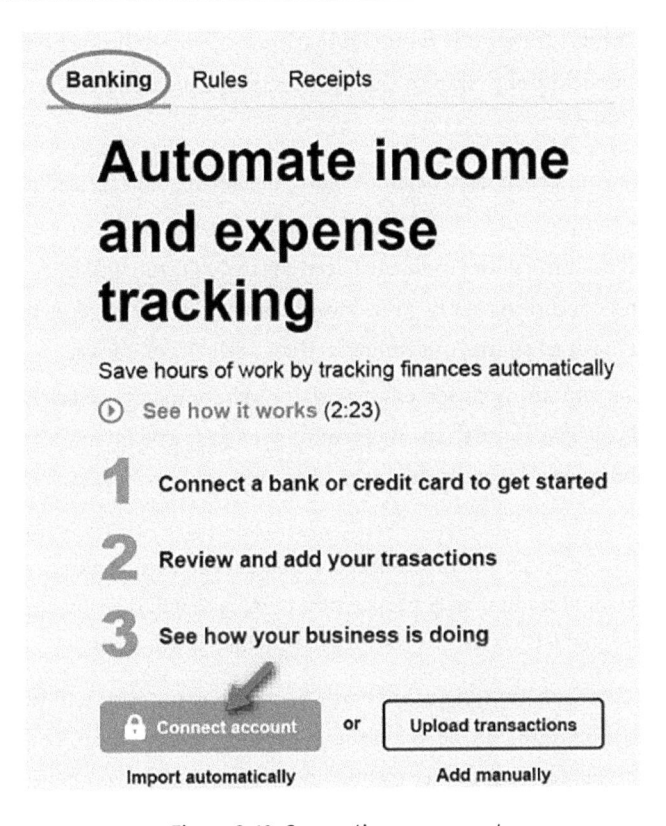

Figure 3.40: Connecting an account

3. To connect your credit card account, select your credit card company by clicking on the icon or typing the name of the financial institution in the search box, as shown here:

Figure 3.41: Selecting your bank

If you cannot locate your financial institution, you will not be able to connect your account to QuickBooks. Skip to the next section, *Uploading credit card transactions from an Excel or CSV file*.

4. Sign in to your credit card account using the secure user ID and password issued by your bank.

5. Before connecting your credit card account to QBO, you will be required to consent to the terms and conditions set by your bank. This consent is used as documentation, proving that you agree to share your financial data with QuickBooks.

6. Follow the remaining onscreen instructions to connect your credit card account to QuickBooks. If you have more than one account with the same financial institution, you will have the option to connect all credit card accounts or just select specific credit card accounts.

Make sure that you only connect *business* credit card accounts to QuickBooks and not personal credit card accounts; otherwise, you will have personal credit card activity mingled with business transactions, which is not ideal.

If you have multiple credit cards for one account, you will want to link the parent account only… or the individual cards only, but not both. The parent account is recommended as it makes reconciling much easier. If you have linked the individual cards, you will need to have them listed as subaccounts on your chart of accounts of a parent card, to be able to reconcile to your monthly statement.

After connecting your credit card accounts to QuickBooks, they will appear in the banking center. From the banking center, you can see the date of the most recent download along with a description and the amount of each transaction downloaded. If your financial institution does not allow you to connect your credit card account to QuickBooks, you will need to upload credit card transactions from an Excel or CSV file.

Uploading credit card transactions from an Excel or CSV file

If your financial institution does not integrate with QuickBooks, you need to download your credit card transactions to an Excel or CSV file. Most banks allow you to download your transactions as a PDF or CSV file. Log in to your credit card account and look for a **Download Transactions** option. If you don't see this option, contact the credit card company and inform them that you need your transactions in a CSV file so you can upload them to QuickBooks.

Chapter 3

> While you cannot use a PDF file to upload transactions to QBO, there are programs that will extract transactions from bank and credit card PDF statements into QBO. **MoneyThumb** is one of many programs that will do this: https://www.moneythumb.com/quickbooks-converters-benefits/.

To upload credit card transactions from an Excel or CSV file to QuickBooks, follow these instructions:

1. At the beginning of this chapter, we showed you how to add a new account to the chart of accounts list. Follow those step-by-step instructions and add your credit card account to QuickBooks.

2. Your credit card account setup screen should resemble the one in *Figure 3.42*:

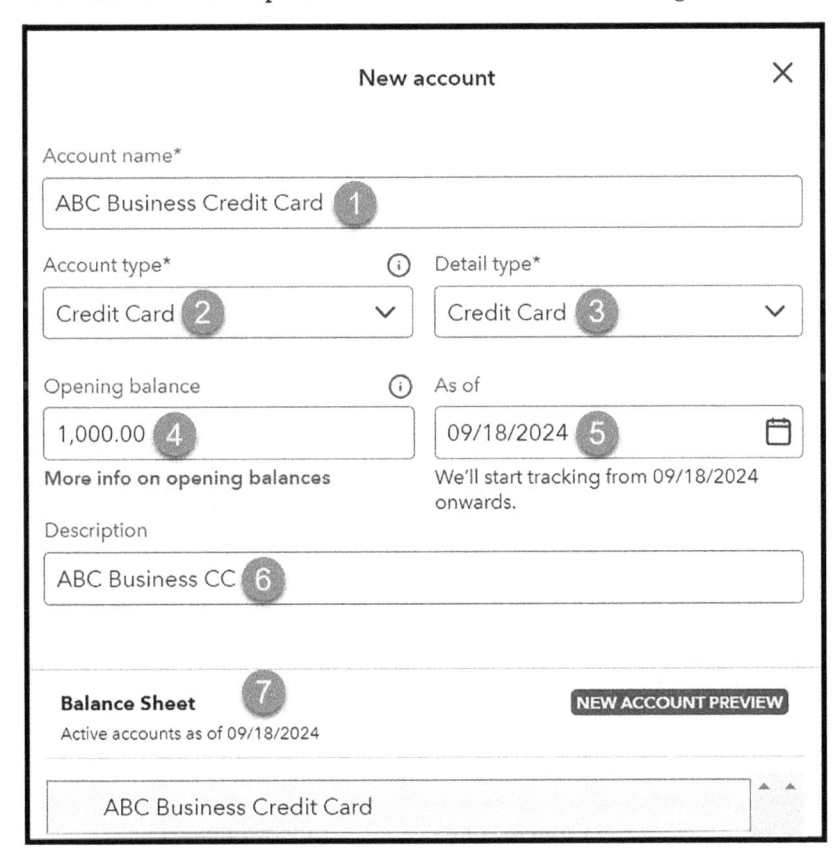

Figure 3.42: Adding account details for a credit card

The following is a brief explanation of the new credit card account fields:

- **Account name (1)**: The name of the credit card belongs in this field. If you have multiple credit card accounts at the same financial institution, you may want to consider entering the last four digits of each account in this field. This will make it easier when you are entering transactions and reconciling accounts.
- **Account type (2)**: The account type will be **Credit Card**.
- **Detail type (3)**: **Detail type** should default to the account type, **Credit Card**.
- **Opening balance (4)**: Enter the current outstanding balance due on your credit card account as of your QuickBooks start date (see *Step 5*). For example, if you began to use QuickBooks as of January 1, enter the balance owed on your credit card as of the last day of the previous period, which would be December 31 of the previous year.
- **As of (5)**: From the drop-down, select the date you want to begin tracking your finances for this account.
- **Description (6)**: You can include a brief description of the account that you are adding in this field or enter the name of the account.
- **NEW ACCOUNT PREVIEW (7)**: In this section, you will see a preview of where on the financial statements this account will appear. In our example, it will appear on the **Balance Sheet** report as a sub-account below **Credit Cards**.

> It's important to have your credit card statements handy as you are adding credit card accounts to QuickBooks. This is to ensure that you enter the correct balance and effective dates. If you leave this field blank, you will not be able to access this field later on; instead, you will have to make a balance adjustment directly in the credit card register.

Chapter 3									91

3. From the gear icon, select **Import data** in the **Tools** column, as shown in *Figure 3.43*:

TOOLS

Order checks

(Import data)

Import desktop

Figure 3.43: The Import data option

4. The **Import Data** screen is where you can import bank and credit card transactions, customers, vendors, a chart of accounts list, a products and services list, and invoices. Select the **Bank Data** option to display the setup screen, as shown in *Figure 3.44*:

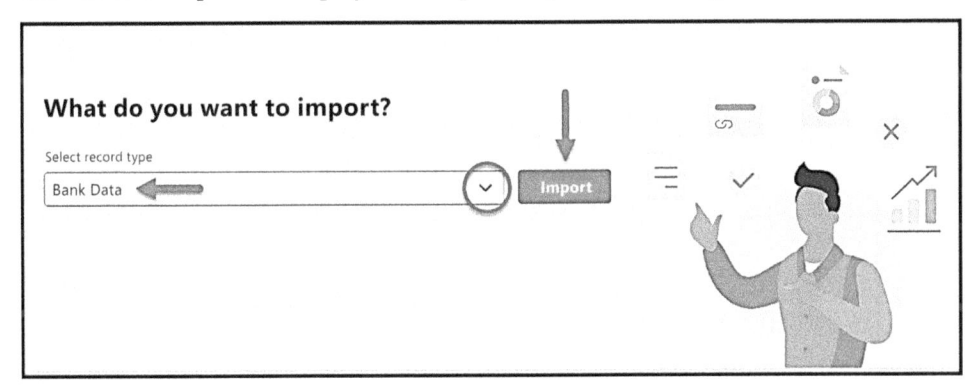

Figure 3.44: The Import Data screen

The following screen appears. Click on **select files** to choose the file that includes your bank data, as indicated below:

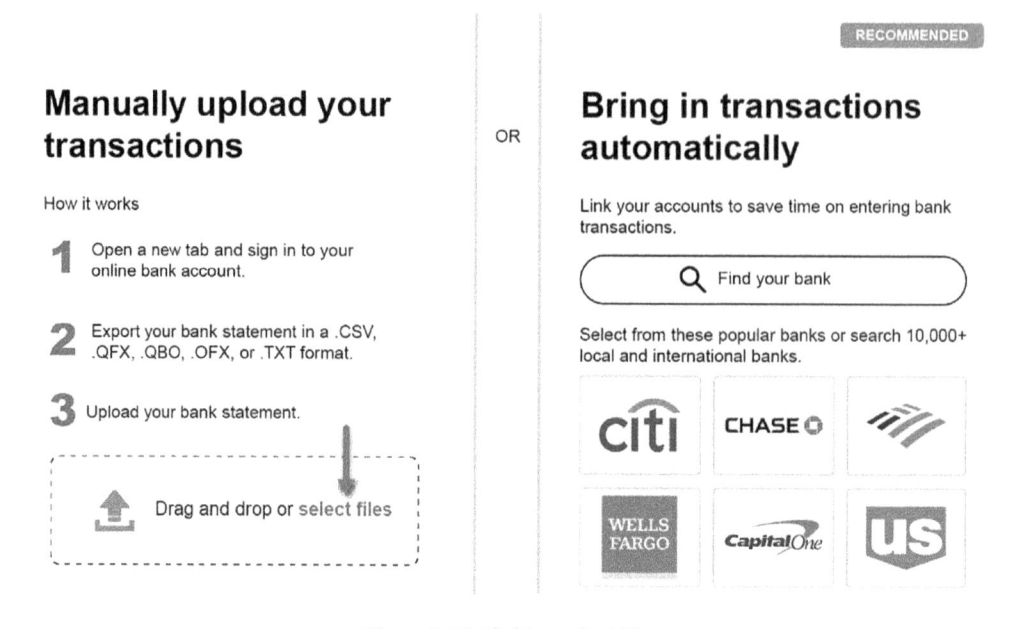

Figure 3.45: Clicking select files

The filename will appear in the field as shown below:

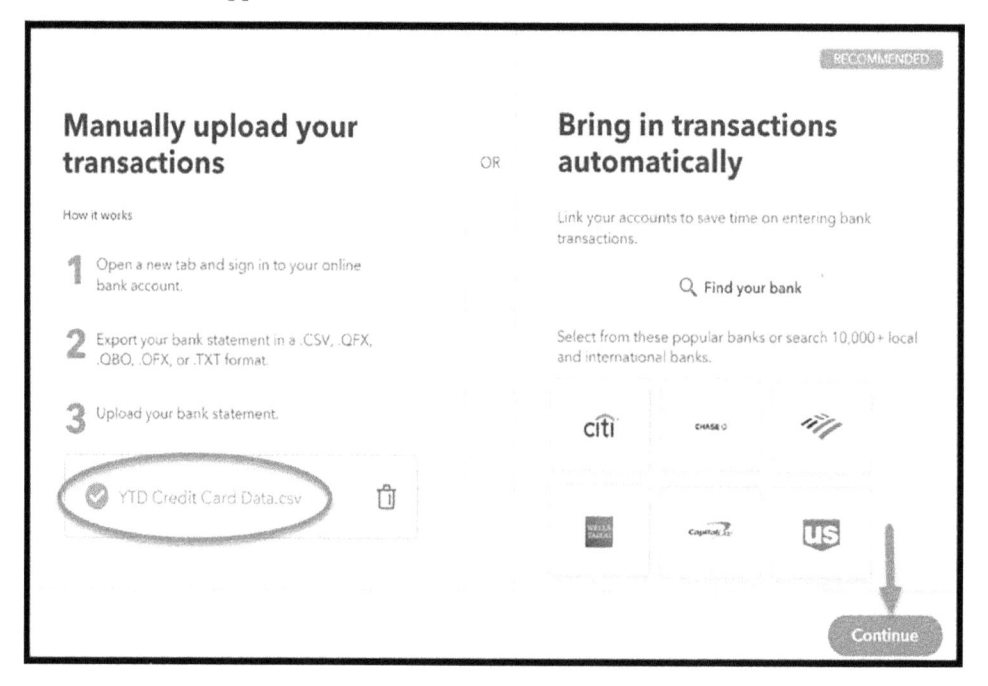

Figure 3.46: Checking the filename

Chapter 3 93

5. Click the **Continue** button to proceed to the next step.
6. In this step, you will select the credit card account for which you want the transactions to be uploaded to QuickBooks. Select the **Business Credit Card** account from the drop-down menu, as shown in *Figure 3.47*:

Which account are these transactions from?

Selected File: **January 2021 Credit Card Data.csv**

Select a QuickBooks account for the bank file you want to upload

QuickBooks Account

[Business Credit Card ▼]

Figure 3.47: Selecting the account

7. Click **Continue** and the following screen appears:

Let's set up your file in QuickBooks

Step 1: Tell us about the format of your data

Is the first row in your file a header?

[Yes ▼]

How many columns show amounts?

[One column ▼]

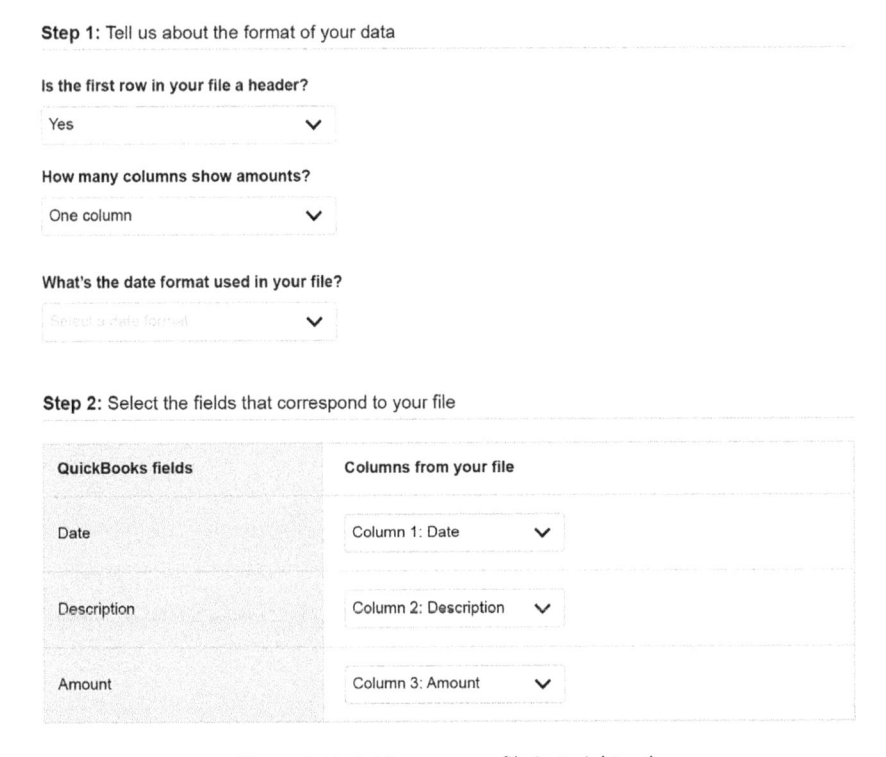

What's the date format used in your file?

[Select a date format ▼]

Step 2: Select the fields that correspond to your file

QuickBooks fields	Columns from your file
Date	Column 1: Date ▼
Description	Column 2: Description ▼
Amount	Column 3: Amount ▼

Figure 3.48: Setting up your file in QuickBooks

On this screen, you will respond to the three questions in **Step 1**, and in **Step 2** you will map the columns in your CSV file to a field in QuickBooks. This is a very important step to ensure that the information is populated into the correct fields in QuickBooks.

> If you have additional columns of information in your Excel or CSV file, that is OK. QuickBooks is only going to pick up the information in the three required fields: **Date**, **Description**, and **Amount**.

8. For each QBO field located on the left, select the column from your import file that includes the corresponding data, as shown in the preceding screenshot. There are three fields that need to be populated in QuickBooks: the transaction date, a brief description, and the transaction amount. You will need to indicate what column in your CSV file includes this information:

   - **Date**: From the drop-down, select the column in the CSV file that includes the dates of the credit card transactions. You can also select the format that the date is in (for example, mm/dd/yyyy).
   - **Description**: Select the column in the CSV file that includes descriptions of the transactions.
   - **Amount**: From the drop-down, select the column in the CSV file that includes the transaction amounts. Amounts can be formatted into one column that includes both positive and negative numbers or into two separate columns, one for positive numbers (credit card charges) and one for negative numbers (credit card payments and credits).

Chapter 3

9. Click **Continue**. On the next screen, there appears a preview of how your data will upload to QuickBooks. It's important to review the data to ensure that the correct fields are populated:

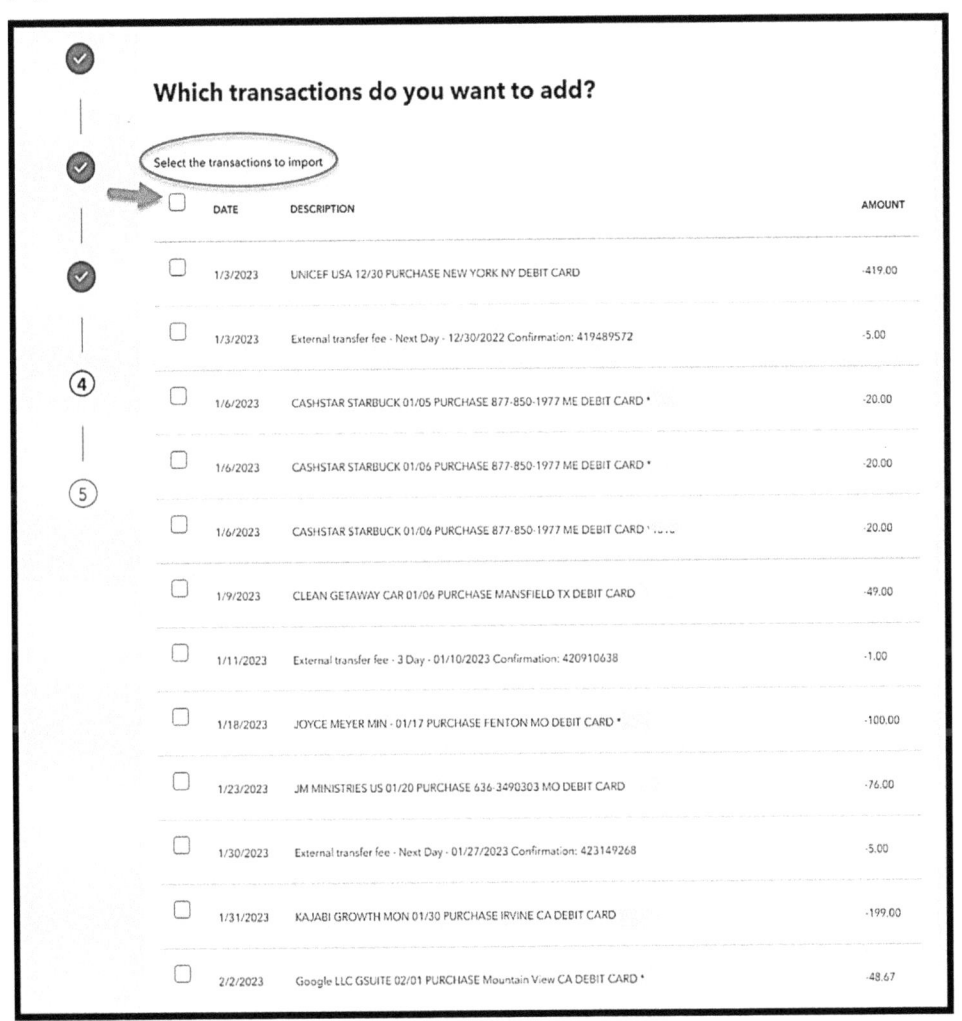

DATE	DESCRIPTION	AMOUNT
1/3/2023	UNICEF USA 12/30 PURCHASE NEW YORK NY DEBIT CARD	-419.00
1/3/2023	External transfer fee - Next Day - 12/30/2022 Confirmation: 419489572	-5.00
1/6/2023	CASHSTAR STARBUCK 01/05 PURCHASE 877-850-1977 ME DEBIT CARD *	-20.00
1/6/2023	CASHSTAR STARBUCK 01/06 PURCHASE 877-850-1977 ME DEBIT CARD *	-20.00
1/6/2023	CASHSTAR STARBUCK 01/06 PURCHASE 877-850-1977 ME DEBIT CARD *...	-20.00
1/9/2023	CLEAN GETAWAY CAR 01/06 PURCHASE MANSFIELD TX DEBIT CARD	-49.00
1/11/2023	External transfer fee - 3 Day - 01/10/2023 Confirmation: 420910638	-1.00
1/18/2023	JOYCE MEYER MIN - 01/17 PURCHASE FENTON MO DEBIT CARD *	-100.00
1/23/2023	JM MINISTRIES US 01/20 PURCHASE 636-3490303 MO DEBIT CARD	-76.00
1/30/2023	External transfer fee - Next Day - 01/27/2023 Confirmation: 423149268	-5.00
1/31/2023	KAJABI GROWTH MON 01/30 PURCHASE IRVINE CA DEBIT CARD	-199.00
2/2/2023	Google LLC GSUITE 02/01 PURCHASE Mountain View CA DEBIT CARD *	-48.67

Figure 3.49: Checking your data

10. Click the **Next** button to proceed.

11. On the following screen, QuickBooks will provide you with the number of transactions to be uploaded. This is your final opportunity to confirm that the data is correct. Once you confirm this, there will be no option to undo it. To proceed with the upload, click the **Yes** button, as shown in the following screenshot:

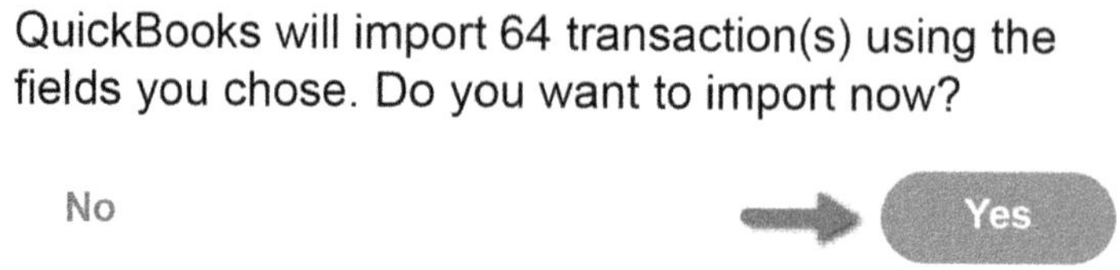

> QuickBooks will import 64 transaction(s) using the fields you chose. Do you want to import now?
>
> No   →   Yes

Figure 3.50: Confirming the import

After confirming the number of transactions to import, your transactions will be added to QuickBooks. To verify the data was imported correctly, head over to the banking center where you should see the dates, descriptions, and number of transactions that were successfully imported from your CSV file.

> Many financial institutions have different ways to connect your bank accounts to QuickBooks. I recommend that you contact the small business banking department at your bank and ask them what your options are for connecting your business bank accounts to QBO. By default, most banks allow you to import the last 90 days. However, if you need to go back further than that, be sure to inform them so that they can provide you with the best solution.

Giving other users access to your QuickBooks data

The ability to give other users access to your data is one of the many benefits of using QBO. Except for QBO Advanced, which includes three accountant users, the other QBO subscriptions include access for two accountant users and access for one or more additional users. There are two main groups that users fall into: **billable roles** and **non-billable roles**.

Billable roles count towards your user limit. For example, QBO Plus is limited to 5 users. Billable roles count toward this limit. There are eight *billable* roles that you can create in QBO:

- Standard all access
- Standard no access
- Accounts receivable manager
- Accounts payable manager
- Standard limited customers and vendors
- In house accountant
- Company administrator
- Primary administrator

Non-billable roles do not count toward your user limit. For example, if you give a contractor **Track time only** access, that access would *not* count toward your user limit because it is a non-billable role. There are two *non-billable* roles that you can create in QBO:

- Track time only
- View company reports

We will discuss each of these in more detail in the following subsections.

Standard all access user

The **Standard all access** user can access everything under customers and sales, as well as vendors and purchases. They also have full access to QBO without admin privileges, plus access to payroll, if QBO Payroll is enabled. This user has partial access to bills and company information. This user **does not** have the ability to change your QBO subscription, nor are they able to add, edit, or delete new users. Go through the following steps to assign the standard all access role to a new user:

1. From the gear icon, select **Manage users** in the **YOUR COMPANY** column, as shown in *Figure 3.51*:

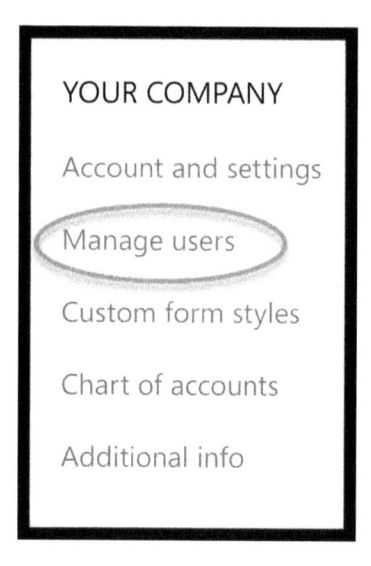

Figure 3.51: The Manage users option

2. Click on the **Add user** button:

Figure 3.52: The Add user button

3. Enter the first name, last name, and email address of the new user as indicated in *Figure 3.53*:

Chapter 3

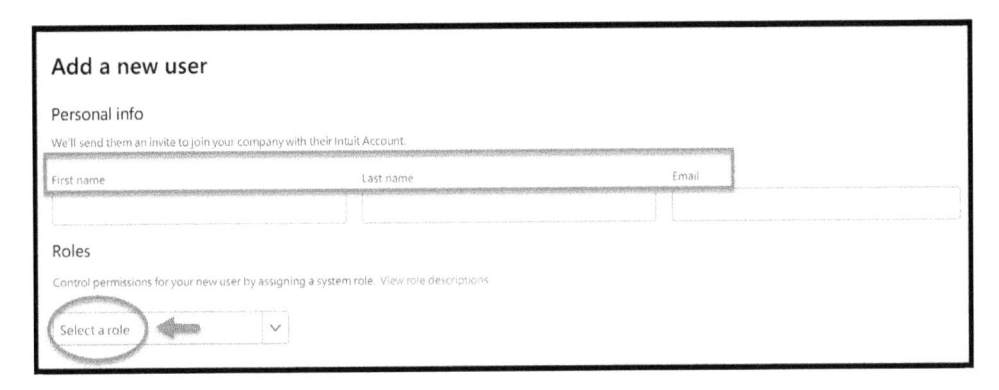

Figure 3.53: Choosing a user type

4. From the drop-down, select **Standard all access** as indicated here:

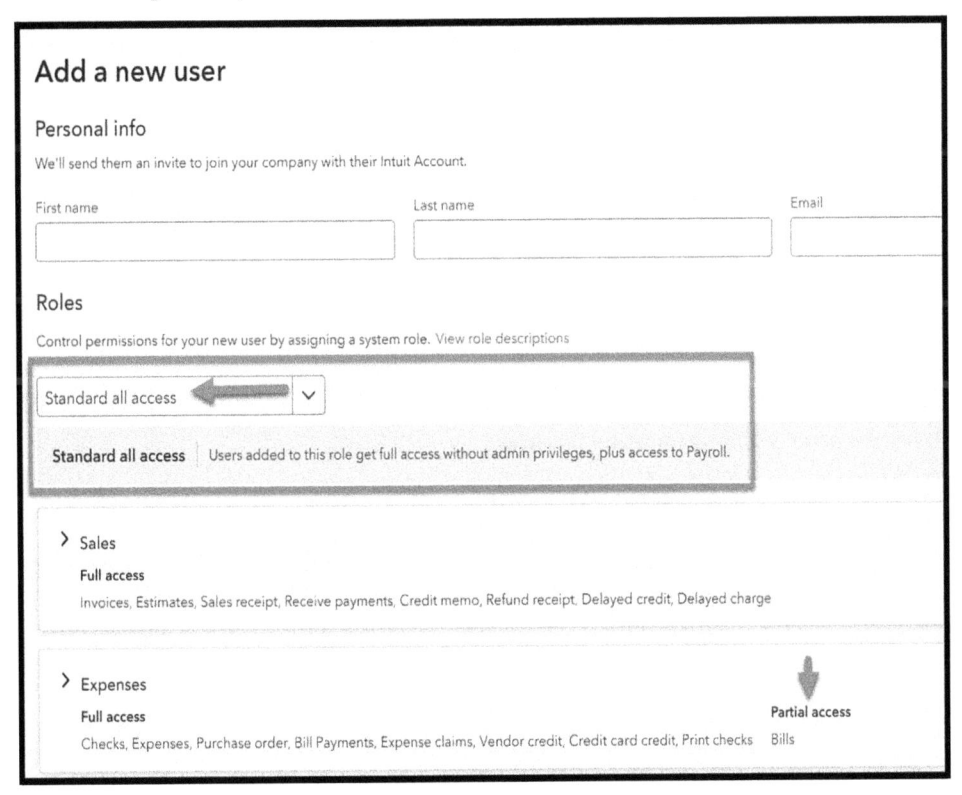

Figure 3.54: Selecting access rights for a new user

A standard all access user will count toward the total number of users included in your QBO subscription. Once you have specified how much access you want the user to have, click the **Send invite** button in the lower-right corner of the screen to send the email invitation to the new user.

To recap, the following is a summary of the number of users that are included in each plan:

- QuickBooks Online Simple Start: 2 accountants and 1 user
- QuickBooks Online Essentials: 2 accountants and 3 users
- QuickBooks Online Plus: 2 accountants and 5 users
- QuickBooks Online Advanced: 3 accountants and 25 users

Standard no access user

The following is a snapshot of the access rights for **Standard no access**:

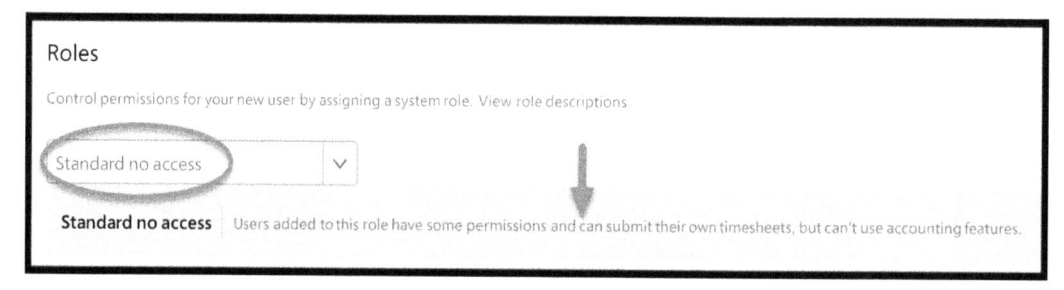

Figure 3.55: Access rights for Standard no access role

Standard no access gives the user some permissions, like submitting their own timesheet, but they have no access to accounting features.

Accounts receivable manager

The following snapshot shows the access rights for the **Accounts receivable manager** role:

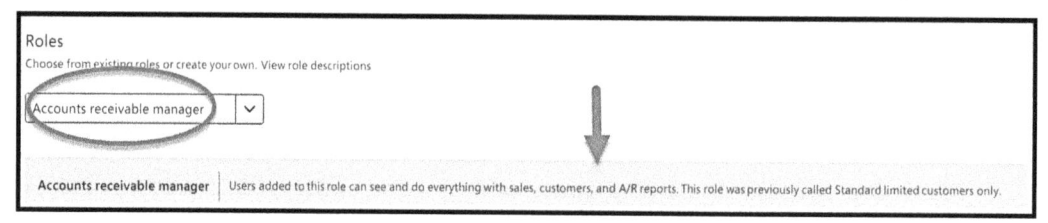

Figure 3.56: Access rights for Accounts receivable manager role

Chapter 3

The **Accounts receivable manager** role gives the user full access to sales, inventory, lists, and some bookkeeping tasks like bank deposits, but no access to employee and vendor lists, bank transactions, expense reports, or payroll reports. This role was previously called *Standard limited customers only*.

Accounts payable manager

Figure 3.57 below shows the access rights for the **Accounts payable manager** role:

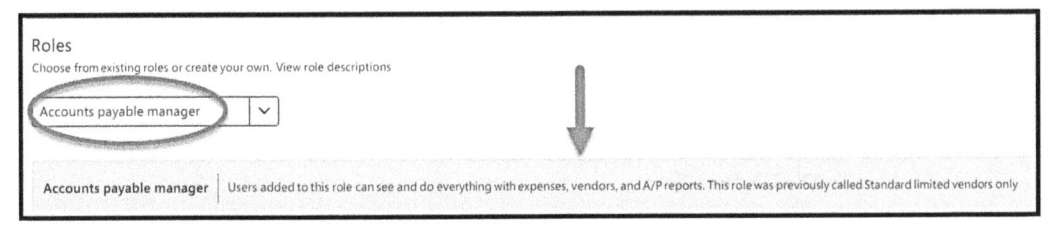

Figure 3.57: Access rights for Accounts payable manager role

The **Accounts payable manager** role can access expenses, vendors, and A/P reports. This role was previously called standard limited vendors only.

Standard limited customers and vendors

The following is a snapshot of the access rights for **Standard limited customers and vendors**:

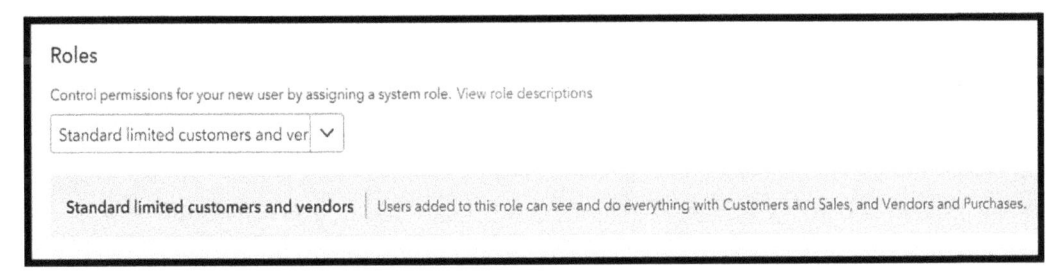

Figure 3.58: Access rights for standard limited customers and vendors

The **Standard limited customers and vendors only** role gives the user the ability to manage all customers and sales transactions and vendors and purchases. This level of access would be ideal for a bookkeeper who manages all aspects of **accounts receivable (A/R)** and **accounts payable (A/P)**.

In house accountant

The following is a snapshot of the access rights for **In house accountant**:

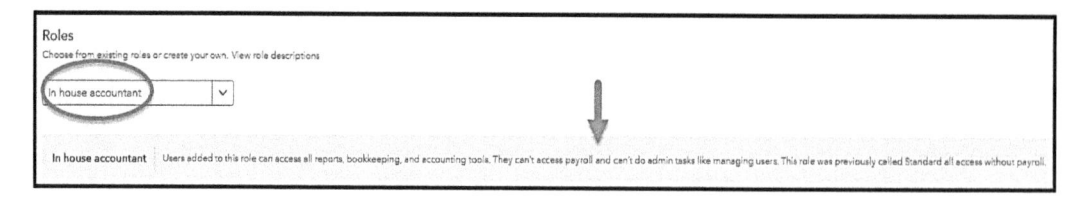

Figure 3.59: Access rights for the In house accountant role (for better visualization, refer to https://packt.link/gbp/9781836649977)

The **In house accountant** role can access all reports, bookkeeping, and accounting tools. However, they can't access payroll and are not able to perform admin tasks like managing users. This role was previously called *Standard all access without payroll*.

Company administrator

The **company administrator role** includes access to every aspect of QuickBooks. This includes adding new users, changing passwords, and having control of your QBO subscription. Because there are no limitations to what this user can do, we recommend that you limit this role to owners of the business, IT personnel, or an officer of the company.

Since the company administrator has access to everything, you will just enter their name and email address to send them an invite to your QBO file. Once they accept, they will have full access to your QBO file.

Primary administrator

The **primary administrator** is the main user who has access to every part of QuickBooks. There can only be one primary admin user for a QBO account. They can manage all users and other admin tasks. By default, the person who sets up the QuickBooks account is automatically assigned as the primary admin. If you need to assign a new primary admin, you can always transfer the role to another user.

You cannot assign this role like the previous roles we have discussed. The only person who can transfer this role to someone is the existing primary administrator. If that person is no longer with the company, you will need to contact the QuickBooks tech support team for assistance.

Book Code for Supplementary Content

Your book code for the supplementary content package included with this book is **3VK4D4D3G8**. Happy learning!

> It is always advised to make the owner of the company the primary administrator since transferring the prior admin role from a former employee can be a hassle.

Reports-only user

The **View company reports only** role is very limited. This role can generate just about any report in QuickBooks except payroll or vendor and customer contact information; however, the reports-only user cannot add, edit, or change any QuickBooks data. They also do not have the ability to view anything outside of reports. This role is ideal for a business partner who wants to periodically review reports but has no day-to-day responsibilities. Unlike the standard and company admin roles, the reports-only role does not count toward your user limit, which means you can give reports-only access to an unlimited number of users, at no additional charge. To add a reports-only user, follow *Steps 1* and *2* in the *Standard all access user* section. In *Step 3*, select **View Company Reports** and follow the onscreen prompts to complete the setup.

Time tracking user

Similar to the **View company reports only** role, the **Track time only** role is also very limited. This role is limited to entering timesheets. It is ideal for employees and contractors who don't need access to any other areas of QuickBooks. Like the reports-only role, the time tracking user does not count toward your user limit. This means that you can add an unlimited number of time tracking users at no additional charge. To add a time tracking user, follow *Steps 1* and *2* in the *Standard all access user* section. In *Step 3*, select **Time tracking only** and follow the onscreen prompts to complete the setup.

Accountant user

Each QBO plan includes at least two accountant users, at no additional cost. The level of access the accountant user has is identical to that of the company administrator.

Accountant users can access all areas of QuickBooks. This includes adding users, editing passwords, and managing your QuickBooks subscription. You should be extremely careful who you give this level of access to; ideally, it should be limited to your **Certified Public Accountant (CPA)**, tax preparer, or bookkeeper.

Go through the following steps to invite an accountant to access your QuickBooks data:

1. Click on the gear icon and select **Manage users** from the company info column, as shown in *Figure 3.60*:

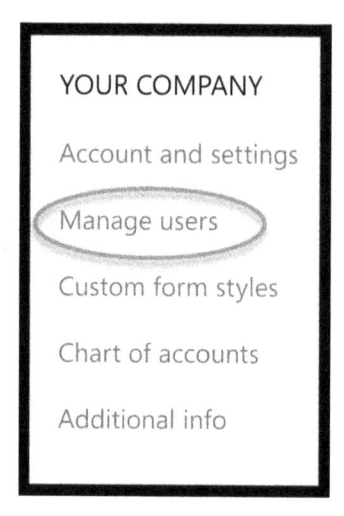

Figure 3.60: The Manage users option

2. On the **Manage users** page, click on **Accountants**, as shown in *Figure 3.61*:

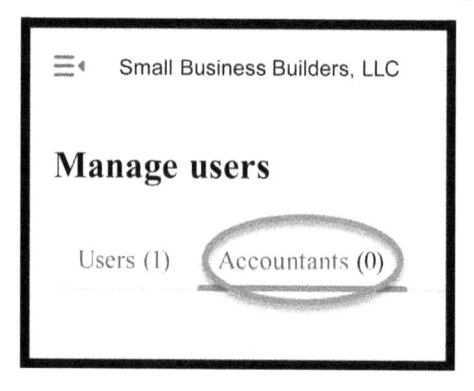

Figure 3.61: The Accountants tab

3. The following screen appears. Type your accountant's email address in the field and click the **Invite** button, as shown in *Figure 3.62*:

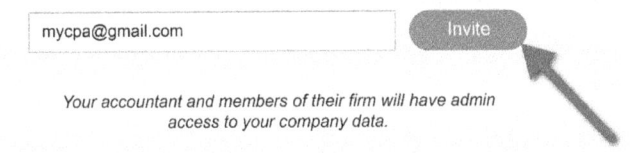

Figure 3.62: Inviting your accountant to your QBO account

Your accountant will then receive an email inviting them to access your QBO account. They will need to accept the invitation and create a secure password. Their user ID will be the email address that you entered in the screenshot above.

Editing user privileges

You can remove or edit access for any user at any time. Follow the steps below to edit a user's access to your QuickBooks file:

1. Navigate to the **Users** page, as shown in the upper left of *Figure 3.63*:

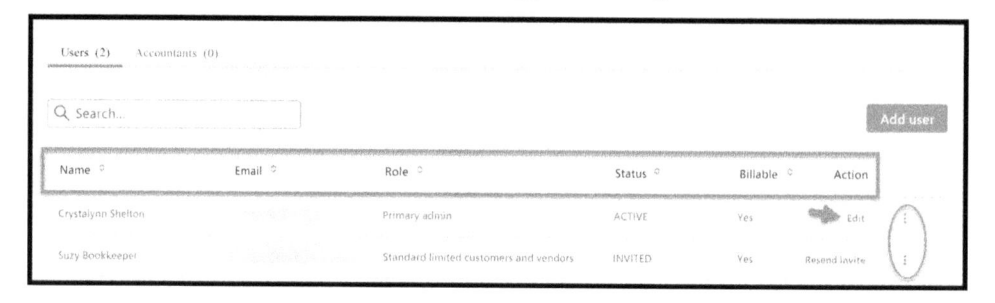

Figure 3.63: Users page in a QuickBooks file (for better visualization, refer to https://packt.link/gbp/9781836649977)

2. Next to the appropriate user, click on **Edit** to change the user's role, or click on the three dots to the right of **Edit** and select **Delete** to remove the user's access altogether, as shown in *Figure 3.63*.

> If a user has the **Primary admin** role (as *Crystalynn Shelton* does in *Figure 3.63*), you will not be able to delete that user. First, you will need to transfer the **Primary admin** access to another user. Once this is complete, you will be able to delete the previous **Primary admin** user.

You should now have a better understanding of the types of users you can set up in QuickBooks (standard – access, no access, limited customers and vendors, accounts receivable manager, accounts payable manager, in-house accountant, company admin, reports-only, time tracking, and accountant). Using the detailed information we have provided on the level of access each user has, you can start inviting your accountant, bookkeeper, and other users to access your QuickBooks data. For more details on the role descriptions and permissions for each role, head over to the online portal to access a complete list: `https://quickbooks.intuit.com/learn-support/en-us/help-article/access-permissions/user-roles-access-rights-quickbooks-online/L66P0fRrI_US_en_US`.

We will wrap this chapter up by showing you how to navigate the QuickBooks Apps Center. Apps are a great way to help you streamline day-to-day business tasks that could otherwise be time-consuming.

Using apps in QBO

There are two types of apps that integrate seamlessly with QBO. First, is the QBO Mobile app, which is available for iPhones, iPads, Android phones, and Android tablets. It allows you to manage your day-to-day business functions on the go, which will transform how you do business.

Below, you will find step-by-step instructions on how to download the QBO Mobile app:

1. Open the App Store **or** Google Play on your device and search for **QuickBooks Online**. (It may not be available in some countries.)
2. Select **Free**, then **Install**.
3. If you are already signed up for QBO, use the same user ID and password to sign in to the app.
4. You may be asked to enter a one-time code to confirm your identity. Once confirmed, you can continue into your account.

> There are a number of functions that can be performed using the app. For a complete list by device, check out this Intuit article for the details: https://quickbooks.intuit.com/learn-support/en-us/help-article/mobile-apps/compare-mobile-app-features/L97TKZ2ck_US_en_US?uid=m26j67uc.

The second type of app that integrates seamlessly with QBO are third-party apps. There are many benefits and a few risks of extending functionality through apps. Some of the **benefits** of using apps in QBO are:

- The ability to expand the functionality of the software so you can have what you need to run all aspects of your business.
- Access to more than 700 apps that integrate seamlessly with QBO, allowing you to manage your inventory, accept online payments, pay your bills, and manage your eCommerce transactions.
- The companies featured in the QuickBooks Apps Center have gone through an extensive vetting process and were approved by Intuit to create apps that will help you simplify tasks, streamline data entry, and sync with QuickBooks.

A couple of the **risks** involved with using apps are:

- The apps are not free, which means the fees charged to use an app will be in addition to what you pay for your monthly QBO subscription, so be sure to do a cost/benefit analysis to ensure you can take on the additional cost.

- You will need to give permission for your data in QBO to be shared with any company whose app you wish to use. You can be confident that your data is secure, since that is also a requirement to become a partner with Intuit.

The app store is organized into categories based on app functionality. Customer reviews are included, along with short video demonstrations to show you how the app works and customer service information if you have additional questions. In this section, we will provide you with an overview of the Apps Center, show you how to find apps that are relevant to your business needs, and show you how to connect apps to QBO.

> Because of the large number of apps that are available, it's impossible for ProAdvisors and accountants to be familiar with all apps. Therefore, you will need to reach out to the technical support team for the app that you choose for assistance with setup, implementation, and training needs. The data in your apps must be maintained and accurate for it to transfer to QBO accurately.

Overview of the QuickBooks App Center

The layout of the App Center is very simple. You can easily search for apps, see a list of the apps you have added, and check out apps that have been recommended based on the type of business you have. Let's take a closer look at the layout:

1. On the left menu bar, click on **Apps** to navigate to the App Center, as follows:

Chapter 3   109

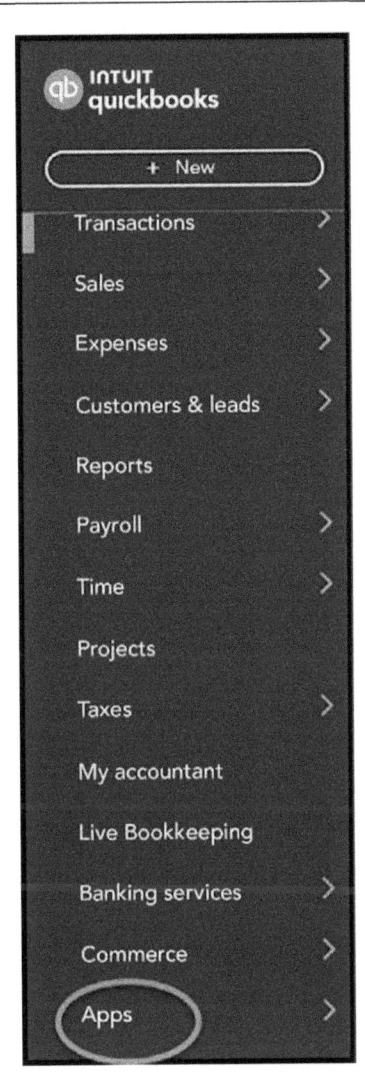

Figure 3.64: Navigating to the QuickBooks App Center

The screen displays as shown in *Figure 3.65*:

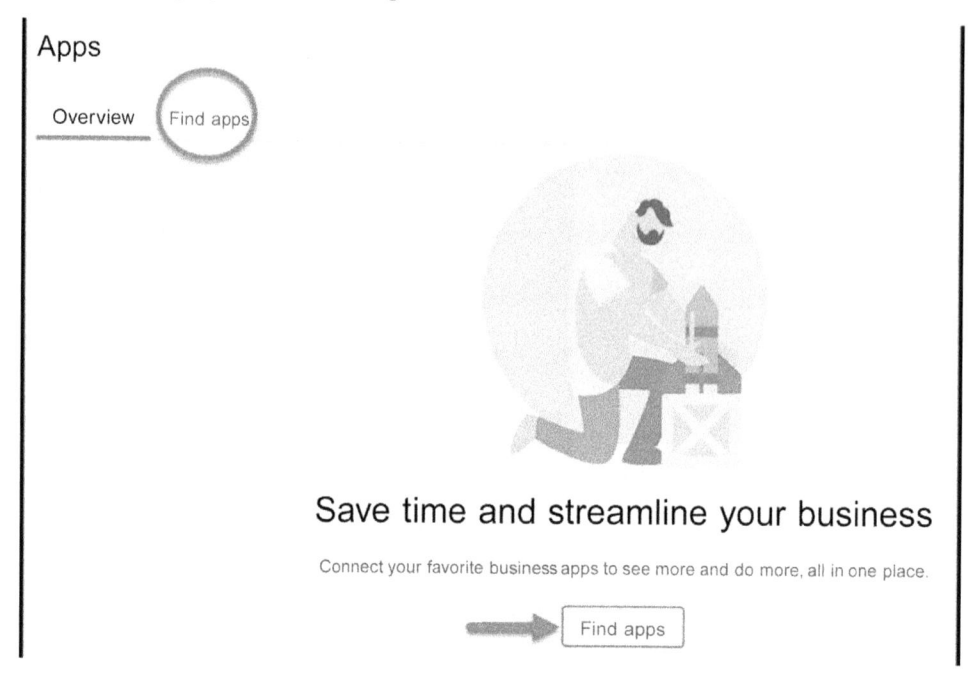

Figure 3.65: The Find apps window displays

2. To start your search, click on the **Find apps** tab next to the **Overview** tab or click the **Find apps** button shown at the bottom of the screen.

3. The App Center will be displayed, as shown in *Figure 3.66*:

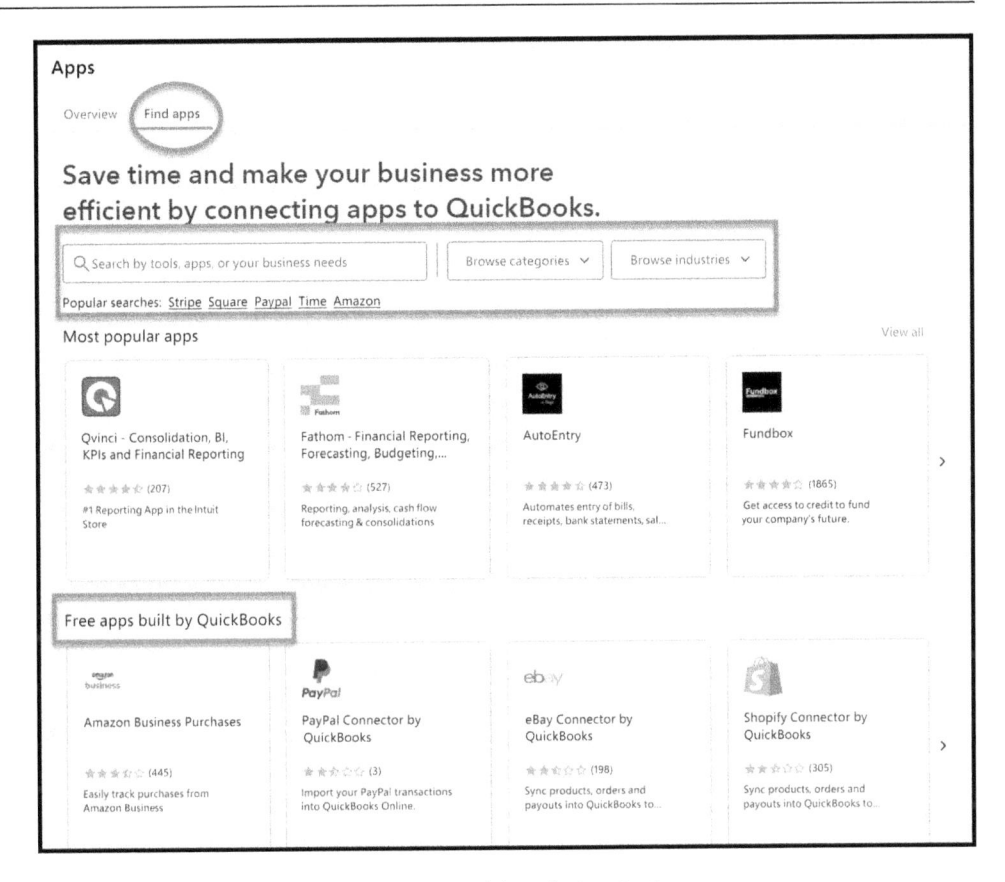

Figure 3.66: QuickBooks App Center

The four key areas of the QuickBooks App Center are as follows:

- **Search options**: If you know the name of the app you are searching for, you can simply type the name of the app into the search box shown in the preceding screenshot. However, if you don't know the name of the app and simply want to search by category, you can do so by clicking on the **Browse categories** button.
- **Browse categories**: There are several categories you can search by, such as **Get customers**, **Get paid**, **Get capital**, **Manage workforce**, **Access advice**, **Be compliant and organized**, **Manage business**, **Manage sales**, and **Manage data**. This will help to narrow down the search so that you can quickly find the apps that you are looking for.
- **Browse industries**: The ability to browse apps by industry is a new one! I love this feature because it allows you to filter your results to the apps that meet your specific industry needs. Some of the industries you will find on this list are: accounting, entertainment, manufacturing, hospitality, technology, retail, and many more.
- **Free apps built by QuickBooks**: In this section, you will find apps that were created by QuickBooks.

If you're not sure which app to choose, I recommend that you schedule a live demo with the app company so that you can see how the app works and get your questions answered. Many companies offer a trial period of 14 days or more so that you can try the app before you buy it. Like QBO, there are no contracts, so you can cancel your subscription at any time. Let's now walk through an example of how to find apps for your business.

Finding apps for your business

As we mentioned previously, there are more than 700 apps in the QuickBooks App Center. While it can be overwhelming at first, you should focus on the needs of your business. There is a lot of information in the center about each app, which will save you the time you would have normally spent doing research. Let's take a look at an app to see what kind of information you can expect to find here.

Scroll down to the **Most Popular** category and click on the **Fathom** app. You will be greeted with the following screen:

Chapter 3

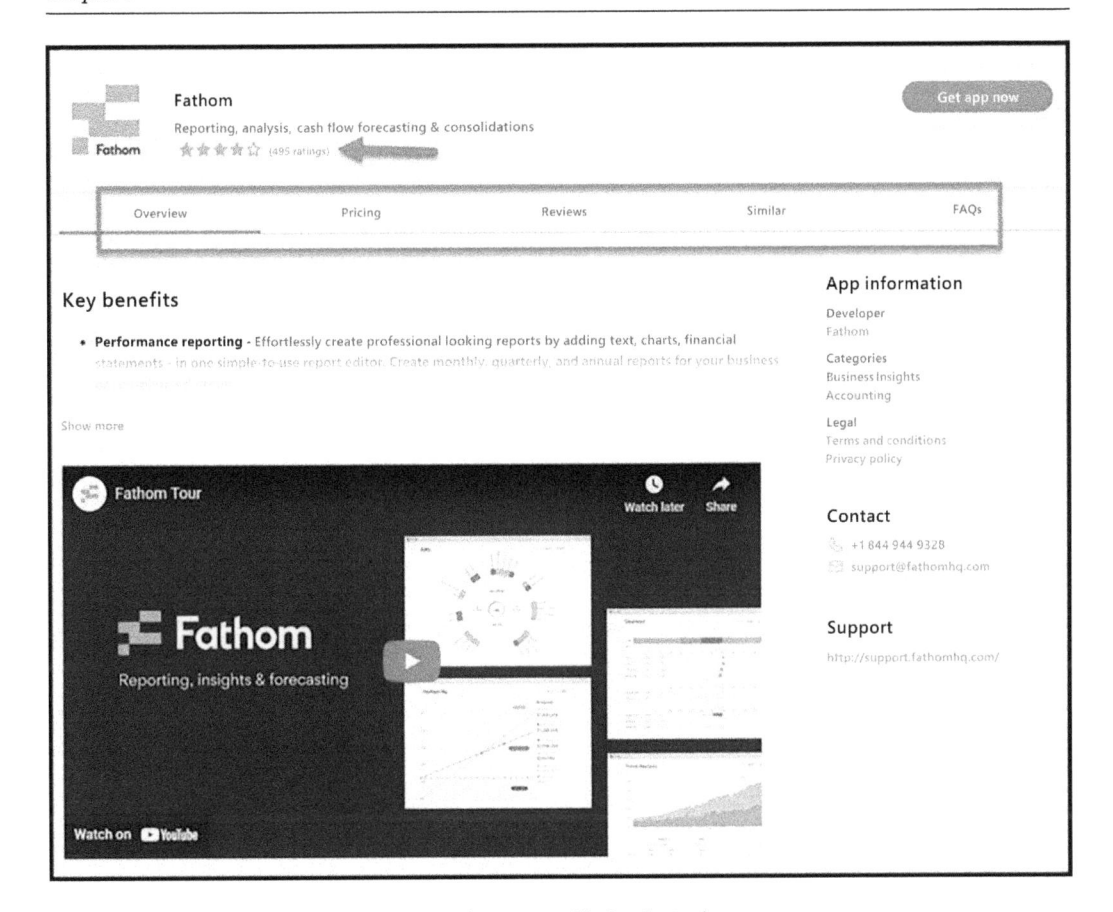

Figure 3.67: The app profile for the Fathom app

The following is a brief description of the information you will find in the app profile:

- **Overview**: The **Overview** tab includes a list of the key benefits the app has, how the app works with QBO, and additional details. Like Fathom, most apps will include a short video to demonstrate how the app works, along with additional screenshots of the user interface.
- **Pricing**: Unfortunately, these apps are not free. Pricing will vary and is usually subscription-based, like QBO. However, you will be billed by the third-party company (in this case, Fathom), not QuickBooks. The good news is that most apps will offer a free trial period of at least 14 days.
- **Reviews**: Like most products, you will see a rating of the app based on customer reviews. Click on the link to see what customers are saying about the app. The more reviews an app has, the better the chance of getting a broad perspective.

- **Similar**: The **Similar** tab shows a list of apps that have similar functionality to the one you are looking at.
- **FAQs**: A list of the most frequently asked questions and answers can be found on this tab.

Once you have decided which app(s) to go with, it's easy to get started. Simply click on the **Get app now** button located on each app profile. Follow the onscreen instructions to complete the app's setup.

> Reaching out to an industry-specific professional organization is a great way to find out the most popular apps used for your industry. This may help narrow down your search for the right fit.

Summary

In this chapter, we showed you how to customize the chart of accounts by adding, editing, deleting, and merging accounts. We covered how to connect your bank and credit card accounts to QuickBooks so that transactions are automatically downloaded into QuickBooks. We also covered how to import banking transactions into QuickBooks from a CSV file. Keep in mind that the bank and credit card transactions are not yet recorded on your books.

After importing the transactions, they are sitting in the banking center and will require you to review and categorize them. In *Chapter 15, Reconciling Uploaded Bank and Credit Card Transactions*, accessible online using this link: `https://packt.link/supplementary-content-9781836649977` we will show you how to do this.

We showed you how to give other users, such as a bookkeeper, business partner, or CPA, full or limited access to your QuickBooks data. Finally, we showed you how to search the QuickBooks App Center for apps that can help streamline your business processes. By now, you should know how to manage your chart of accounts, bank, and credit card accounts, how to add additional users, as well as how to delete users, and how to navigate the QBO App Center.

In the next chapter, we will show you how to manage customers, vendors, and products and services in QBO. This will include how to add, edit, and inactivate customers, vendors, and products and services.

Join our community on Discord

Join our community's Discord space for discussions with the authors and other readers:

https://packt.link/powerusers

4

Managing Customer, Vendor, and Products and Services Lists

Now that you've created your company files, it's time to add the people you do business with on a regular basis. This includes the customers to whom you sell your products and services and the vendors from whom you purchase services and supplies. We will also cover how to create a products and services list in **QuickBooks Online (QBO)** so that you can keep track of your sales.

One of the benefits of adding customers and vendors to QBO is the ability to manage contact information such as the mailing address, telephone number, and primary contact. This allows you to use QBO as your one-stop shop not just for sales data but also when you need to make a quick call to your customer or vendor; all the pertinent information is just a few clicks away. By the same token, keeping track of the products and/or services you sell to customers gives you access to detailed reports that will show you what your top-performing products/services are as well as which products or services are not selling. Having access to this kind of information has been critical to my small business clients when trying to determine whether to implement a marketing campaign to promote slow performers or discontinue selling them altogether.

In this chapter, we will cover the following key concepts:

- Managing customer lists in QBO
- Managing vendor lists in QBO
- Managing products and services lists in QBO

By the end of this chapter, you will understand how to add, edit, delete, and merge customers, vendors, and the products and services that you sell.

> The US edition of QBO was used to create this book. If you are using a version that is outside of the US, results may differ.

Managing customer lists in QBO

A customer is anyone that you sell products or services to. A customer can be an individual or a business.

Some of the information QBO allows you to keep track of related to customers includes contact information, such as their telephone number and email address, payment terms, invoicing, and payment history. You can enter customer information manually or import it from an Excel spreadsheet. If you need to make changes to the contact information for a customer, you can do so easily. If you stop doing business with a customer, you can make customers inactive so that they no longer appear in the customer listing. You can also merge customers if you have duplicates. In this section, we will show you how each of these works, beginning with manually adding customers.

Manually adding customers in QBO

In order to add new customers to QBO, you need to have the basic contact details of your customer. This includes their company name, billing address, business telephone number, and the first and last name of the primary contact. You should also know what payment terms you will extend to customers (for example, net 30 days or net 60 days).

Follow these steps to add a new customer in QBO:

1. Navigate to **Customers** by selecting **Sales** from the left menu bar and then **Customers**, as shown in *Figure 4.1*:

Chapter 4

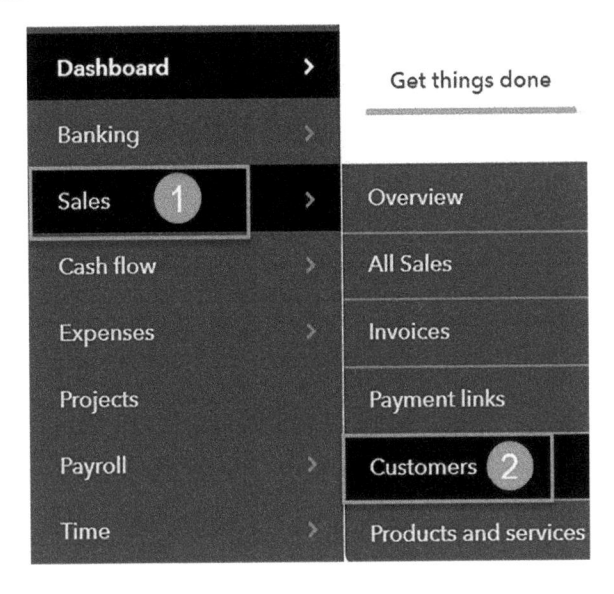

Figure 4.1: Navigating to Customers

The following screen will appear:

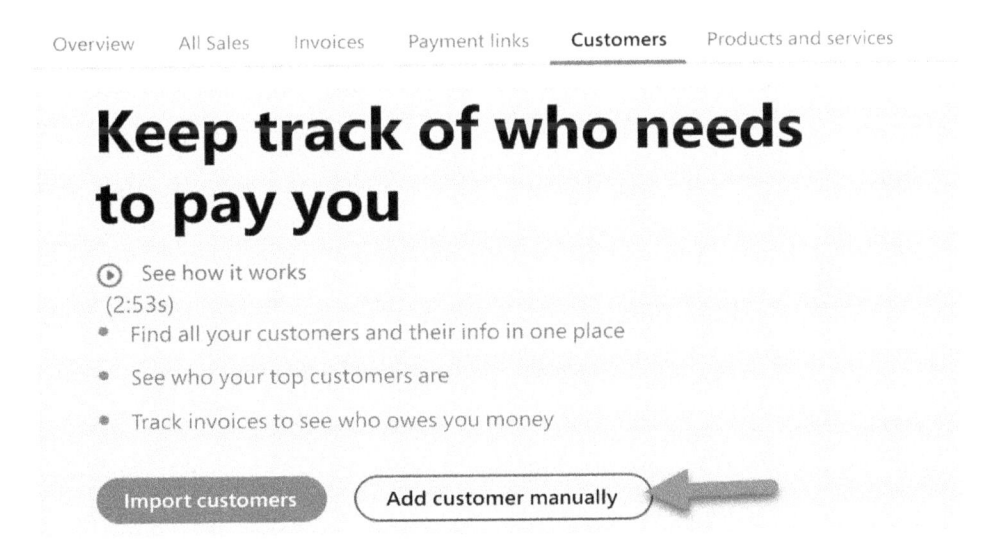

Figure 4.2: The Add customer manually button

2. Click on the **Add customer manually** button. Note that this button will not appear if you have added customers previously to QuickBooks.
3. Fill in the fields on the **Customer** information screen, as shown in *Figure 4.3*:

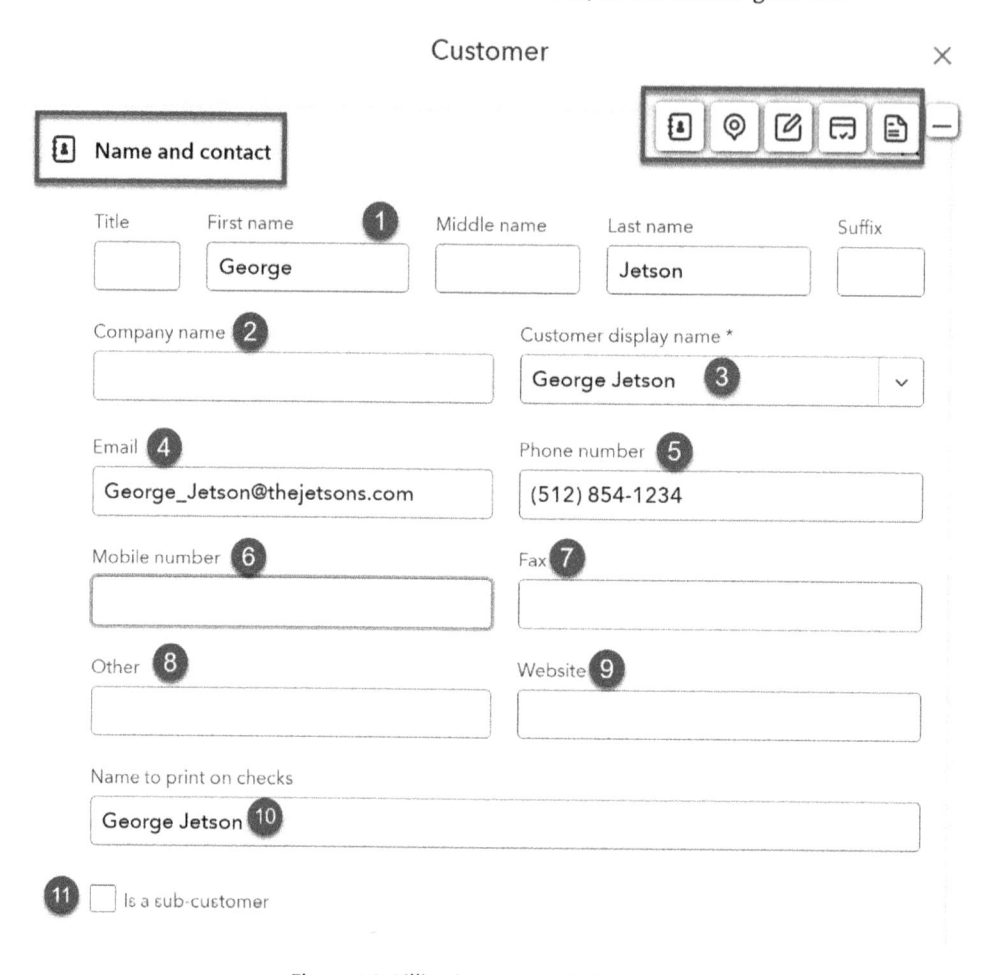

Figure 4.3: Filling in customer information

4. When adding a new customer, there are five key areas that need to be completed: **Name and contact**, **Addresses**, **Notes and attachments**, **Payments**, and **Additional information**. You can navigate to each area using the icons located in the top-right corner of the screen, as indicated in *Figure 4.3*.

   i. The following is a brief description of the 11 fields of information you can enter in the **Name and contact** section. While the only required field is the **Customer display name** field, I recommend that you take the time to add as much information as you can about your customers:

      - **First name** and **Last name** (1): If the customer is an individual, enter their first and last names in these fields. If the customer is a business, leave these fields blank. Note that if a business is a sole proprietorship or a single-member LLC and you want to keep track of the name of the business owner and the legal business name, complete both fields. Be sure to periodically review your customer list for duplicates. If you have more than one person adding customers, you want to make sure that they are consistent when adding customers using the first name and last name fields and/or adding them using the business name field. A good rule of thumb is to use the first/last name fields for customers who don't have a company name and use the business name field for those that have a **doing business as (DBA)**.

      - **Company name** (2): If the customer is a business, enter the business name in this field. If the customer is an individual, leave this field blank.

      - **Customer display name** (3): There is no need to input anything in this field; it will automatically populate with the information you entered in the **Company name** or **First name** and **Last name** fields. This field is important because the information will be displayed in the customer list found in the customer center.

      - **Email** (4): Enter the business email address for customers in this field.

      - **Phone number** (5): Enter the business telephone number for customers in this field.

      - **Mobile number** (6): Enter the mobile number for customers in this field.

      - **Fax** (7): Enter the fax number (if applicable) for customers in this field.

- **Other** (8): Enter an additional contact phone number in the **Other** field.
- **Website** (9): Enter the website address for the business if you have one.
- **Name to print on checks** (10): Similar to the **Customer display name** field, this field will automatically populate with the information that you entered in the **Company name** or **First name** and **Last name** fields. If you need to change the payee name, enter the name you would like to appear on checks. Typically, you would issue a check to a customer in the case of a refund, so it is important to have the correct payee name in this field.
- **Is a sub-customer** (11): If you have more than one job or project you are working on for the same customer, you can create sub-customers to keep track of the income and expenses for each job separately. For example, if a contractor is working on a kitchen remodel and a bathroom remodel for the same customer, each of these jobs can be set up as a sub-customer so that you can track income and expenses for each job (sub-customer) separately. This will allow you to easily run reports by sub-customer (job, project) so that you can see the profitability of each one.

> Before you can create a sub-customer, the main customer must be added to QuickBooks first. Going back to our contractor example, the customer must be added to QuickBooks first before adding kitchen remodel and bathroom remodel as sub-customers.

ii. Complete the following fields in the **Addresses** section:

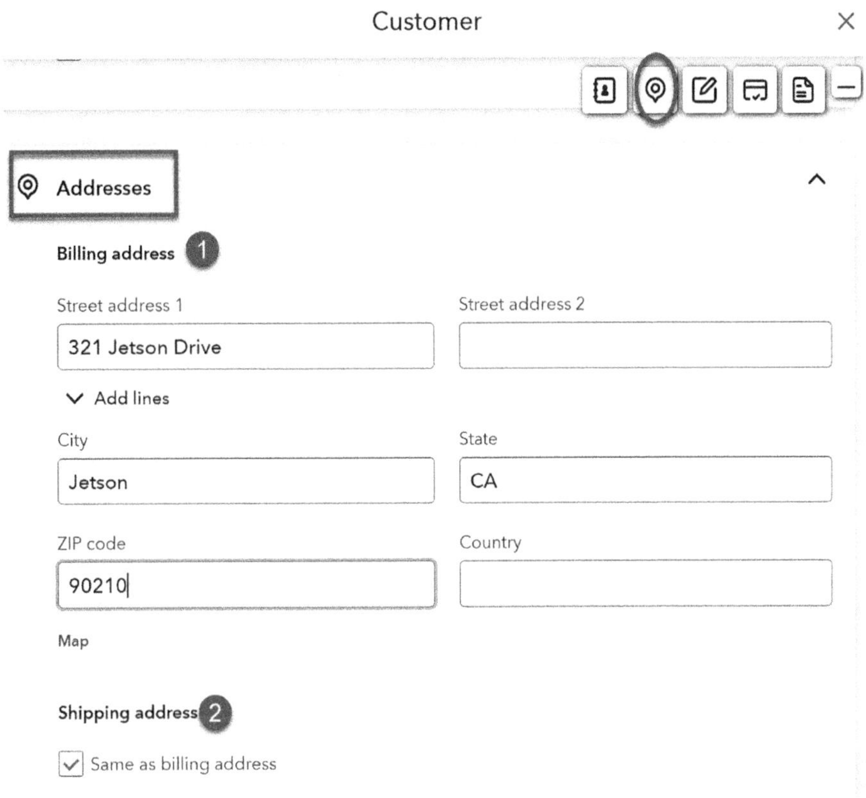

Customer ✕

Addresses

Billing address ①

Street address 1 | Street address 2
321 Jetson Drive |

∨ Add lines

City | State
Jetson | CA

ZIP code | Country
90210 |

Map

Shipping address ②

☑ Same as billing address

Figure 4.4: Addresses section of the Customer information screen

The following is a brief description of the fields of information you can enter in the **Addresses** section:

- **Billing address** (1): Enter the address where your customers would like their invoices to be mailed to and/or where correspondence should be sent. Even if you plan to email all the invoices and other correspondence, we recommend that you keep an address on file for all customers.

- **Shipping address** (2): The address entered in the **Billing address** field will automatically be copied to the **Shipping address** field. This can be edited if necessary. The billing address will be used to mail invoices to customers, and the shipping address is where products are shipped, if applicable.

iii. Complete the following fields in the **Notes and attachments** section:

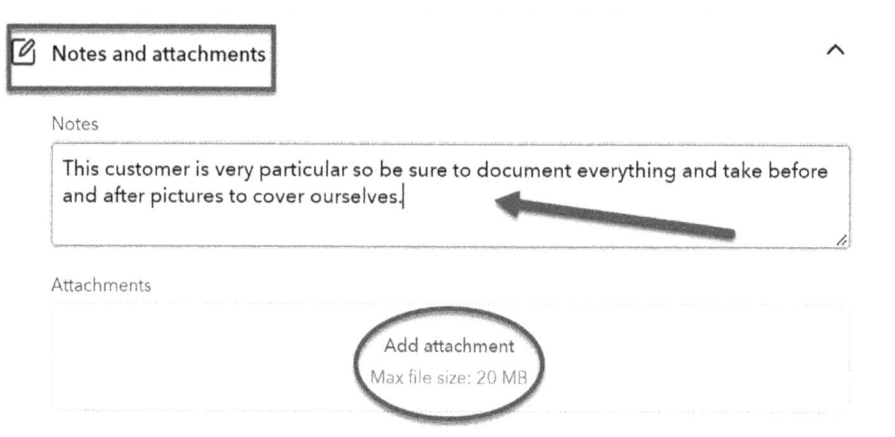

Figure 4.5: Descriptive note and button to add an attachment

- **Notes:** This field is optional but can be used to enter additional information about your customers, such as any preferences they have, or even to document previous incidents or issues. This information is for internal use only and is not visible to the customer.

- **Attachments:** You can store important documents such as contracts, engagement letters, or proposals in QuickBooks. Simply scan the document into your computer and attach it to the customer with whom it is associated.

iv. Complete the following four fields in the **Payments** section:

[Payments section showing four fields: Primary payment method: Check (1); Terms: Net 30 (2); Sales form delivery options: None (3); Language to use when you send invoices: English (4)]

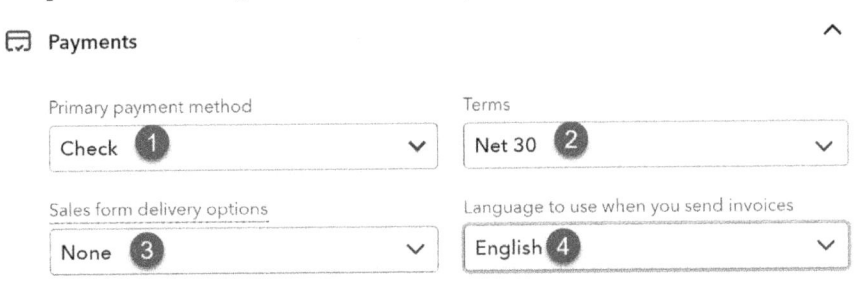

Figure 4.6: Payments section of the Customer information screen

- **Primary payment method** (1): Choose from the drop-down list the payment method used most by the customer. **Cash**, **Check**, and **Credit card** are the options available, but you can also add new payment methods, such as Cash App or Zelle.

- **Terms** (2): Select the payment terms for customers in this field. For example, **Net 30** means the customer has 30 days from the invoice date to remit payment. If payment is not received by the due date, QuickBooks will flag the invoice as past due. You can set QuickBooks up to automatically send a reminder email to customers when invoices are coming due or past due. Refer to *Chapter 2, Company File Setup*, to learn how to do this.

- **Sales form delivery options** (3): From the dropdown, you can select the method with which you typically provide customers their invoices (**Email**, **Printed copy**, **Default method**, or **None** are the options).

- **Language to use when you send invoices** (4): From the dropdown, you can select the language you would like to invoice customers in. Currently, the choices are **English**, **French**, **Spanish**, **Italian**, **Chinese (Traditional)**, and **Portuguese (Brazil)**.

v. Complete the following fields in the **Additional info** section:

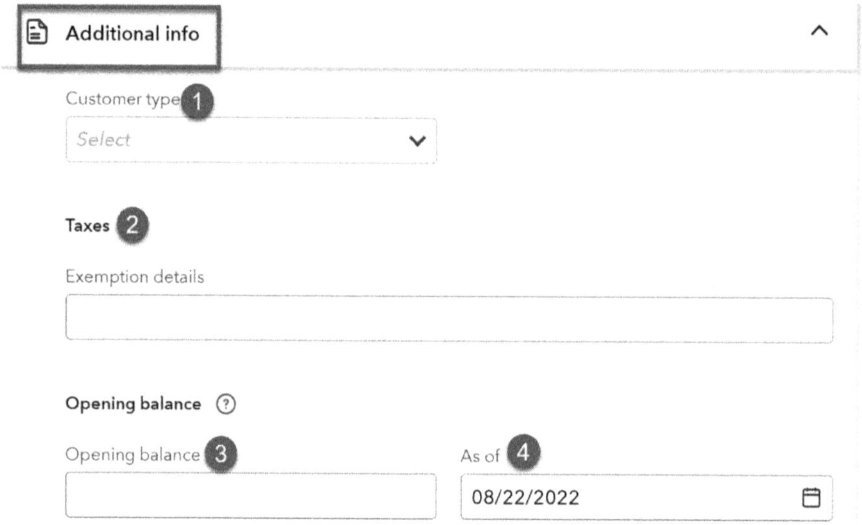

Figure 4.7: Additional info screen of the Customer information screen

- **Customer type** (1): If you need to categorize your customers into different types (for example, wholesaler or retailer), you can create custom types and assign each customer to a type. This will allow you to run reports and filter by customer type to get detailed information, such as sales by customer type.

- **Taxes** (2): Enter the details for tax-exempt customers such as their resale certificate number. In addition, you should request a copy of the certificate and attach it in the **Notes and Attachments** section. This will cover you if you ever have a sales tax audit and need to provide supporting information on why you did not charge a customer sales tax.

- **Opening balance** (3): Generally, you wouldn't use this field unless converting from another accounting software. This field is useful for recording the existing accounts receivable balance that customers have with you at the time of converting from your old accounting system to QuickBooks. However, if you plan to enter unpaid invoices into QuickBooks, leave this field blank.

Chapter 4

- **As of** (4): If you entered an opening **accounts receivable (A/R)** balance in *step 3*, enter the effective date in this field. This would typically be the date you start using QuickBooks to track your business finances.

5. Be sure to click the **Save** button at the very bottom of the screen to save the customer information in QuickBooks.

If you have more than a handful of customers to add to QuickBooks, I recommend you put the customer information into an Excel spreadsheet and import the data into QuickBooks.

Importing customers into QBO

You can import all of your customer details from a CSV file into QuickBooks. A template can be found here: https://github.com/PacktPublishing/Mastering-QuickBooks-2025-Sixth-Edition/tree/main/Chapter05.

Follow these steps to import customers into QBO:

1. Navigate to **Customers** by selecting **Sales** from the left-hand menu bar and then **Customers**, as shown in *Figure 4.8*:

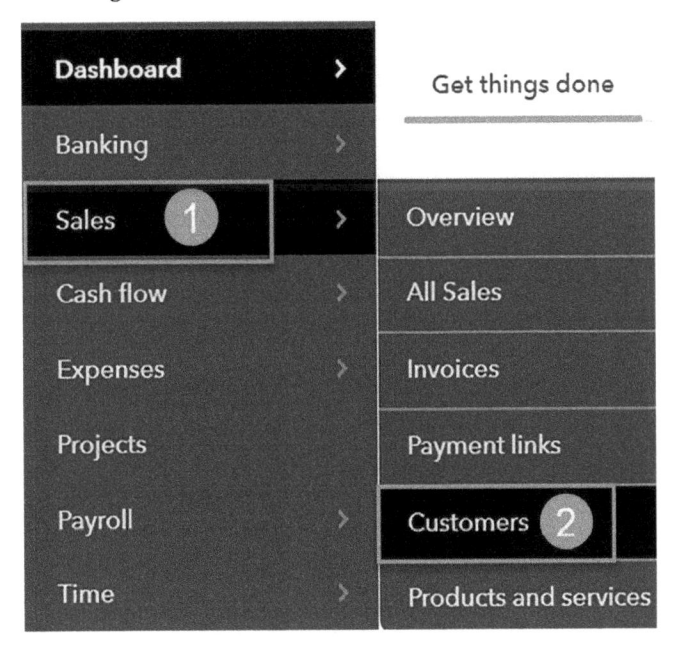

Figure 4.8: Navigating to Customers

2. Click the drop-down arrow next to the **New customer** button, located in the upper-right corner, and select **Import customers**, as shown in *Figure 4.9*:

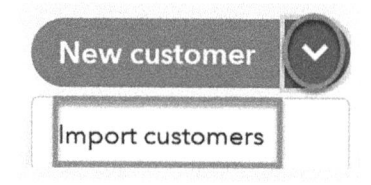

Figure 4.9: The Import customers option

3. On the **Import customers** screen, click the **Browse** button to upload the Excel or CSV file from your computer, as shown in *Figure 4.10*:

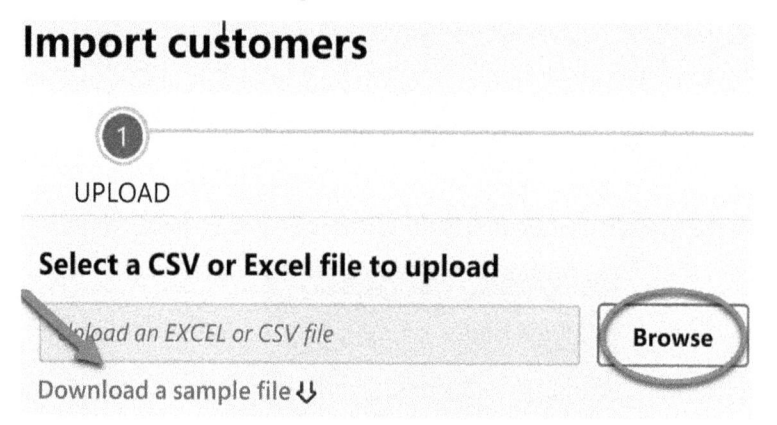

Figure 4.10: Uploading a CSV or Excel file

4. You can click on the blue hyperlink to download the sample file (shown in the preceding screenshot). This file includes all of the fields of information you can upload for customers. Save this file and use it as your template.

5. Follow the onscreen instructions to import your customer data into QBO.

> A common error made when importing data is the use of special characters. QuickBooks will not accept the use of special characters (for example, &, !, and $), so be sure to avoid doing this. For additional tips on troubleshooting errors during importing, you can download the troubleshooting guide using this link:
>
> https://github.com/PacktPublishing/Mastering-QuickBooks-2025-Sixth-Edition/tree/main/Chapter05

Making changes to existing customers in QBO

There may be times when you need to correct or update a customer's information. For example, if a customer's address changes or their primary contact changes, you will need to update your records with the new information. Updating customer information is easy to do in QuickBooks – all you need to do is navigate to the Customer Center and select the customer that you need to make changes to.

Follow these steps to edit an existing customer in QBO:

1. Navigate to **Customers** by selecting **Sales** from the left-hand menu bar and then **Customers**, as shown in *Figure 4.11*:

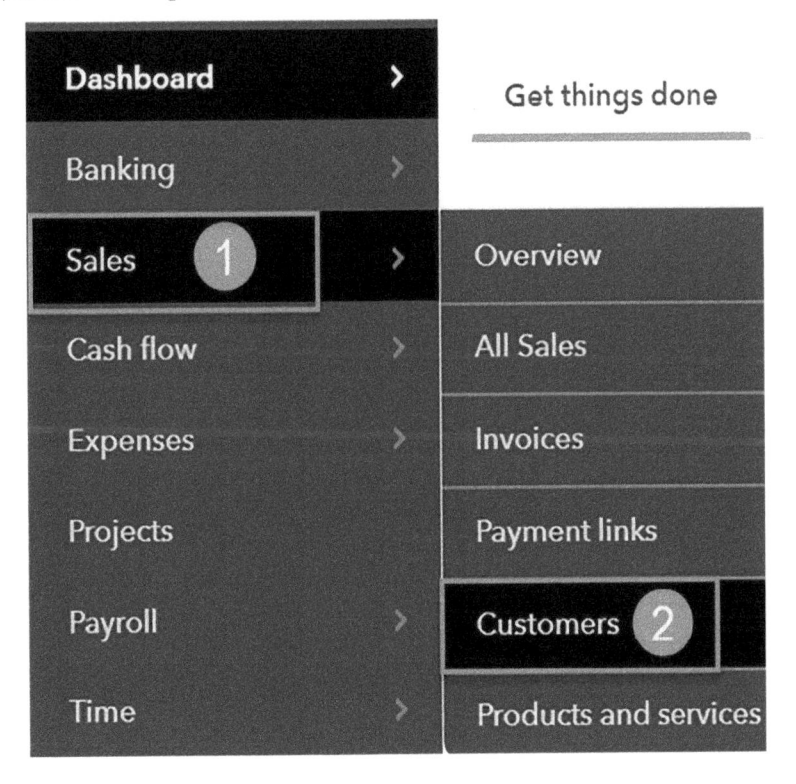

Figure 4.11: Navigating to Customers

2. The **Customer Center** will appear on the next screen. Click on the customer name, as indicated in *Figure 4.12*:

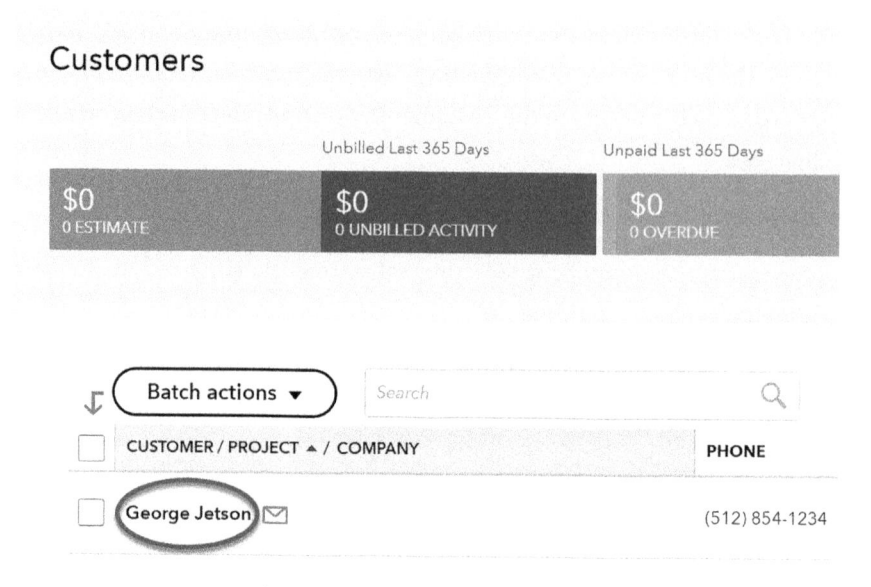

Figure 4.12: Editing customer details

3. The following screen appears. Click the **Edit** button shown in *Figure 4.13* and make the necessary changes:

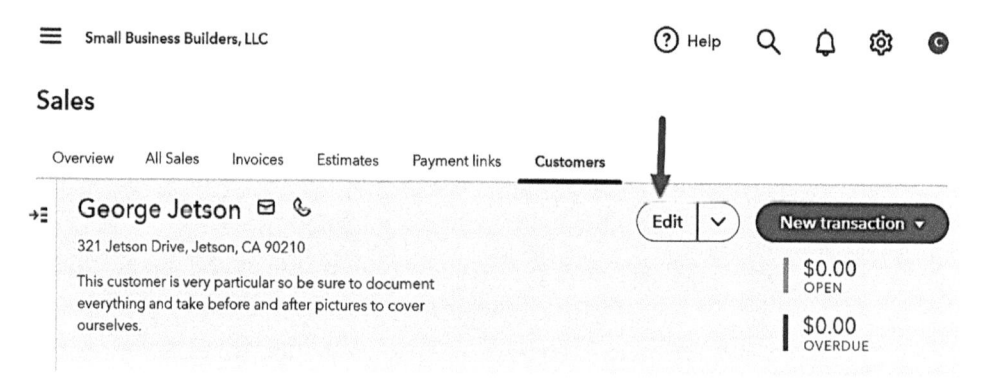

Figure 4.13: Edit button for a customer listed in the Customer Center

You can update the information you have on file for your customers at any time. Having up-to-date information will ensure that invoices, sales receipts, and other documents contain the most recent contact information, such as billing and shipping address information, on file.

Inactivating customers in QBO

You cannot delete customers, vendors, or products in QBO. However, similar to accounts on the chart of accounts (discussed in the previous chapter), you can inactivate customers, vendors, and products, which will keep the existing transactions recorded in QuickBooks but "hide" the customer, vendor, or item from the drop-down list.

Follow these steps to inactivate customers in QBO:

1. Navigate to **Customers** by selecting **Sales** from the left-hand menu bar and then **Customers**, as shown in *Figure 4.14*:

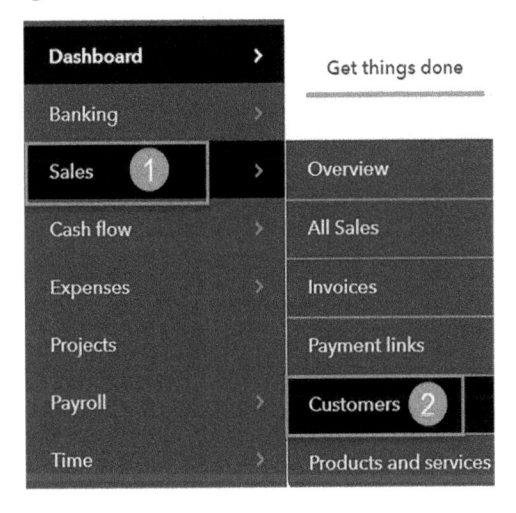

Figure 4.14: Navigating to Customers

2. Put a checkmark next to the customer you want to inactivate, click the arrow next to **Batch actions**, and select **Make inactive**, as shown in *Figure 4.15*:

Figure 4.15: The Make inactive option

This **Make inactive** action will prevent someone from selecting customers you no longer wish to use, while preserving the historical transactions that have been recorded for each customer. We will cover how to make vendors and items inactive later on in this chapter.

Merging customers in QBO

A common issue that you may encounter is duplicate customers. If you have more than one person setting up customers in QuickBooks or you don't have an established way of adding new customers, you will have this issue. The best way to avoid having duplicate customers is to establish a process to add new customers. For example, have only one person who is responsible for adding customers in QuickBooks, and establish whether you will enter customers by first name, last name, or last name, first name.

If you do encounter duplicate customers, you can combine the information entered for the duplicate customers to create one customer profile.

Follow the steps below to merge customers:

1. Navigate to the **Customer Center** and identify the duplicate customers:

CUSTOMER ▲ / COMPANY	PHONE	OPEN BALANCE	ACTION
Astro Jetson Astro Jetston & Associates	(818) 678-2345	$0.00	Create invoice ▼
Elroy Jetson ✉ Elroy Jetson, Inc	(818) 876-5432	$0.00	Create invoice ▼
George Jetson ✉	(512) 854-1234	$21.90	Receive payment ▼
Jane Jetson ✉ Jane Jetson Industries	(818) 234-5678	$0.00	Create invoice ▼
Jetson, Astro		$0.00	Create invoice ▼

Figure 4.16: Identifying duplicate customers in the Customer Center

2. In *Figure 4.16*, **Astro Jetson** and **Jetson, Astro** are the same customer. Since the owner would like all customer information entered as "first name followed by last name," the customer profile we want to keep is the one at the top of the list, **Astro Jetson**.

Chapter 4 133

3. Click once on the customer profile you plan to remove. In our example, this is **Jetson, Astro**. The following appears once we click on **Jetson, Astro**:

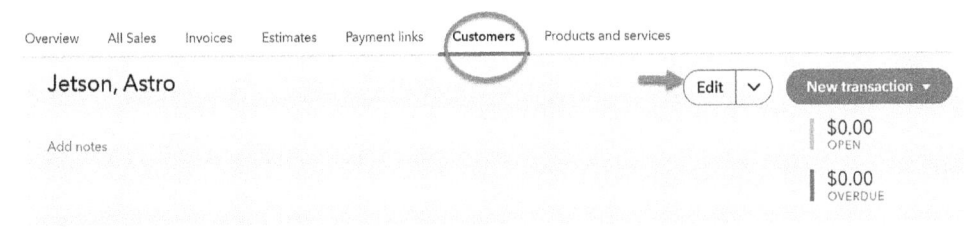

Figure 4.17: Viewing customer information

4. Click the **Edit** button and the **Customer** information screen will appear:

Figure 4.18: Editing information for an existing customer

5. Click once in the **Customer display name** field, and type the name exactly as it appears in the customer profile that you wish to keep. In our example, this would be **Astro Jetson**, as shown below:

Figure 4.19: Editing the Customer display name field

6. Click the **Save** button in the lower-right corner.

The following message will appear:

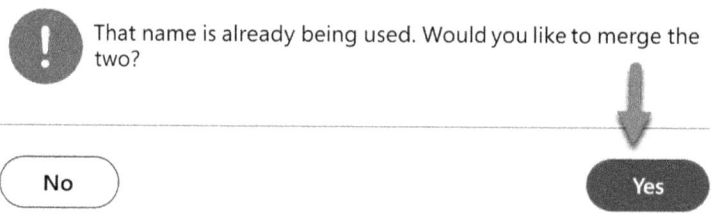

Figure 4.20: Confirming the merging of customers

Chapter 4

7. Click **Yes** and the customer profiles will be combined into one, as shown in *Figure 4.21*:

CUSTOMER ▲ / COMPANY	PHONE	OPEN BALANCE	ACTION
Astro Jetson Astro Jetston & Associates	(818) 678-2345	$0.00	Create invoice ▼
Elroy Jetson ✉ Elroy Jetson, Inc	(818) 876-5432	$0.00	Create invoice ▼
George Jetson ✉	(512) 854-1234	$21.90	Receive payment ▼
Jane Jetson ✉ Jane Jetson Industries	(818) 234-5678	$0.00	Create invoice ▼
Judy Jetson ✉ Judy Jetson, LLC	(818) 567-8900	$0.00	Create invoice ▼

Figure 4.21: The Customer Center with both profiles combined

As you can see, the duplicate profile (**Jetson, Astro**) is no longer on the customer list. All of the transactions recorded for that customer have been moved to the **Astro Jetson** profile. With that, we have shown you how to manually add, import, edit, inactivate, and merge customers. In the next section, we will show you how to add, import, edit, inactivate, and merge vendors.

> While you do not have to complete anything other than the customer name to begin working, we recommend that you keep as much information as possible about your customer in QBO so that your records are complete and accurate.

Managing vendor lists in QBO

A vendor is an individual or a business that you pay. Vendors can be 1099 contractors, which are independent contractors whom you pay $600 or more in a calendar year, utility companies, or businesses you purchase products from. Similar to customers, you can keep track of all vendor information, such as the company's address, telephone number, email address, and federal tax ID number for 1099 reporting. 1099 reporting is required for contractors that you have paid $600 or more to within a calendar year.

In this section, we will show you how to add new vendors, edit existing vendors, inactivate vendors, and merge vendors in QuickBooks.

Manually adding vendors in QBO

To add new vendors to QBO, you need to have each vendor's contact details. This includes a business telephone number, remit to address, email address, and tax ID number (or social security number) for 1099 vendors. You can also enter the payment terms your vendor has extended to you. Entering these payment terms will allow QuickBooks to remind you when bills are due or past due.

Follow these steps to manually add vendors in QBO:

1. Navigate to **Vendors** by clicking on **Expenses** on the left-hand menu bar and selecting **Vendors**, as shown in *Figure 4.22*:

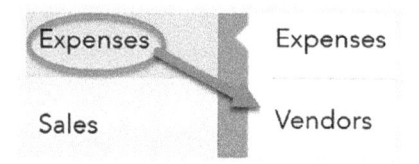

Figure 4.22: Selecting Vendors

2. Click the **New Vendor** button located in the upper-right corner, as shown in *Figure 4.23*:

Figure 4.23: The New Vendor button

If this is the first time you are accessing the Vendors Center, you will see the option **Add vendor manually** instead of the **New Vendor** button. However, both options take you to the screen in *Figure 4.24*.

3. Fill in the fields in the **Vendor** window, as shown here:

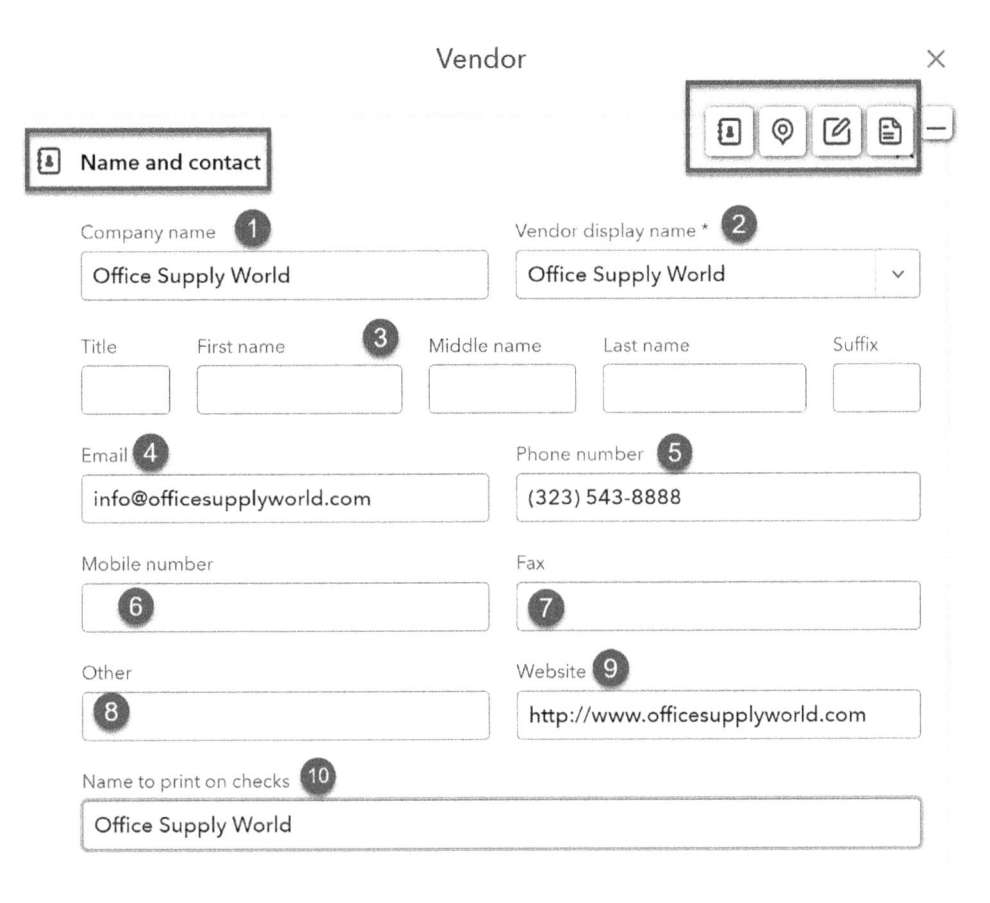

Figure 4.24: Filling in the Vendor window

The following is a brief description of the 10 fields of information you can enter for new vendors:

- **Company name** (1): Enter the name of the business that you are purchasing from. If the vendor is an individual, such as a 1099 contractor, leave this field blank and complete the **First name** and **Last name** fields instead.

> If you have an existing customer who is also a vendor, you will need to set them up as a vendor in QuickBooks. Since QuickBooks does not allow you to use duplicate names, we recommend you add additional verbiage after the name, such as "V" or "Vend," to differentiate between the customer profile and the vendor profile. For example, if Cameras-R-Us is already set up in QuickBooks, we would set it up as a vendor as Cameras-R-Us-V or Cameras-R-Us-Vend.

- **Vendor display name** (2): This field will automatically populate with the company name that was entered in *step 1*.
- **First name** and **Last name** (3): If purchasing from an individual and not a business, enter the name of the individual you are purchasing goods or services from. If the vendor is a sole proprietorship or LLC and you want to keep the name of the business owner, enter both.
- **Email** (4): Enter the primary email address for the vendor in this field. This email address will be used to send purchase orders and other vendor-related documents directly from QuickBooks.
- **Phone number** (5): Enter the vendor's telephone number in this field.
- **Mobile number** (6): Enter the vendor's cell phone number in this field.
- **Fax** (7): Enter the vendor's fax number in this field.
- **Other** (8): Enter any additional contact information in this field.
- **Website** (9): Enter the vendor's website information in this field.
- **Name to print on checks** (10): The information entered for the company name (1) or the first and last name (3) will automatically appear in this field. If necessary, you can edit this information.

4. Enter the address where you mail your payments. If you don't mail payments, you still want to complete these fields if you have the info:

Address

Street address 1

444 Bedrock Lane

Street address 2

∨ Add lines

City

Bedrock

State

CA

ZIP code

95432

Country

Figure 4.25: Adding vendor address details

> If you make your payments online or via credit card, it's still a good idea to keep an address on file for each vendor. This is especially important to do for 1099 contractors because you are required to mail a 1099 form to them at the end of the year for tax reporting purposes. It is important to keep up to date on rules for issuing 1099s. If you are unsure if a vendor should receive a 1099, please reach out to a tax professional for guidance.

5. Complete the **Notes and attachments** section, as shown in *Figure 4.26*:

Notes and attachments

Notes

Include our account number on all payments. Our account number is 1234567.

Attachments

Add attachment
Max file size: 20 MB

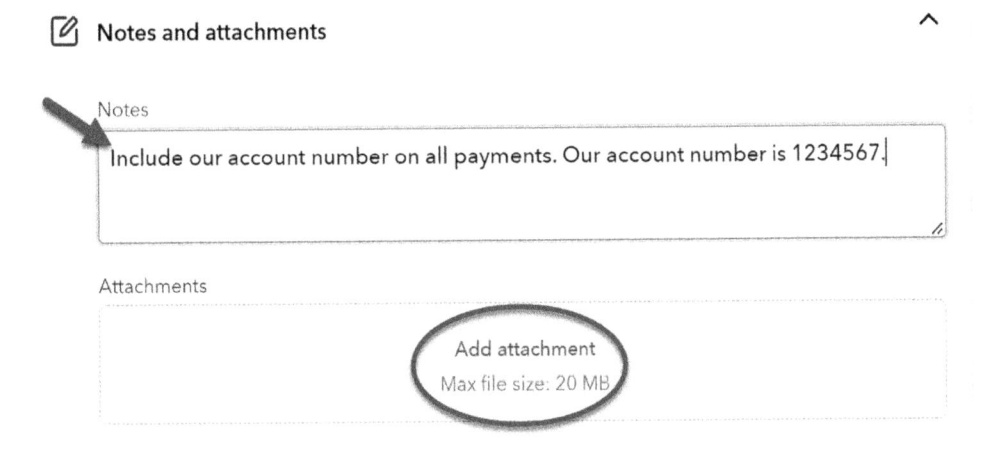

Figure 4.26: Notes and attachments section of the Vendor information screen

Like customers, you can add notes about your vendors and suppliers that are for *internal purposes only*. Any information added to this section is not visible to vendors. In addition, you can attach contracts, files, emails, and other pertinent documents in the section labeled **Add attachment**, as shown in *Figure 4.26*.

6. Complete the fields in the **Additional info** section:

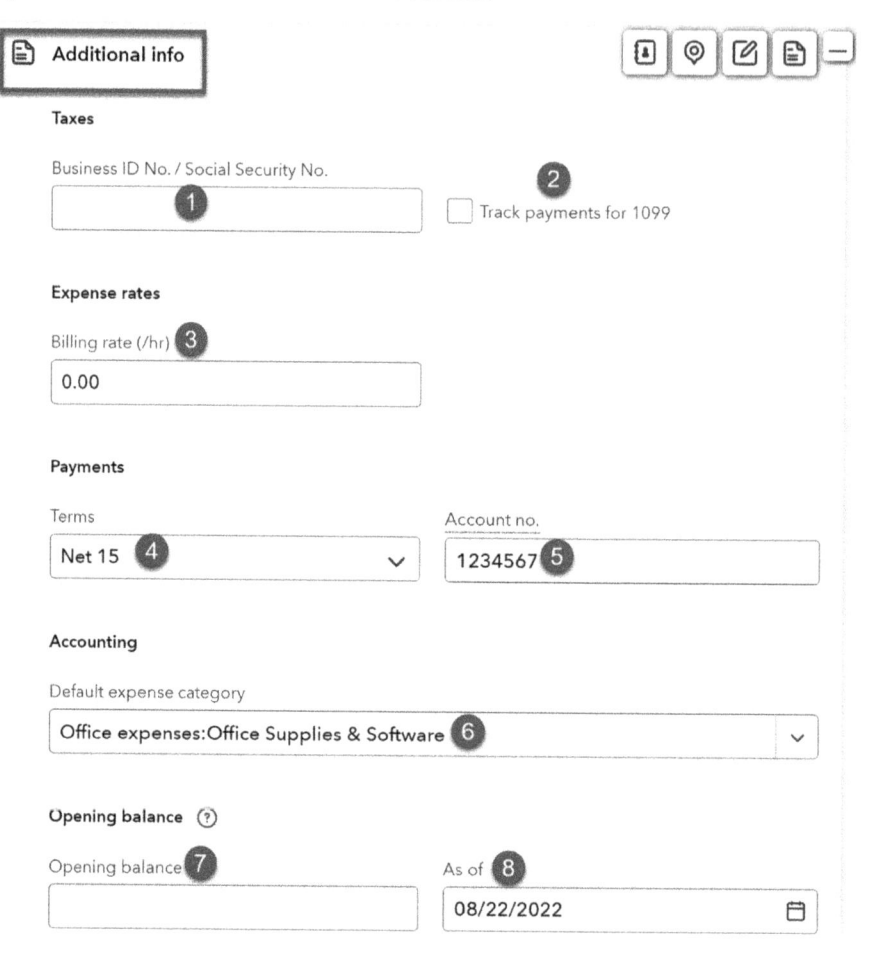

Figure 4.27: Additional info section of the Vendor information screen

- **Business ID No.** (1): Enter the social security number or federal tax ID number for all 1099 vendors in this field. If a business is incorporated, there is no need to obtain this information.

> It's good practice to request a W9 form from all 1099 contractors before you remit payment. A W9 form includes an individual's first and last names, **DBA** company name, mailing address, business entity (for example, sole proprietor or LLC), and social security or federal tax ID number. In *Chapter 8, Managing Employees and 1099 Contractors in QuickBooks Online*, we cover how to invite a new contractor to complete an electronic W9 form.

- **Track payments for 1099** (2): Select this checkbox for any individuals you purchase goods and services from that are not incorporated. By marking this box, QuickBooks will flag these vendors so that they appear on the 1099 report at the end of the year.

  > In the US, if you pay $600 or more to a 1099 contractor during the year, you are required to provide that contractor with a 1099 form at the end of the year. If total payments during the year do not equal $600 or more, you are not required to provide a 1099 form. In *Chapter 8, Managing Employees and 1099 Contractors in QuickBooks Online*, we will introduce you to the Contractors Center. In the Contractors Center, you can add, edit, and pay 1099 contractors as well as complete your annual 1099 report filings.

- **Billing rate** (3): If you have an agreed-upon billing rate that does not change, enter that information in this field. However, if the billing rate varies, leave this field blank.
- **Terms** (4): Select the payment terms the vendor has extended to you (for example, net 30 days, net 15 days, or due upon receipt). It's important to select payment terms so that QuickBooks can use this information to remind you when bills are due or past due.
- **Account no.** (5): If your vendor has given you an account number, enter it in this field. Otherwise, you can leave this field blank.

- **Default expense category** (6): If you use the same category for all payments to a vendor, you can select the category from the dropdown. This will allow QuickBooks to automatically populate the category field each time you record a new transaction for this vendor. If the category varies, leave this field blank.
- **Opening balance** (7): If you are converting from other accounting software to QuickBooks, you can enter the outstanding accounts payable balance for suppliers in this field. However, if you plan to manually enter unpaid bills into QuickBooks, leave this field blank.
- **As of** (8): If you entered an opening balance, enter an effective date in the **As of** field. In general, this date will be the same as the date you start tracking your income and expenses in QuickBooks.

Similar to customers, you can include a wealth of information in QuickBooks pertaining to your vendors. By including this information in QuickBooks, you can easily create purchase orders, bills, and other forms and documents without needing to enter this information over and over.

Importing vendors into QBO

If you have more than a few vendors to add to QuickBooks, you may want to consider importing the information instead of manually inputting it into QuickBooks. Similar to customers, you can import your vendor details from a CSV file. This template can be found here: https://packt.link/MQ23chapter5.

Follow these steps to import vendors into QBO:

1. Navigate to **Vendors** by clicking on **Expenses** on the left-hand menu bar and selecting **Vendors**, as shown in *Figure 4.28*:

Figure 4.28: Selecting Vendors

Chapter 4

2. Click on the arrow to the right of the **New vendor** button, located in the upper-right corner, and select **Import vendors**, as shown in *Figure 4.29*:

Figure 4.29: The Import vendors option

3. On the **Import vendors** screen, click the **Browse** button to upload the Excel or CSV file from your computer, as shown in *Figure 4.30*:

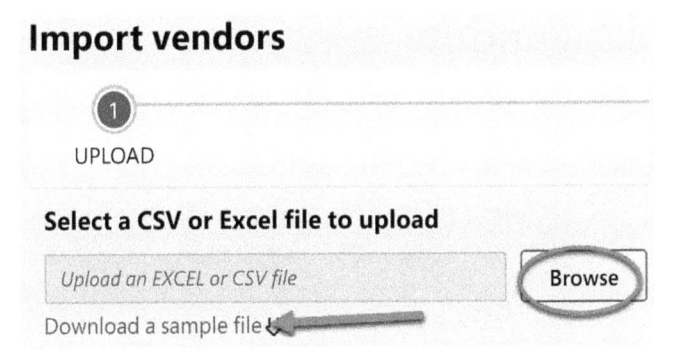

Figure 4.30: Uploading a CSV or Excel file

4. You can click on the blue link to download the sample file (shown in the preceding screenshot). This file includes all of the fields of information you can upload for vendors. Save this file and use it as your template.

5. Follow the onscreen prompts to import your vendors into QBO.

Review the vendor information to ensure accuracy. If you do find errors, you can easily fix them. Let's see how!

Making changes to existing vendors in QBO

Similar to customers, the information that you have on file for vendors can change. For example, the remit address where payments are mailed could change, or the telephone number may need to be updated. When it does, you can quickly update your records in QuickBooks. You will need to navigate to the Vendors Center and select the vendor that you need to make changes to.

Follow these steps to edit an existing vendor in QBO:

1. Click on **Expenses** on the left-hand menu bar and select **Vendors**, as shown in *Figure 4.31*:

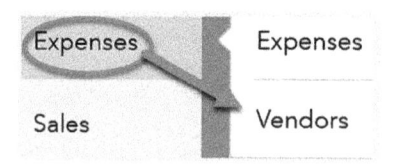

Figure 4.31: Selecting Vendors

2. Select the vendor you want to edit by clicking on the vendor's name, as shown in *Figure 4.32*:

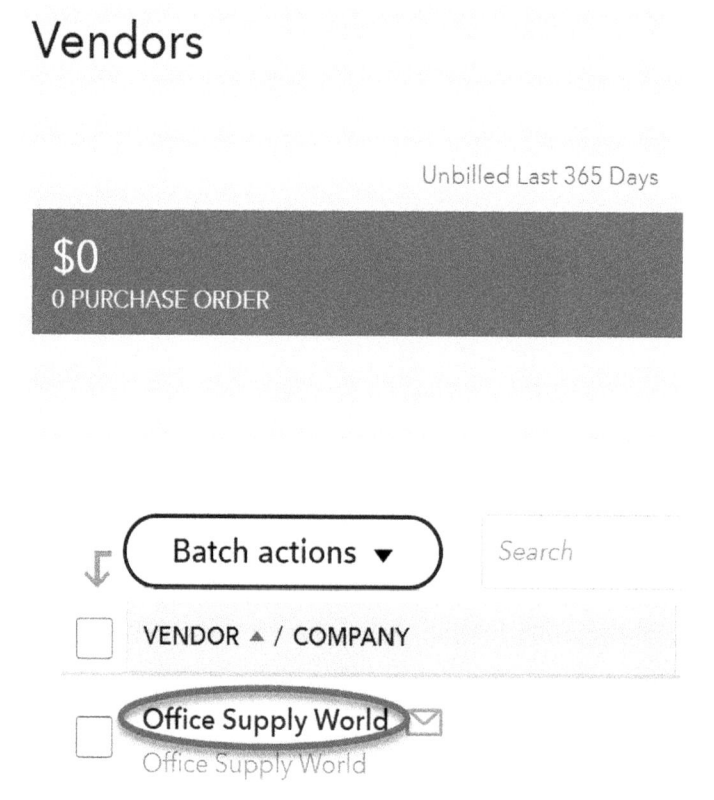

Figure 4.32: Clicking on a vendor name

Chapter 4

3. The Vendors Center will be displayed on the next screen. Click on the **Edit** button to make changes:

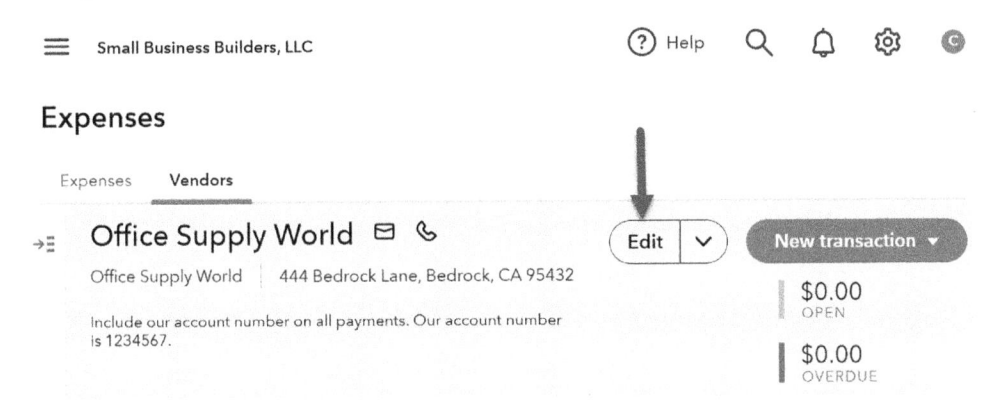

Figure 4.33: Editing a vendor

QuickBooks makes it easy to update vendor contact information. Having up-to-date vendor information will ensure that all purchase orders, bills, and reports are accurate. If you decide you no longer want to do business with a vendor, but you have existing transactions in QuickBooks, you can inactivate vendors. Let's look at this next.

Inactivating vendors in QBO

Similar to customers, you cannot delete vendors, but you can inactivate any vendors you no longer do business with. As with inactivating accounts and customers, this **Make inactive** action will maintain your existing vendor transactions that were previously recorded but remove the vendor from the Vendors Center.

Follow these steps to inactivate vendors in QBO:

1. Click on **Expenses** on the left-hand menu bar and select **Vendors**, as shown in *Figure 4.34*:

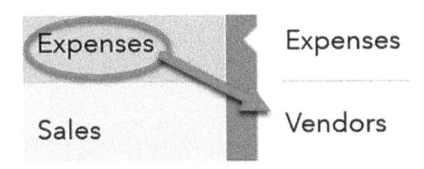

Figure 4.34: Selecting Vendors

2. Put a checkmark in the box next to the vendor you want to inactivate and select **Make inactive**, as shown in *Figure 4.35*:

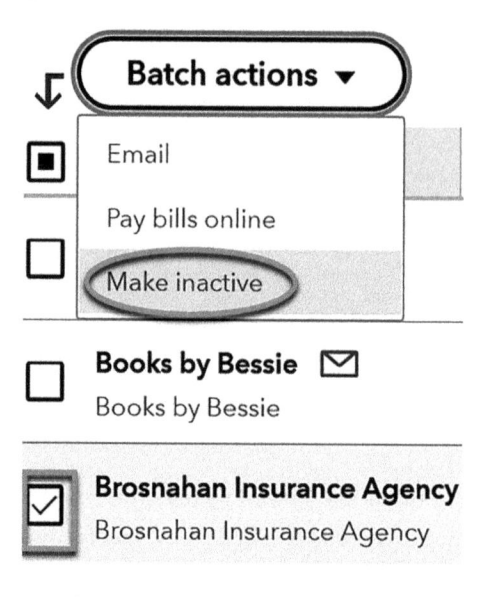

Figure 4.35: Making a vendor inactive

When you inactivate a vendor, QuickBooks will preserve the existing historical transactions but remove the vendor from the drop-down list so that it cannot be used in future transactions, such as purchase orders and bills.

Merging vendors in QBO

Similar to customers, you could run into an issue where you have inadvertently added a vendor twice. Like customers, you can easily merge duplicate vendors. Follow the steps below to merge two vendor profiles:

1. Navigate to the Vendors Center and identify the duplicate vendors:

Chapter 4

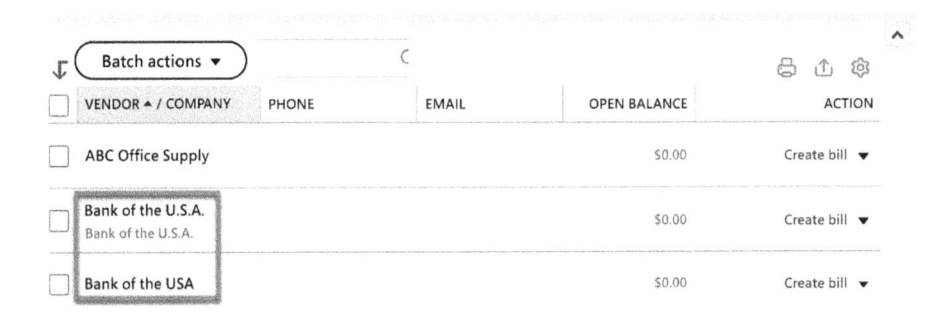

Figure 4.36: Duplicate vendors in the Vendors Center

2. Notice we have one vendor that includes a period after each letter in U.S.A. and another vendor without the periods in between. These are duplicate vendors, and we will keep the vendor that does not include the periods, **Bank of the USA**.

3. Click once on the vendor you do not wish to keep. In our example, that is **Bank of the U.S.A.** The following screen appears after clicking once on **Bank of the U.S.A.**:

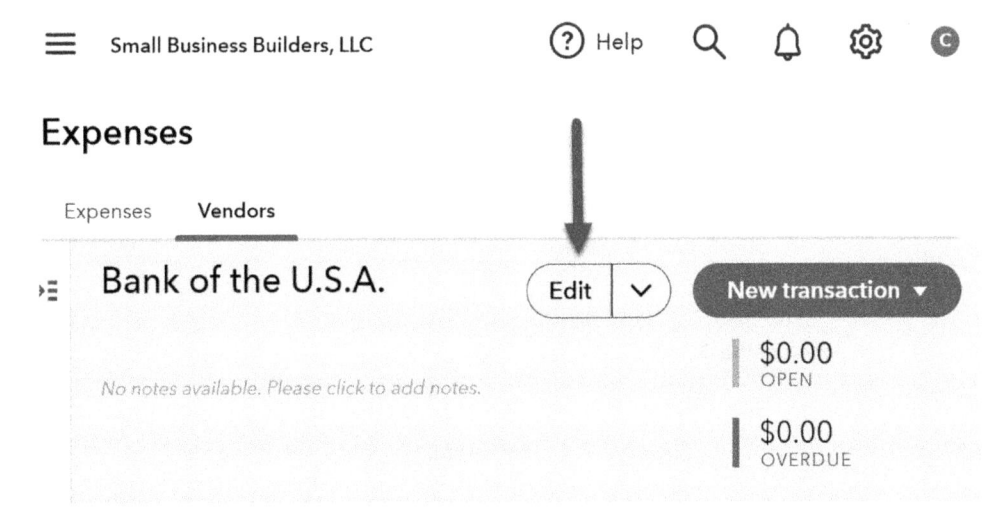

Figure 4.37: Viewing vendor information

4. Click on the **Edit** button, as indicated above, and the **Vendor** information window will appear:

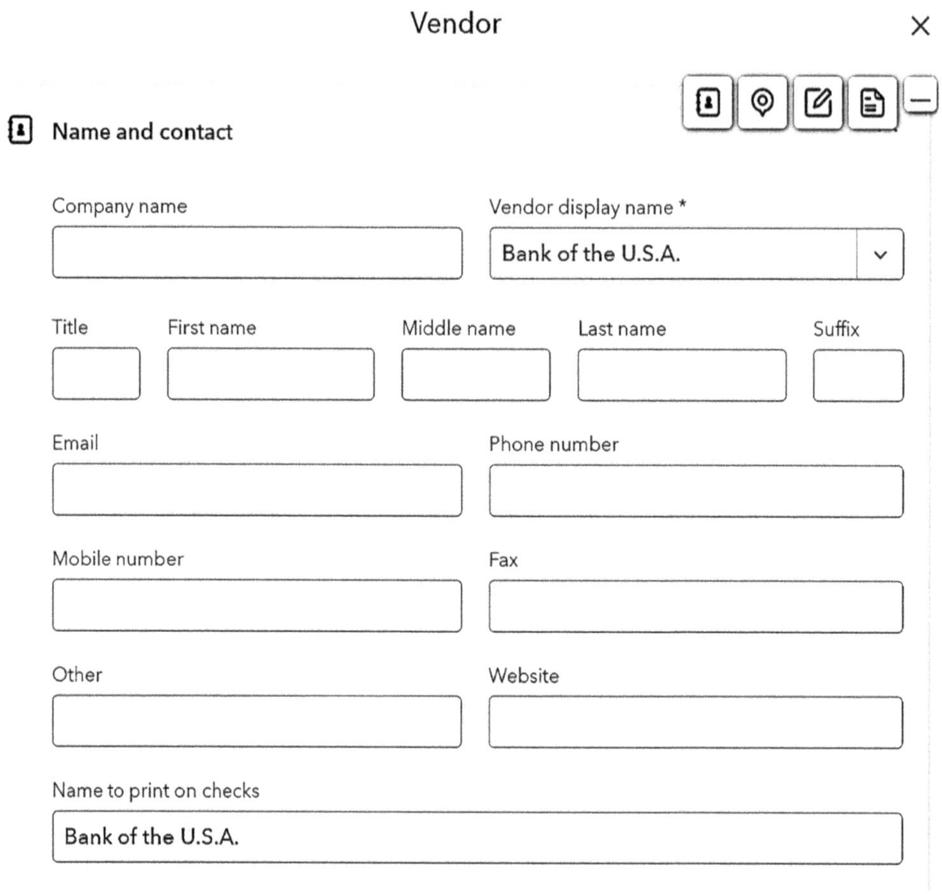

Vendor

Name and contact

Company name

Vendor display name *

Bank of the U.S.A.

Title   First name   Middle name   Last name   Suffix

Email

Phone number

Mobile number

Fax

Other

Website

Name to print on checks

Bank of the U.S.A.

Figure 4.38: Editing information for an existing vendor

5. Click once in the **Company name** field and type the name exactly as it appears in the vendor profile that you wish to keep. In our example, this would be **Bank of the USA**. Repeat these steps for the **Vendor display name** field, as shown below:

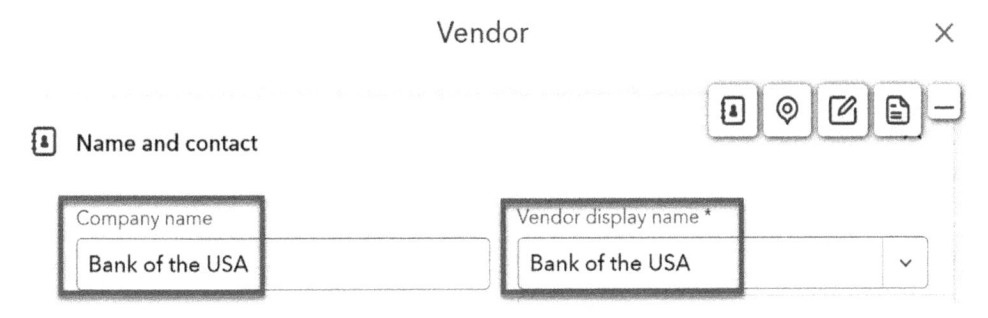

Figure 4.39: Editing the Company name and Vendor display name fields

6. Click the **Save** button in the lower-right corner. The following message will appear:

Please Confirm

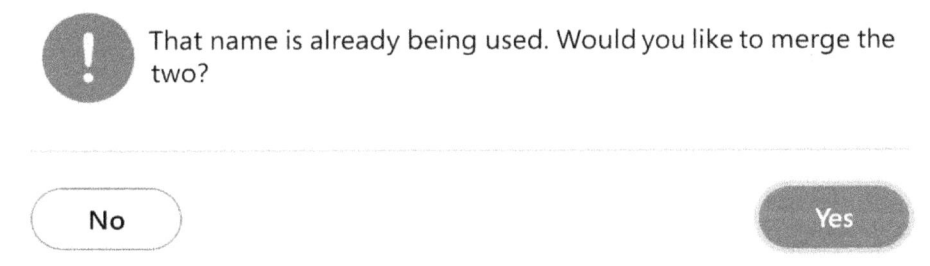

That name is already being used. Would you like to merge the two?

No   Yes

Figure 4.40: Confirming the merge of duplicate vendors

7. Click **Yes**, and the two vendor profiles will be combined into one:

VENDOR ▲ / COMPANY	PHONE	EMAIL	OPEN BALANCE	ACTION
ABC Office Supply			$0.00	Create bill ▼
Bank of the USA			$0.00	Create bill ▼
Cameras - R- Us ✉ Cameras - R- Us	(323) 543-8888	camerasrus@camerasrus.com	$0.00	Create bill ▼
The Phone Company			$450.00	Schedule payments ▼
USPS			$0.00	Create bill ▼

Figure 4.41: The Vendors Center with the vendors merged

As you can see, the duplicate profile (**Bank of the U.S.A.**) is no longer on the vendor list. All of the transactions recorded for that vendor have been moved to the **Bank of the USA** profile. We have now covered how to manually add vendors, how to import vendors, how to make changes to vendors, and how to inactivate and merge vendors. Next, we will cover how to perform those very same actions for products and services that you sell.

Managing products and services lists in QBO

The products and services that you sell are referred to as **items** in QuickBooks. You can track all your products and services in QBO. This includes the product name, product (item) number, product description, cost, selling price, and quantity on hand. It's important to set up products and/or services so that you can easily invoice customers for their purchases. In addition, these items are linked to an account on the chart of accounts so that QuickBooks can do the accounting behind the scenes for you. Once you have added products and services to QuickBooks, you will be able to run detailed reports on the products and services you sell.

In this section, we will cover how to manually add items, import items, modify existing items, inactivate items, and merge items in QBO. You will need to create items in order to invoice customers.

Keep in mind that you must have a QuickBooks Plus or QuickBooks Advanced subscription to track inventory items.

Manually adding products and services in QBO

In order to add products and services in QuickBooks, you need to have a list of the products or services you plan to sell, along with the cost, sales price, and a brief description that you want to appear on invoices.

Chapter 4   151

Follow these steps to add a new item in QBO:

1. Navigate to the gear icon and select **Products and Services**, as shown in *Figure 4.42*:

Lists

All Lists

Products and Services

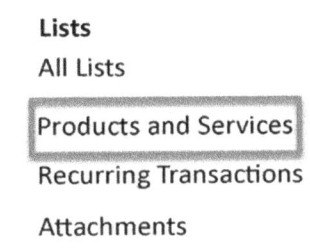

Recurring Transactions

Attachments

Figure 4.42: Selecting Products and Services

2. Click on the **New** button, as indicated here:

Figure 4.43: The New button

3. If this is your first time adding a product/service, you will see the **Add an item** button instead, as shown in *Figure 4.44*:

Start adding products and services

Save time creating your next invoice or receipt.

⊙ See how it works (2:22s)

• Item management
  Add products, bundles, and services

• Basic inventory tracking
  Quantity tracking and inventory alerts by QuickBooks Plus

Add an item ⟵

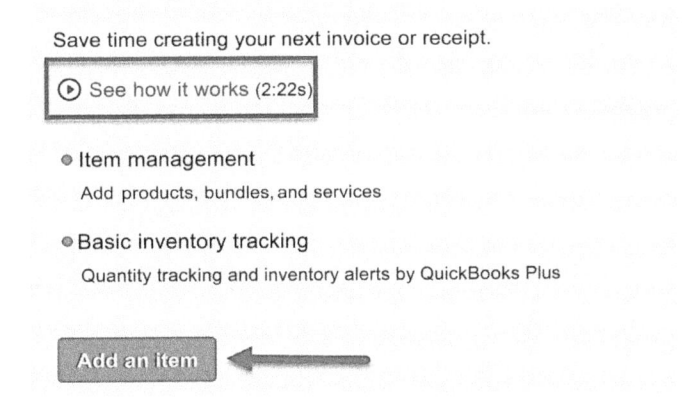

Figure 4.44: Button for adding an item for the first time

4. On the next screen, select the appropriate item type, as shown in *Figure 4.45*:

Product/Service information

Inventory
Products you buy and/or sell and that you track quantities of.

Non-inventory
Products you buy and/or sell but don't need to (or can't) track quantities of, for example, nuts and bolts used in an installation.

Service
Services that you provide to customers, for example, landscaping or tax preparation services.

Bundle
A collection of products and/or services that you sell together, for example, a gift basket of fruit, cheese, and wine.

Figure 4.45: Selecting an item type

There are four item types to choose from. A brief description of each item type follows:

- **Inventory**: Products that you buy and sell and want to track in the inventory should be set up as **Inventory** items – for example, a retail T-shirt store that purchases T-shirts and resells them, or a grocery store that needs to keep track of the items they've purchased and sold.

Chapter 4 153

- **Non-inventory**: The **Non-inventory** type is used to track items you sell but don't keep in inventory. For example, a photographer may purchase photo paper to print pictures but does not keep track of the quantity of photo paper they've purchased.
- **Service**: This is typically used for services that you sell – for example, bookkeeping services, photography services, or landscaping services.
- **Bundle**: A **bundle** is a collection of products that are sold together – for example, a gift set that includes all the James Bond movies.

5. Fill in the following fields to add a new **Service** item:

Product/Service information

① Service Change type

Name*
Initial Consultation ②

SKU
③

Category
Consulting Services ④

Description
☑ I sell this product/service to my customers.
Complimentary New Client Consultation ⑤

Sales price/rate
⑥

Income account ⑦
Sales:Consultation Income

⑨

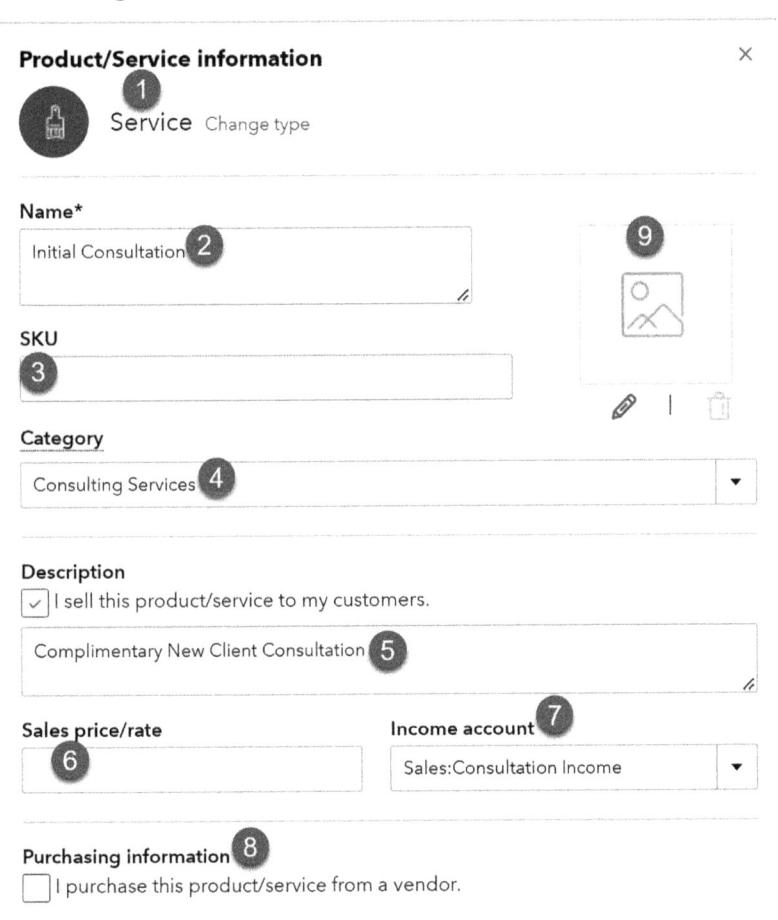

Purchasing information ⑧
☐ I purchase this product/service from a vendor.

Figure 4.46: Adding a new product or service

A brief description of the eight fields you will complete in order to add a new service item in QBO follows:

- **Item type** (1): This is the item type selected in the previous screen. In our example, **Service** is selected.
- **Name** (2): Enter the name of the service you will be selling to customers.
- **SKU** (3): A **stock-keeping unit** (**SKU**) is a scannable bar code printed on product labels in a retail store. If applicable, enter the SKU for the product you are selling. In general, an SKU applies to products and not service items.
- **Category** (4): This field is *optional*. If you want to categorize the products and services you sell, you can do so by creating categories. For example, in addition to general consulting, Small Business Builders offers a variety of coaching services such as business plans, marketing plans, bookkeeping, and tax planning. They would like to track their sales by each category. In our example, the initial consultation is a complimentary service that will be tracked in the **Consulting Services** category. To create a category, just type the name of the category in the field and save it.
- **Description** (5): Enter a brief description of the item in this field. In our example, it is `Complimentary Initial Consultation`. This description will appear on all customer invoices and sales receipts. However, you can always change the information directly on the invoice/sales receipt if needed.
- **Sales price/rate** (6): Enter the sales price for the item if it is generally the same for all customers. However, if the price varies by customer, you can leave this field blank and complete it when you create an invoice to bill your customers. Since the service we are setting up is complimentary, there is no charge, so we will leave this field blank.
- **Income account** (7): This is a required field. From the dropdown, select the appropriate income account where you want sales for this item to be recorded on the financial statements. In our example, we have selected **Consultation Income**.

> Every item you create in QuickBooks will be mapped to an account. Using this information, QuickBooks will record the debits and credits for you in the background so that you don't have to.

Chapter 4   155

- **Purchasing information** (8): If you are setting up an item that you purchase from a vendor/supplier, you will need to enter this information to track the cost of each item.

6. Fill in the following fields to set up an **Inventory** item:

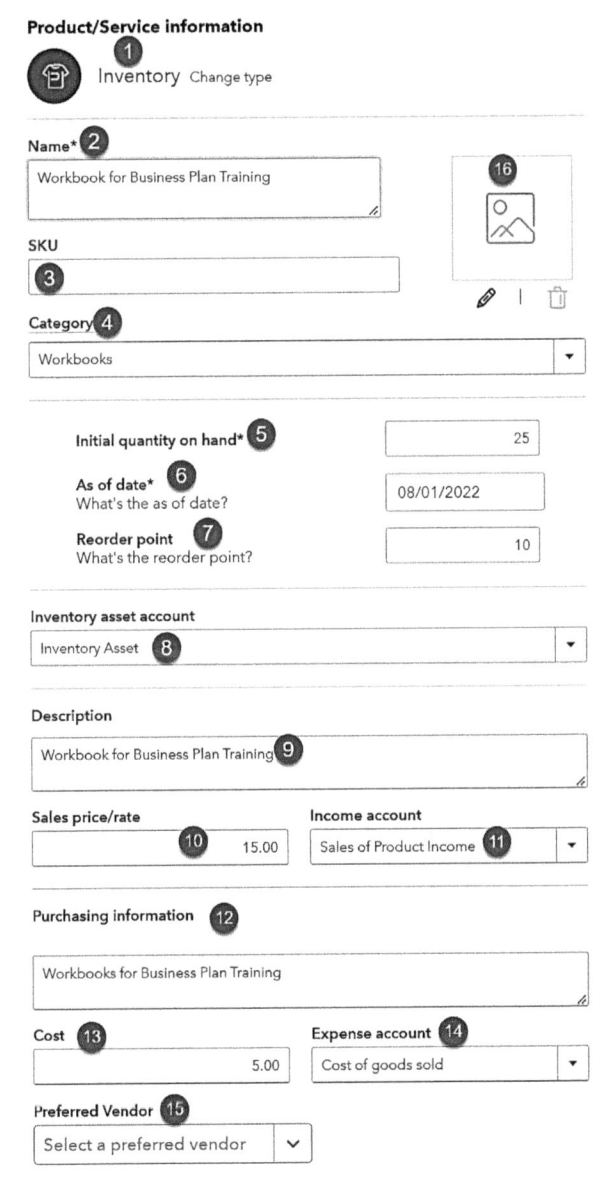

Figure 4.47: Adding an inventory item

Here are some brief descriptions of the fields you will fill in when setting up an **Inventory** item:

- **Item type** (1): Select the type of item you are setting up. In our example, it is an inventory item.
- **Name** (2): Enter the name of the product or item.
- **SKU** (3): In general, an SKU applies to products and not service items, so it is more likely to be relevant here than when we covered service items previously.
- **Category** (4): This field is *optional*. If you want to categorize the products and services you sell, you can do so by creating categories. In our example, we have created a category called **Workbooks**. You can easily create a category by simply typing the name of that category in this field and clicking **Save**.
- **Initial quantity on hand** (5): This should represent the total quantity for each item you have in your inventory as of the date the inventory was counted.

> You need to perform a physical inventory count before setting up inventory items in QBO. If you don't have the inventory quantity when setting up the item, you won't be able to add it to this screen later on. Instead, you will have to create an inventory adjustment journal to record the inventory. You will learn how to record inventory adjustments in *Chapter 9, Closing the Books in QuickBooks Online*.

- **As of date** (6): Enter the date when the inventory was counted.
- **Reorder point** (7): The reorder point is the minimum you want your inventory count to go down to before QuickBooks alerts you to place an order. In our example, when the inventory goes down to 10 workbooks, QuickBooks will alert us to place an order.
- **Inventory asset account** (8): All inventory is recorded as an asset and the default account is **Inventory Asset**, as indicated in our example.
- **Description** (9): Enter the description that you want to appear on customer sales receipts and invoices. In our example, it is Workbook for Business Plan Training.
- **Sales price/rate** (10): Enter the price you sell the item for. If it varies, leave it blank, and you can complete it when you create the customer invoice. In our example, the sales price is **15.00** per workbook.

- **Income account** (11): Enter the account you want to track all sales of for this product. In our example, we are going to use the **Sales of Product Income** account.
- **Purchasing information** (12): Enter the description that you want to appear on purchase orders when placing an order with your supplier. In our example, that is `Workbooks for Business Plan Training`.
- **Cost** (13): Enter the amount that you pay your vendor/supplier for this item. *The cost reflected here is for information purposes only and will be determined by QuickBooks after bills are entered*. In our example, the cost of each workbook is **5.00**.
- **Expense account** (14): The default expense account is the **cost of goods sold** for products. However, if you prefer to track these costs in a different account, you can click on the dropdown and add a new account.
- **Preferred Vendor** (15): This field is *optional*. If you choose to use it, you can add the vendor that you purchase this item from most often. If the vendor is not in the drop-down menu, you can select **Add** to set up the vendor in QuickBooks.
- **Product image** (16): You can add a picture of the product for easy reference by clicking on the pencil icon and selecting the image saved on your computer.

If you don't have the time to enter your products and services manually, you can import this data into QuickBooks, as we have demonstrated already for accounts, customers, and vendors.

Importing products and services in QBO

Similar to customers and vendors, you can import a products and services list in QuickBooks. This can save you a lot of time if you have a sizeable list of products or services that you sell. You can import this information from a CSV file into QBO. This template can be found here: `https://github.com/PacktPublishing/Mastering-QuickBooks-2025-Sixth-Edition/tree/main/Chapter05`.

Follow these steps to import products and services into QBO:

1. Navigate to the **Products and Services** list by clicking on the gear icon and selecting **Products and Services**, as shown in *Figure 4.48*:

Lists

All Lists

Products and Services

Recurring Transactions

Attachments

Figure 4.48: Selecting Products and Services

2. Click on the arrow next to the **New** item button located in the upper-right corner and then click on **Import**, as shown in *Figure 4.49*:

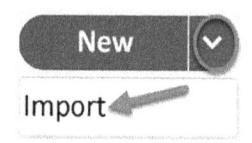

New

Import

Figure 4.49: The Import option

3. Click the **Browse** button to upload the Excel or CSV file from your computer, as shown in *Figure 4.50*:

Import products and services

1

UPLOAD

Select a CSV or Excel file to upload

Upload an EXCEL or CSV file   Browse

Download a sample file ⇊

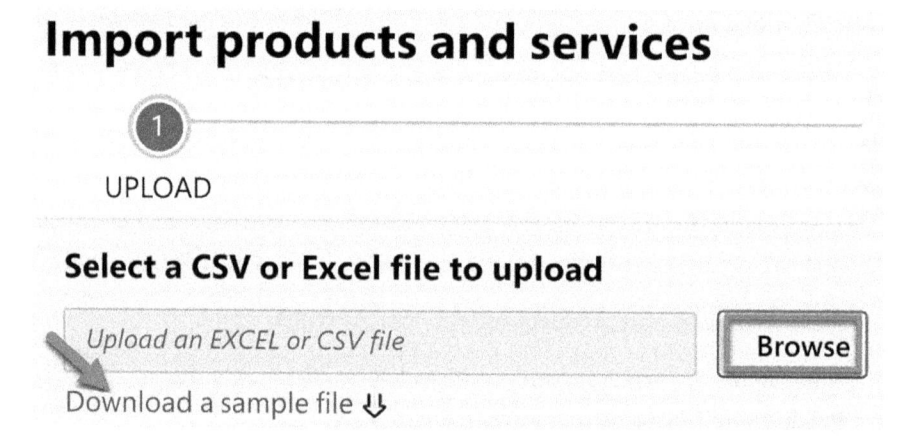

Figure 4.50: Uploading a CSV or Excel file

4. You can click on the blue link to download the sample file (shown in the preceding screenshot). This file includes all of the fields of information you can upload for items. Save this file and use it as your template.

5. Follow the onscreen prompts to import your products and services into QBO.

Chapter 4 159

Be sure to review the data imported to ensure accuracy. If you do find that corrections are needed, you can easily make them.

Making changes to existing products and services in QBO

You can change any fields in existing products and services except the item type. If you have already used an item in a transaction, QuickBooks will not allow you to change the item type. Instead, you will need to inactivate the old item and add a brand-new item with the correct item type.

Follow these steps to make changes to existing products and services in QBO:

1. Navigate to the gear icon and select **Products and Services**, as shown in *Figure 4.51*:

Lists

All Lists

Products and Services

Recurring Transactions

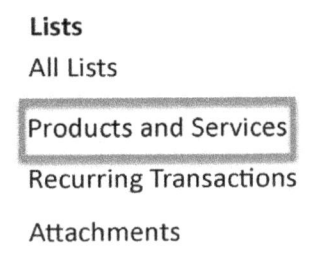

Attachments

Figure 4.51: Selecting Products and Services

2. Select the product or service you would like to make changes to by clicking on the **Edit** button in the far-right column, as shown in *Figure 4.52*:

NAME ▲	TYPE	SALES DESCRIPTION	SALES PRICE	COST	ACTION
Hours	Service				Edit ▼
Photography Services	Service	Photography Services	150		Edit ▼
Picture Frame - 8X10	Inventory	8X10 Picture Frame	20	10	Edit ▼
Sales	Service				Edit ▼

Figure 4.52: Editing a product or service

As we mentioned previously, you can change an item type if you haven't used it in a transaction in QuickBooks. However, if you have used an item in a transaction and the item type is incorrect, you will need to create a new item with the correct item type and inactivate the old item.

Inactivating products and services in QBO

As we discussed when we talked about customers and vendors, you cannot delete products and services in QBO once you have created them; however, you can inactivate them. This will preserve the existing transactions and remove the product or service from the items list so that it cannot be used in new transactions.

Follow these steps to inactivate a product or service in QBO:

1. Navigate to the gear icon and select **Products and Services**, as shown in *Figure 4.53*:

Lists

All Lists

Products and Services

Recurring Transactions

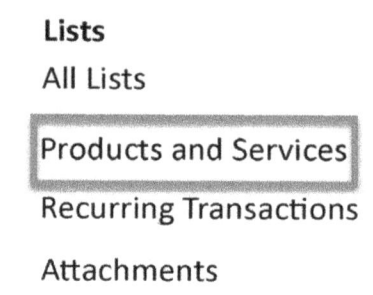

Attachments

Figure 4.53: Selecting Products and Services

2. Scroll down the items list to the product (or service), click on the **Edit** button, and select **Make inactive**, as shown in *Figure 4.54*:

Figure 4.54: Making a product or service inactive

Similar to customers and vendors, inactivating a product or service will remove it from selection for future transactions. However, the existing data will remain intact to ensure reports are accurate for tax and other reporting purposes.

Merging products and services in QBO

Like vendors and customers, you can also merge duplicate services that have been entered into QuickBooks by mistake. Unfortunately, you cannot merge duplicate inventory items because of the complexity of inventory tracking. Instead, you will need to inactivate one of the duplicate inventory items and record inventory adjustments to manage the transactions that have been recorded.

> Consult your accountant before making any inventory adjustments since this can have a *significant* impact on your books.

Follow the steps below to merge duplicate services:

1. Navigate to the **Products and Services** list and identify the duplicate items:

NAME ▲	TYPE	SALES DESCRIPTION
Complimentary Consultation	Service	Complimentary Consultation for new clients
Consulting Services		
Initial Consultation	Service	Complimentary New Client Consultation

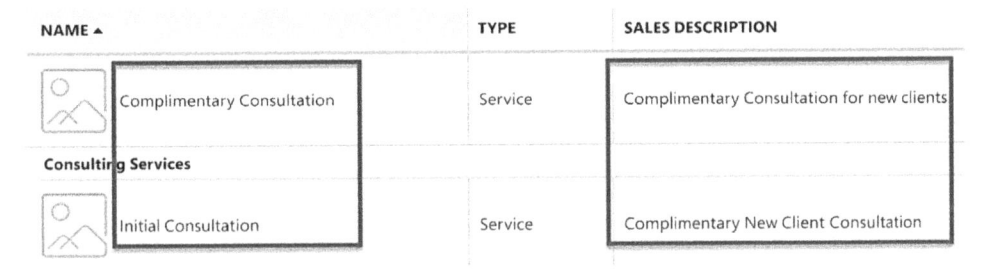

Figure 4.55: Identifying duplicate services in the Products and Services list

2. As you can see in the image above, there is an item called **Complimentary Consultation** and a duplicate item called **Initial Consultation**. To maintain accurate records, we must merge them into one. The item we will keep in our example is **Initial Consultation**.
3. Click on the item that you wish to remove – **Complimentary Consultation** in our example.

4. After you click on **Complimentary Consultation**, the **Product/Service information** window will appear:

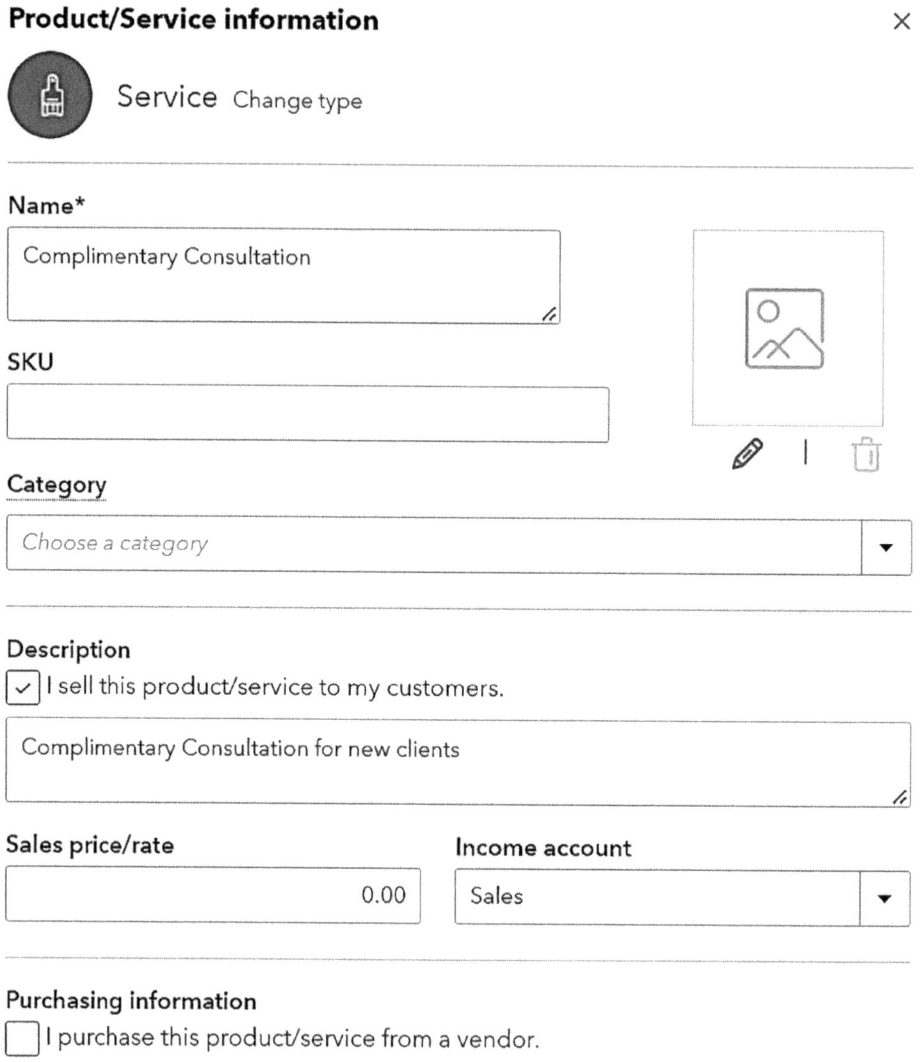

Product/Service information

Service Change type

Name*

Complimentary Consultation

SKU

Category

Choose a category

Description

☑ I sell this product/service to my customers.

Complimentary Consultation for new clients

Sales price/rate

0.00

Income account

Sales

Purchasing information

☐ I purchase this product/service from a vendor.

Figure 4.56: Displaying products and services information

Chapter 4

5. Click once in the **Name** field and type in the item name you want to merge with - `Initial Consultation` in our case. Select **Consulting Services** in the **Category** field. Type `Complimentary New Client Consultation` in the **Description** field, as shown below:

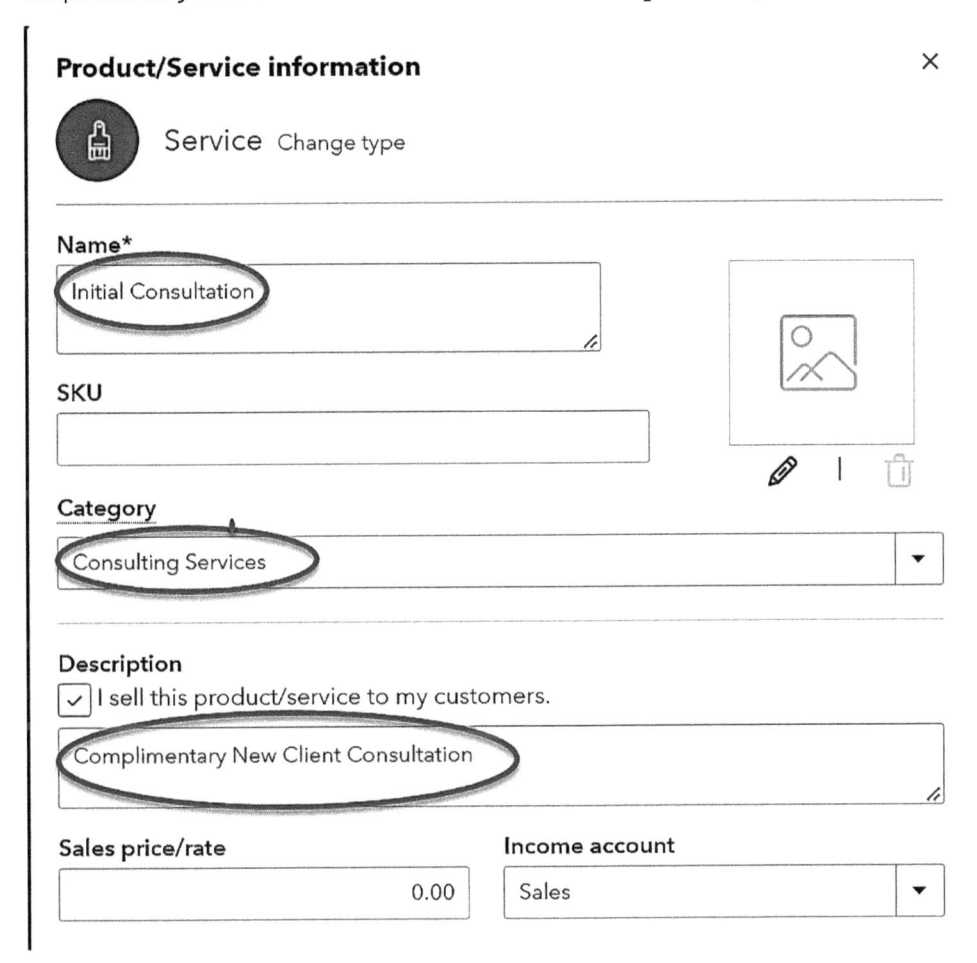

Figure 4.57: Editing product and services information

6. Click the **Save and Close** button in the lower-right corner. The following message will appear:

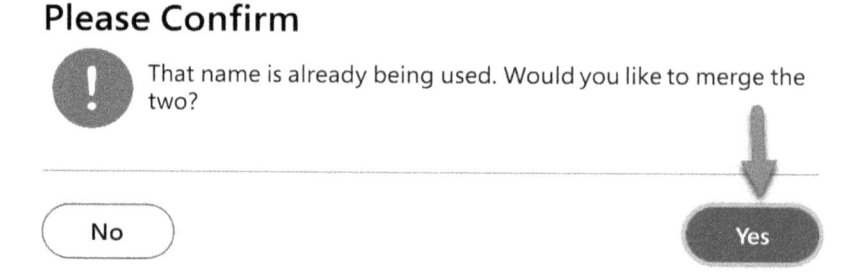

Please Confirm

That name is already being used. Would you like to merge the two?

No   Yes

Figure 4.58: Confirming the merging of duplicate service items

7. Click **Yes** and the two service items will be combined:

NAME	TYPE	SALES DESCRIPTION	SALES PRICE	COST	QTY ON HAND	REORDER
Consulting Services						
Initial Consultation	Service	Complimentary New Client Consultation				
Hours	Service					
Sales	Service					
Workbooks						
Workbook for Business Plan Training	Inventory	Workbook for Business Plan Training	15	5	25	10

Figure 4.59: The Products and Services list with the merged item

Notice the **Complimentary Consultation** item is no longer shown because it has been merged with **Initial Consultation**.

We have now covered how to manually add products and services, import products and services, make changes to existing products and services, inactivate products and services (also known as items), and merge items.

Summary

In this chapter, we covered how to manage customer data by manually adding and importing the information, editing existing customers, and inactivating customers you no longer do business with.

In addition, we covered how to manage vendor data by manually adding and importing the information, editing existing vendors, inactivating vendors you no longer do business with, and merging duplicate customer and vendor records.

Finally, we showed you how to manage products and services, also referred to as items, including how to add and import data, how to edit existing products and services, how to inactivate products and services, and how to merge service items in QBO.

Keep in mind that you will need to update the customer, vendor, and products and services lists when the information changes. For example, if customers and vendors move, you will need to update your records with their new mailing address. In addition, if you start selling new products and services, you will need to add them to the list. By the same token, if you discontinue a product or service, you should inactivate these items to keep your records current.

Now that you understand how to manage your customers, it's time to learn how to set up and manage sales tax. In the next chapter, we will show you how to set up sales tax, create an invoice that includes sales tax, and run sales tax reports.

Join our community on Discord

Join our community's Discord space for discussions with the authors and other readers:

`https://packt.link/powerusers`

Part 2

Recording Transactions in QuickBooks Online

This part is all about mastering the art of recording and tracking transactions in QuickBooks Online. You'll learn how to handle sales tax, create customized invoices, and record sales and expenses seamlessly. We'll also cover tips for managing recurring transactions and reconciling bank accounts, ensuring your financial records stay accurate and up-to-date. With practical examples and advice, you'll feel confident managing your business's finances.

This part comprises the following chapters:

- Chapter 5, *Managing Sales Tax*
- Chapter 6, *Recording Sales Transactions in QuickBooks Online*
- Chapter 7, *Recording Expenses in QuickBooks Online*

5
Managing Sales Tax

In the United States, sales tax is typically applied to the sale of products. However, some states and local tax jurisdictions also apply sales tax to certain types of services. The way sales tax works is that the tax is paid by customers who purchase your products. The business that collects the sales tax from its consumer is responsible for reporting the sales tax collected on a sales tax return and submitting it to the appropriate state and/or local tax authority. The tax is typically due on a monthly, quarterly, or annual basis, depending on the amount collected. If you fail to file and/or pay sales tax, you will incur penalties and interest until the tax is paid. It's, therefore, important to consult with your CPA or tax professional to determine which laws apply in your geographical location as well as how often you need to file and when payment is due.

In this chapter, we will cover how to manage sales tax in **QuickBooks Online** (**QBO**). While you cannot pay sales tax directly from QBO, we will cover how to record the payment in QBO after you have paid your tax authority.

We will cover the following topics in this chapter:

- Setting up sales tax in QBO
- Creating an invoice that includes sales tax
- Sales tax reports
- Paying sales tax when it comes due

> The US edition of QBO was used to create this book. If you are using a version that is outside of the US, results may differ.

Do you need to charge sales tax?

Before we dive into the mechanics of setting up sales tax, you may be wondering whether you need to charge sales tax or not. The short answer is *yes* if you sell any type of product, such as T-shirts, books, a cup of coffee, and so on. If you don't sell a product but you do sell services, such as bookkeeping, legal, or consulting, then the answer is *maybe*. Because the answer is dependent on the rules and regulations of your state/local jurisdiction, it's important that you seek the advice of a CPA or tax preparer.

However, there are a couple of resources that we recommend you check out. First, this article from the QuickBooks blog, *Do I need to charge sales tax?*: `https://quickbooks.intuit.com/r/taxes/need-collect-sales-tax-much/`. Another great resource is **Avalara**, a company that specializes in sales tax compliance. Not only do they offer sales tax compliance services but they are also a great resource for any questions you may have regarding whether or not you need to charge sales tax and how to go about making sure you are in compliance.

Setting up sales tax in QBO

If you are required to collect sales tax from customers, it is important to complete the sales tax setup in QuickBooks prior to invoicing customers. If you create an invoice without sales tax, you will ultimately underpay the sales tax you are required to submit to your local tax authority. This could lead to additional taxes and penalties, which can add up quickly. Setting up sales tax in QuickBooks from the start allows QuickBooks to automatically calculate and keep track of the amount of sales tax that you owe.

Perform the following steps to set up sales tax:

1. Click **Taxes** and select **Sales tax** on the left menu bar, as indicated in *Figure 5.1*, to navigate to the Sales Tax Center:

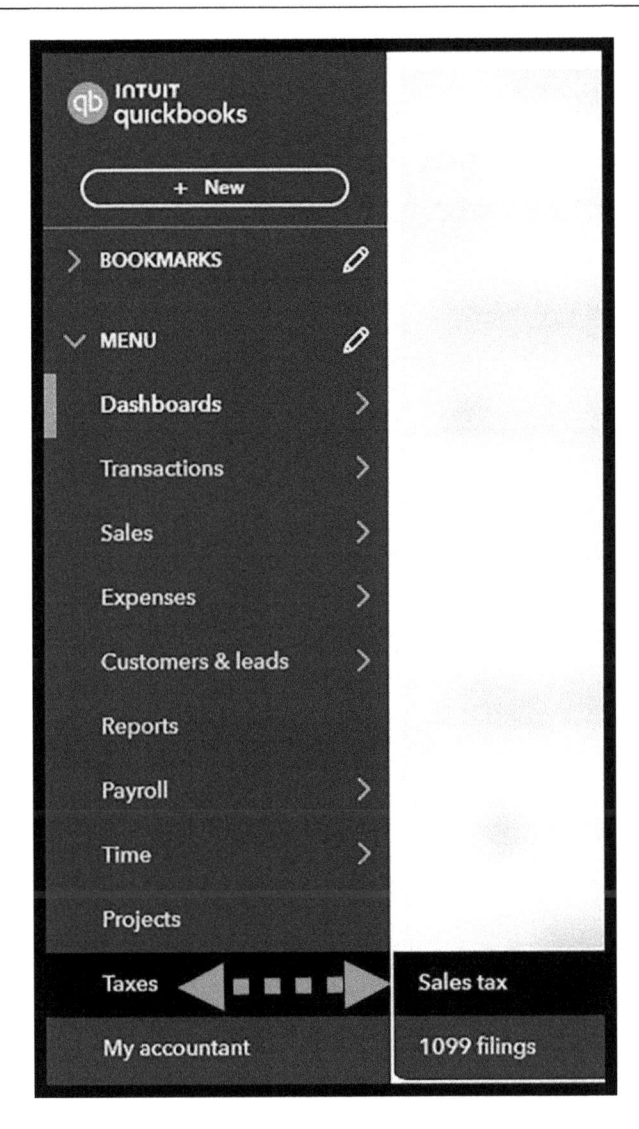

Figure 5.1: Navigating to the Sales Tax Center

2. The following message will appear. Click the **Use Automatic Sales Tax** button, as indicated in *Figure 5.2*:

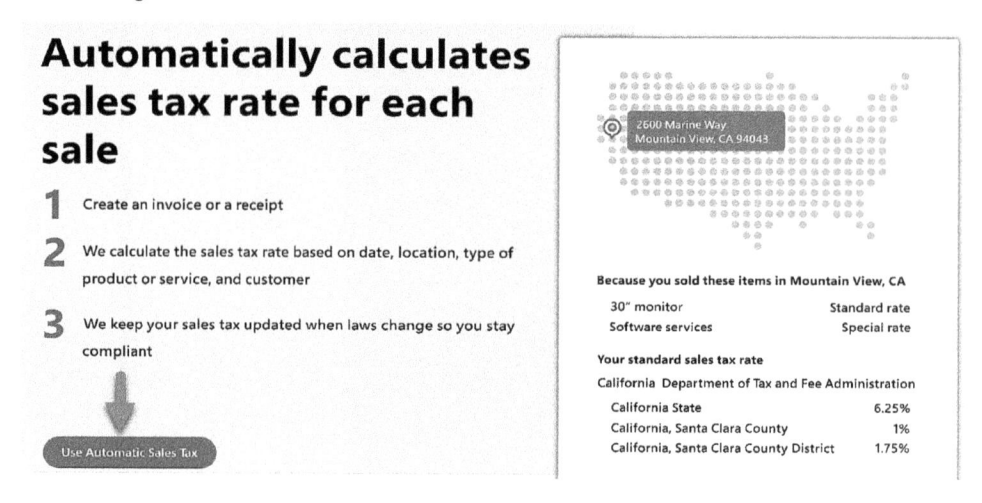

Figure 5.2: Sales Tax Center welcome page

The following window will appear:

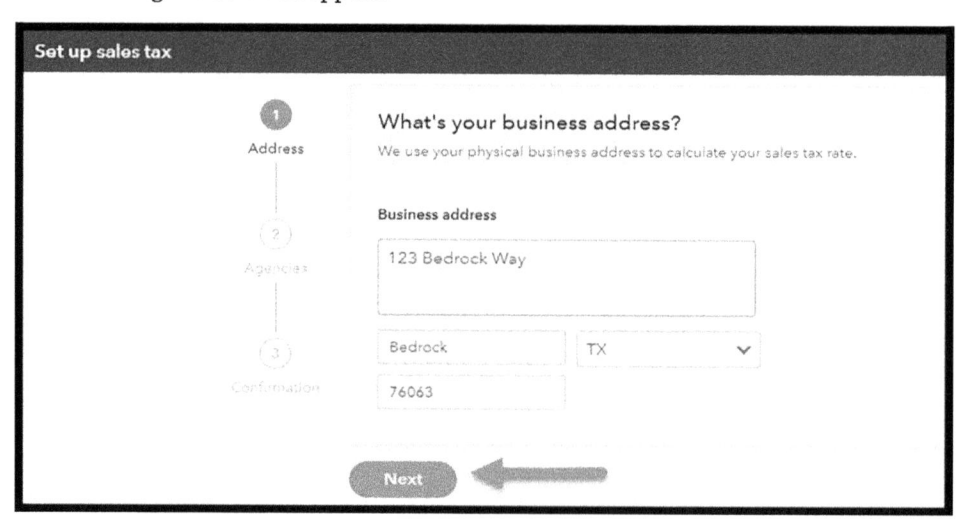

Figure 5.3: Entering the business address used to calculate sales tax

Chapter 5

3. Your business address should automatically populate the fields (as indicated in *Figure 5.3*). If it does not, complete any missing fields and click **Next**. The following screen will appear:

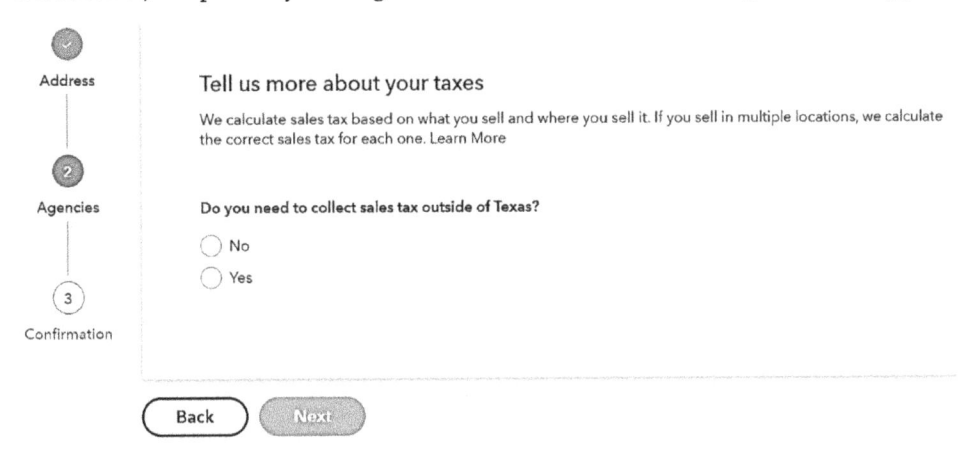

Figure 5.4: Sales tax information outside of your state

4. If you are not required to collect sales tax outside of your state, select **No**, and the tax agency that you should remit payment to will be listed, as indicated in *Figure 5.5*; click **Next**:

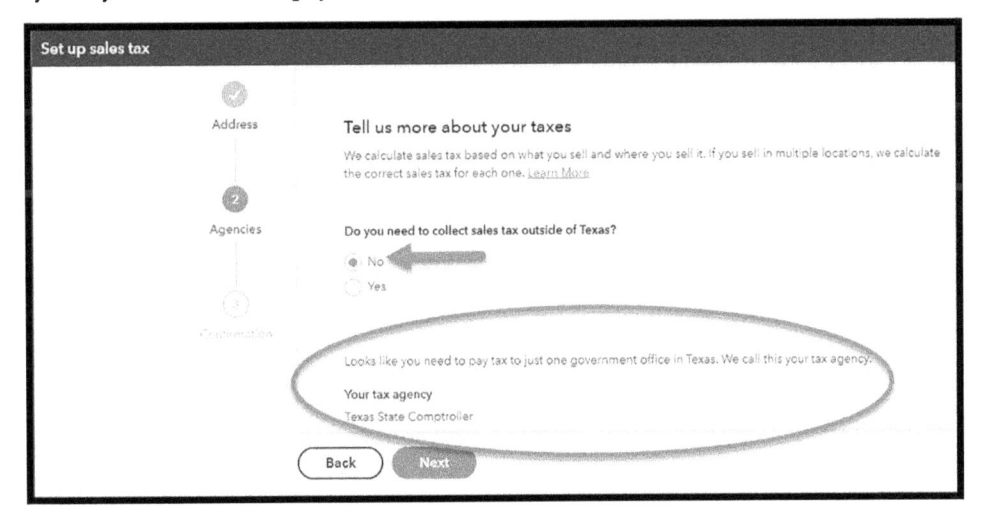

Figure 5.5: Sales tax information within your state only (for better visualization, refer to https://packt.link/gbp/9781836649977)

5. If you are required to collect sales tax outside of your state, select **Yes** and click on the drop-down arrow below the **Your tax agency** field to select all of the jurisdictions you are required to collect sales tax from, as indicated in *Figure 5.6*:

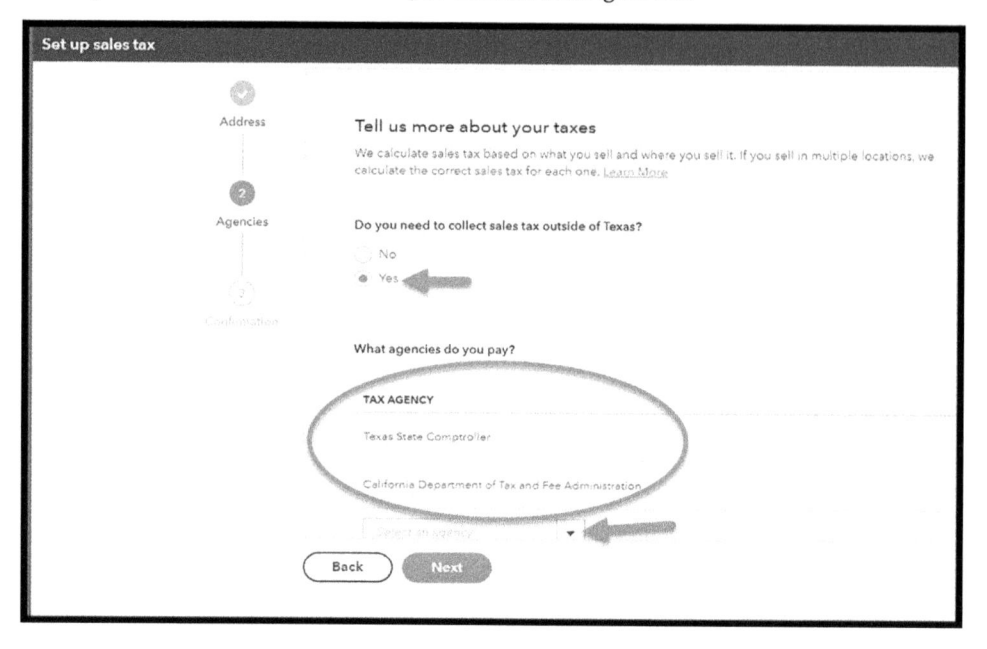

Figure 5.6: Sales tax information in other jurisdictions (for better visualization, refer to https://packt.link/gbp/9781836649977)

> Most businesses are not required to collect sales tax outside their state. If you are not sure, you need to consult with your tax professional or CPA on this matter.

6. Click **Next** and the following screen will appear, indicating that the automatic sales tax setup is complete:

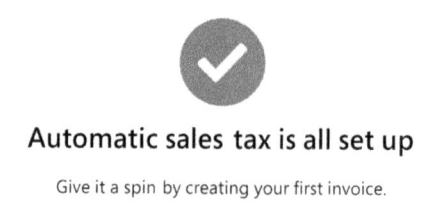

Figure 5.7: Confirmation that automatic sales tax is set up

Chapter 5

7. Click **X** in the upper-right corner of the screen to bypass the preceding message and navigate to the **How often do you file sales tax?** screen:

    ## How often do you file sales tax?

    You can find this info on your sales tax business registration. If you can't find it or it changed, check out the table to see where your business fits.

    Agency
    Texas State Comptroller   1 of 1

    Filing frequency
    [Select frequency ▾]

    Texas filing frequency requirements

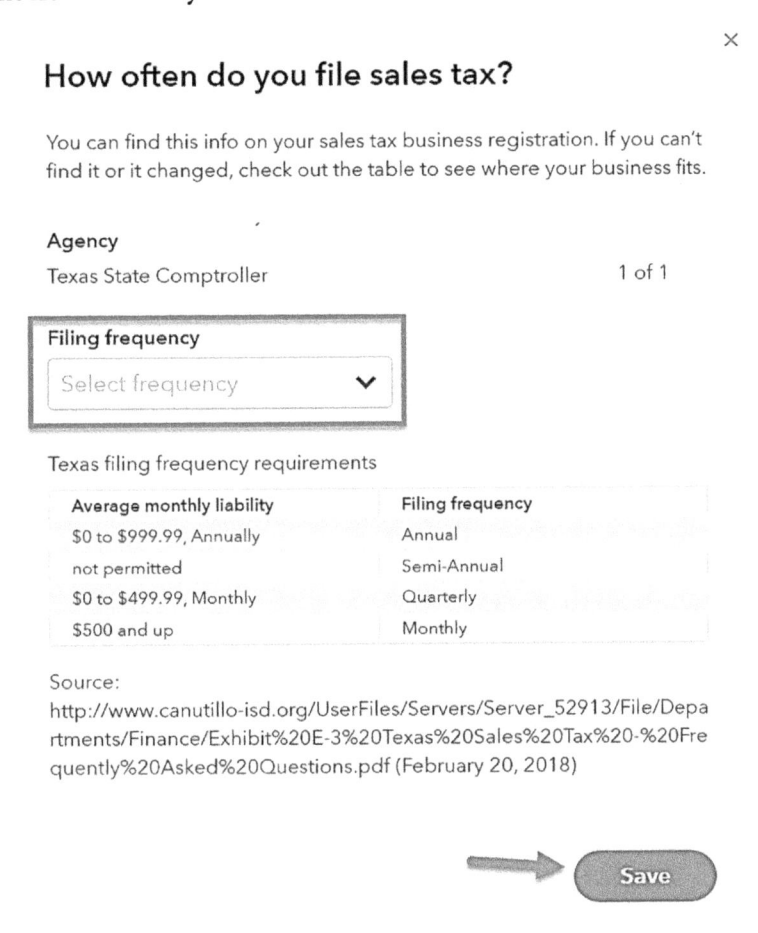

Average monthly liability	Filing frequency
$0 to $999.99, Annually	Annual
not permitted	Semi-Annual
$0 to $499.99, Monthly	Quarterly
$500 and up	Monthly

    Source:
    http://www.canutillo-isd.org/UserFiles/Servers/Server_52913/File/Departments/Finance/Exhibit%20E-3%20Texas%20Sales%20Tax%20-%20Frequently%20Asked%20Questions.pdf (February 20, 2018)

    → **Save**

    Figure 5.8: Filing frequency for sales tax

    Based on the state where your business is located, the **Agency** field will automatically be populated.

8. From the **Filing frequency** drop-down menu, select the frequency with which you file sales tax. The options are **Monthly**, **Quarterly**, and **Yearly**.

    > If you are not sure how often you need to submit sales tax, refer to the chart that appears below the **Filing frequency** field or contact the tax agency directly.

9. Click the **Save** button to keep your changes. The Sales Tax Center will appear:

Figure 5.9: Sales Tax Center

10. Within the Sales Tax Center, you can see the amount of tax due for each agency that you collect sales tax for:

    - (1) Select the agency from the drop-down menu and it will appear, as shown in *Figure 5.9*.
    - (2) The agency (**TEXAS STATE COMPTROLLER**), in our example, appears in this section, along with the tax period due and the accounting method.
    - (3) Select the status and tax period date using the drop-down menus.
    - (4) In this section, you will see a summary of your selections for **AGENCY**, **PERIOD**, **DUE DATE**, **AMOUNT**, **STATUS**, and **ACTION** items.
    - (5) Review your **Sales Tax Settings** and make any necessary changes.
    - (6) Review your **Economic Nexus**. If you have a question about Nexus, I recommend that you reach out to a tax professional or contact Avalara.
    - (7) Generate sales tax reports. Since we don't currently have any taxable sales recorded, we will create an invoice with sales tax next.

Chapter 5

Creating an invoice that includes sales tax

After completing the setup for sales tax, you are ready to create invoices and sales receipts with sales tax. In this section, we will create an invoice and show you how to include sales tax. Perform the following steps:

1. From the left menu bar, click on **Sales** and then select **Invoices**, as indicated in *Figure 5.10*:

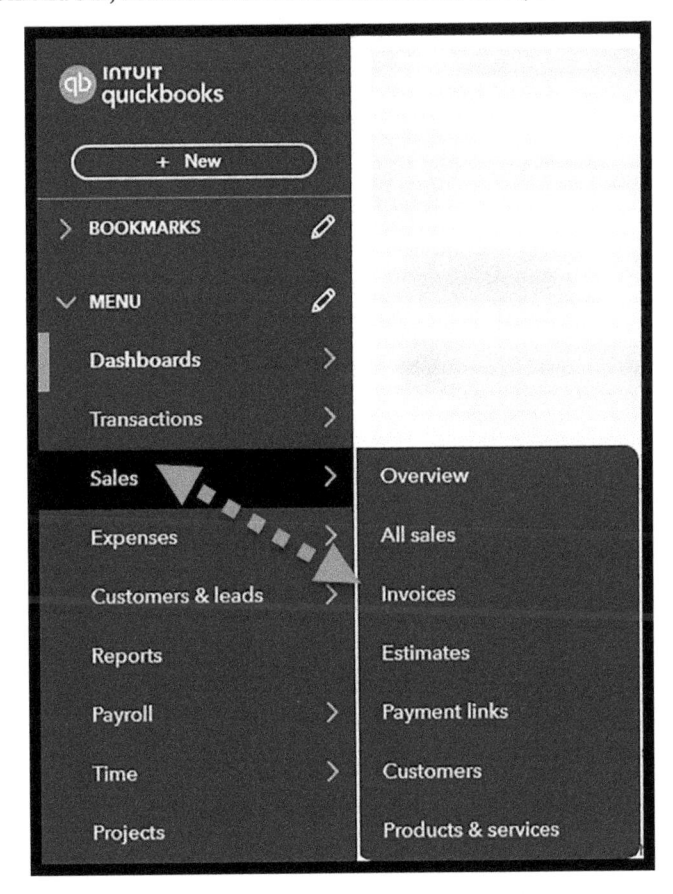

Figure 5.10: Navigating to Invoices

2. Click the **Create invoice** button, as indicated in *Figure 5.11*:

Figure 5.11: Creating an invoice

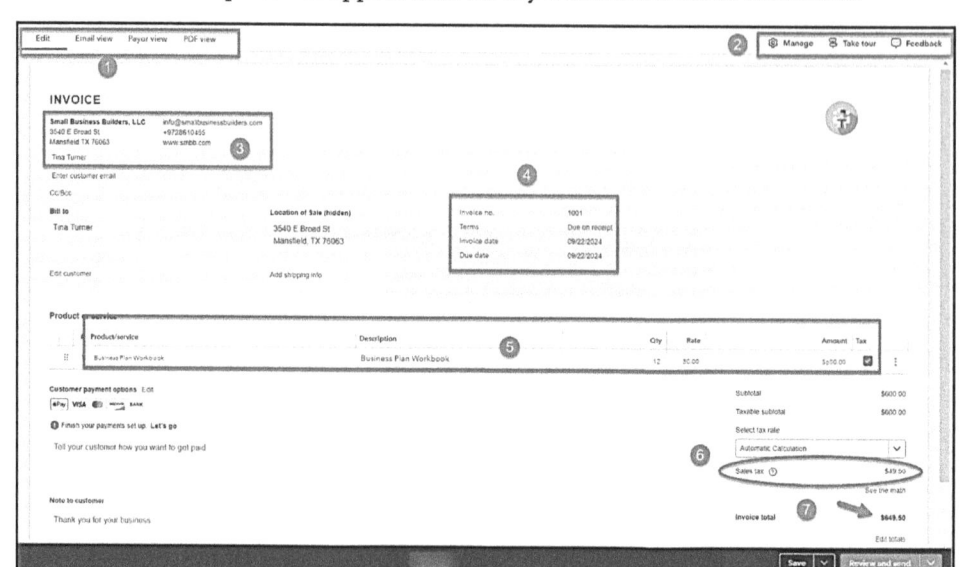

3. A blank invoice template will appear with six key areas that need to be filled in:

Figure 5.12: Completed Invoice with Sales tax (for better visualization, refer to https://packt.link/gbp/9781836649977)

- **Invoice view** (1): There are four different views for the invoice template. The default mode is **Edit**, which is the mode you want to be in when making changes to the invoice; **Email view** is the view that your customers will see when they receive the invoice via email; **Payor view** is the preview of the invoice when the customer receives it. **PDF view** is the appearance of the invoice as a PDF document.

- **Other options** (2): In this section, you can manage invoice settings, take a tour of the features available for invoicing, and provide feedback to Intuit about your experience using the invoice template.

- **Your company information and customer information** (3): Your company mailing address, telephone number, and website information will appear in this section. This is the information that was entered when you set up the company preferences in *Chapter 2, Company File Setup*. Below this information is a drop-down field where you can select the customer you wish to create an invoice for.

- **Invoice details** (4): Within this section of the invoice, you will find the invoice number, which is automatically generated by QBO, and the payment terms, which you set up back in *Chapter 2, Company File Setup*. The invoice date and the due date will also appear in this section. All of these fields can be edited as needed.
- **Billing details** (5): From the drop-down menu, you will select the items you are billing your customer for. In *Chapter 4, Managing Customer, Vendor, and Products and Services Lists,* we covered how to add your products and services to QBO.
- **Sales tax** (6): Since we turned automatic sales tax on, you should see the sales tax amount automatically calculated as **$49.50** in our example. If you don't see sales tax here, return to the Sales Tax Center and review the settings for accuracy.
- **Invoice total** (7): The grand total of the invoice, including sales tax, will appear in this field. In our example, this is **$649.50**.

> QuickBooks will automatically use your business address as the sales location. Be sure to confirm if the location of the sale is correct. If necessary, you may need to charge a different sales tax based on the city/county/tax jurisdiction for each sale. You can even update your business address if needed within the account and settings. In *Chapter 2, Company File Setup*, we show you how to do this but be sure to consult with your tax preparer or accountant for additional guidance.

4. Click the **Save** button to save the invoice and click **X** in the upper-right corner to close the invoice.

5. Navigate back to the Sales Tax Center by clicking on **Taxes** from the left menu bar. The following window will appear:

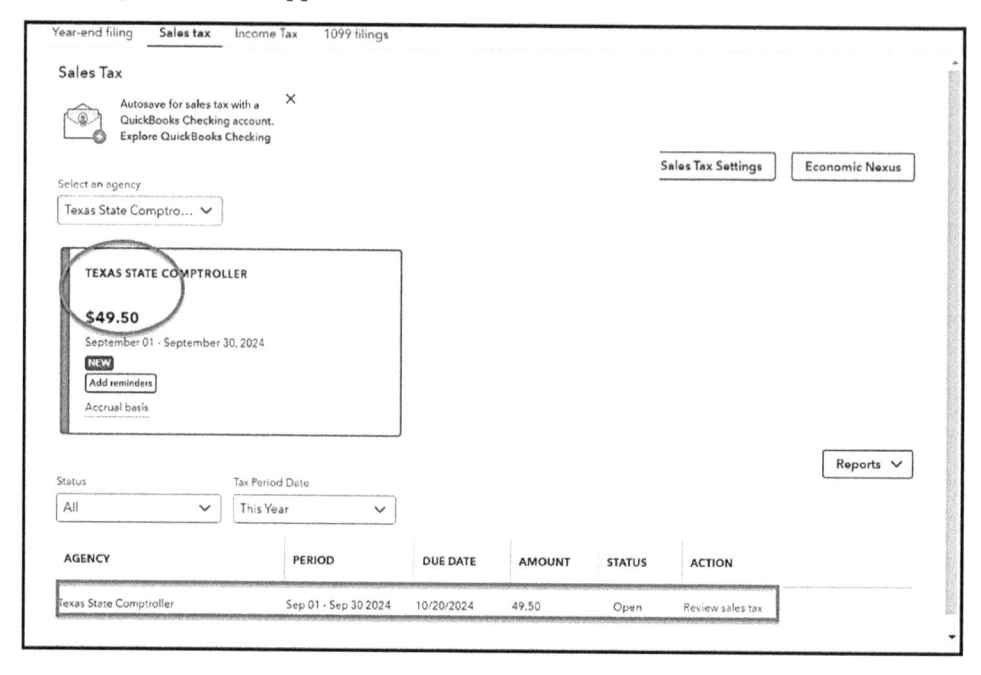

Figure 5.13: Sales Tax Center with updated sales tax amount

As you can see, the tax of **$49.50** now shows up as upcoming sales tax that will be due sometime in the future. Once the sales tax becomes due, the status will change to **Due**.

Next, we will cover the sales tax reports you can generate to determine how much sales tax you owe and when it is due. Sales tax reports are also used to complete the sales tax return.

Sales tax reports

QuickBooks makes it easy to stay on top of the sales tax collected, which will ensure that you pay the correct amount when it is due. There are three reports available to help you stay on top of the sales tax you owe: a tax liability report, a taxable customer report, and a non-taxable transaction review report.

Chapter 5 181

Within the Sales Tax Center, click on the **Reports** link to access the sales tax reports, as indicated in *Figure 5.14*:

Figure 5.14: Sales tax reports

The first report is the **Tax Liability** Report. This report will show you the sales tax collected for a specific period of time. The report will show gross sales, taxable sales, non-taxable sales, and the tax amount.

In the report shown below, there are four columns: **GROSS TOTAL, NON-TAXABLE, TAXABLE AMOUNT,** and **TAX AMOUNT**. The gross total amount is **$600.00**, the non-taxable amount is **$0**, the taxable amount is **$600.00**, and the total tax amount is **$49.50**:

Small Business Builders, LLC
Sales Tax Liability Report
January 1 - September 22, 2024

TAX NAME	GROSS TOTAL	NON-TAXABLE	TAXABLE AMOUNT	TAX AMOUNT
Texas State Comptroller				
Texas State	600.00	0.00	600.00	37.50
Texas, Mansfield City	600.00	0.00	600.00	12.00
Total for Texas State Comptroller				**$49.50**

Figure 5.15: Sales tax liability report

The second option is the **Taxable customer** report, which will list all customers who are subject to sales tax, along with their billing address, shipping address, taxable sales, and tax rate. Below is a snapshot of what this report looks like:

Small Business Builders, LLC

Customer Contact List

CUSTOMER	BILLING ADDRESS	SHIPPING ADDRESS	TAXABLE	TAX RATE
Tina Turner	321 Pleasant Drive Mansfield Texas 76063 United States	321 Pleasant Drive Mansfield Texas 76063 United States	Yes	TX-Mansfield (8.25%)

Figure 5.16: Taxable customer report

As you can see, it is easy to keep track of sales tax in QuickBooks. You can use the tax liability report and the taxable customer report to prepare your sales tax return. In addition, you can use these reports to determine the amount owed.

> Be sure to select the correct accounting method (cash or accrual) before running your reports. Refer to the *Chapter 13, Small-Business Bookkeeping 101*, available as bonus content online at https://packt.link/supplementary-content-9781836649977 to learn the difference between cash and accrual accounting.
>
> Unfortunately, you cannot pay sales tax within QBO. You must visit the website of your state tax authority and submit payment online or mail a check before the due date.

Summary

In this chapter, we have discussed the importance of setting up sales tax in QuickBooks so it can automatically calculate sales tax for you. We have shown you how to create an invoice and include sales tax, and we have covered the key reports available to help you stay on top of your sales tax liability.

It's important to make sure you set up sales tax and use the correct sales tax rate. This will help you avoid penalties or fees for under-reporting and underpaying sales tax to your state tax office. To ensure proper setup of sales tax, I recommend that you reach out to an accountant or tax professional who can review your setup for accuracy. Remember, you can give them access to view company reports only. That way, they can view the sales tax setup without having the ability to make changes without your permission.

In the next chapter, we will cover how to record invoices and sales receipts in QBO.

Join our community on Discord

Join our community's Discord space for discussions with the authors and other readers:

https://packt.link/powerusers

6
Recording Sales Transactions in QuickBooks Online

In *Chapter 4, Managing Customer, Vendor, and Products and Services Lists*, you learned how to customize QuickBooks by adding customers, vendors, and the products and services you sell to QuickBooks. Now that you have completed your QuickBooks setup, it's time to learn how to record transactions. Recording sales transactions will allow you to keep track of how much money your business is making. This information is important and will help you determine whether or not your business is profitable.

In this chapter, we will focus on recording sales transactions in **QuickBooks Online** (**QBO**) as well as how to customize sales templates. We will cover the three types of sales transactions, when you should use them, how to record each transaction, and the behind-the-scenes accounting that QuickBooks does for you. We will also show you how to record customer payments, how to manage credit card payments, and how to issue credit memos and refunds to customers.

In this chapter, we will cover the following key concepts:

- Entering sales forms—sales receipts, deposits, and sales invoices
- Customizing sales templates
- Recording payments received from customers
- Managing credit card payments
- Recording payments to the *payments to deposit* account
- Issuing credit memos and refunds to customers

Entering sales forms

Recording income for a business can be accomplished in a variety of ways. There are three primary ways to record income in QBO. First, a **sales receipt** is used when you receive payment at the same time as you provide products and/or services to your customers. Second, you can use a **deposit** to record income for a specific customer, from multiple customers at any one time, or to record miscellaneous deposits such as a tax refund check. Third, you can use a **sales invoice**, which allows you to bill a specific customer, who will pay you based on payment terms that are agreed upon upfront.

In the following sections, we will cover when and how to record income using a sales receipt, a deposit, and a sales invoice. We will also show you the accounting that takes place behind the scenes for each transaction. This will include the debits and credits recorded for each transaction.

Recording income using a sales receipt

A sales receipt is used when the sale of a product or service and the receipt of the customer payment take place simultaneously. For example, retail businesses, such as restaurants or clothing stores, will receive payment at the same time as they provide their service (for example, serving food to customers) or products (for example, clothing items for purchase). In general, you would record a sales receipt immediately upon making the sale so that you can either give a copy to your customer or send it via email. For a restaurant or coffee shop, you may only record sales receipts on a daily or weekly basis, especially if you have a **point of sale** (**POS**) system that you can use to keep track of your daily sales. You can record a sales receipt in QuickBooks by completing a couple of simple steps.

Follow these steps to record a sales receipt:

1. From the **+ New** menu, select **Sales receipt**, as indicated in *Figure 6.1*:

Chapter 6

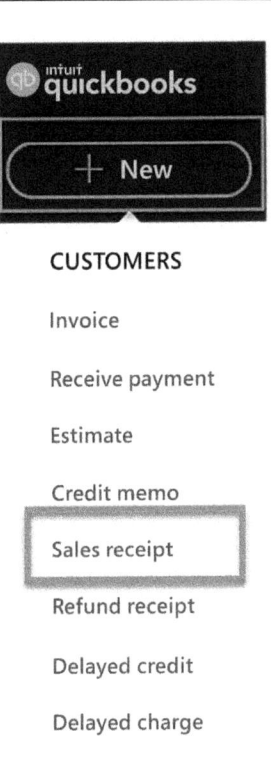

Figure 6.1: Navigating to the Sales receipt form

Figure 6.2 shows a completed sales receipt:

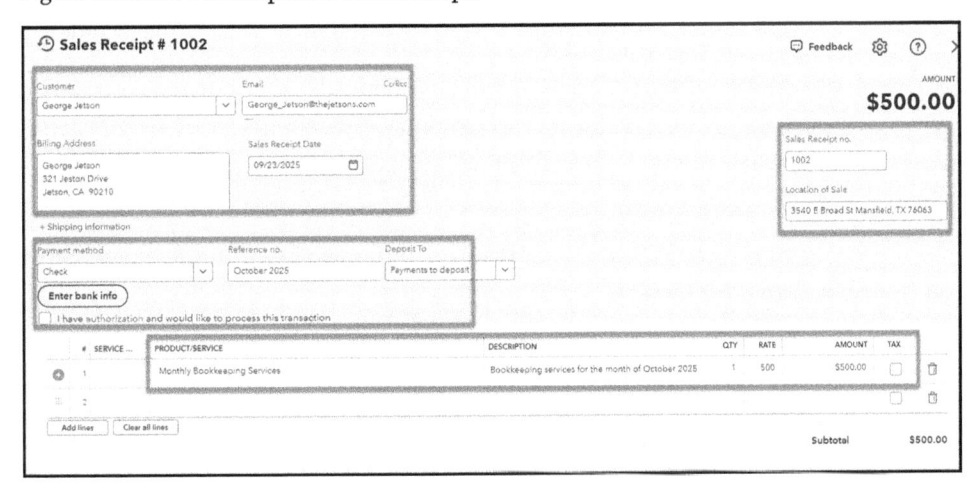

Figure 6.2: Completing the Sales Receipt form (for better visualization, refer to https://packt.link/gbp/9781836649977)

2. You can complete the sales receipt using the information in *Figure 6.2* and below *or* enter the information that is relevant for your customer.

There are several fields of information that need to be completed on the **Sales Receipt** form. The following is a brief description of the information you need to include in each field:

- **Customer**: Select the customer you sold the product or service to by clicking on the drop-down arrow in this field. **George Jetson** is the customer in our example. If you have not added any customers yet, you can add a new customer by typing the customer's name in this field.

> If you need to record sales for an event for multiple customers at once, you can enter the event name and date or the week instead of a specific customer; for example, sales for the week of 2/1/25 to 2/7/25. You can also set up a generic customer called Daily Sales or Weekly Sales, depending on how often you record sales in QuickBooks.

- **Email**: This field will automatically be populated with the email address you have on file for the customer. The email address in our example is `George_Jetson@thejetsons.com`. If the field is blank, you can type an email address directly in this field.

QuickBooks will email the sales receipt to the email address you include in this field.

- **Billing Address**: This field will automatically be populated with the billing address you have on file for this customer. The billing address in our example is `321 Jetson Drive., Jetson, CA 90210`. If you don't have an address on file, you can enter one directly in this field.

- **Sales Receipt Date**: Enter the date of the sale in this field, which is `09/23/2025` in our example.

- **Payment method**: Select the payment method by clicking the drop-down arrow. We have selected **Check** in our example.

- **Reference no.**: If your customer paid by check, enter the check number in this field. If payment was made by cash or credit card, you can select it from the drop-down and enter a reference number, or leave this field blank. The reference number is October 2025 in our example.

- **Deposit To**: From the drop-down menu, select the bank account to which you will deposit this payment. In our example, the funds will be deposited into the **Payments to deposit** account.

  > If you plan to deposit payments for multiple customers on the same day, select the **Payments to deposit** account (formerly **Undeposited funds**), instead of the **Business Checking** account as the **Deposit To** account. Later, you will be able to select the specific deposits made on each day. This will make it much easier to reconcile the bank account.

- **Sales receipt no.**: QuickBooks will automatically generate this number, which is 1002 in our example.
- **Location of Sale**: For sales tax purposes, this field will automatically be populated with the business address of our sample company. The business address in our example is 3540 E Broad St Mansfield, Tx 76063.
- **PRODUCT/SERVICE**: From the drop-down menu, select the type of service (or product) sold to the customer. In our example, it is a bookkeeping service. **Monthly Bookkeeping Services** has not been added, so you will need to select **Add New** and complete the following fields to add it to the list:
    - **Name**: Monthly Bookkeeping Services
    - **Description**: Bookkeeping for the month of October 2025
    - **Rate**: $500.00
- **DESCRIPTION**: This field will automatically be populated based on the product/service selected. In our example, the description is **Bookkeeping for the month of October 2025**.
- **QTY**: Enter the quantity of items sold or the total hours of service provided. In our example, the quantity is 1.
- **RATE**: Enter the hourly rate for your services or the unit cost of the product sold. This field should automatically populate with the rate that was set. In our example, the rate is $500.

- **AMOUNT**: You don't need to enter anything in this field. QuickBooks will multiply the quantity by the rate to automatically calculate the total amount of the sales receipt. In our example, the total amount is `$500`.
- **TAX**: This box may automatically be turned on. If so, remove **X** from this field since this service is not taxable.

This Intuit video tutorial summarizes the steps we have covered on how to create a sales receipt: `https://quickbooks.intuit.com/learn-support/en-us/sales-receipts/how-to-record-a-sales-receipt/00/344860`.

As mentioned in *Chapter 1, Getting Started with QuickBooks Online*, one of the benefits of using QuickBooks is that you don't need to have knowledge of debits and credits to use the software. QuickBooks will automatically debit and credit the appropriate accounts for you. However, it is important for you to understand the impact of recording transactions in QuickBooks.

The following table shows the journal entry that is recorded behind the scenes in QuickBooks for the sales receipt displayed previously in *Figure 6.2*:

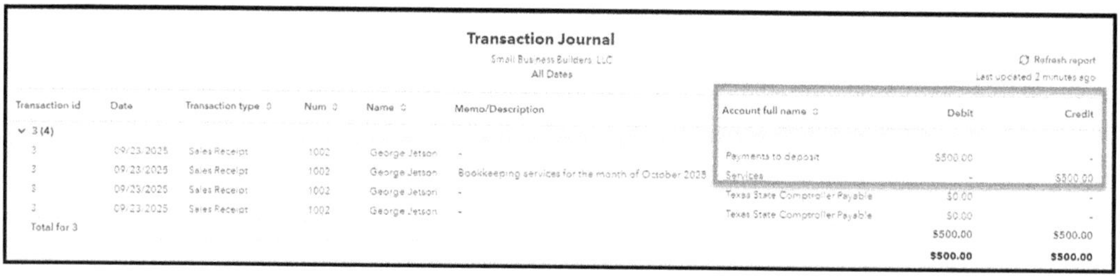

Transaction Journal
Small Business Builders LLC
All Dates
Refresh report
Last updated 2 minutes ago

Transaction id	Date	Transaction type	Num	Name	Memo/Description	Account full name	Debit	Credit
3 (4)								
3	09/23/2025	Sales Receipt	1002	George Jetson	-	Payments to deposit	$500.00	-
3	09/23/2025	Sales Receipt	1002	George Jetson	Bookkeeping services for the month of October 2025	Services	-	$500.00
3	09/23/2025	Sales Receipt	1002	George Jetson	-	Texas State Comptroller Payable	$0.00	-
3	09/23/2025	Sales Receipt	1002	George Jetson	-	Texas State Comptroller Payable	$0.00	-
Total for 3							$500.00	$500.00
							$500.00	**$500.00**

Figure 6.3: Transaction journal entry recorded for a sales receipt (for better visualization, refer to https://packt.link/gbp/9781836649977)

When you create a sales receipt in QuickBooks, it has an impact on the balance sheet and the income statement.

In *Chapter 18, Business Overview and Cash Management Tools and Reports*, available online using this link: `https://packt.link/supplementary-content-9781836649977` we show you how to generate these reports. In our example, the **Payments to deposit** account is increased by `$500`, which increases the total assets on the balance sheet report. **Services** has also increased by `$500`, which increases the total income on the profit and loss (income statement).

Chapter 6

You can access the **Transaction Journal** entry for a sales receipt by clicking on the **More** button at the very bottom of the screen and then selecting **Transaction journal** as shown below:

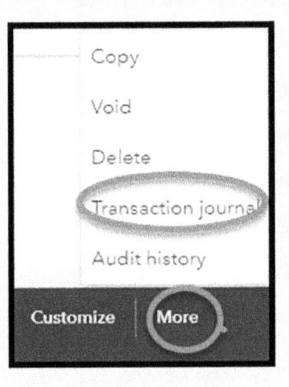

Figure 6.4: Navigate to Transaction journal

Now that you know how to use a sales receipt to record income, we will show you how to record income using a deposit, and the impact deposits have on financial statements.

Recording income using a deposit

Another method used to record income in QuickBooks is that of a deposit. The downside to using this method is that you won't have a detailed record of the type of service that was performed, since there is no field to select the service or product provided. This method should be used if you don't need to record your sales by the type of product or service that was sold. An example of a business that might use this method is a real estate agent recording commission income. You can record a lump-sum deposit amount for multiple checks, or you can record deposits for a specific customer. Recording a deposit in QuickBooks can be done in just a couple of steps.

Follow these steps to record income in QuickBooks using a deposit:

1. From the **+ New** menu, select **Bank deposit** in the **OTHER** column, as indicated in *Figure 6.5*:

Figure 6.5: Navigating to Bank Deposit

Figure 6.6 shows a completed **Bank Deposit** form:

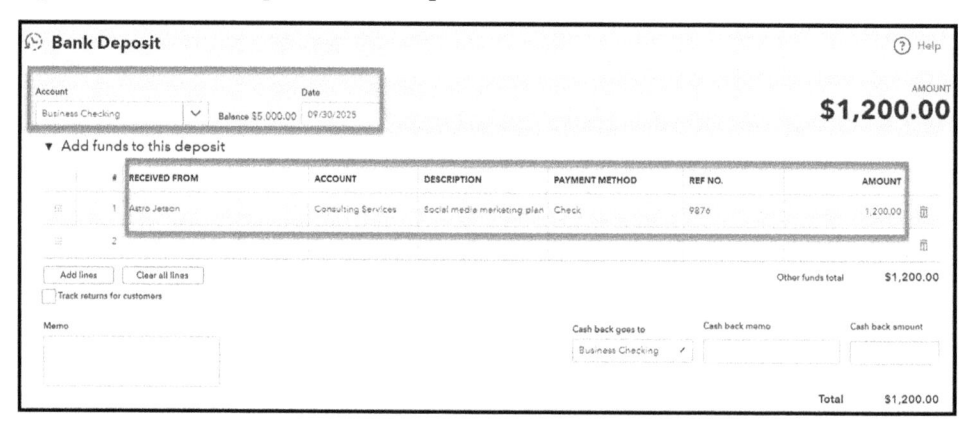

Figure 6.6: Bank Deposit form (for better visualization, refer to https://packt.link/gbp/9781836649977)

2. Use the information in *Figure 6.6* to complete the bank deposit form or use your own information to complete the form.

   Brief descriptions of the fields that need to be completed in a deposit slip are given here. All fields are required except for the **DESCRIPTION**, **PAYMENT METHOD**, and **REF NO.** fields:

   - **Account:** Use the drop-down arrow to select the bank account to which the deposit will be made. In our example, we have selected the **Business Checking** account.

- **Date**: Enter the date on which you will make the deposit with your bank. This deposit was made on 09/30/2025.
- **RECEIVED FROM**: Click in this field and select the customer from whom you received the payment. If you prefer not to track income according to the customer, you can leave this field blank. Our deposit was received from **Astro Jetson**.
- **ACCOUNT**: From the drop-down menu, select the appropriate account to which this income should be categorized. This is generally an income account and should be based on the type of product or service provided. The account in our example is **Consulting Services**.
- **DESCRIPTION**: In this field, you can type a brief description of the product or service provided. The description in our example is **Social media marketing plan**.
- **PAYMENT METHOD**: In this field, you can indicate the method of payment received (that is, by credit card, cash, or check). The payment method in our example is **Check**.
- **REF NO.**: If the payment method was **Check**, enter the check number in this field. For all other payment methods, you can leave this field blank. The reference number is 9876 in our example.
- **AMOUNT**: Enter the amount of the sale in this field. The total amount of the above deposit is $1200.

When you create a deposit transaction in QuickBooks, it affects the balance sheet and profit and loss (income statement) reports. The bank account where the deposit will be made goes up, which increases the assets section of the balance sheet report. The profit and loss report is increased by the product or service that was sold.

Click on the **More** button and select **Transaction journal** to see the report:

Transaction id	Date	Transaction type	Num	Name	Memo/Description	Account full name	Debit	Credit
∨ 4 (2)								
4	09/30/2025	Deposit	-	Astro Jetson	-	Business Checking	$1,200.00	-
4	09/30/2025	Deposit	-	Astro Jetson	Social media marketing plan	Consulting Services	-	$1,200.00
Total for 4							$1,200.00	$1,200.00
							$1,200.00	$1,200.00

Figure 6.7: Transaction Journal entry to record a bank deposit (for better visualization, refer to https://packt.link/gbp/9781836649977)

In our example, the **Business Checking** account increased by $1200, which will increase the total assets on the balance sheet report. **Consultation Services** also increased by $1200, which will increase the total income on the profit and loss report (income statement).

> This method can also be used to record miscellaneous deposits, such as a refund check from a vendor or the IRS. In addition, if you receive a rewards check from a credit card company, that can be recorded as a deposit. However, if your credit card statement has a credit for rewards or a refund, that would be entered in the credit card register.

Now that you know how to record income using a deposit, we will show you how to record income using a sales invoice.

Recording income using a sales invoice

A sales invoice is used to record income from customers who have been given extended payment terms. This means the customer does not pay at the time the product is sold or services are rendered; instead, they pay you sometime in the future. The most common payment term is **net 30**, which means the invoice is due 30 days from the sale date or the invoice date.

Unlike the sales receipt and deposit forms, which record both the sale and the receipt of payment in a single transaction, recording a sales invoice and payment is done in two steps. In this section, we will cover the first step: recording a sales invoice. We will cover recording customer payments later in the chapter.

Chapter 6   195

To record a sales invoice in QBO, follow these steps:

1. Navigate to the **+ New** menu and select **Invoice** under **CUSTOMERS**, as indicated here:

Figure 6.8: Navigating to the Invoice form

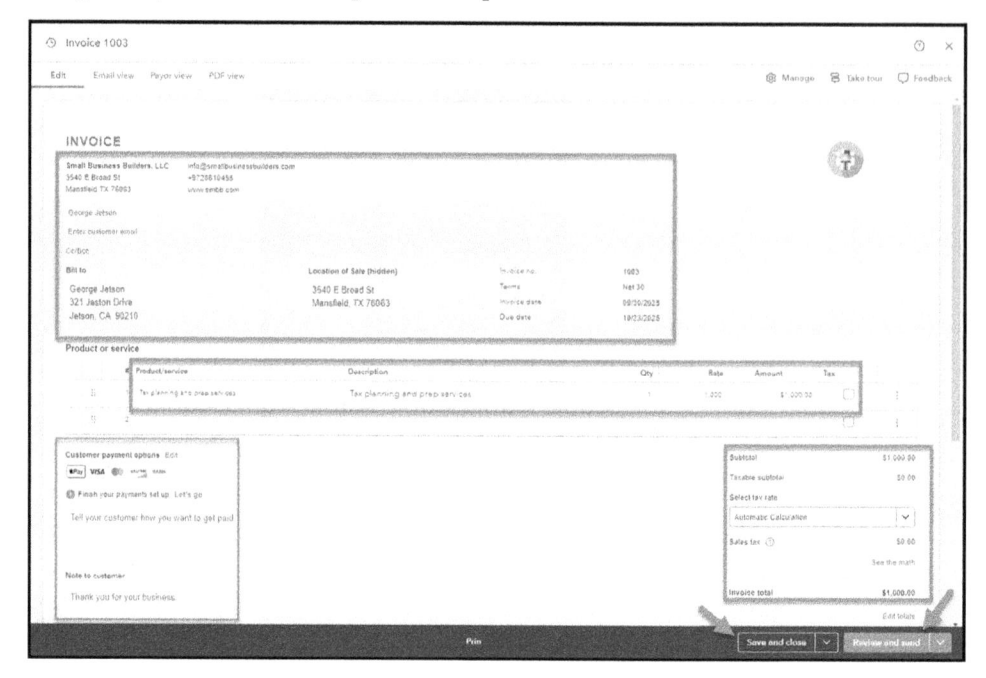

In *Figure 6.9*, we have an example of a complete sales invoice form:

Figure 6.9: The Invoice form

2. Use the information in *Figure 6.9* to complete the invoice form or use your own information to complete the form.

   Here are the fields that need to be completed in a sales invoice. All fields are required except for the **Description, Qty**, and **Note to customer** fields:

   - **Customer**: Select the customer from the drop-down menu. **George Jetson** is the customer selected in our example.
   - **Bill to**: This field will automatically be populated with the address information you have on file for your customer. If you have not set up the address information, you can type it directly in this field. The billing address in this field is `321 Jetson Drive, Jetson, CA 90210`.
   - **Terms**: This field will automatically be populated with the payment terms you have set up for your customer. In our example, we have set payment terms of **Net 30**, which means the invoice is due 30 days from the invoice date. If you have not set up payment terms, you can select these from the drop-down menu.
   - **Invoice date**: Enter the date of the sale in this field. The invoice date is `09/30/2025` in our example.

- **Due date:** This field is automatically calculated by QuickBooks. Since the payment terms are **Net 30**, it adds 30 days to the invoice date in order to compute the date payment is due. The due date is `10/23/2025` in our example.

- **Invoice no.:** QuickBooks will automatically populate this field with the next available invoice number. In our example, the invoice number is `1003`.

- **Product/service:** From the drop-down menu, select the product and/or services provided to the customer. In our example, the product sold is **Tax planning and preparation**. Select **Add new** from the drop-down menu to add this service to the list.

- **Description:** This field will automatically be populated based on the product/service selected in the previous field. The description of the product sold in our example is **Tax planning and preparation**. You can edit this field as needed directly on the invoice.

- **Qty:** Enter the quantity of the product or the total hours to bill the customer. In our example, the fee is a flat amount, so the **Qty** field will automatically populate with **1**.

- **Rate:** This field will automatically be populated based on the product/service selected. However, if you don't have a rate set up, you can enter the price per unit or the hourly rate in this field. In our example, the rate for tax planning and preparation is `$1,000.00`.

- **Amount:** QuickBooks will automatically calculate the total invoice amount by taking the quantity and multiplying it by the rate. In our example, the total amount due is `$1,000.00`.

- **Note to customer:** This field is optional. You can type a personal thank you message to your customer and it will appear on the invoice. In our example, we have entered the following message: **Thank you for your business**.

You have the option to print the sales invoice, email it, or save it as a PDF document. If you would like to allow customers to pay their invoices online, you can sign up for the Intuit Payments service. This service allows you to accept payments from customers via eight payment methods: Apple Pay, Visa, Mastercard, Discover Card, Amex, ACH, PayPal, and Venmo. Using Intuit Payments is a fast and efficient way to get paid.

> You can now send invoices in one of six languages: English, French, Spanish, Italian, Portuguese (Brazil), and Chinese (traditional). To select the preferred language for a customer, navigate to the customer profile and click on the **Language** tab.

When you create a sales invoice in QuickBooks, it has an impact on the balance sheet as well as the profit and loss statement. The accounts receivable account will increase, which will result in an increase in the total assets on the balance sheet report. Income will also increase the profit and loss statement.

Figure 6.10 shows the transaction journal entry that will be recorded in QuickBooks for our sample sales invoice shown in *Figure 6.9*:

Transaction id	Date	Transaction type	Num	Name	Memo/Description	Account full name	Debit	Credit
∨ 5 (4)								
5	09/30/2025	Invoice	1003	George Jetson	-	Accounts Receivable (A/R)	$1,000.00	-
5	09/30/2025	Invoice	1003	George Jetson	Tax planning and prep services	Services	-	$1,000.00
5	09/30/2025	Invoice	1003	George Jetson	-	Texas State Comptroller Payable	$0.00	-
5	09/30/2025	Invoice	1003	George Jetson	-	Texas State Comptroller Payable	$0.00	-
Total for 5							$1,000.00	$1,000.00
							$1,000.00	$1,000.00

Figure 6.10: Automatic journal entry recorded for the invoice (for better visualization, refer to https://packt.link/gbp/9781836649977)

The amount owed by customers—also known as accounts receivable—goes up by $1,000.00, and **Services** is increased by $1,000.00. In the *Recording customer payments* section of this chapter, we will show you how to apply payments to open accounts receivable balances.

Now that you know how to record income using a sales invoice, we will cover how to customize sales templates. Understanding how to customize sales templates with your company name and logo will allow you to make your brand style consistent across different forms.

Customizing sales templates

QuickBooks allows you to create custom sales forms to match your brand and style. Taking the time to customize sales templates will allow you to create professional-looking forms so your customers can easily see what they owe and make payments online in just a few minutes. You can customize invoices, estimates, and sales receipt templates.

Chapter 6

Follow these steps to learn how to customize these sales templates:

1. Click on the gear icon and select **Custom form styles** from the **YOUR COMPANY** column, as shown here:

Figure 6.11: Navigating to Custom form styles

2. Click on the **New style** button and select a sales template to customize:

Figure 6.12: Clicking the New style button

3. The following window will display three areas you can customize for sales templates:

Figure 6.13: Three customization options for sales templates

The following is a brief explanation of the information you can customize in each of these areas:

- **Design:** The **Design** section allows you to create your template style and format. You will select a template design, add your company logo, add your brand colors, and choose the font size and style.

- **Content:** For **Content**, you can select what information you would like to appear on the sales template, including your basic contact information, such as a business telephone number and mailing address. You can also add your website and email address to the form. In the billing section, you can determine how much detail you would like to include in the sales form. For example, an invoice should include a list of each product or service you are billing the customer for.

- **Emails:** QuickBooks allows you to email a sales form directly to customers. In this section, you can decide whether you want any details of the form to be included in the body of the email. Also, you can choose to have a PDF document attached to the email. In *Figure 6.14* below, you can see the email options on the left and the actual preview of what your customer will see on the right:

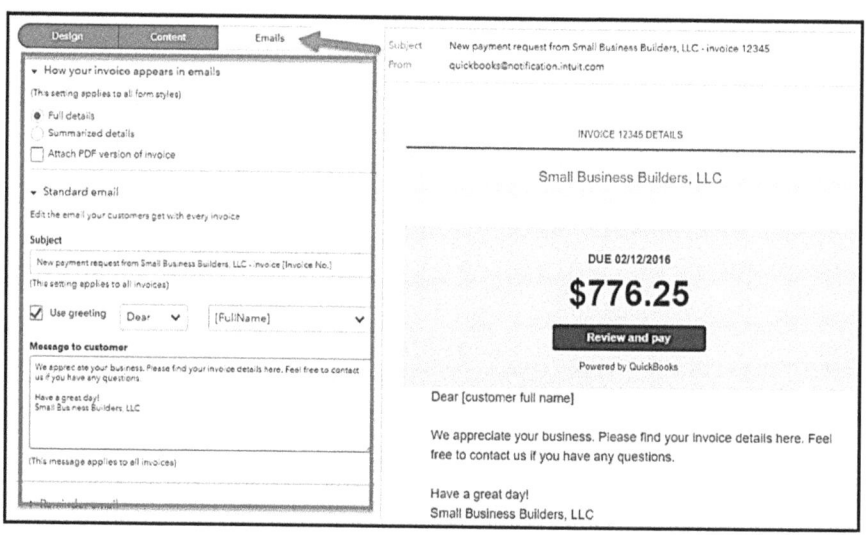

Figure 6.14: Review email options and print preview (for better visualization, refer to https://packt.link/gbp/9781836649977)

4. After completing each section, click the **Done** button at the bottom of the screen to save your changes. A preview of your customized sales form should appear, as shown in *Figure 6.15*:

Small Business Builders, LLC
3540 E Broad St
Mansfield, TX 76063
US

www.smallbusinessbuilders.com

INVOICE

BILL TO
Smith Co.
123 Main Street
City, CA 12345

INVOICE   12345
DATE   01/12/2016
TERMS   Net 30
DUE DATE   02/12/2016

DATE		DESCRIPTION	QTY	RATE	AMOUNT
12/01/2016	Item name	Description of the item	2	$225.00	$450.00
01/12/2016	Item name	Description of the item	1	$225.00	$225.00

SUBTOTAL $675.00
TAX $101.00
TOTAL $776.00

BALANCE DUE **$776.25**

Figure 6.15: Sample custom invoice for Small Business Builders, LLC

You can create an unlimited number of templates for various types of sales and customers. It is easy to make changes to them anytime. The best part is that you don't have to create any templates from scratch.

After completing the invoice form as shown in *Figure 6.9*, you can click on the **Review and send** button in the bottom-right corner of the screen. This will display a screen that resembles the one in *Figure 6.16* below. Within that screen, you can also select the option to text the invoice link to your customer. You'll also notice the option at the top of the screen to enter the customer's phone number and confirm that you have permission to send invoices via text.

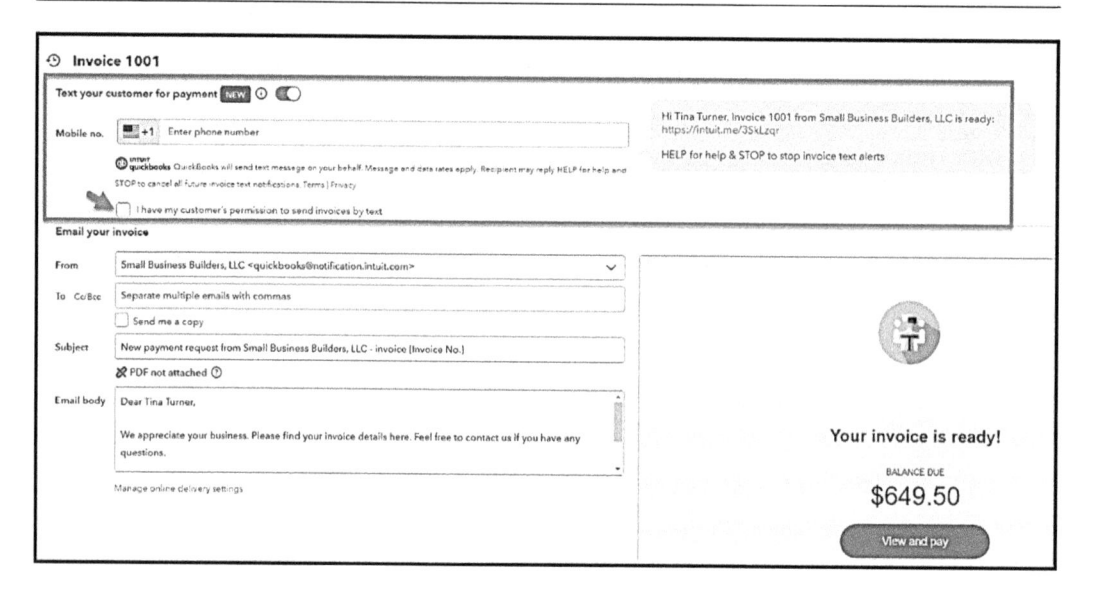

Figure 6.16: Text invoices to customers in QBO (for better visualization, refer to https://packt.link/gbp/9781836649977)

> Learn how to customize sales forms with this Intuit video tutorial with tips and tricks on customizing sales forms in QBO: `https://www.youtube.com/watch?v=b51wvS-4g1w`.

Since texting invoices to customers is a brand-new feature, you definitely need to obtain your customer's permission to do this. I'm not big on texting but I do recommend sending your invoices via email over snail mail. Nowadays, people like to make online payments because they are much faster. Giving your customers the option to make online payments will help you get paid faster, which can help you maintain positive cash flow.

Now that you know how to record income using a sales invoice and how to customize sales templates, we will cover the second step, which is receiving customer payments. You must correctly apply customer payments to outstanding sales invoices to ensure that your accounts receivable balance is always up to date.

Chapter 6

Recording customer payments

If you record income using a sales invoice, you will receive payment based on the terms you have agreed with your customer. When customer payments are received, you must apply payments to an outstanding sales invoice to reduce the accounts receivable balance. As mentioned previously, you can accept multiple payment methods in QuickBooks, including check, cash, Apple Pay, Visa, Mastercard, Discover Card, Amex, ACH, PayPal, and Venmo. To learn more about managing credit card payments, refer to *Chapter 10*, *Handling Special Transactions in QuickBooks Online*.

Follow these steps to receive payment from a customer:

1. Click on the **+ New** menu.
2. Navigate to **Receive payment**, located below **CUSTOMERS**, as indicated here:

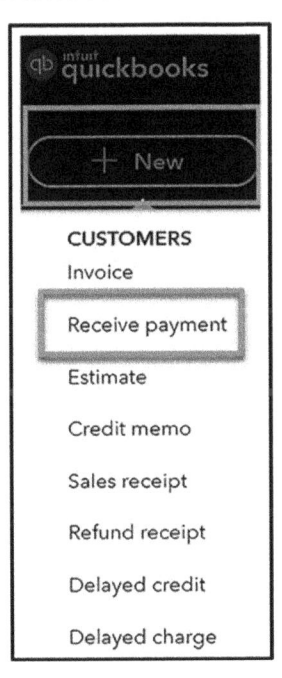

Figure 6.17: Navigating to Receive payment

3. Complete the fields, as indicated in *Figure 6.18*, to record the customer payment:

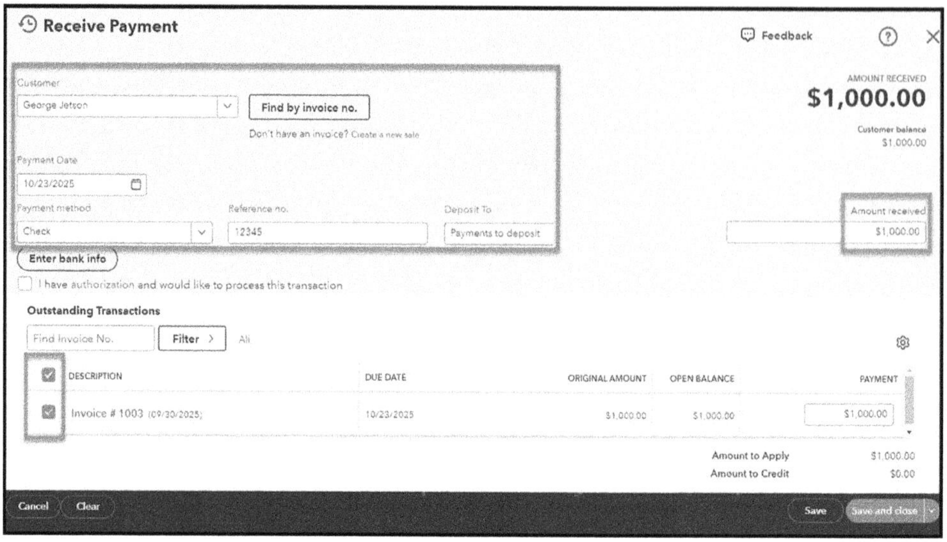

Figure 6.18: The Receive Payment window (for better visualization, refer to https://packt.link/gbp/9781836649977)

The following are the key fields you need to fill before receiving customer payments:

- **Customer**: Select the customer by clicking the drop-down arrow. **George Jetson** is the customer selected in our example.

- **Payment date**: Enter the date payment was received. The payment date is 10/23/2025 in our example.

- **Payment method**: From the drop-down menu, select the payment method received (that is, by credit card, check, or cash). The payment method is **Check** in our example.

- **Reference no.:** If payment was made by check, enter the check number in this field. If another payment method was used, you can leave this field blank. The reference number is 12345 in our example.

- **Deposit To**: Select the bank account to which you will deposit this payment. **Payments to deposit** (formerly **Undeposited funds**) is the **Deposit To** account in our example.

- **Amount received**: Enter the amount of the payment received. The amount received in our example is $1,000.00.

Chapter 6

- **Outstanding Transactions**: A list of unpaid invoices will appear in this section. Based on the amount entered in the **Amount received** field, QuickBooks will select the invoice that matches that amount and is closest to the date of the transaction. In our example, **Invoice # 1003** for **$1,000.00** is the invoice that payment has been received for. If QuickBooks selects the wrong invoice, you can remove the checkmark and manually select the correct invoice(s) to apply the payment to.

Recording customer payments affects the balance sheet report but not the income statement, if you are on an accrual basis. However, if you are on a cash basis, both the income statement and the balance sheet report will be affected. *Figure 6.19* shows the transaction journal entry that will automatically be recorded in QuickBooks for this customer payment of $1,000.00:

Transaction Id	Date	Transaction type	Num	Name	Memo/Description	Account full name	Debit	Credit
✓ 6 (2)								
6	10/23/2025	Payment	12345	George Jetson	-	Payments to deposit	$1,000.00	-
6	10/23/2025	Payment	12345	George Jetson	-	Accounts Receivable (A/R)	-	$1,000.00
Total for 6							$1,000.00	$1,000.00
							$1,000.00	$1,000.00

Figure 6.19: Automatic journal entry recorded for customer payment received (for better visualization, refer to https://packt.link/gbp/9781836649977)

The **Payments to deposit** account is increased by $1,000.00, which will result in an increase in the assets section of the balance sheet report. **Accounts Receivable** will decrease by $1,000.00, which will result in a decrease in the **Assets** section of the balance sheet report.

The **Receive payments** method should be used when an invoice has previously been issued. Using **Receive payments** without an invoice will result in a credit balance on the customer account. By the same token, do not record a customer payment using the deposits form if there is an open invoice that it should be applied to. This will cause you to double up your income and the open invoice will never be reconciled with the payment.

The **Accounts receivable aging summary** report shows all open invoices and credits for each customer. It should be reviewed periodically to capture any credits on customer accounts. We will review this report in detail in *Chapter 14, Customer Sales Reports in QuickBooks Online*, available online using this link: `https://packt.link/supplementary-content-9781836649977`.

Managing credit card payments

In addition to traditional payments such as cash and checks, you can accept credit cards as another form of payment from your customers. QBO has a built-in credit card processor called QuickBooks Payments. QuickBooks Payments is a merchant account that allows you to accept credit cards, PayPal, Venmo, Apple Pay, and ACH (bank transfers) from your customers. While there are fees associated with accepting credit card payments, you can choose which payment method your customers can use to make their payments. There are several benefits to accepting online payments. First, you can get paid faster with a credit card than waiting to receive a check in the mail.

Second, if you sign up for a QuickBooks Payments account (https://quickbooks.intuit.com/payments/?sc=seq_intuit_pay_click_ft), you can email customers their invoice, which includes a payment link. They can click on the link, enter their payment information, and pay their invoice in a matter of minutes, which is much faster than waiting to receive a check in the mail. Best of all, QuickBooks will mark the invoice as *paid*, which automatically reduces your accounts receivable balance. As we discussed in *Chapter 3, Customizing QuickBooks for Your Business*, you can send your customers payment reminder emails, which will include a copy of the open invoices, along with a payment link.

In this section, we will show you how to record credit card payments that have been received from customers via QuickBooks Payments and a third-party credit card processing company.

Before you can perform the steps, you will need to have an active QuickBooks Payments account that is connected to your QBO account. Visit QuickBooks Payments (https://quickbooks.intuit.com/payments/?sc=seq_intuit_pay_click_ft) to apply for a QuickBooks Payments account and learn more about how this works.

If you are using a third-party processor, you may be able to connect your account to QuickBooks. For example, PayPal and Square have apps within the QBO app center. In *Chapter 3, Customizing QuickBooks for Your Business*, we cover how the integration between apps works. If you are not sure if your credit card processor works similarly to this, contact your credit card processor to find out if they are compatible with QBO.

Chapter 6

Follow these steps to record a credit card sale if you have a QuickBooks Payments account:

1. Click on the **+ New** button and select **Sales receipt** from the **Customers** column, as shown in *Figure 6.20*:

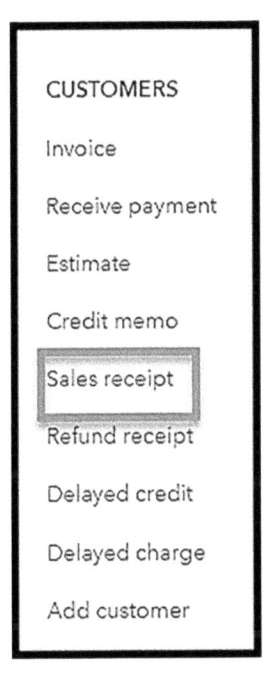

Figure 6.20: Navigating to Sales receipt

2. Fill in the fields in the sales receipt form, as shown in *Figure 6.21*:

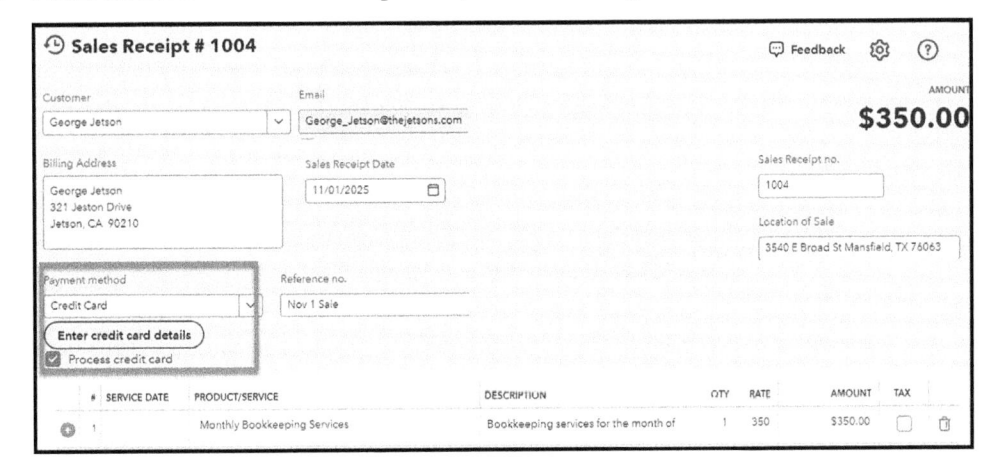

Figure 6.21: Completing the Sales Receipt form

After selecting the customer from the drop-down menu, the **Email** and **Billing Address** fields will automatically be populated with the information you have on file.

3. Next, select a payment method from the drop-down menu. When you select **Credit Card** as the payment method and you have a QuickBooks Payments account, you will see an option to enter credit card details directly below the **Payment method** field.

   The following screen will appear so that you can enter the required credit card information, as shown in *Figure 6.22*:

   Figure 6.22: Completing the credit card payment information

   In *Figure 6.22*, the credit card number has been removed for security reasons. Be sure to complete all the necessary fields and click the **Use this info** button to save the information.

   > After entering the customer's credit card information, QuickBooks will keep this information on file. You won't have to enter it again unless your customer would like to use a different payment method or the credit card expires.

4. This will take you back to the sales receipt form, where you can fill in the details of the services/products provided and the amount. When you click the **Save** button, the credit card payment will be processed and an email with the sales receipt attached will be sent to the customer.

> If you don't have a QuickBooks Payments account, you can still enter the credit card information and save it. However, you will need to process the credit card payment outside of QuickBooks using your third-party merchant company. When the payment is deposited into your bank account, you will need to match it up with the sales receipt in the Banking Center. To learn more about matching transactions, read *Chapter 15, Reconciling Uploaded Bank and Credit Card Transactions*, available online using this link: https://packt.link/supplementary-content-9781836649977.

You now know the benefits of accepting credit card payments from customers and how to manage these payments in QuickBooks.

Recording payments to the payments to deposit account

In the previous examples, each of the payments that have been recorded from customers, whether on a sales receipt, deposit slip, or invoice, were all deposited to the business checking account. This is ideal if you don't deposit more than one check (customer payment) at a time.

However, like most businesses, you will probably wait until you have multiple checks before you head to the bank to make a deposit. In that case, you will need to record all customer payments to an account called **payments to deposit** (formerly "undeposited funds"). The payments to deposit account is an account that is automatically created by QuickBooks. It acts like a cash drawer, where all customer payments are held until you record a deposit in QuickBooks.

After you make a deposit with the bank, you need to record that deposit in QuickBooks. Follow the steps below to record a deposit that includes multiple checks (customer payments):

1. Click on the **+ New** button and select **Bank deposit**, as shown below:

OTHER
Bank deposit
Transfer
Journal entry
Statement
Inventory qty adjustment
Pay down credit card

Figure 6.23: Navigating to Bank deposit

2. The **Bank Deposit** form will appear:

Figure 6.24: The Bank Deposit form

3. Select the bank account to which the deposit will be made. **Business Checking** is the account selected in our example. In the **Date** field, select the date of the deposit; in our example, it is 11/01/2025.

4. Below the **Select the payments included in this deposit** heading, put a checkmark next to each payment included in this deposit. In our example, there are three payments from one customer (George Jetson), which total 1850.00 dollars.

5. Click the **Save** button to record the deposit.

When this deposit is recorded in QuickBooks, the following transaction journal entry is automatically recorded behind the scenes:

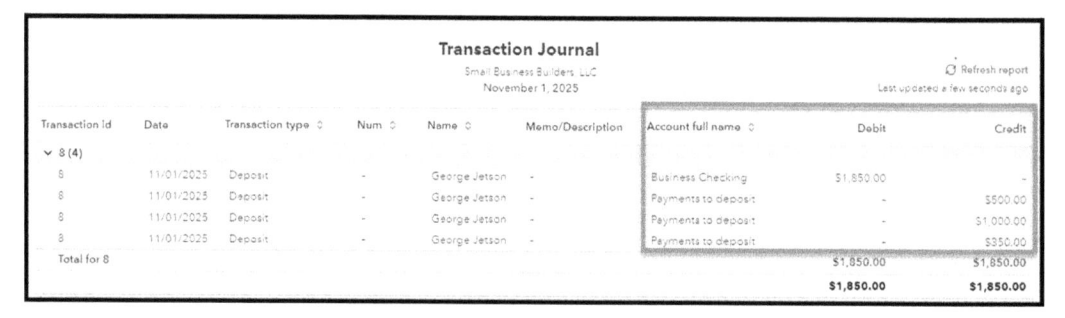

Figure 6.25: Journal entry to transfer payments from payments to deposit to the checking account

> You can also print a deposit slip from the screen shown in *Figure 6.24*, which you can take to your bank along with the checks you are depositing.

When this deposit is recorded in QuickBooks, it only affects the balance sheet report. The business checking account (an asset) increases by the total deposit amount, and the payments to deposit account (also an asset) decreases by the total deposit amount. To ensure you are in balance when you reconcile your bank accounts, always make sure that you have recorded all deposits in QuickBooks. If you have any payments sitting in the payments to deposit account (and they were actually deposited), you will be out of balance. To learn more about how to reconcile bank accounts, head over to *Chapter 15, Reconciling Uploaded Bank and Credit Card Transactions*, available online using this link: https://packt.link/supplementary-content-9781836649977.

Now that you know how to record income and apply payments to outstanding customer invoices, we will show you how to handle customer returns and refunds in the next section.

Issuing credit memos and refunds to customers

There may be times when a customer returns merchandise, or you need to refund a customer due to an issue with the services or products you have provided. When that happens, you can create a credit memo in QuickBooks that can be applied to a future invoice, or you can refund the customer instead by clicking on **+ New**, selecting **Refund receipt**, and following the onscreen instructions.

Follow these steps to create a credit memo in QBO:

1. Click on the **+ New** menu and select **Credit memo** below **CUSTOMERS**, as indicated in *Figure 6.26*:

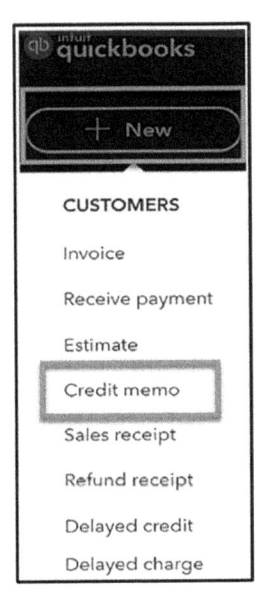

Figure 6.26: Navigating to the Credit Memo form

2. Complete the key fields indicated here for the credit memo:

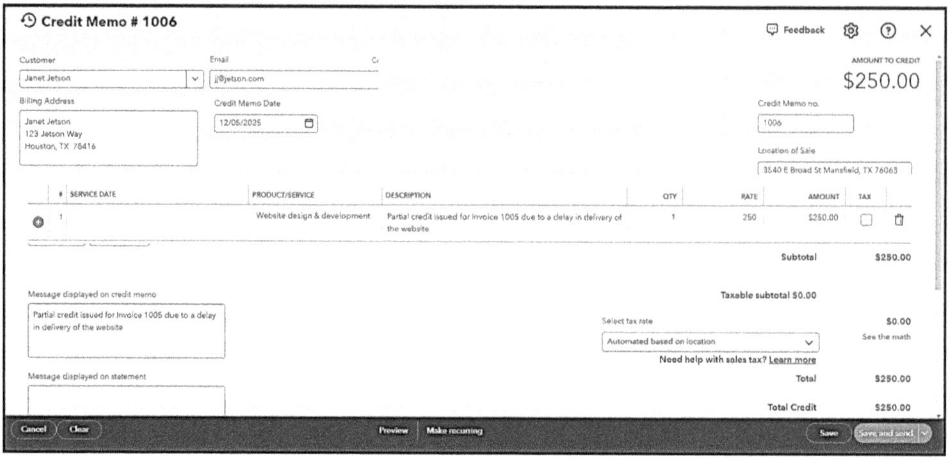

Figure 6.27: Credit Memo form (for better visualization, refer to https://packt.link/gbp/9781836649977)

The following are brief descriptions of the key fields to complete for a credit memo. All fields are required except for the **QTY, DESCRIPTION**, and **Message displayed on credit memo** fields:

- **Customer**: From the drop-down menu, select the customer you need to refund. **Janet Jetson** is the customer selected in our example.

- **Email**: This field will automatically be populated with the email address you have on file. If you don't have an email address on file, you can enter the email address in this field if you would like to email the credit memo to the customer. The email address for Janet Jetson is `jj@jetson.com`.

- **Billing Address**: This field will automatically be populated with the billing address you have on file. If you don't have a billing address on file, you can enter it directly in this field. The billing address for Janet Jetson is `123 Jetson Way, Houston, TX 78416`.

- **Credit Memo Date**: Enter the date for which you are creating this credit memo. The credit memo is dated **12/05/2025**.

- **PRODUCT/SERVICE**: From the drop-down menu, select the product or service for which you are providing a refund. The product in our example is **Website design & development**. If you prefer to create an account specifically for refunds, you can do so by adding a new account to the chart of accounts called **REFUNDS**. This will show up as a separate line on your profit and loss statement.

Chapter 6											213

- **DESCRIPTION**: This field will be populated automatically, but you should edit this to specify the reason for the credit as well as the original invoice number used to bill the customer. In our example, the description is **Partial credit issued for invoice 1005 due to a delay in delivery of the website**.
- **QTY**: Enter the number of items or hours for which you are refunding the customer. The quantity in our example is 1.
- **RATE**: This field will automatically be populated based on the product/service selected. However, if there is no rate set up, you can enter the rate in this field. The rate is $250 in our example.
- **AMOUNT**: This field is automatically calculated by multiplying the quantity by the rate. You do not have to enter anything in this field. The total amount to be credited to the customer is $250.00 in our example. Since the customer has not paid the invoice yet, we will apply this credit to the open invoice. However, if the invoice had already been paid, you would have issued a refund to the customer.
- **Message displayed on credit memo**: In this field, you can add the original invoice number for which you are providing a full or partial credit or a brief description of the reason for the credit. The message on our credit memo is **Partial credit issued for invoice 1005 due to a delay in delivery of the website**. Recording a credit memo in QuickBooks will have an impact on the balance sheet and income statement reports. The income account (consultation income) will decrease, which will reduce the total income on the profit and loss report. If the original invoice has **not** been paid, the credit memo can be applied to that invoice to reduce the total amount due from the customer. The accounts receivable balance will decrease since the amount due from the customer has been reduced.

The journal entry for the preceding credit memo will automatically be recorded in QuickBooks as follows:

Transaction id	Date	Transaction type	Num	Name	Memo/Description	Account full name	Debit	Credit
∨ 10 (4)								
10	12/05/2025	Credit Memo	1006	Janet Jetson	-	Accounts Receivable (A/R)	-	$250.00
10	12/05/2025	Credit Memo	1006	Janet Jetson	Partial credit issued for Invoice	Consulting Services	$250.00	-
10	12/05/2025	Credit Memo	1006	Janet Jetson	-	Texas State Comptroller Payable	$0.00	-
10	12/05/2025	Credit Memo	1006	Janet Jetson	-	Texas State Comptroller Payable	$0.00	-
Total for 10							$250.00	$250.00
							$250.00	$250.00

Figure 6.28: Automatic journal entry recorded for the credit memo (for better visualization, refer to https://packt.link/gbp/9781836649977)

Applying a credit memo to an open invoice

After recording a credit memo for a customer, the credit will immediately be applied to the open balance for that customer. Let's assume that Janet Jetson has sent a payment in for invoice #1005. Navigate to the **Receive Payment** window, select **Janet Jetson** from the **Customer** drop-down, and the following screen will display:

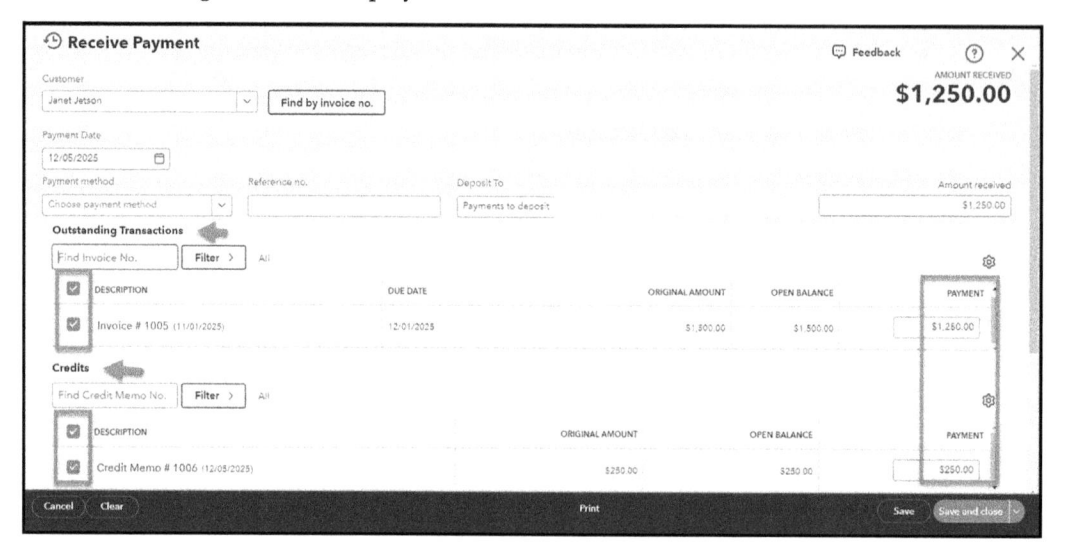

Figure 6.29: Janet Jetson invoice with credit memo applied

As you can see, the original invoice amount was $1,500.00, and now that the credit has been recorded, the open balance has been reduced by the $250 credit amount (shown in *Figure 6.29*) to $1,250.00.

> If you do not invoice customers through QuickBooks, you can issue a refund check by going to **+ New** and selecting **Check**, listed below the **Vendors** column. This will allow you to refund a customer instead of creating a credit memo since you will never have an invoice to apply it to.

Summary

In this chapter, you have learned how to record sales transactions for the sale of products and services using a sales receipt, a deposit, and a sales invoice. You now know when to use each sales transaction and how to record them in QBO. We have also covered the journal entry that is recorded behind the scenes by QuickBooks for each transaction. To put your best foot forward, we have shown you how to create professional-looking invoices, sales receipts, and estimates by adding your brand colors and logo. In addition, you have learned how to record customer payments so that they are correctly applied to open invoices. We have also covered how to manage credit card payments by signing up for a QuickBooks Payments account. Finally, we covered how to issue credit memos and refunds to customers. Recording sales transactions will allow you to keep track of how much money your business is making. This is important so that you can determine whether your business is profitable or not. In the next chapter, we will look at how to record the money that flows out of your business to cover expenses.

Join our community on Discord

Join our community's Discord space for discussions with the authors and other readers:

`https://packt.link/powerusers`

7

Recording Expenses in QuickBooks Online

Managing expenses incurred by a business is one of the primary reasons why many businesses decide to use QuickBooks. Most businesses know when they are generating income, but when it comes to where their money is going, it's a whole different story. For a business to be profitable, it must be able to control expenses that directly affect the bottom line.

In this chapter, we will show you four ways to record expenses, also known as **money-out** transactions: (1) entering and paying bills, (2) managing recurring expenses, (3) writing and printing checks, and (4) capturing and categorizing receipts and bills.

Entering a bill is ideal for suppliers who have extended credit to you. You receive your purchases immediately and payment is due sometime in the future. However, expenses that require immediate payment should be paid via check, debit card, or credit card. In *Chapter 15, Reconciling Uploaded Bank and Credit Card Transactions*, available online using this link: `https://packt.link/supplementary-content-9781836649977` we will show you how to record payments made with a debit or credit card. Entering a check allows you to record both the expense and the payment at the same time.

Using one or more of these methods will give you access to detailed reports that will give you insight into all of your money-out transactions. This is a key component in having the ability to control expenses.

In this chapter, we will cover the following topics:

- Adding and paying bills
- Managing recurring expenses

- Writing checks
- Printing checks
- Editing, voiding, and deleting expenses
- Capturing and categorizing receipts and bills

By the end of this chapter, you will know how to add and pay your bills, and how to create recurring expenses for rent, utilities, and other recurring costs. Plus, you will understand how to write a check and print it directly from QuickBooks, and you will become familiar with the various ways in which you can upload receipts and bills in QuickBooks.

> The US edition of QBO was used to create this book. If you are using a version that is outside of the United States, results may differ.

Adding and paying bills

For purchases made on the account, adding bills to QuickBooks and paying them a few days before they become due is the best way to manage your cash flow. If you add bills to QuickBooks as you receive them, you can run reports that will show you which bills are due or nearly due, so that you can plan ahead and ensure you have sufficient cash on hand to pay them. Unpaid bills are also referred to as **accounts payable**, or **A/P** for short. In the following sections, we will first cover how to add bills, and then we will discuss how to pay bills in **QBO**.

> There are a number of apps available to help automate the bill entry process. From the left navigation bar, select **Apps**. In the search box, type the keywords `bill pay`, and several options, such as **Bill Pay for QuickBooks Online** and **bill.com**, will display. To learn more about the Intuit Apps marketplace, refer to *Chapter 10, Handling Special Transactions in QuickBooks Online*.

Entering bills into QuickBooks Online

As advised earlier, adding your bills into QuickBooks before they come due will help you manage your cash flow. You can easily run reports, such as the **Unpaid Bills** report or the **A/P Aging** report, to see which bills are coming due or are past due. There are a couple of ways to add your bills to QuickBooks. You can upload a bill that you have saved on your computer, or you can manually create the bill. First, we will cover how to manually create a bill.

Chapter 7

Follow these steps to create a bill in QBO:

1. Click on the **Expenses** tab from the left menu bar as indicated in *Figure 7.1*:

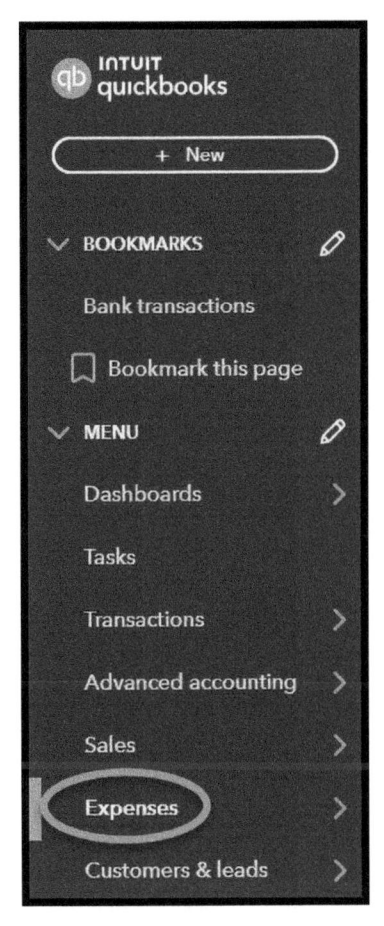

Figure 7.1: Navigating to Expenses from the left menu bar

2. On the screen that appears, click on the **Add bill** button in the upper-right corner as shown here:

Figure 7.2: Bill pay window displays (for better visualization, refer to https://packt.link/gbp/9781836649977)

3. Select **Create Bill** and complete the fields in the **Bill** pay form as indicated:

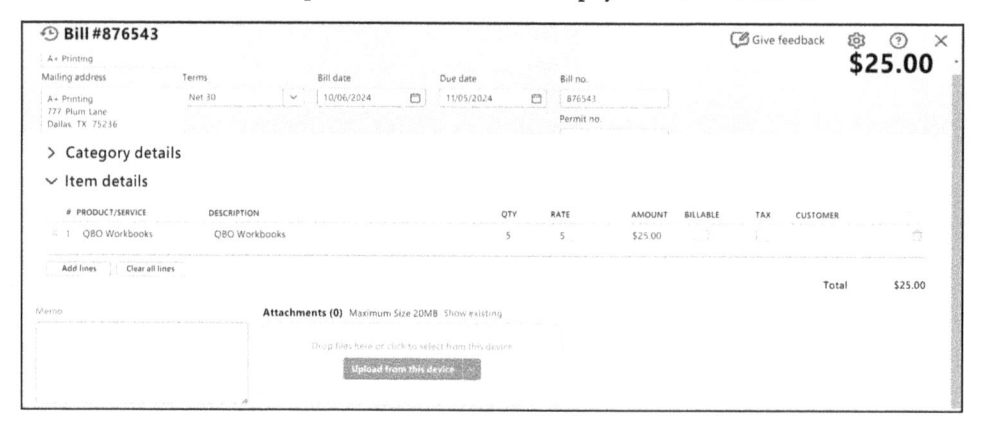

Figure 7.3: Completing the Bill form for a vendor (for better visualization, refer to https://packt.link/gbp/9781836649977)

4. The following is a brief description of the key fields in the **Bill** form. All fields must be completed:

   - **Vendor:** Select a vendor from the drop-down menu, or add a new vendor if they have not been previously set up in QuickBooks. You can do this by selecting **Add New** from the drop-down menu. In our example, A+ Printing is the vendor.
   - **Mailing address:** This field will automatically populate for vendors you have previously created in QuickBooks. If this is a new vendor, you can enter the address in this field. In our example, the address is 777 Plum Lane, Dallas, TX 75236.

Chapter 7　　221

- **Terms**: This field will automatically populate with the vendor terms you have set up. If you have not previously set up vendor terms, you can select the appropriate payment terms from the drop-down menu. The payment terms should be **Net 30** for **A+ Printing**.
- **Bill date**: Enter the date that appears on the vendor bill. Our bill date is 10/06/2024.
- **Due date**: The due date will be calculated automatically based on the payment terms selected. If payment terms were not selected, you can also enter the due date directly in this field. The due date in our example is 11/05/2024.
- **Bill no.**: The bill number is the invoice number assigned by the vendor supplier. If the bill does not include a unique number, create one. Having a unique bill number is very important so that QuickBooks can track bills and alert you if there is a duplicate bill number used. If a bill does not include a bill number, utilize the bill date, or something unique, for each bill. The bill number in our example is 876543.
- **Category details**: Complete this section if you have purchased services from the vendor. Since we have purchased workbooks that are tracked in our inventory, we will complete the **Item details** section right below **Category details**.
- **Item details**: Complete this section if you have purchased a product that you need to keep in inventory so that you can track the quantity and/or costs. If the items purchased are not put into inventory, use the **Category details** tab. From the drop-down menu, select the product/service purchased. If the item has not been added to QuickBooks, you can do so on this screen by selecting the **Add new** option. The **New item** window will display so that you can complete the item setup for QBO Workbooks. For more information on adding a new item to the products and services list, see *Chapter 4, Managing Customer, Vendor, and Products and Services Lists*.
- **DESCRIPTION**: Enter a brief description of what was purchased in this field. For this example, the description is QBO Workbooks.
- **QTY**: Enter the quantity of the item purchased. In our example, 5 workbooks were purchased.
- **RATE**: This field should automatically populate with the rate entered when setting up the item. If no rate was added, you can enter it directly in this form. The rate is 5 in our example.
- **AMOUNT**: QuickBooks will automatically calculate the total amount by multiplying the quantity entered by the rate. In our example, the total amount calculated is $25.00.

- **Save** or **Save and schedule payment**: You have the option to save the bill and schedule payment at a later date, or schedule payment now. We will save the bill for now and cover how to schedule payment later in this chapter.

In our example, this bill only has an impact on the balance sheet. There is no impact on the profit and loss (income statement) reports. Inventory (which is an asset) increases by $25.00, and A/P also increases, which, in turn, increases current liabilities on the balance sheet report.

The journal entry that is recorded in QuickBooks for the preceding bill is shown in *Figure 7.4*:

Transaction id	Date	Transaction type	Num	Name	Memo/Description	Account full name	Debit	Credit
∨ 13 (2)								
13	10/06/2024	Bill	876543	A+ Printing	-	Accounts Payable (A/P)	-	$25.00
13	10/06/2024	Bill	876543	A+ Printing	QBO Workbooks	Inventory Asset	$25.00	-
Total for 13							$25.00	$25.00
							$25.00	$25.00

Figure 7.4: Journal entry to record a vendor bill

In our example, we have used the **Item details** section, because the product is placed in inventory. If you are recording the purchase of an expense (such as consultation services or office supplies), instead of inventory, an expense account, such as **Consulting expense** or **Office supplies**, can be used in the **Category details** section. This would increase expenses on the profit and loss report. Accounts payable would still increase by the amount that was purchased.

In order to stay on top of your bills, it's a good idea to enter them as soon as you receive them. Be sure to enter the date of the bill and the due date; this will ensure that QuickBooks will calculate the correct due date and alert you when a bill is coming due. At the bottom of the bill form, you can even attach a copy of the bill to this transaction.

Uploading bills to QuickBooks

The second way you can add bills to QBO is by uploading them from your computer. You will follow *Steps 1* through *3* as indicated previously for manually creating a bill. For *Step 4*, you will select **Upload from computer** as shown here:

Chapter 7

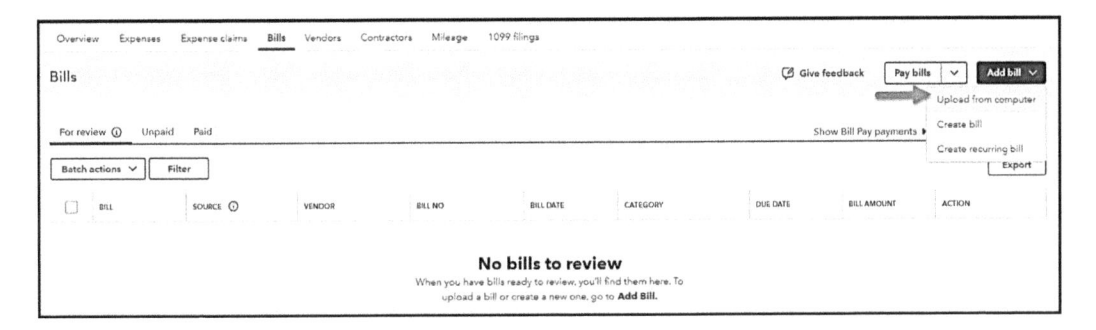

Figure 7.5: Uploading bills from a computer to QBO (for better visualization, refer to https://packt.link/gbp/9781836649977)

1. On the screen that displays, click the **Upload** button as shown in *Figure 7.6*, and select the bill you want to upload:

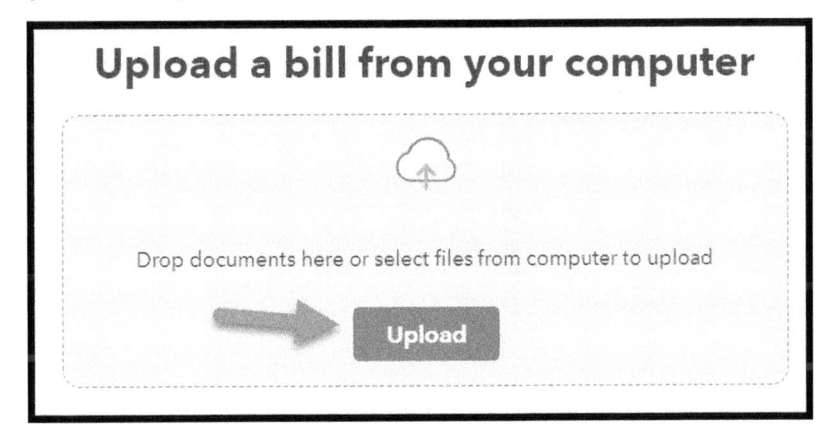

Figure 7.6: Upload bills from your computer

> If the bill is not saved on your computer, do that first and then return to this step.

2. Once the upload is complete, your screen should resemble the one in *Figure 7.7*. Bills that have been uploaded can be found on the **For review** tab, which provides you with a summary of the information QBO has captured for the bill:

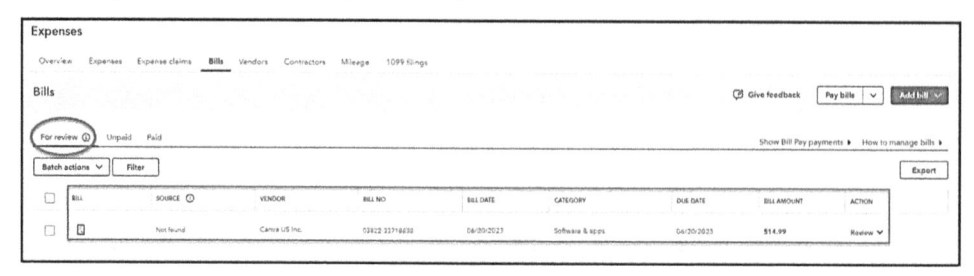

Figure 7.7: Bills for review

3. Click on the **Review** link located to the far right, below the **Action** column (shown in *Figure 7.7*) and a snapshot of the bill along with the fields to be completed will display:

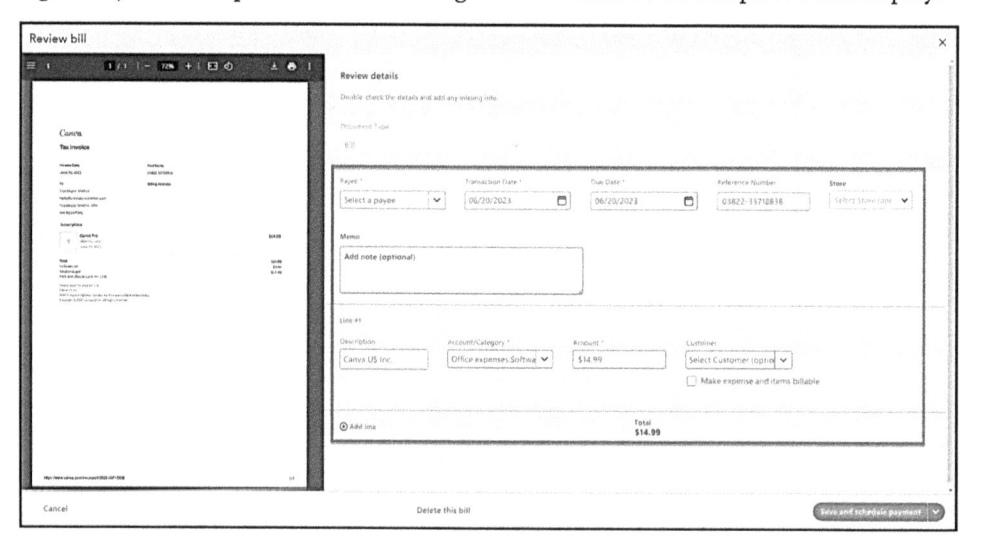

Figure 7.8: Review details of bill uploaded to QBO

The following fields are **required** as indicated by an asterisk (*) in *Figure 7.8*:

- **Payee:** This field indicates the vendor or supplier who you need to pay. In our example, it would be Canva. If Canva is not already set up in QBO, you can easily click on the drop-down menu and select **Add Vendor**.
- **Transaction Date:** The date of the bill is reflected in this field. Notice that QBO has completed this field for us.

- **Due Date**: This field has also been completed by QBO but it is not correct. We can easily edit this field to select the appropriate due date.
- **Account/Category**: This field has been populated by QBO based on the account previously used to pay this type of bill. Similar to the due date, you can edit this field if needed.
- **Amount**: This field has been automatically populated by QBO.

Other fields of information that you may want to complete are as follows:

- **Reference Number**: The invoice or bill number belongs in this field. As shown, QBO has automatically completed this field.
- **Memo**: Any additional information you would like to add can be added in this field. This memo field is for internal purposes only so your vendor/supplier will not have visibility to this information.
- **Description**: QBO has automatically populated this field with the payee name. You can edit this field to include a detailed description.
- **Customer**: If this purchase was made on behalf of a customer, you can select the customer from the drop-down menu. If you would like to bill the customer back for this purchase, be sure to mark the `Make expense and items billable` box that is directly below this field.

4. Click the arrow to the right of the **Save and schedule payment** button shown in the bottom-right corner of *Figure 7.8* to save the bill.

Now that you know how to add your bills to QBO, we will discuss how to pay bills next.

Paying bills in QuickBooks Online

After you enter a bill into QuickBooks, you will need to pay it before the due date. Paying bills in QuickBooks will ensure that the A/P balance is always up to date. It will also allow you to run reports, and see which bills have been paid or need to be paid.

Follow these steps to pay bills in QBO:

1. Click on the **+ New** button and select **Pay Bills** in the **Vendors** column, as indicated:

    Vendors

    Expense

    Check

    Bill

    Pay Bills

    Figure 7.9: Navigating to Pay Bills from the Vendors menu

1. The **Pay Bills** form should appear:

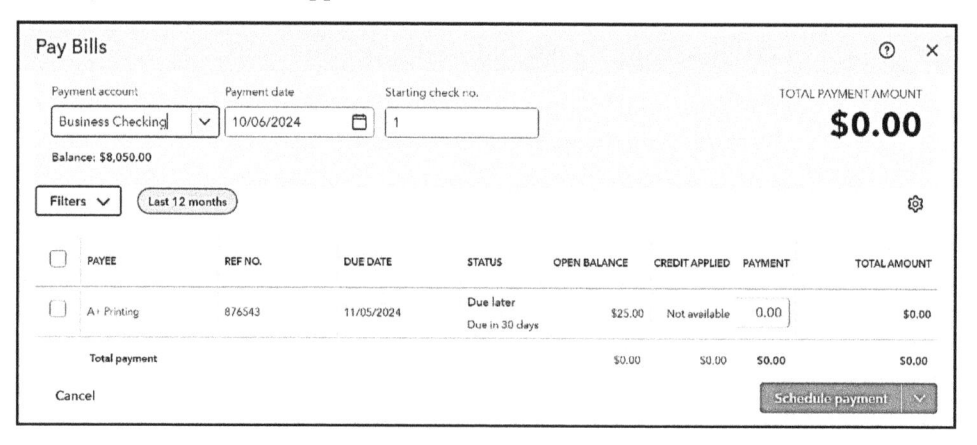

    Figure 7.10: The Pay Bills form displays

2. Complete the fields as indicated below to record the bill payment:

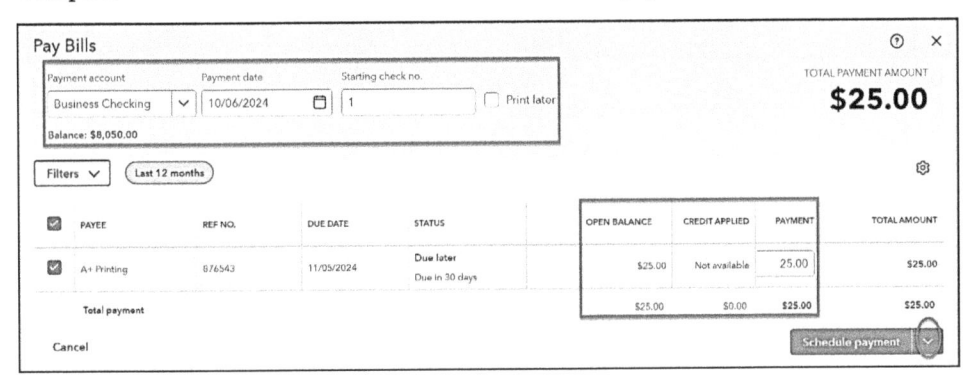

Figure 7.11: Completing the Pay Bills form

The following is a brief description of the fields in the **Pay Bills** form; all fields must be completed:

- **Payment account**: Select the bank or credit card account from which you want to deduct this bill payment. **Business Checking** is the account selected in our example.

- **Balance**: The amount next to the payment account is the current balance per QuickBooks.

> Please note that if you have banking transactions that have not been reviewed and added to QuickBooks, this balance will not match your actual bank account. Be sure to double-check your actual bank balance before making payments.

- **Payment date**: Select the date on which you will pay this bill. If writing a check, this will be the check date. The payment date is 10/06/2024 in our example.

- **Starting check no.**: If you are writing a check, make sure the check number is the next available number. The starting check number is 1 in our example.

- **Print later**: Put a checkmark in this box if you don't plan to print the check now, but will print it later on. We will show you how to print checks later in this chapter.
- **PAYEE**: This field will include a list of the payees with open bills. To select a bill for payment, put a checkmark in the box to the left of the **PAYEE** field. In our example, we have one payee with an open bill: `A+ Printing`.

> If you have more than one invoice for a vendor and your vendor prefers separate checks for each invoice, select the first invoice and save it, and then select each invoice one at a time, clicking **Save** in between each. Then, when you print checks, there will be separate checks for each invoice. An example where this might be useful is paying utility bills. Many utility companies prefer separate checks per account for which you are paying a bill.

- **REF NO.**: This field will include the invoice number (or bill number) that was entered when the bill was saved in QuickBooks. In our example, 876543 is the reference number for the `A+ Printing` bill.
- **DUE DATE**: This field will automatically populate with the due date that was entered when the bill was saved in QuickBooks. In our example, the due date for the `A+ Printing` bill is 11/05/2024.
- **OPEN BALANCE**: This field will automatically be populated with the unpaid amount of the bill. The open balance for the `A+ Printing` bill is $25.00.
- **CREDIT APPLIED**: If you have any open credits for a vendor, you will see them listed in this column. You can choose to use the credit or leave it and use it later on. In our example, A+ Printing has no open credits at this time.
- **PAYMENT**: Enter the amount you would like to pay in this field. You can pay the bill in full or make a partial payment. If you make a partial payment, QuickBooks will keep track of the remaining balance due for you to pay in the future. The payment amount is $25.00 for the `A+ Printing` bill. However, if you wish to pay less than the bill amount, you can do so by entering the amount you want to pay in this field.
- **TOTAL AMOUNT**: This column is automatically calculated for you. You cannot edit this field.

Chapter 7   229

3. You have the option to pay your bills online using your bank account (ACH) or debit/credit card information. There is a basic plan, which is free, and two paid plans starting at $15.00/month, plus transaction fees. To learn more about bill payment services, select the **Schedule Payments Online** button. However, if you prefer to manually write checks or print them from QuickBooks, click on the arrow to the right of **Schedule Payments Online** and select **Save**. We will cover how to write checks in QuickBooks later in this chapter.

When you pay a bill in QuickBooks, it only has an impact on the balance sheet report. The A/P balance goes down because you no longer owe your vendor for the bill, and the business checking account goes down because a payment has been made. If you pay the bill with a credit card, the credit card balance goes up, which increases liabilities.

The following report shows the journal entry recorded for the preceding bill if you are on accrual basis:

Transaction id	Date	Transaction type	Num	Name	Memo/Description	Account full name	Debit	Credit
∨ 14 (2)								
14	10/06/2024	Bill Payment (Check)	1	A+ Printing	-	Business Checking	-	$25.00
14	10/06/2024	Bill Payment (Check)	1	A+ Printing	-	Accounts Payable (A/P)	$25.00	-
Total for 14							$25.00	$25.00
							$25.00	$25.00

Figure 7.12: Journal entry to pay bills

In our example, the debit to A/P decreases total liabilities on the balance sheet report by $25.00. In addition, the credit to the business checking account decreases the total assets on the balance sheet report by $25.00. If you are on a cash basis, the debit would be to an expense account like printing, and reproduction costs and the credit would be to the business checking account.

In this way, paying bills in QuickBooks will give you access to detailed information about your expenses. You can run reports to show how much you are spending, which vendors you purchase from, and how often you purchase from them. These reports will help you control what you are spending your money on, which allows you to properly manage your expenses. In *Chapter 17, Vendor and Expenses Reports*, available online using this link: https://packt.link/supplementary-content-9781836649977 we cover reports in detail.

There may be times when you need to return merchandise or request a vendor credit. Let's cover how to enter vendor credits next.

Entering vendor credits into QuickBooks Online

If you overpay a vendor or receive a credit for damaged or returned merchandise, you can enter the credit memo into QuickBooks. By entering the credit memo into QBO, you can easily apply it to future purchases from the vendor. However, if you don't plan to order from that vendor again, you should request a refund. In our example, we received a credit on the order for the workbooks because the shipment was short by five workbooks, and we can apply the vendor credit to future purchases.

To enter vendor credits into QBO, you will need to complete the following steps:

1. Click on the **+ New** button and select **Vendor credit** in the **Vendors** column, as indicated here:

VENDORS

Expense

Check

Bill

Pay bills

Purchase order

Vendor credit

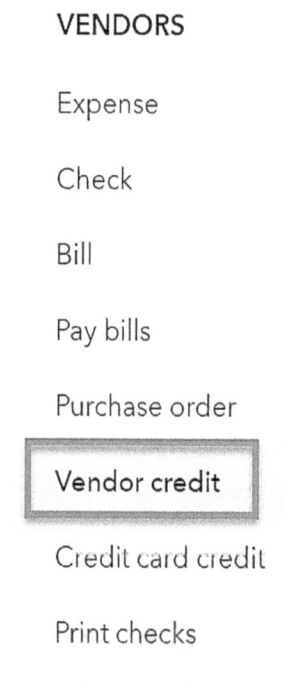

Credit card credit

Print checks

Figure 7.13: Navigating to the Vendor Credit form

2. The **Vendor Credit** form will appear. Complete the fields in this form as shown here:

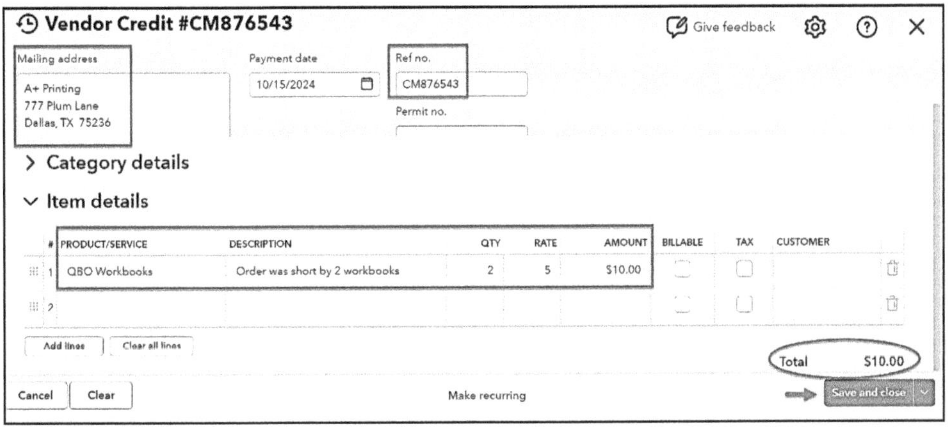

Figure 7.14: Completing the Vendor Credit form

The following is a brief description of the key fields in the **Vendor Credit** form. All fields must be completed, except for the **DESCRIPTION** field, which is optional but recommended:

- **Vendor**: Select a vendor from the drop-down menu. In our example, **A+ Printing** is the vendor.

- **Mailing address**: This field will automatically populate for vendors you have previously created in QuickBooks. If this is a new vendor, you can enter the address in this field. In our example, the address is 777 Plum Lane, Dallas, TX 75236.

- **Payment date**: Enter the date that appears on the vendor credit memo. Our payment date is 10/15/2024.

- **Ref no.**: The reference number is the vendor credit memo number assigned by the vendor supplier. If the vendor credit memo does not include a unique number, create one. Having a unique vendor credit memo number allows QuickBooks to track vendor credits and alert you if there is a duplicate number used. If a vendor credit memo does not include a number, I typically use the letters **CM**, short for credit memo, and the original bill number paid. The vendor credit memo number in our example is CM876543.

- **Category details:** Complete this section if you have purchased services or non-inventory expenses from the vendor. Since we have purchased workbooks that are tracked in our inventory, we will complete the **Item details** section right below **Category details**.

- **Item details:** Complete this section if you have purchased an item added on QuickBooks that you need to keep track of quantity and/or costs for. From the drop-down menu, select the product/service purchased. If the item has not been added to QuickBooks, you can do so on this screen by selecting the **Add new** option. The new item window will display so that you can complete the item setup. For more information on adding a new item to the products and services list, see *Chapter 4, Managing Customer, Vendor, and Products and Services Lists*.

- **DESCRIPTION**: Enter a brief description of what was purchased in this field. In our example, the description is `Order was short by 2 workbooks`.

- **QTY:** Enter the total number of items the credit is for. In our example, the quantity is 2.

- **RATE:** This field should automatically populate with the rate that was set for the item. If not, enter the rate in this field. In our example, the rate is 5.

- **AMOUNT:** QuickBooks will multiply the **QTY** field by the **RATE** field to get the total amount of the credit. The total amount is $10 for the vendor credit from A+ Printing.

If you receive the credit before paying the original bill, when you enter the vendor credit into QBO, the A/P account will be reduced by the credit, and the inventory will be reduced by the same amount. Both of these accounts will only impact the balance sheet report; there is no impact on the income statement.

The journal entry that is recorded in QuickBooks for the preceding vendor credit is shown here:

Transaction id	Date	Transaction type	Num	Name	Memo/Description	Account full name	Debit
∨ 15 (2)							
15	10/15/2024	Vendor Credit	CM876543	A+ Printing	-	Accounts Payable (A/P)	$10.00
15	10/15/2024	Vendor Credit	CM876543	A+ Printing	Order was short by 2 workbooks	Inventory Asset	-
Total for 15							$10.00
							$10.00

Figure 7.15: Journal entry to record a vendor credit

Chapter 7   233

In our example, the debit to **Accounts Payable** decreases the current liabilities on the balance sheet report by $10.00, and the credit to **Inventory** decreases the total inventory on the balance sheet by $10.00. Creating recurring expenses can save you a lot of time, so let's cover this next.

Managing recurring expenses

In this section, we will show you how to create a template for recurring (repeat) expenses. Most businesses purchase goods and services from the same vendors. For example, rent and utilities are examples of recurring expenses that are generally paid monthly. Instead of creating these expenses from scratch each month, you can create a recurring expense, which is a template you can save with the vendor, amount, account, and other pertinent information.

When you are ready to pay a recurring expense, you can schedule the expense to be recorded automatically on a certain day. You can manually generate the expense when you need to pay it or have QuickBooks send you an alert when it's time to make a payment. Using recurring expense templates will save you time and will reduce the amount of manual data entry required.

Follow these steps to create a recurring expense in QuickBooks:

1. Navigate to the gear icon and select **Recurring Transactions** from the **Lists** column, as indicated here:

    Lists

    All Lists

    Products and Services

    Recurring Transactions

    Attachments

    Figure 7.16: Selecting Recurring Transactions from the Lists menu

2. Click the **New** button in the upper-right corner:

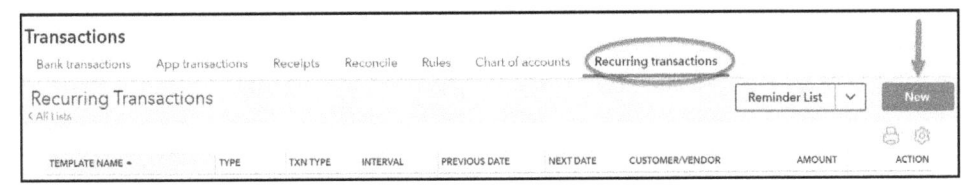

    Figure 7.17: Clicking New to create a new recurring transactions template

1. Select the transaction type from the drop-down menu, as indicated below, and click the **OK** button:

Select Transaction Type
Select the type of template to create

Transaction Type

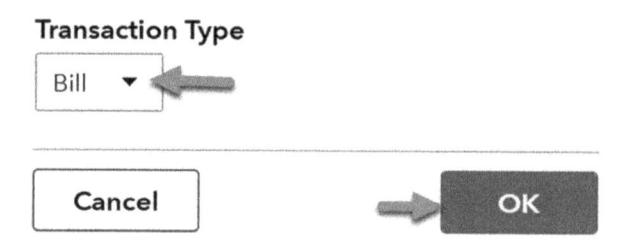

Bill ▼

Cancel   OK

Figure 7.18: Selecting the transaction type for a recurring transactions template

You can create a recurring transaction for several different types of transactions besides a bill. The other options available from the drop-down include **Check**, **Credit card credit**, **Credit memo**, **Deposit**, **Estimate**, **Expense**, **Invoice**, **Journal entry**, and a few others. While the screens may differ slightly, they will be very similar to what you see in this example.

2. Click **OK** to select **Bill** and a blank recurring transactions template will appear, called **Recurring Bill**. Complete the fields as indicated here:

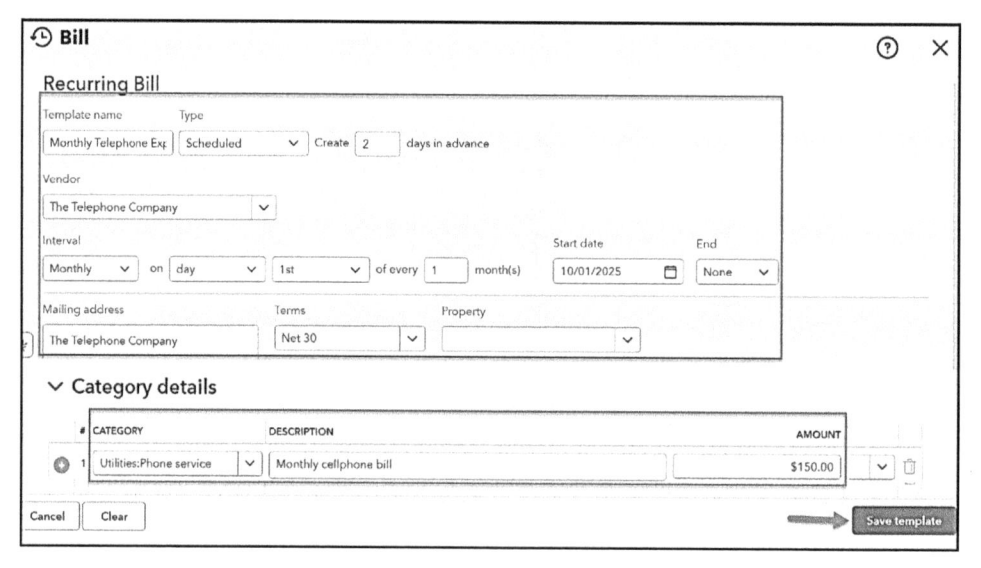

Figure 7.19: Completing the recurring transactions template (for better visualization, refer to https://packt.link/gbp/9781836649977)

Chapter 7

The following is a brief description of the information required to complete the recurring transactions template:

- **Template name:** This field should include the type of expense or the payee's name. **Monthly Telephone Expense** is the template name in our example.
- **Type:** From the drop-down menu, you can select **Scheduled**, **Reminder**, or **Unscheduled**. **Scheduled** is the type of template we are setting up.
- **Create X days in advance:** QuickBooks will create the transaction in advance of the due date. 2 days in advance is selected in our example.
- **Vendor:** Select the payee from the drop-down menu. If you have not added vendors to QuickBooks, you can add a new vendor by selecting **Add new** in the drop-down field. **The Telephone Company** is the vendor in our example.
- **Interval:** This field refers to how often you would like to create this recurring transaction. The options are **Daily, Weekly, Monthly,** or **Yearly. Monthly** is the interval selected in our example.
- **Start date/End:** Select the date on which you would like to start using the recurring transaction and, if applicable, you can select an end date, or select **None**. The start date is 10/01/2025 and the end date is **None** in our example.
- **Mailing address:** If you plan to mail your payment, you need to add a mailing address to this field. However, if the payment is automatically deducted from your business checking account or made using a credit card, you can leave this field blank.
- **Terms:** Include the payment terms for the vendor in this field. Payment terms are **Net 30** in our example.
- **CATEGORY:** From the drop-down menu, select the account that accurately describes the type of purchase made. The category is `Utilities: Phone service` for our example.
- **DESCRIPTION:** Include a brief description of the expense in this field. `Monthly cellphone bill` is the description in our case.
- **AMOUNT:** Enter the amount of the expense in this field. The amount is `$150.00` in our example.

3. Be sure to click **Save template** when you are done. After saving the template, the **Recurring Transactions** template list will appear, as indicated here:

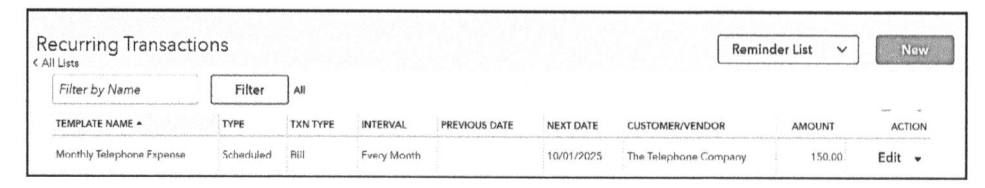

Figure 7.20: Recurring transactions template (expense)

4. In the **Recurring Transactions** template list, you will see the information previously entered in the template. The following info appears in *Figure 7.20*:

    - **TEMPLATE NAME:** Monthly Telephone Expense
    - **TYPE:** Scheduled
    - **TXN TYPE:** Bill
    - **INTERVAL:** Every Month
    - **NEXT DATE:** 10/01/2025
    - **CUSTOMER/VENDOR:** The Telephone Company
    - **AMOUNT:** 150.00
    - **ACTION:** From the drop-down menu in this column, you can choose **Edit**, **Use** (record), **Duplicate**, **Pause**, **Skip**, or **Delete**. **Edit** simply allows you to make changes to the template; **Duplicate** allows you to create a template with the same information; **Pause** allows you to stop the recurring transaction temporarily; **Skip** allows you to skip a recurring transaction; and **Delete** allows you to delete the template.

5. In addition to creating recurring transactions such as bills to pay expenses, you can also create the following types of recurring transactions:

    - **Check:** This is for payments made via check for products or services purchased.
    - **Credit card credit:** Credit card credit is money that was refunded to you from a previous credit card charge. This could also be a cashback rebate given to you by your credit card merchant for meeting a certain spending threshold.
    - **Credit memo:** A credit memo is issued to customers for a product they have returned or for services that were not provided.

- **Deposit**: A deposit is money received from customers, which is then deposited into your bank account. If you have customers who pay via wire transfer or **Automated Clearing House (ACH)** bank transfer on a periodic basis, you could set these deposits up as recurring.
- **Estimate**: An estimate is a bid or quote, created to provide customers with an approximate cost of your products or services.
- **Expense**: An expense is a payment for services received from a vendor/supplier.
- **Invoice**: An invoice is a sales form, used to record the sale of products or services provided on credit.
- **Journal entry**: A journal entry form is used to make adjustments to the financial statements before closing the books.
- **Refund**: A product returned by you or your customer will result in a refund of the payment that was made for the returned goods or unfulfilled services.
- **Sales receipt**: A sales receipt is used to record sales whereby payment is made immediately by the customer (for example, businesses such as clothing stores or restaurants).
- **Transfer**: A transfer is used to move money between bank accounts, such as business checking and savings accounts.
- **Vendor credit**: A vendor credit is a refund issued to you by a vendor supplier for a product you have returned or for services that were not performed.

Recurring transactions are ideal for loan payments or other cash disbursements for which you may not receive a monthly bill.

If you need to pay a bill that was unexpected or past due, *you don't need to enter it as a bill and then pay it*. Instead, you can pay it with a debit or credit card and categorize it when it comes into the banking center, *or* you can go directly to the check register and write a check. We will cover writing checks in the next section.

Writing checks

So far, we have discussed how to pay expenses by entering them as bills and paying them at a later date, and how to set up recurring expenses. A third way in which you can record expenses for your business is by writing checks. The benefit of writing checks directly in QuickBooks is that you don't have to waste time manually writing a check.

Instead, you can create checks and print them directly from QuickBooks. This is ideal for vendors that typically don't accept debit or credit card payments.

Follow these steps to write checks in QBO:

1. Click on the **+ New** button and select **Check** in the **Vendors** column, as indicated below:

    Vendors

    Expense

    Check

    Bill

    Pay Bills

Figure 7.21: Navigating to Check

1. The following screenshot shows the fields of information to be completed in the **Check** form:

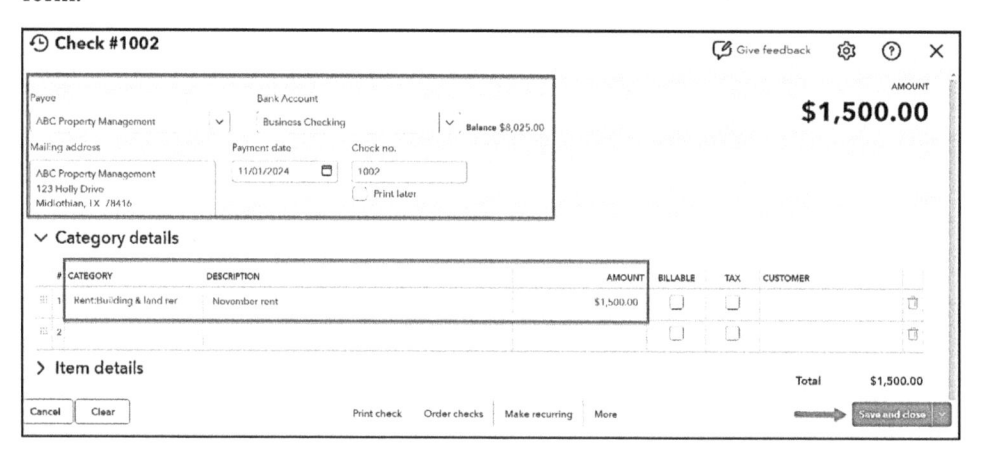

Figure 7.22: Completing the Check form

2. The following is a brief description of the information in the **Check** form:

    - **Payee**: From the drop-down menu, select the vendor to whom you are making a payment. If you haven't added vendors, you can do so by selecting **Add new** from the drop-down menu. `ABC Property Management` is the payee in our example.

- **Bank Account**: This field will automatically populate with your business checking account. However, if you have more than one checking account, be sure to select the correct account from the drop-down menu. `Business Checking` is the bank account in our example.
- **Balance**: Based on the bank account selected, you will see the current balance (per QuickBooks) of the business checking account you have selected. The current balance in the business checking account is `$8,025.00` in our case.
- **Mailing address**: This field will automatically be populated with the information on file for the payee. In our case, the mailing address is `123 Holly Drive, Midlothian, TX 78416`.
- **Payment date**: This date should reflect the check date. In our example, the payment date is `11/01/2024`.
- **Check no.**: The check number will automatically be populated with the next available check number. The check number is `1002` in our example.

> You can also use the **Check** form to record expenses paid with a debit card. Instead of entering a check number in the **Check no.** field, you would use **DB** or **Debit**, indicating the expense was paid with a debit card. To record ACH transactions, you would put **ACH** in the check number field.

- **CATEGORY**: Select the category (account) that best describes the items purchased. In our example, the category is `Rent: Building & land rent`.
- **DESCRIPTION**: Enter a detailed description of the items purchased. `October Rent` is the description in our example.
- **AMOUNT**: Enter the amount of the purchase. The amount in our example is `$1,500.00`.

When entering a check into QuickBooks, it can have an impact on accounts that appear on both the balance sheet and the profit and loss (income statement). The balance sheet will always be affected because the bank account is included in the assets section of the balance sheet. However, the profit and loss will only be affected if you are buying services or purchasing items that you can expense like office supplies. Otherwise, if you purchase a product for resale (inventory), it will only have an impact on the balance sheet.

The following screenshot shows the journal entry recorded for the check in *Figure 7.23*:

Transaction id	Date	Transaction type	Num	Name	Memo/Description	Account full name	Debit	Credit
∨ 17 (2)								
17	11/01/2024	Check	1002	ABC Property Management	-	Business Checking		$1,500.00
17	11/01/2024	Check	1002	ABC Property Management	November rent	Rent:Building & land rent	$1,500.00	-
Total for 17							$1,500.00	$1,500.00
							$1,500.00	$1,500.00

Figure 7.23: Journal entry to record payment of a bill by check

In our example, Rent Expense increased by $1,500, which increases expenses on the profit and loss (income statement). The Business Checking account decreased by $1,500.00, which means assets have gone down on the balance sheet report.

After entering a check, you can choose to print the check immediately, or wait and print a batch of checks later on. In the next section, we will show you how to print checks.

Printing checks

In order to print checks, you must purchase check stock that is compatible with QBO. You can order checks from a variety of places, such as your financial institution, or directly from Intuit. Visit the *Intuit Checks and Supplies* (https://intuitmarket.intuit.com/checks) website to learn more.

Follow these steps to print checks:

1. Click on the **+ New** button and select **Print Checks** in the **Vendors** column, as indicated here:

   Vendors

   Expense

   Check

   Bill

   Pay Bills

   Purchase Order

   Vendor Credit

   Credit Card Credit

   (Print Checks)

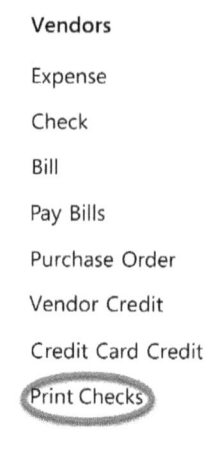

Figure 7.24: Navigating to Print Checks

Chapter 7 241

1. Follow the steps on the next screen to ensure that your printer is set up properly:

   Print checks setup

   ①

   PRINT SAMPLE

   ### Select a check type and print a sample

   a. Select the type of checks you use:

      ● Voucher   ○ Standard

      You can order checks from Intuit.

   b. Load blank paper in your printer.

   c. View preview and print sample

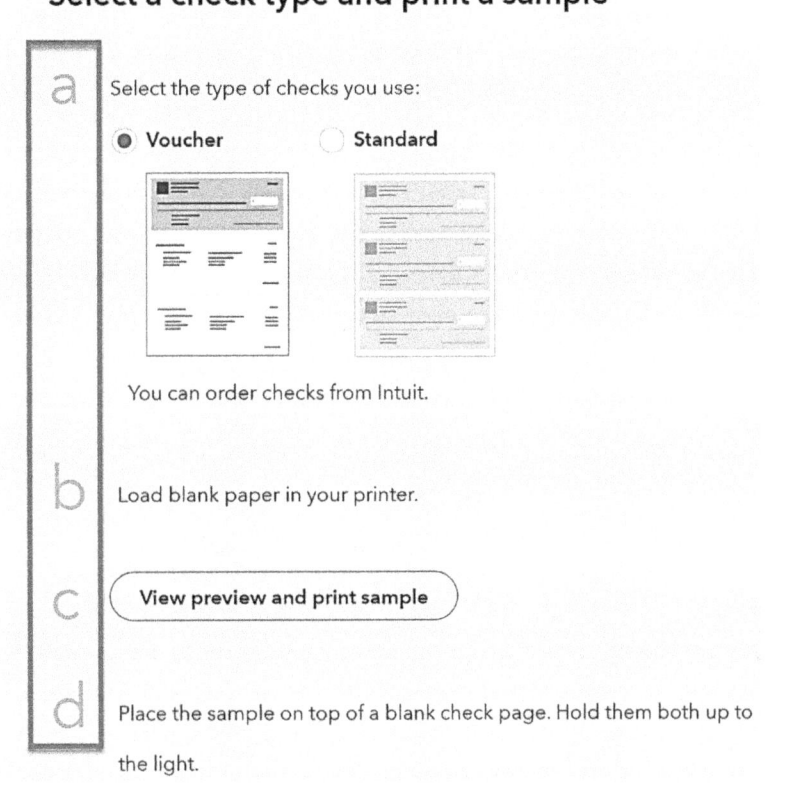

   d. Place the sample on top of a blank check page. Hold them both up to the light.

   Figure 7.25: Selecting the check type for printing checks

   a. **Select the type of checks you use**: There are two types of checks: **Voucher** and **Standard**. The **Voucher** check includes one check per page and two printed vouchers (one for you and one for the payee). The **Standard** check has three checks per page and no voucher.

   > A voucher is a printout of the payment details, including the bill number, amount, and check number.

b. **Load blank paper into your printer**: Before loading real check stock, run a test using a blank paper. Draw an arrow on the top of the first sheet of paper to see how the information will print so that you know how to load the check stock in your printer.

c. **View preview and print sample**: You can preview a sample check to see whether it is aligned properly. If not, follow the on-screen instructions to fix any issues before using real check stock. Checks will print to a preview screen where you can select your printer.

As discussed, printing checks directly from QuickBooks will save you time when you reconcile your bank account. Since expenses paid with a check are automatically recorded in QuickBooks when you save the check, you won't have to worry about manually entering them later on. One way to have quick access to source documents is to attach receipts and bills to transactions by using the capture and categorize receipts feature. We will discuss this shortly.

> Let's say you have pizza delivered to the office and you need to quickly print one check. Click the **+ New** button, select **Check**, enter the payment details, and select **Print check** at the bottom of the screen.

Editing, voiding, and deleting expenses

Like most transactions in QuickBooks, you can edit bills up until they are paid. However, after you have paid a bill, you will need to either record a credit memo if you overpaid or request a new bill if you have underpaid. You can still make changes to a paid bill if the changes do not affect the amount. To edit a bill, you need to go to the Vendor Center, select the vendor, and then click on the bill you wish to make changes to. After making the necessary changes, save the bill and close it.

You can also edit checks in a similar manner. As long as you haven't printed the check, you can make any changes necessary. Navigate to the check register, locate the check, and make the necessary changes. After you have printed a check, you will need to void it if it is incorrect. From the check register, select the check that needs to be voided. Click the **Edit** option and the check will display on your screen.

At the very bottom of the page, you will see a tab that says **More**; click on it and the following menu will appear:

Copy

Void

Delete

Transaction journal

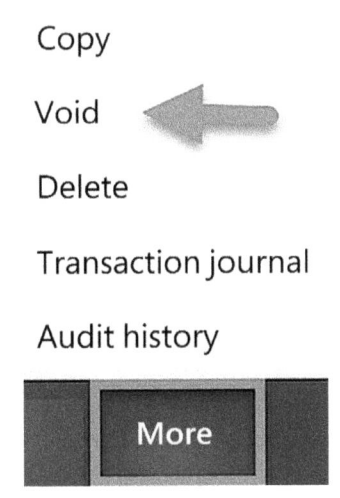

Audit history

More

Figure 7.26: Reaching the option for voiding an expense from the More button

For expenses in general, if you have not closed the books or reconciled the bank account for the period, you can make changes to expenses that were previously recorded.

> If you have closed the books or reconciled the bank account for the period, you *cannot* make changes to the transaction date or amount. If a correction to the books is required, you will need to consult with your accountant to discuss recording a journal entry. See *Chapter 9, Closing the Books in QuickBooks Online*, to learn more about journal entries.

Capturing and categorizing receipts and bills

Receipt capture allows you to attach receipts and bills to transactions in QuickBooks. As a result, you will be able to quickly access source documents when needed. This feature works in two different ways. First, you can attach receipts and bills to transactions previously entered into QBO. Second, you can use receipt capture to record a transaction for the first time. Of course, you can use both methods interchangeably.

Perform the following steps to capture a receipt or bill:

1. Navigate to **Transactions** and select **Receipts**.

2. The following screen will appear (make sure you are on the **Receipts** tab, as indicated here):

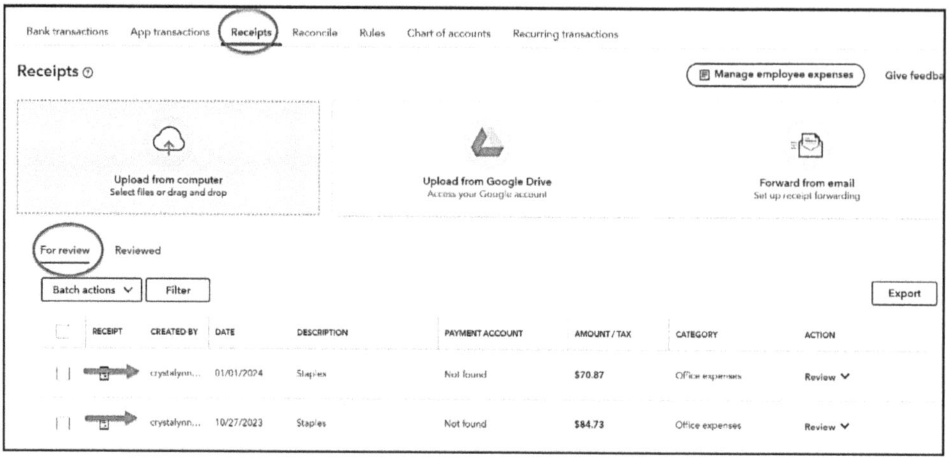

Figure 7.27: Reviewing and Uploading receipts to QBO (for better visualization, refer to https://packt.link/gbp/9781836649977)

3. There are three options available to capture receipts:

    - **Upload from computer**: If the bill or receipt is saved to your computer, select this option and navigate to where the receipt or bill is located on your computer.
    - **Upload from Google Drive**: If the receipt or bill is located in your Google Drive account, you can access it by clicking on this icon and following the on-screen instructions to locate the file in Google Drive.
    - **Forward from email**: By selecting this option, QuickBooks will take you through a few setup screens to create a custom email address that can be used to forward receipts and bills to QuickBooks.

    > Keep in mind that for each of the receipt capture options, there should only be *one receipt per file*. If you try to include more than one receipt in a file, QuickBooks will not be able to process the receipt capture.

4. Once you add receipts to QuickBooks, they will show up in the **For review** section just below the receipt capture options, as shown in *Figure 7.27*.

Chapter 7

5. You can click on the review link in the **ACTION** column located on the far right and the following info will display:

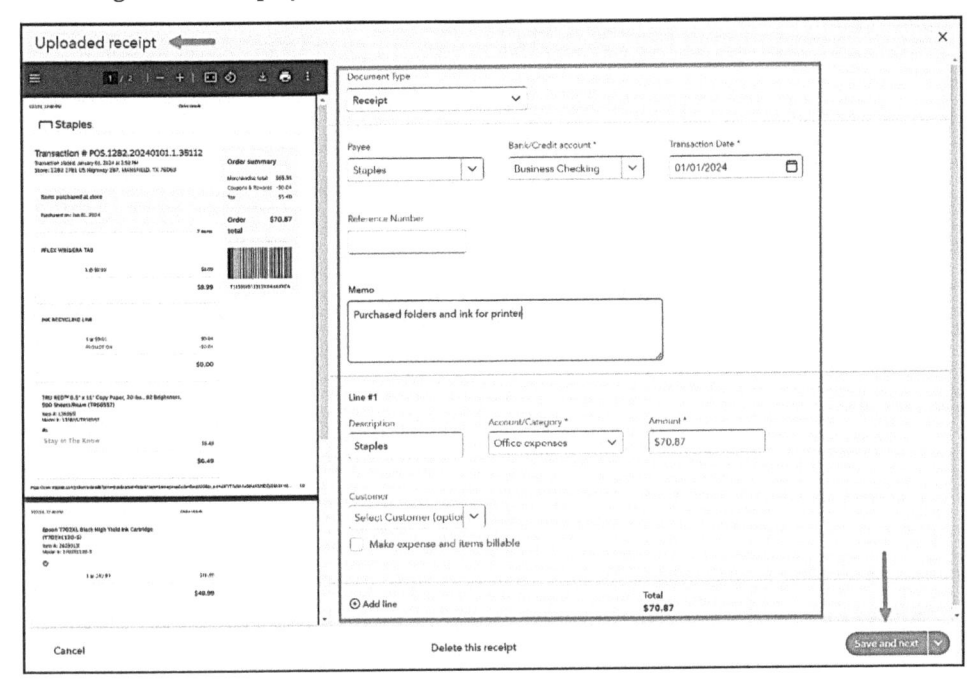

Figure 7.28: Reviewing a selected receipt in QBO

6. Complete any empty fields and review the information for accuracy in the fields that QuickBooks has automatically completed. Once you are satisfied with the information, you can save it, and it will be recorded in your books.

> 💡 You can also add receipts to transactions using the paperclip (**Attachments**) feature located at the bottom of the screen when you have an individual transaction open such as a bill.

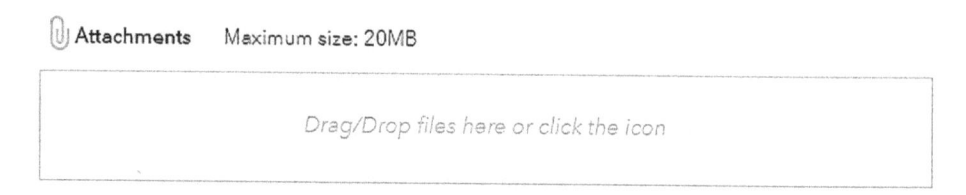

Figure 7.29: Button for attaching a receipt to a transaction

To summarize, we have covered how to use the capture and categorize receipts and bills feature, which allows you to attach source documents, such as bills, to existing transactions. In addition, you can create new transactions using this feature, which will save you the time you normally would have spent entering the data manually.

Summary

In this chapter, we showed you how to enter and pay your bills, how to enter vendor credits, how to manage recurring expenses, how to write checks, and how to print checks. We also covered the three ways in which you can upload bills and receipts to QuickBooks. Having a good understanding of the various options you have to record your expenses will ensure that they have been recorded properly. By recording your expenses in a timely manner, you have a good idea of what your obligations are, which helps you stay on top of your cash outflow.

In the next chapter, we will shift gears and discuss another core activity in the financial management of your business: the importance of properly setting up the employees and contractors that work for you.

Join our community on Discord

Join our community's Discord space for discussions with the authors and other readers:

https://packt.link/powerusers

Part 3

Managing Employees and Contractors

Managing employees and contractors can feel overwhelming, but QuickBooks Online simplifies the process. In this section, I'll guide you through setting up payroll, filing tax forms, and generating reports. You'll also learn how to work with 1099 contractors, including what forms you'll need and how to make payments. This part should give you the tools to handle your workforce efficiently and stay compliant with ease.

This part comprises the following chapter:

- *Chapter 8, Managing Employees and 1099 Contractors in QuickBooks Online*

8

Managing Employees and 1099 Contractors in QuickBooks Online

Managing payroll is one of the most important aspects of your business. If not done right, it could negatively impact your employees since they may not be paid the right amount. It could also result in interest and penalties if payroll taxes are not filed and paid on time.

There are four main aspects of managing payroll: setting up your employees with the proper deductions and benefit elections, processing payroll by ensuring the hours paid are correct and on time, generating payroll reports to gain an insight into total payroll costs, and filing payroll tax forms and making payments on time. In this chapter, we will cover the information required to properly set up payroll, how to subscribe to an Intuit payroll subscription, payroll reports that will provide you with insight into payroll costs, and the importance of filing payroll tax forms and making payments on time.

If you do not understand how payroll works or you do not wish to do your own payroll, it is highly recommended you subscribe to the QBO Elite payroll plan, which is the full-service payroll option. QBO Elite is equivalent to third-party payroll services like ADP and Paychex. We will provide additional details about the QBO Payroll Elite plan later on in this chapter.

We will show you how the Contractors Center is a one-stop shop to help you set up, manage, and pay independent contractors. One of the tasks that can be time-consuming is 1099 reporting. We will show you how the Contractors Center automates this process, which will save you the time you normally would have spent tracking down key information so that you can provide 1099 reports to both the contractors and the IRS each year.

In this chapter, we will cover the following topics:

- Setting up payroll
- Generating payroll reports
- Filing payroll tax forms and payments
- Managing 1099 contractors in QuickBooks Online
- Introducing QuickBooks Time

> The US edition of QBO was used in this book. If you are using a version that is outside of the US, results may differ.

Setting up payroll

The most important aspect of ensuring an accurate payroll is to set up the payroll properly before you run your first payroll. Setting up payroll involves gathering information about your employees, such as their names, mailing addresses, and Social Security numbers. As an employer, you will need a federal tax ID number and a business bank account for payroll checks and payroll taxes. You will need to determine what benefits you will offer employees, how often you will pay employees (for example, weekly, bi-weekly, or monthly), and the payment method you will use (for example, paper check or direct deposit).

> It is best practice to manage payroll out of a separate checking account from all other operating expenses. That way, you ensure the funds for the payroll taxes remain in the account until you remit payment to the state and federal government.

In the following sections, we will provide you with a checklist of information you need to have handy to complete your employer profile and set up employees. However, we will not actually set up payroll in this chapter because the details will vary depending on your business needs. First, we will show you how to set up payroll in QBO.

Payroll setup checklist and key documents

As discussed, the key to ensuring the accuracy of payroll checks, payroll tax forms, and payments is to ensure your payroll is set up properly. To set up payroll, you will need to gather information from your employees. Also, you will need to have certain documents and information handy to complete the employer information section. This information may vary state by state, so it is important while following this guide that you refer to your local employment development office for specific requirements.

The following table shows a summarized checklist of the information required to set up your payroll:

Employee info	Employer info
Hire date	Federal Employer Identification Number (FEIN)
Form W-4: Employee withholding info	State employer ID number (if applicable)
Form I-9: Employment Eligibility Verification	
Salary or hourly rate	Bank account information
Sick leave or vacation accrual rate	Employee benefits
Payroll deductions and contributions	Employee travel reimbursement policy
Payment method	Other compensation: bonuses, commissions
Direct deposit authorization form (if applicable)	Other deductions: wage garnishment

Table 8.1: Checklist of employee and employer info needed to set up payroll

The following is a brief explanation of the *employee* information required to set up payroll:

- **Hire date**: This is the official start date for an employee. This information will be used to determine benefits eligibility as well as vacation and sick pay if that is something you offer to your employees.

- **Form W-4**: This is an official form issued by the **Internal Revenue Service** (**IRS**) to gather employee withholding information, which determines the amount of federal tax withheld from paychecks. You can download this form from http://irs.gov and include it in your employee new hire packet. Be sure to check your state's Department of Revenue website for any withholding forms that are needed.

- **Salary or hourly rate:** This is the agreed-upon salary or hourly rate for an employee.
- **Sick leave or vacation accrual rate:** The number of hours an employee can earn toward sick or vacation leave.
- **Payroll deductions and contributions:** These are the deductions or contributions for health care, 401(k), or other benefits an employee has agreed to participate in. Deductions can be post-tax or pre-tax. Please check with your accountant if you are unsure of the taxability of any deductions.
- **Payment method:** Most employers will pay their employees in the form of a check or direct deposit. If the employee signs up for direct deposit, they will need to complete a direct deposit authorization form.
- **Direct deposit authorization:** If an employee would like their paycheck to be electronically deposited into their bank account, this form gives the employer the authority to do so. Employers must save this form on file along with other payroll information.

> Employee files are important for all businesses and should comply with all federal, state, and local requirements. When in doubt, seek guidance from a **Certified Public Accountant (CPA)** or human resource professional. New hire packets should be part of your normal business practices. These packets will generally include all of the necessary paperwork required under the employment law.

The following is a brief explanation of the *employer* information required to set up payroll:

- **Federal employer identification number (FEIN):** Employers are required to have a federal tax ID number before they can process payroll for employees. This number is used by the IRS to keep track of employee and employer payroll tax payments and filings. If you don't have an FEIN, you can apply for one at http://irs.gov.
- **State employer ID number:** If you live in one of the nine states that are subject to income tax, you will need to apply for a state employer identification number. Similar to the FEIN, the state employer ID number is used to keep track of payroll tax payments and filings.

> Most states have a website where business owners can apply for their state payroll tax IDs. It is important to know which taxes apply to your state and to consult an advisor regarding payroll tax withholding requirements for remote employees.

- **Bank account information**: As discussed, I recommend that you set up a separate bank account to keep track of payments made to employees in the form of payroll checks or direct deposits. Also, all payroll tax payments made to the IRS or your state need to be made out of this account. Since most payments are made electronically, you will need the routing number of your financial institution and the full account number.

    Similar to your business checking account, you will need to add the payroll bank account to your chart of accounts list in QuickBooks. Refer to *Chapter 3, Customizing QuickBooks for Your Business*, where we cover how to add an account to the chart of accounts list.

- **Employee benefits**: Details regarding benefits provided to employees will need to be entered into QuickBooks. This includes the employee and employer portions of health care, 401(k) plans, and sick leave and vacation pay.

- **Employee travel reimbursement policy**: If employees travel on behalf of your business and incur expenses, such as business meals, airfare, and hotel costs, you need to set up your payroll to reimburse employees for these.

    A simpler way to handle employee reimbursements is to process the payments outside of payroll. This would involve setting up an employee as a vendor and writing a check to reimburse them for business expenses paid with personal funds. Refer to *Chapter 4, Managing Customer, Vendor, and Products and Services Lists*, for instructions on how to add an employee as a vendor.

- **Other compensation**: If you pay bonuses or commissions, or make other forms of payment to employees, you will need to include this information in your payroll setup.

- **Other deductions**: On occasion, you may receive wage garnishments for employees who owe back taxes or child support. These are court-ordered requests that you cannot ignore. Instead, you must set up the garnishment amount as a deduction for the employee. These requests will typically have an end date that is based on the total outstanding amount. Be sure to set these payments up exactly as they are outlined in the letter. If you don't, you could be subject to penalties as a result.

Now that you have a good understanding of the key documents and information required to properly set up payroll, you are ready to sign up for an Intuit payroll subscription.

Signing up for an Intuit payroll subscription

Setting up payroll in QBO can be done in six easy steps:

1. Click on **Payroll** on the left menu bar to navigate to the Payroll Center, as shown here:

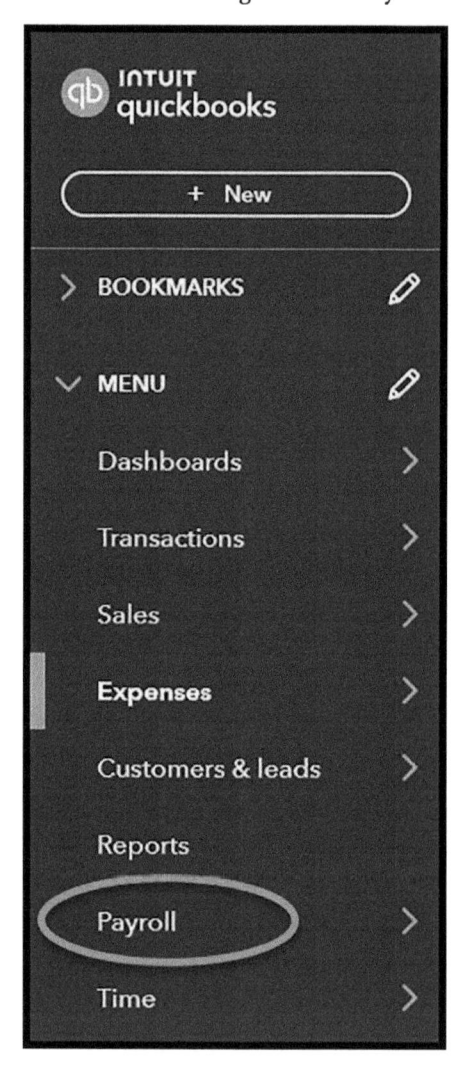

Figure 8.1: Navigating to the Payroll Center

Chapter 8 255

2. Select **Employees** and click the **See plans & pricing** button, as shown in *Figure 8.2*:

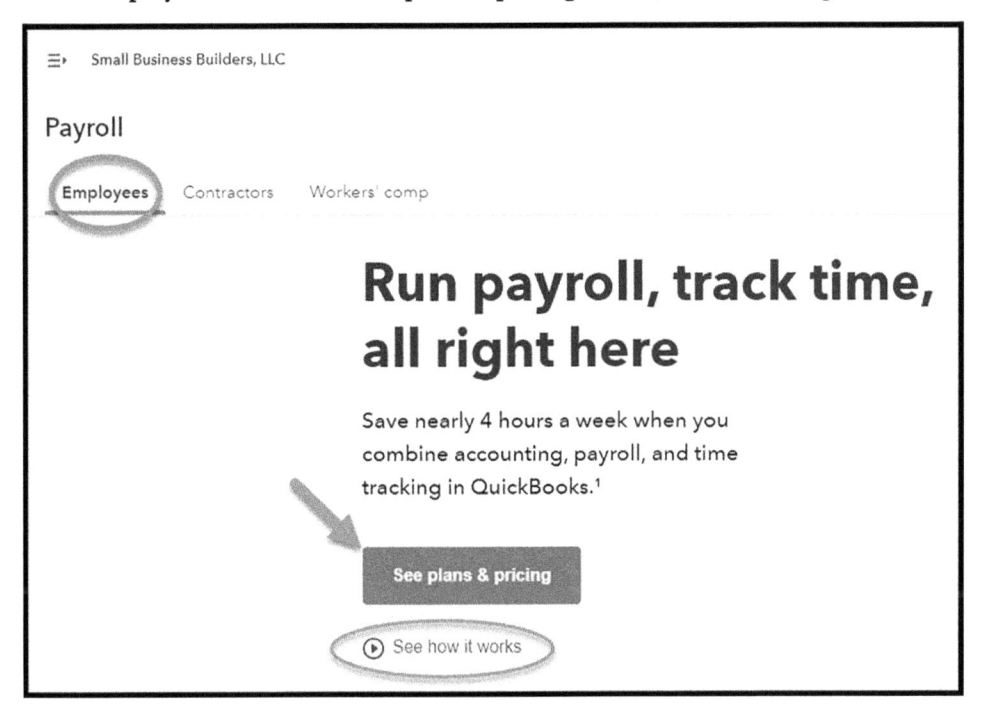

Figure 8.2: Review payroll plans & pricing

Directly below the button is a **See how it works** link. Click on this link to watch a short demo of how QBO Payroll works.

3. On the next screen, you will have the option of selecting a payroll plan, as indicated in *Figure 8.3*:

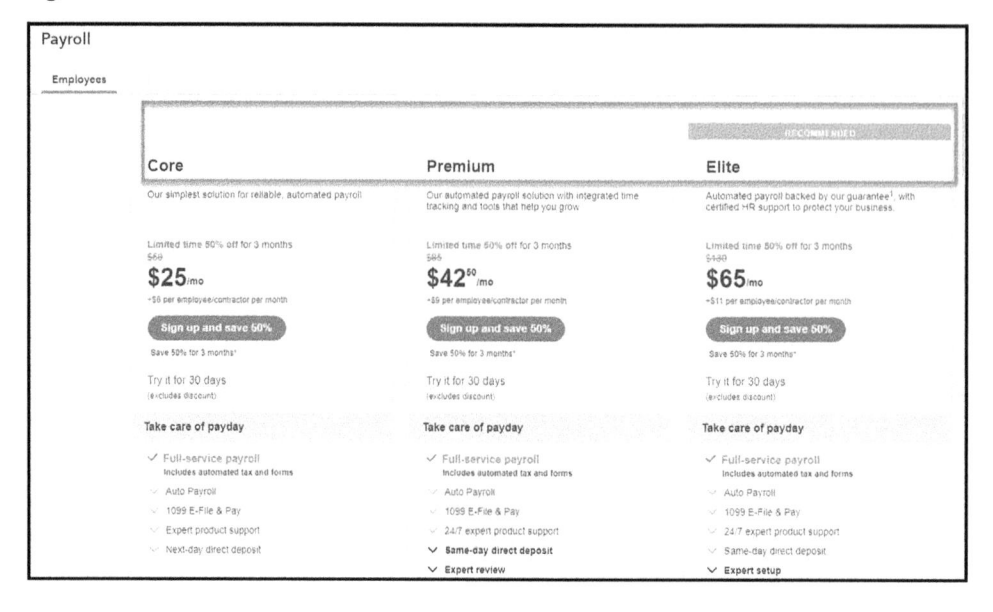

Figure 8.3: Selecting payroll features to begin setting up payroll

Based on your selections, the recommended payroll plan will show up to the right of these selections. In our example, **Elite** is the plan recommended for Small Business Builders, LLC.

> Pricing is based on the current rates and is subject to change. Please visit https://www.intuit.com/ (click on **Products** and select **QuickBooks**) for the most up-to-date information.
>
> As of the writing of this book, Intuit will no longer provide printing and mailing W-2s and 1099s as part of subscriptions. It will incur an additional fee of $4 per employee or contractor. Be sure to visit the website for the most up-to-date information on this.

The following is a brief explanation of each QBO payroll plan currently available:

- **Core**: This plan is ideal for employers who prefer to manage their payroll in-house. The subscription fee includes updated payroll tax tables that are used to automatically calculate payroll taxes and payroll checks for you—no manual calculation is required! With this plan, you can process payroll checks, electronically make payroll tax payments for state and federal taxes, and file payroll tax forms for state and federal taxes only. This plan does not offer local tax payments and filings. You will need to print the forms and upload them to the necessary local sites as required. This plan also includes *next-day direct deposit*.

    The Core plan is recommended for small payrolls and someone with payroll experience. This is due to the fact that the responsibility for local payroll tax filings and payments will remain with the business owner.

- **Premium**: This plan includes all of the features outlined in the Core plan plus automated local tax filings, *same-day direct deposit, workers' comp administration, an HR support center*, a QuickBooks expert who will review your payroll setup, and the ability to allow employees to track time using their mobile device. When setting up payroll, links will be available for applying for certain state ID numbers that are required.

- **Elite**: This plan includes customized setup by a QBO payroll expert, payroll processing, completion of tax forms, and automated payroll tax payments for federal, state, and local governments. Unlike the Core and Premium plans, it includes multi-state payroll filings, the ability to track projects from any mobile device, time tracking, tax penalty protection up to $25,000, access to a personal HR advisor, and 24/7 product support, which can be beneficial if there is an issue with a payroll or an individual paycheck. Voids and corrections must be made by the payroll service.

QuickBooks payroll is available in all 50 states and all payroll plans include the following key features:

- Unlimited payroll runs
- Calculated paychecks and taxes
- Automated taxes and forms
- Workforce portal
- Custom user access by setting permission levels

- Garnishment and deductions management
- Payroll reports
- Unlimited chat and telephone support at no additional cost

> It is advised to check local payroll tax filing requirements to confirm that the payroll subscription you have chosen can handle all necessary filings.

Depending on your business needs, setting up payroll and running payroll will vary based on the benefits offered and the applicable taxes. Therefore, we recommend you follow the step-by-step instructions within QuickBooks to learn how to set up and run payroll. To get started, click on the **Payroll** tab located on the left navigation bar. If you run into an issue, contact the payroll support team. You can do this within the software by clicking on the **Help** menu. Be sure to get payroll set up before you start running reports.

Generating payroll reports

By now, you know that QBO includes a library of preset reports that provide business owners with insights into every aspect of their business. There are several summary and detailed reports you can generate to gain insight into your payroll costs, payroll deductions and contributions, vacation and sick leave, and payroll taxes. If you have the Core plan, these reports will help you complete payroll tax forms and make payroll tax payments to the local tax authorities.

> It's important to note that if you have not signed up for a payroll subscription plan, you will *not* see the payroll reports covered in this chapter. These reports are only available to payroll subscribers.

Follow these steps to generate payroll reports:

1. Click on **Reports** on the left navigation bar, as indicated in *Figure 8.4*:

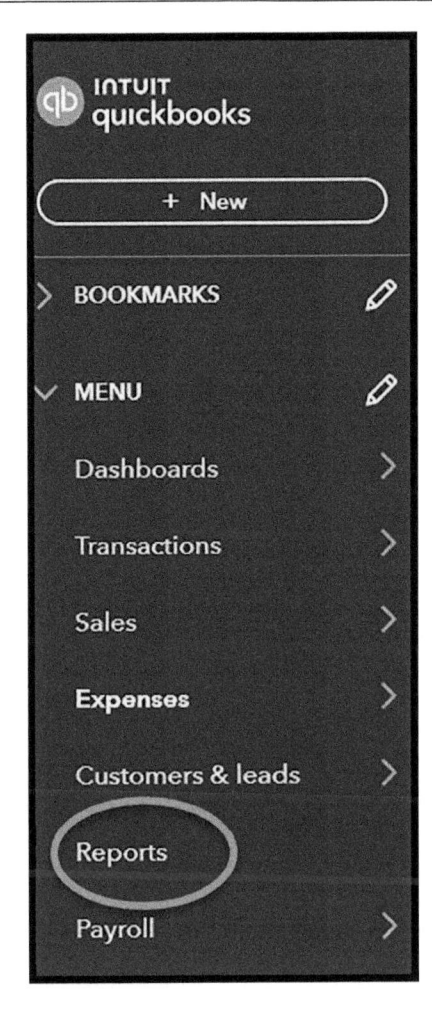

Figure 8.4: Navigating to the Reports Center

2. Scroll down to the **Payroll** section and you will see several reports, as indicated in *Figure 8.5*:

```
Payroll

Contractor Payments                    Payroll Tax Liability
Employee Details                       Payroll Tax Payments
Employee Directory                     Payroll Tax and Wage Summary
FFCRA CARES Act Report                 Recent/Edited Time Activities
Multiple Worksites                     Retirement Plans
[Paycheck History] ★                   State Mandated Retirement Plans
Payroll Billing Summary                Time Activities by Employee Detail
[Payroll Deductions/Contributions] ★
                                       Total Pay
Payroll Details                        [Total Payroll Cost] ★
Payroll Item List                      [Vacation and Sick Leave] ★
[Payroll Summary by Employee] ★
                                       Workers' Compensation
Payroll Summary
```

Figure 8.5: Payroll reports available for QBO Payroll subscribers

While you will find a number of great reports to help manage your payroll, I have found that there are five key reports that will help you stay on top of your payroll costs:

- **Paycheck History:** This report includes a list of paychecks that have been issued. You can use this report to edit check numbers, print pay stubs, and more.
- **Payroll Deductions/Contributions:** This report details payroll deductions by employee as well as employer contributions made for each pay period.
- **Payroll Summary by Employee:** This is a comprehensive report that includes wages, deductions, and taxes totaled by the employee or payroll period.
- **Total Payroll Cost:** This report includes all costs associated with paying employees, such as total pay, net pay, deductions, company contributions, and taxes.

- **Vacation and Sick Leave**: This report details the total vacation and sick pay that has been used as well as the remaining balance left.

3. To generate a report, simply click on the report and select the pay period you would like to see data for. Similar to other QBO reports, you can save payroll reports as PDF files or export them to Excel. Refer to *Chapter 16, Reports Center Overview*, available online using this link: https://packt.link/supplementary-content-9781836649977 for step-by-step instructions on how this works.

One of the key benefits of generating reports is that they include the information you need in order to file payroll tax forms and make payroll tax payments. In the next section, we will discuss your options for filing and making payroll tax payments.

Filing payroll tax forms and payments

Employers are required to file payroll tax forms and make payroll tax payments at the federal, state, and sometimes local levels. The due dates will vary by employer and are generally based on the dollar amount of the payroll and other factors specific to your business. The good news is that all QBO Payroll plans will take care of calculating, paying, and filing payroll taxes at the state and federal levels. As discussed, the Core plan is the only one that does not automatically take care of the local tax authority.

There are a few key reports that you should generate to help you understand the total cost of payroll to your business. These reports are also shown in *Figure 8.5*:

- **Payroll Tax Liability**: This report provides you with the details of how much payroll tax you are required to pay and how much you have already paid to state and federal tax authorities for a specified period of time.
- **Payroll Tax Payments**: This report provides you with the details of all tax payments you have made for a specific period of time.
- **Payroll Tax and Wage Summary**: This report shows total and taxable wages that are subject to federal and province/region/state withholding for a specific period of time.

While QBO Payroll handles the tax payments and filings on your behalf, it is still your responsibility to make sure that the tax forms and payments are submitted to the proper tax authorities on time. Otherwise, you could be subject to hefty penalties and fines. All payroll plans include unlimited tech support. Therefore, be sure to contact the Intuit payroll support team with any questions or concerns you may have regarding taxes.

> It is recommended that you keep a checklist of when your payroll taxes are due and when the related filings must be submitted.

Managing 1099 contractors in QBO

If you hire an individual to perform services for your business and they are not an employee, they are considered an independent contractor, also known as a **1099 contractor**. Payments to 1099 contractors must be tracked so that you can report this information to the IRS at the end of the year.

To ensure payments are tracked properly, you will need to set up contractors in QuickBooks, add an account to post all payments to, pay contractors with a paper check (or an **electronic fund transfer** (EFT), or debit/credit card), and provide a 1099 form to all the contractors who meet the threshold at the end of the year. If the total payments to a contractor equal $600 or more, you must issue a 1099 form and report this information to the IRS. Failure to track and report payments to 1099 contractors could lead to penalties and fines.

> To determine what constitutes a 1099 vendor vs an employee, be sure to visit http://irs.gov to learn more about whether someone qualifies as a 1099 vendor. The laws around this are updated each year so be sure to visit the IRS website to stay up to date on changes made each year.

Let's get started with setting up 1099 contractors in QuickBooks Online.

Setting up 1099 contractors

It's important to set up 1099 contractors correctly in QuickBooks to ensure payments are tracked for 1099 reporting purposes. Within the last year, there have been *significant* improvements made in QBO to streamline the process of setting up and tracking payments to 1099 contractors. In previous years, you would have to set up a contractor in the Vendor Center and flag the vendor as a 1099 contractor. In the most recent version of QBO, there is now a Contractors Center that allows you to collect the information normally provided on a W-9 form electronically. A W-9 form is similar to a W-4 form for an employee. It includes the vendor's name, mailing address, business entity type (sole proprietor, partnership, S-Corp, or C-Corp), tax ID number, and signature.

To set up a new contractor, you simply send an invitation to them, which requires them to create a user ID and password. Once they do so, they can complete the W-9 form online. Once the form is completed, you will be notified and can go into QBO and view the electronic W-9 form.

Chapter 8　　　　　　　　　　　　　　　　　　　　　　　　　　　　　　　　　　　　　263

Within the Contractors Center, you can also process contractor payments and generate reports as needed.

> It is best practice to obtain a completed W-9 form from each contractor before you make your first payment to them. Having this information is important because you will need it to create a 1099 form, if applicable.

Follow these steps to set up a 1099 contractor in QuickBooks:

1. Navigate to **Payroll** and the **Contractors** tab, as shown in *Figure 8.6*:

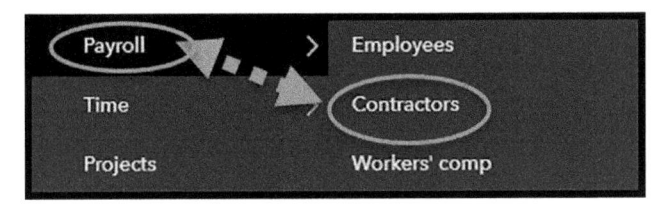

Figure 8.6: Navigating to the Contractors Center

2. Ensure that you are on the **Contractors** tab and click **Add your first contractor**. If you already have contractors in QBO, your screen will look slightly different and you will see the option to **Add a contractor**:

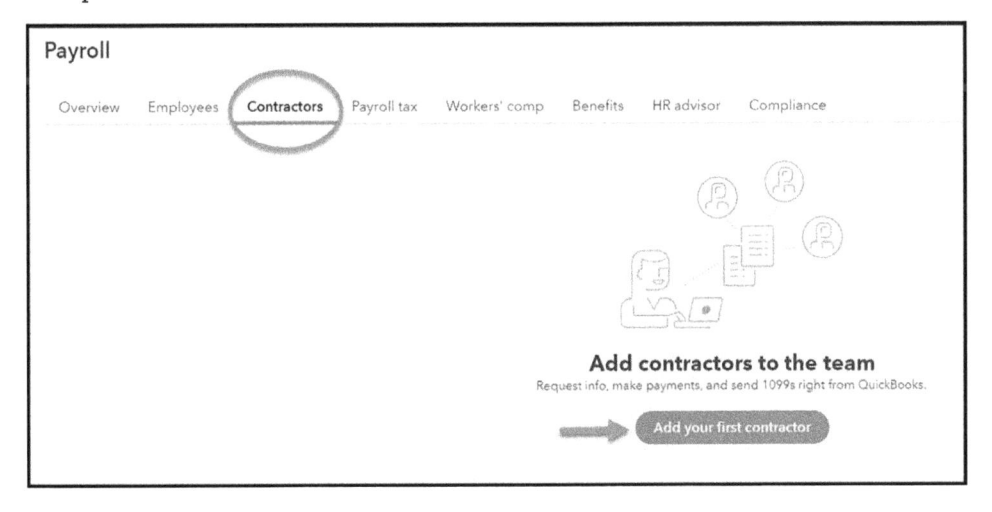

Figure 8.7: Clicking on Add your first contractor

3. The following screen will display. Complete the fields and click on the **Add contractor** button, as shown in *Figure 8.8*:

Figure 8.8: Completing the fields to add a new contractor

Before QBO allows you to add a contractor, you will see a popup that requires you to enter a security code that will be sent to you via text message or email. You will not be allowed to proceed until you enter this code. This level of security is to ensure that the person who is adding a contractor is authorized to do so. Once the code is entered, the email invitation will be sent to the contractor, per the note right below the **Email** field shown in *Figure 8.8*. Contractors will gain access to a portal where they can manage W-9 information, banking information if they would like to be paid via direct deposit, and 1099 information.

Chapter 8 265

4. After completing the necessary fields, you will see the new contractor listed in the **Contractors Center**, as shown in *Figure 8.9*:

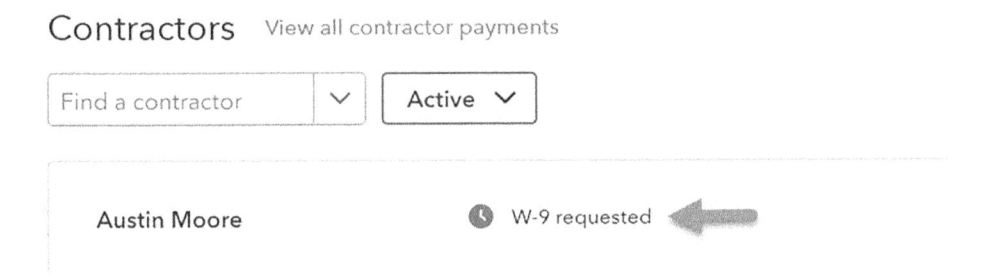

Figure 8.9: Status of the new contractors listed in the Contractors Center

After adding a new contractor, you will see them listed within the Contractors Center along with a note indicating that the W-9 form has been requested.

5. Once the W-9 form has been completed, the status will change to **W-9 ready**, as shown in *Figure 8.10*:

Figure 8.10: Reviewing the W-9 status for contractors

Repeat these steps for each 1099 contractor you pay throughout the year. Once you have added all of your contractors to QuickBooks, you are ready to make payments. We will discuss how to track and pay 1099 contractors next.

Tracking and paying 1099 contractors

The simplest way to keep track of payments to 1099 vendors is to create an account called **Contractor labor expense**. This account should be added to your chart of accounts list and used to post all 1099 payments. For more information on adding accounts to the chart of accounts, refer to *Chapter 3, Customizing QuickBooks for Your Business*.

You can pay 1099 contractors within the Contractors Center. Follow the steps below to set up a payment to a contractor:

1. Navigate to the Contractors Center (**Payroll | Contractors**).

   The following screen will display:

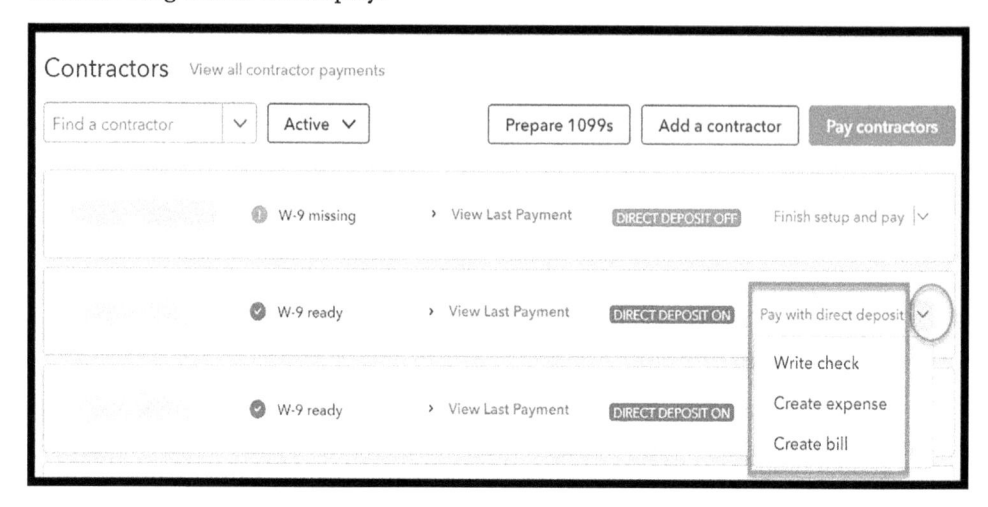

   Figure 8.11: Paying contractors within the Contractors Center

2. In the far-right column, click on the arrow to select the payment method (**Pay with direct deposit, Write check, Create expense,** or **Create bill**). Please note that if you would like to pay contractors with direct deposit, you will need to enter their payment details (bank account and bank routing number) before you can do so. This information can be entered by selecting the **Finish setup and pay** link that is shown in *Figure 8.11*.

3. If you select direct deposit, you will see the screen shown here:

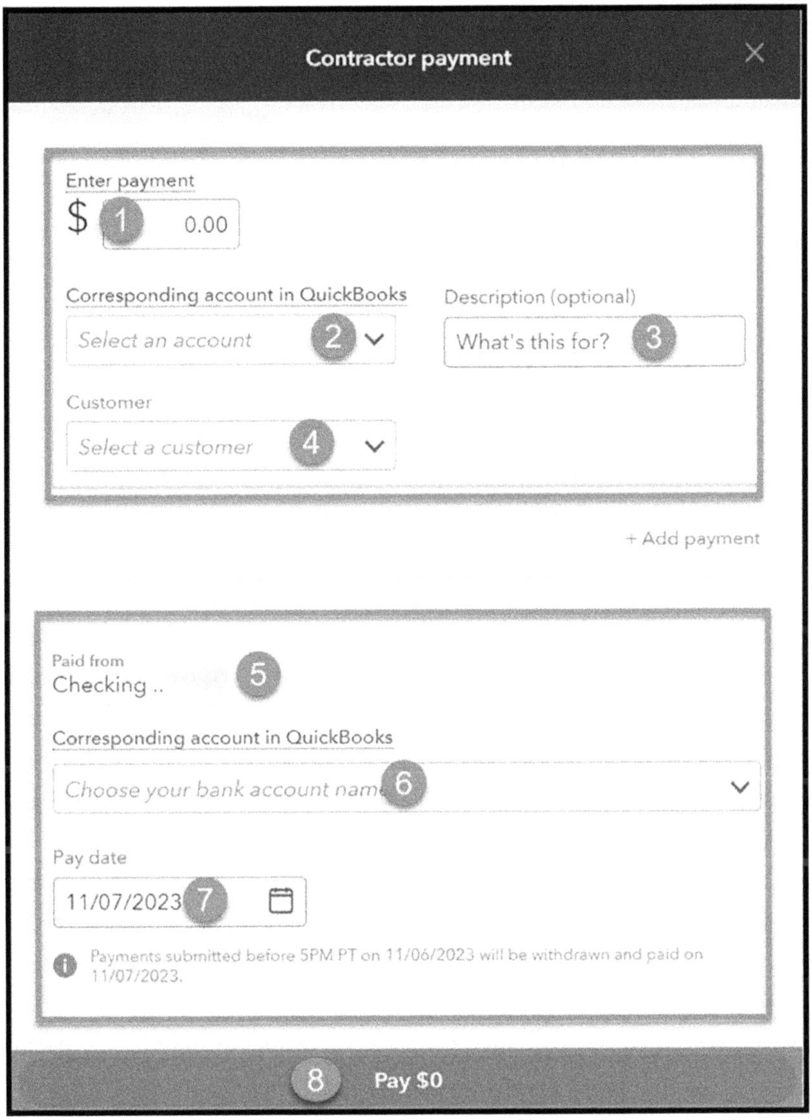

Figure 8.12: Paying a contractor via direct deposit in QBO

Complete the fields indicated in *Figure 8.12* as follows:

- **Enter payment (1)**: Enter the total amount of the payment.
- **Corresponding account in QuickBooks (2)**: From the dropdown, select the expense account (e.g., contractors expense, website design, etc.).
- **Description (3)**: Enter a brief description of the type of services provided by the contractor (e.g., monthly social media marketing). This field can also indicate the time period the payment is for (e.g., services for 11/01 to 11/15).
- **Customer (4)**: If you do have customers that you bill back for time worked by contractors, you can select the customer from the dropdown. This payment will also be included in the unbilled expenses account, which you can add to a customer's invoice in order to be reimbursed.
- **Paid from (5)**: You will see the bank account that the payment will be deducted from. This will typically be the business checking account or your payroll account if you have a separate account for employee and contractor payments.
- **Corresponding account in QuickBooks (6)**: From the dropdown, select the bank account in QuickBooks that corresponds to the actual bank account the payment will be deducted from in point 5 above.
- **Pay date (7)**: Select the date you would like the payment to be made. QBO allows you to set a date in the future. Typically, this will be the next business day as long as you submit it before 5 PM PT, as indicated in *Figure 8.12*.
- **Pay (8)**: Click on the **Pay** button to submit the payment.

After the payment is submitted, you will receive an email indicating that this payment is in process. If you have added their email address in QBO, the contractor will also receive an email to let them know the payment is in process. The email will include the payment amount and the date the payment has been scheduled for.

Now that you know how to add independent contractors to QuickBooks, set up an account to track payments, and make payments, it's time to discuss what you will do with this information.

1099 year-end reporting

1099 year-end reporting consists of printing and mailing 1099 forms to contractors who meet the $600 threshold and reporting this information to the IRS by January 31st each year. This date is subject to change, so be sure to visit http://irs.gov each year to confirm the due date.

Similar to a **W-2 form** or **Wage and Tax Statement** for an employee that includes the amount paid in wages for a calendar year, the 1099 form includes the amount you have paid to a contractor within the calendar year.

This form is used by independent contractors to report their earnings for the year on their tax returns. Failure to provide this information to the IRS and the contractors could result in fines and penalties.

When you are ready to generate 1099 forms, the process is very simple. First, you review the accuracy of your information and the basic contact information for each contractor. Then, you review the payments that have been flagged as 1099 payments. If this information is correct, you can have Intuit process your 1099 forms electronically for a fee. Another option is to manually print and mail the 1099 forms yourself.

There are various types of 1099 forms. The most common are Form 1099-DIV, which is issued for dividends and distributions, Form 1099-INT, which is issued for interest income, and Form 1099-MISC, which is for miscellaneous income.

> Currently, the IRS requires you to exclude payments made to a 1099 vendor via debit card, credit card, or gift card from Form 1099-MISC. In addition, payments made through third-party payment networks, such as PayPal and QuickBooks Payments, should also be excluded. Instead, these payments are reported by the card issuers and third-party networks on Form 1099-K. The 1099 vendor will receive a copy of Form 1099-K directly from the card issuers.

Follow these steps to learn how to do 1099 reporting:

1. Navigate to the **Contractors Center**, as shown in *Figure 8.13*:

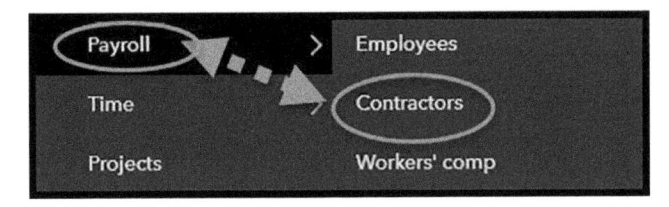

Figure 8.13: Navigating to the Contractors Center

2. Click on **Prepare 1099s**, as shown in *Figure 8.14*:

Figure 8.14: Clicking the Prepare 1099s button

3. If this is your first time preparing 1099s, the following screen will appear. Click the **Let's get started** button:

Figure 8.15: Clicking Let's get started to file your 1099 forms

If you have prepared 1099s in QBO before, you will see the deadline for e-filing 1099s and the deadline for printing and mailing 1099s for the upcoming tax season.

Chapter 8

4. On the next screen, you can review your company information and make any necessary corrections:

Figure 8.16: Reviewing your company info for accuracy

5. Click the **Save** button when you are done.

6. Click **Next** at the bottom of the screen. Then, select the box and the account you have categorized 1099 payments to, from the list shown in *Figure 8.17*:

Map your QuickBooks contractor payments to 1099 boxes

1. First select the checkbox for each type of contractor payment you recorded last year. Each payment type corresponds to two most common types.)
2. Then for each payment type selected, select all the QuickBooks expense accounts you used last year. Need more help

If you're not sure which expense accounts you used, you can run a report of all last year's expenses marked for 1099.

Common payment types

- [ ] Non-employee compensation (most common) Box 1 1099-NEC
- [ ] Rents Box 1 1099-MISC

Direct sales

- [ ] Direct Sales - NEC Box 2 1099-NEC
- [ ] Direct Sales - MISC Box 7 1099-MISC

Other payment types

- [ ] Royalties Box 2 1099-MISC
- [ ] Other Income Box 3 1099-MISC
- [ ] Medical Payments Box 6 1099-MISC
- [ ] Substitute Payments in lieu of dividends or interest Box 8 1099-MISC
- [ ] Crop Insurance Proceeds Box 9 1099-MISC
- [ ] Gross Proceeds Paid to an Attorney Box 10 1099-MISC
- [ ] Fishing Boat Proceeds Box 5 1099-MISC
- [ ] Fish Purchased for Resale Box 11 1099-MISC

Federal tax withheld (very uncommon) When should I withhold taxes?

- [ ] Federal Tax Withheld - NEC Box 4 1099-NEC
- [ ] Federal Tax Withheld - MISC Box 4 1099-MISC

Figure 8.17: Mapping QuickBooks contractor payments to 1099 boxes (for better visualization, refer to https://packt.link/gbp/9781836649977)

> In general, you will select the first box, **Non-employee compensation (most common)**, on the 1099 forms you generate for the contractors you have paid. In the dropdown below this box, select the account (category) these payments were posted to (e.g., **Contract labor**). To learn more about which box to select, refer to the IRS instructions for Form 1099. You can find this information at http://irs.gov.

7. On the next screen, review your contractors' information to ensure that it is accurate:

Review your contractors' info
Make sure your contractors' details are correct. To see which contractors meet the 1099 threshold, click **Next**.
Need to add anyone?

CONTRACTOR NAME	ADDRESS	TAX ID	EMAIL	ACTION
Fred Flintstone	456 Bedrock Avenue Beverly Hills CA 90210	95-6789543	flintstone@bedrock.com	Edit
Wilma Flintstone	456 Bedrock Avenue Beverly Hills CA 90210	95-1234567	wflintstone@bedrock.com	Edit

Figure 8.18: Reviewing contractors' info for accuracy

Note that you cannot print 1099 forms if your contractor's mailing address and tax ID (or Social Security number) are missing. You must obtain this information prior to printing the 1099 forms.

8. A list of contractors that meet the 1099 threshold will be displayed on the next screen:

Check that the payments add up
Only those contractors you paid above the threshold (usually $600) get a 1099.
IMPORTANT: Credit card payments to contractors should be **excluded**. Why?
Need to add or edit payments?

2018 | 1099 contractors that meet threshold

CONTRACTOR	BOX 7	TOTAL	EXCLUDED	ALL PAYMENTS
Fred Flintstone	$1,200.00	$1,200.00		$1,200.00
Wilma Flintstone	$600.00	$600.00		$600.00

Figure 8.19: Reviewing 1099 payments for accuracy

To meet the 1099 threshold, contractors must have received payments totaling $600 or more within the calendar year. If a contractor was paid less than $600, you are not required to issue a 1099 form and the contractor won't show up in the preceding list.

9. On the next screen, select the 1099 plan that works best for you:

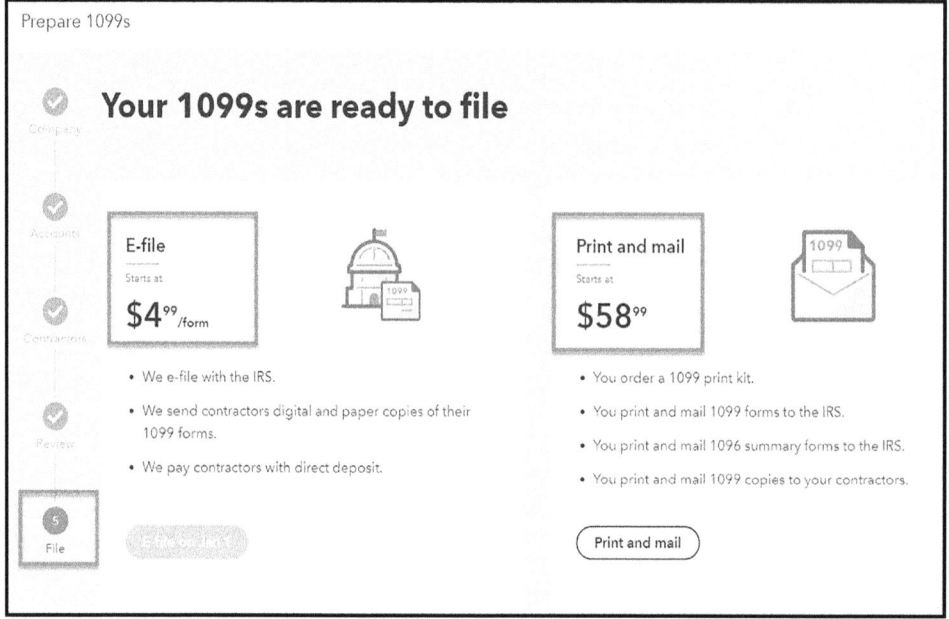

Figure 8.20: Choosing the method you wish to use to file 1099 forms

The two 1099 plans available are:

- **E-file**: This plan starts at $4.99/form and is a full-service plan. Intuit will e-file 1099 forms with the IRS on your behalf, and send contractors digital and paper copies of their 1099 forms. If you choose to, you can also pay contractors with direct deposit at no additional cost.

  > This is the most efficient way to process your 1099 forms. They will be sent to contractors as well as the IRS. You will also have a copy to keep on file for your records. While printing and mailing is an option, it is recommended to file electronically if possible.

- **Print and mail**: This plan starts at $58.99 and is ideal for business owners who prefer to process their 1099 forms in-house. Intuit will mail you a 1099 kit that will include blank 1099 forms you can print on. You are responsible for mailing all 1099 forms to your contractors and sending copies to the IRS before the deadline.

Please note that the pricing of these plans may differ. Visit `https://www.intuit.com/` for the most up-to-date pricing plans available. To select a plan, just click on the plan you want to choose and follow the onscreen prompts to complete filing your 1099 forms.

Another way that you can track the hours worked by employees and contractors is to use the QuickBooks Time feature. QuickBooks Time allows you to ensure that all billable hours are accounted for so that your customer invoices are accurate.

Introducing QuickBooks Time

If you have a service-based business that relies on the ability to keep track of billable hours, **QuickBooks Time (QB Time)** is a great solution. Similar to QBO Payroll, there are three QuickBooks Time plans: Basic, Premium, and Elite. The Basic plan is included in all QBO subscriptions at no additional cost. However, you (or your employees/contractors) will have to enter time manually with the basic plan.

Below is a comparison chart of the features included in the Premium and Elite plans:

	Premium	**Elite**
Cost	$20/month + $8 per user per month	$40/month + $10 per user per month
Seamless QuickBooks integration	✓	✓
Streamlined payroll and invoicing	✓	✓
Workforce mobile app	✓	✓
Mobile crew time entry	✓	✓
Web-and cloud-based time tracking	✓	✓
See who's working	✓	✓
Track time to jobs and customers	✓	✓
Real-time reports	✓	✓

Calculate billable hours	✓	✓
Unlimited live customer support	✓	✓
Assign jobs and projects to employees		✓
Track time to projects		✓
Track project progress to plan		✓
Project estimates vs. actuals reporting		✓
Project activity feed and messaging		✓

Table 8.2: Comparing Premium and Elite QuickBooks Time plans

As you can see in the preceding table, both the Premium and Elite plans include the following features:

- **Seamless QuickBooks integration**: One of the benefits of using QB Time over a third-party company is you can manage time tracking directly in QuickBooks. There are no spreadsheets to import or journal entries to record to get the data into QBO; it's automatically there!

- **Streamlined payroll and invoicing**: When you add employees and/or contractors to QB Time, their hours can be added to payroll to pay hourly employees, contractor payments, or customer invoices whose invoices are based on billable hours for a job or project.

- **Workforce mobile app:** With the Workforce app, employees can clock in and out and access their paystubs, W-2s, time off, and much more. As an employer, you can review and approve time sheets, verify who is on-site at a job or on the road, and so much more.

- **Mobile crew time entry:** Users have a variety of options for clocking in and out. For example, mobile workers can use their smartphone app.

- **Web- and cloud-based time tracking:** In addition to mobile workers using their smartphone app, office-based employees can use their web browsers, and shift-based workers can use an on-site tablet-based digital punch card called Time Clock Kiosk.

- **See who's working**: Using GPS technology, you can see where your team is working and when they clocked in/out so that you can schedule new jobs anytime from anywhere.
- **Track time to jobs and customers**: To ensure accurate customer billing, you can easily track the time for all jobs and customers so those hours can be included on the invoice.
- **Real-time reports**: QuickBooks Time includes a library of reports to help you manage all employee and contractor hours. You won't have to create reports from scratch; these reports are automatically included with your subscription to a QuickBooks Time plan.
- **Calculate billable hours**: As mentioned previously, QuickBooks Time will automatically keep track of billable hours. Whether you are an attorney who needs to bill clients back for hours worked or a plumber, QuickBooks Time allows you to ensure that you are paid for all hours worked on a project or job.
- **Unlimited live customer support**: Similar to all QBO subscription plans, there is a dedicated support team available to answer your questions. Unlimited support is available at no additional charge.

As you can see in the table above, the Elite plan is double the monthly cost of the Premium plan; $40/month vs. $20/month. In addition, the cost per user is $8/user for Premium and $10/user for Elite. If you are not tracking time by project or job, the Premium plan should work for you. However, if you do need to keep track of billable hours by job/project, you should choose the Elite plan.

Summary

To recap, you now know what information is required to set up employees, and what payroll reports are available so that you can gain insight into your total payroll costs, and we discussed the importance of filing payroll tax forms and submitting payroll tax payments on time. Be sure to consult with a CPA, HR professional, or payroll expert to ensure payroll is set up properly. Otherwise, you run the risk of encountering errors, which could result in steep penalties.

In addition to payroll, we have also discussed how to set up 1099 contractors in QuickBooks, how to track payments that have been made to 1099 contractors, the various ways you can pay 1099 contractors, and how to report and file 1099 forms at the end of the year. If you hire individuals such as an attorney or a bookkeeper to provide services to your business, you now know how to set them up in QuickBooks and track payments that are made to them throughout the year. You also know that the threshold for reporting 1099 payments is $600 in payments within a calendar year. We have also shown you how to sign up for the 1099 service provided by Intuit so that you can print and mail 1099 forms. Finally, we introduced you to QuickBooks Time, which helps you to keep track of billable hours for employees and contractors.

Payroll tax returns, W-2s, and 1099 reporting are just a few of the many tasks that must be performed at the end of the year. In the next chapter, we will discuss other tasks that must be completed so that we can close the books for the year.

Join our community on Discord

Join our community's Discord space for discussions with the authors and other readers:

https://packt.link/powerusers

Part 4

Closing the Books and Handling Special Transactions

Closing the books might sound daunting, but it doesn't have to be. In the next part, I'll show you how to wrap up your financial records each month or year with confidence. From reconciling accounts to recording year-end adjustments, you'll know exactly what to do. We'll also tackle some tricky situations, like managing loans, tracking petty cash, and recording delayed charges, so you're prepared for anything your business throws at you.

This part comprises the following chapters:

- *Chapter 9, Closing the Books in QuickBooks Online*
- *Chapter 10, Handling Special Transactions in QuickBooks Online*

9
Closing the Books in QuickBooks Online

After you have entered all of your business transactions into QuickBooks for the year, you will need to finalize your financial statements so that you can hand them off to your accountant to file your taxes. To ensure you have recorded all business transactions for the financial period, we have included a checklist that you can follow to close your books. Closing your books will ensure that no additional transactions are entered into QuickBooks once you have finalized your financial statements. If you have a bookkeeper or an accountant who manages your books, they should ensure that all of the steps have been completed.

In this chapter, we will cover each item on the checklist. This includes reconciling all bank and credit card accounts, making year-end accrual adjustments (if applicable), recording fixed asset purchases made throughout the year, recording depreciation, taking a physical inventory, adjusting retained earnings, and preparing financial statements.

Many of the tasks in this section are typically performed by an accountant. Adding your tax preparer or **Certified Public Accountant (CPA)** as a user will allow them to access your QuickBooks data – this will allow the accountants to run reports and review the items that are needed so that they can perform these tasks in preparation for your tax return. Later in this chapter, I will show you how to give your accountant access to your data.

The chapter topics are summarized as follows:

- Recording journal entries
- Reviewing a checklist to close your books
- Reconciling all bank and credit card accounts
- Making year-end accrual adjustments
- Reviewing new fixed asset purchases and adding them to the chart of account
- Making depreciation journal entries
- Taking a physical inventory and recording inventory adjustments
- Adjusting retained earnings for owner/partner distributions
- Setting a closing date and password
- Preparing key financial reports
- Giving your accountant access to your data

By the end of this chapter, you will know all of the tasks you need to complete in order to close your books for the year. While most small businesses close their books annually, if you close your books on a monthly or quarterly basis, you will still need to follow the steps outlined in this chapter.

> The US edition of QBO was used to create this book. If you are using a version that is outside the US, the results may differ.

Recording journal entries

Before we dive into the details of the checklist, let's discuss recording journal entries. Since many of the items on the checklist will require a journal entry, we will cover the details of what a journal entry is and how to create one.

A **journal entry** is used to adjust your books for transactions that have not been recorded throughout the year. Depreciation expenses for fixed assets, income and expense accruals, and adjustments to retained earnings are three examples we have already mentioned in this chapter. Journal entries are used to record items that cannot be recorded at the transactional level (through checks, deposits, transfers, etc.).

Chapter 9

Follow these steps to record a journal entry in QuickBooks:

1. Click the **+ New** button and select **Journal entry**, as indicated in *Figure 9.1*:

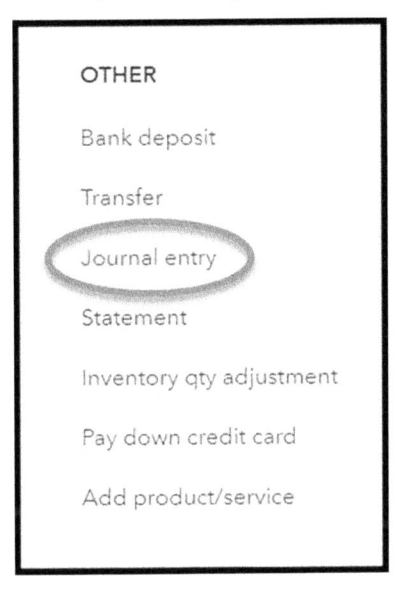

Figure 9.1: Selecting Journal entry in the OTHER column

2. A screen will appear, similar to the one shown in the following screenshot:

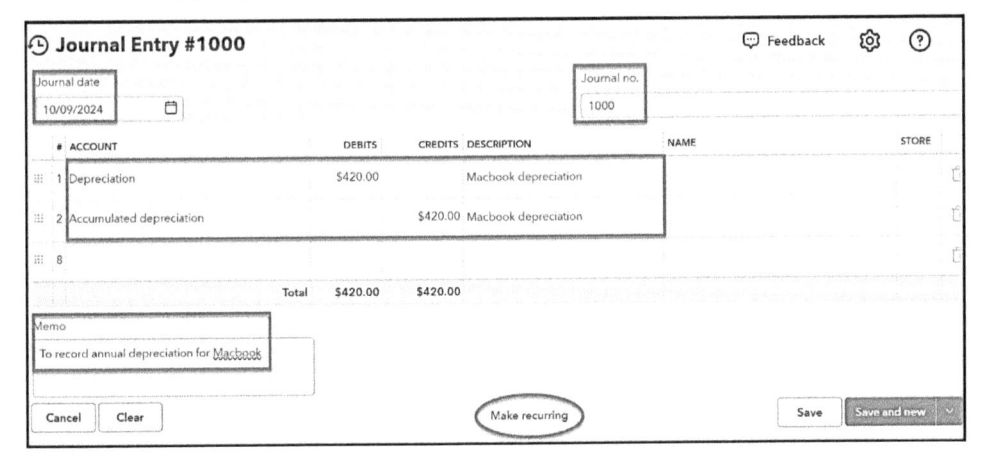

Figure 9.2: Journal Entry template (for better visualization, refer to https://packt.link/gbp/9781836649977)

The following is a brief explanation of the fields that need to be completed in order to record a journal entry:

- **Journal date**: Enter the effective date of the journal in this field.
- **Journal no.**: QuickBooks will automatically populate this field with the next available journal number. If this is the first journal entry you have recorded, you can enter a starting number (such as **1000**), and QuickBooks will increment each journal entry number thereafter. Otherwise, QBO will start with number 1 (as shown in *Figure 9.7*).
- **ACCOUNT**: Select the account from the drop-down menu.
- **DEBITS**: Enter the debit amount in this field.
- **CREDITS**: Enter the credit amount in this field.
- **DESCRIPTION**: Type a detailed description of the purpose of the journal entry in this field. Adding a detailed description is recommended; it is helpful when referring to a journal entry to have an explanation of why it was made.
- **NAME**: If this journal entry is associated with a customer, you can select that customer from the drop-down list in this field.
- **Memo**: Include a brief description of the fixed asset that you are recording this journal entry for.
- **Attachments**: If you have any source documentation you would like to include, you can attach those documents directly to this transaction.
- **Make recurring**: To help you stay on top of these types of adjustments, you can make this journal entry recurring. This means you can set up this journal entry to automatically record on the date you specify. If you don't want QBO to automatically record the journal entry for you, you can also just receive a reminder to record the journal entry. To learn more about how to set up recurring transactions, refer to *Chapter 7, Recording Expenses in QuickBooks Online*.

Be sure to record all journal entries prior to generating financial statements. If you give your CPA or accountant access to your data, they can record all of the necessary journal entries and then generate the financial reports required to file your tax returns. We are now ready to dive into our checklist.

Reviewing a checklist for closing your books

As discussed, there are several steps you will need to take in order to close your books for the financial period. How often you close your books (for example, monthly, quarterly, or annually) will determine how often you need to complete these steps. Remember the importance of closing your books, as this will ensure that all transactions for the financial period have been recorded and that your financial statements are accurate, which is important because your accountant will use them to file your business tax return.

The following is a checklist of the steps you need to complete in order to close your books. You should complete them in the order presented:

1. Reconciling all bank and credit card accounts
2. Making year-end accrual adjustments
3. Reviewing new fixed asset purchases and adding them to the chart of accounts
4. Making depreciation journal entries
5. Taking a physical inventory and recording inventory adjustments
6. Adjusting retained earnings for owner/partner distributions
7. Setting a closing date and password
8. Preparing key financial reports

The purpose of closing the books is to ensure that the elements that impact the financial statements are reviewed and deemed accurate before finalizing the financial statements, which will in turn be used to file your business tax return. We will discuss each of these eight steps in detail, starting with reconciling all bank and credit card accounts.

1. Reconciling all bank and credit card accounts

In the online chapter, *Chapter 15, Reconciling Uploaded Bank and Credit Card Transactions*, available online using this link: https://packt.link/supplementary-content-9781836649977 which you can find at https://packt.link/supplementary-content-9781836649977, you learned how to reconcile your bank and credit card accounts. Loans and lines of credit should also be reconciled, and we will cover how to manage a business loan and/or a line of credit from your financial institution in *Chapter 10, Handling Special Transactions in QuickBooks Online*. It's important for you to reconcile these accounts before closing the books so that you can ensure that all income and expenses for the period have been recorded in QuickBooks.

This will ensure that your financial statements are accurate and that you don't miss out on any tax deductions.

2. Making year-end accrual adjustments

If you are on the **accrual** basis of accounting, you need to make sure that all income and expenses that have been incurred for the period are recorded. In the online chapter, *Chapter 13, Small Business Bookkeeping 101*, available online using this link: https://packt.link/supplementary-content-9781836649977 we discuss what accrual basis accounting versus cash basis account is. Some examples of accruals that may be required are inventory purchases that you have received the product for but not the bill and employee wages. Be sure to consult with your accountant for the proper recording of these transactions. We will discuss journal entries in more detail later in this chapter.

> Record all accounts receivable for the end of the period, which means invoicing all customers for work performed. This will ensure that all income is recorded and shows up on your profit and loss (income statement) report. Similarly, be sure to record all accounts payable (vendor bills) for any expenses incurred in the period. This will ensure that all expenses show up on the profit and loss (income statement).

3. Reviewing new fixed asset purchases and adding them to the chart of accounts

If you purchased any fixed assets during the year, you should add these to QuickBooks. As mentioned in the online chapter, *Chapter 13, Small Business Bookkeeping 101*, available online using this link: https://packt.link/supplementary-content-9781836649977, fixed assets can be equipment purchased for your business such as computers or printers. Furniture such as desks and chairs are also considered fixed assets.

Fixed assets are subject to **depreciation**, which is a **tax-deductible expense**. Depreciation is the reduction of the value of a fixed asset due to wear and tear. Tax-deductible expenses can reduce your tax bill, so you want to make sure that you take all of the deductions to which you are entitled. If you have not recorded new fixed asset purchases, then you will not have depreciation expenses recorded, which means you will miss out on what could be a significant tax deduction.

Your tax preparer should have a detailed list of fixed assets that have been reported on previous tax returns. It is a good idea to review this list annually to ensure it includes new purchases and/or disposal of assets. It's also important to conduct a physical check to ensure that all of the assets on the books still exist and have not been disposed of.

Chapter 9

One of the newest features available in QBO is the ability to manage fixed assets. If you are using the QBO Advanced plan, QBO will automatically calculate depreciation and record monthly depreciation expenses for you. Refer to the online chapter, *Chapter 21, QuickBooks Online Advanced*, available online using this link: https://packt.link/supplementary-content-9781836649977 for step-by-step instructions on how to use this new tool.

For those of you who are not on the QBO Advanced plan, follow the steps below to add your fixed assets to QBO.

> Please note that if you have already entered the fixed asset as an expense into QBO, do not record it as a fixed asset. For businesses located in the US, the IRS recommends that you record purchases as expenses if they are $2,500 or less. Anything that is more than $2,500 you should enter as a fixed asset.

To add fixed assets to QuickBooks, you will need to have the following information on hand since it will be used to calculate depreciation:

- Date of purchase
- Purchase price
- Type of asset
- Make and model (if applicable)
- Year

Follow these steps to add a fixed asset to QuickBooks:

1. From the left menu bar, click on **Transactions**, as indicated in *Figure 9.3*:

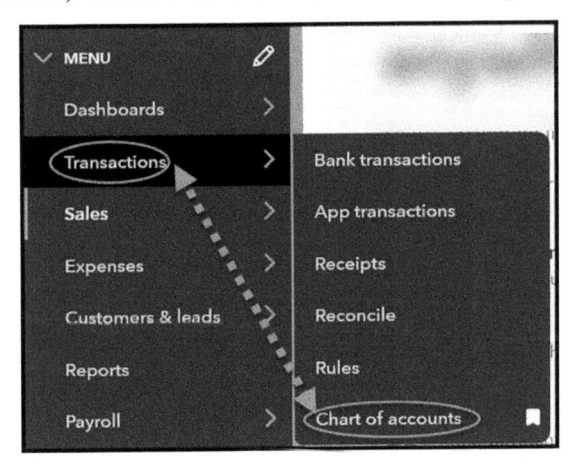

Figure 9.3: Navigating to Chart of accounts

2. Select **Chart of accounts**, and then click the **New** button, as indicated in *Figure 9.4*:

Figure 9.4: Clicking the New button

3. For a new fixed asset, complete the fields, as shown in *Figure 9.5*:

New account

Account name*
MacBook Air

Account type*
Fixed Assets

Detail type*
Fixed Asset Computers

☐ Make this a subaccount

Original cost
2,100.00

As of
10/09/2024

☐ Create a category to keep track of depreciation. **What's depreciation?**

Description
owner's computer

Balance Sheet
Active accounts as of 10/09/2024

NEW ACCOUNT PREVIEW

Land

Long-term office equipment

MacBook Air ⬅

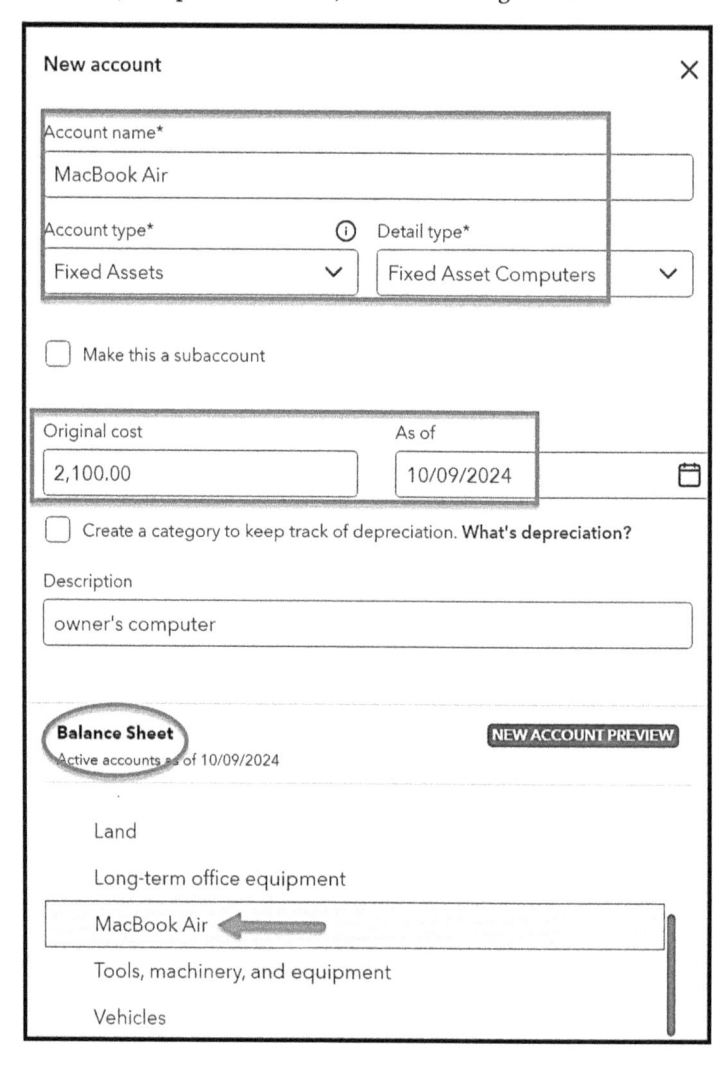

Tools, machinery, and equipment

Vehicles

Figure 9.5: Entering details for a fixed asset

Chapter 9

The following is a brief explanation of the fields that need to be completed for a new fixed asset:

- **Account name**: Type the name of the fixed asset in this field. In our example, this is **MacBook Air**.
- **Account type**: Select **Fixed Assets**, as shown in *Figure 9.5*.
- **Original cost**: In our example, the original cost is **$2,100**. This amount will be used to calculate depreciation.
- **As of**: Enter the date the asset was purchased in this field. In our example, the purchase date was **10/09/2024**.
- **Description**: Type a more detailed description of the fixed asset in this field, or you can enter the account name again. In our example, we have entered **owner's computer**.
- **New Account Preview**: In this section, you will see the financial statement this account will appear in. In our example, the balance sheet is the report all assets will show up in.

4. Click the **Save and Close** button to add the asset to your chart of accounts list.

Be sure to complete these steps for each fixed asset you have purchased during the accounting period, provided that you have not already entered the items as an expense. Please be sure to consult with your tax professional to ensure fixed asset purchases are recorded properly on your books. Remember, fixed assets include items that cost more than **$2,500** as per the latest IRS standards. After adding fixed assets to QuickBooks, you need to record depreciation expenses for the period.

4. Making depreciation journal entries

After adding fixed assets to QuickBooks, you need to record depreciation expenses for the period. As established earlier, **depreciation** is the reduction in the value of an asset, due to wear and tear after it has been in service for a period of time. To reflect the reduced value, you must record the depreciation expense in your books. Depreciation is also a tax-deductible expense, which can help to reduce your overall tax liability.

As mentioned previously, if you subscribe to the QBO Advanced plan, QuickBooks will automatically compute and record depreciation for you. However, if you don't have QBO Advanced, you will need to calculate depreciation manually or have your accountant do this for you. In the *Recording journal entries* section of this chapter, I will show you how to record journal entries in QuickBooks.

If you do have QBO Advanced, please refer to the online chapter, *Chapter 21, QuickBooks Online Advanced*, available online using this link: `https://packt.link/supplementary-content-9781836649977` where I will show you how the new fixed asset manager works.

5. Taking a physical inventory and recording inventory adjustments

Reconciling inventory involves making sure that the products you have on your shelf match what your books reflect as on-hand inventory. You should take a physical inventory count at least once a year, if not more often. After taking a physical count, any discrepancies between the books and the physical count should be recorded in QuickBooks as inventory adjustments. After recording these inventory adjustments, your books and your warehouse will be in sync.

Follow these steps to record inventory adjustments in QuickBooks:

1. Click on the **+ New** button, and select **Inventory qty adjustment** in the **OTHER** column, as indicated in *Figure 9.6*:

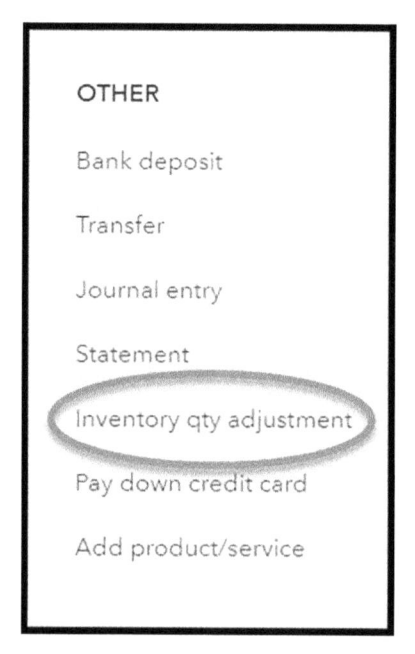

Figure 9.6: Choosing Inventory qty adjustment

Chapter 9   291

2. Complete the fields for the inventory adjustment, as indicated in *Figure 9.7*:

Inventory quantity adjustment #2					
Adjustment date 10/06/2024	**Reference number** 2				
Adjustment reason Damaged Goods	**Inventory adjustment account** Inventory Shrinkage				
#	PRODUCT/VARIANT	SKU	QTY ON HAND	NEW QTY	CHANGE IN QTY
1	QBO Workbooks		35	33	-2
Memo Per physical inventory count on 09/30, two workbooks were severely damaged and had to be thrown away.					

Figure 9.7: Completing the fields to record the inventory adjustment

The following is a brief explanation of the fields that need to be completed in order to record an inventory adjustment:

- **Adjustment date:** Enter the effective date of the adjustment. This date should be on or before the last day of the closing period. In our example, the inventory count was taken on 10/06/2024.
- **Reference no.:** This field will automatically populate with a number. If you prefer to customize the reference number, you can do so by typing directly into this field. In our example, the reference number is 1000.
- **Adjustment reason:** From the drop-down menu, select the reason for the adjustment. The options available are **Damaged Goods**, **Stock write-off**, **Inventory count**, **Shrinkage**, **Inventory Revaluation**, **Stolen Goods**, **Expired**, **Returned Goods**, and **Marketing/Promotion**.
- **Inventory adjustment account: Inventory Shrinkage** is the default account that will appear in this field. However, you can click the drop-down arrow and select a different account, or add a new one.
- **PRODUCT/VARIANT:** From the drop-down menu, select the item for which you are making an adjustment. In our example, QBO Workbooks has been selected.
- **SKU:** If your products have an SKU, this information will automatically populate once you select the product.

- **QTY ON HAND**: This field will automatically be populated with what you currently have recorded in QuickBooks. This field cannot be adjusted.
- **NEW QTY**: Enter the quantity, based on the physical count that was taken in this field.
- **CHANGE IN QTY**: QuickBooks automatically computes the adjustment required by taking the difference between the **QTY ON HAND** and **NEW QTY** values entered.
- **Memo**: Enter a brief explanation of why the adjustment was made.

If you have extensive inventory tracking requirements that go beyond what's available in QBO, visit the Intuit app marketplace, where there are over 700 add-on programs that integrate seamlessly with QBO. In *Chapter 10, Handling Special Transactions in QuickBooks Online*, I'll show you how to navigate the QuickBooks App Center.

6. Adjusting retained earnings for owner/partner distributions

Retained earnings are the cumulative amount of your income and expenses for the prior period(s). This amount will be posted to the retained earnings account at the end of your fiscal/calendar year. QuickBooks will automatically make this entry for you. Depending on the type of organization (corporation, partnership, LLC, sole proprietorship, or non-profit), you may need to move this balance to other equity accounts.

To distribute profits to the owners, you will need to create a journal entry to an equity account entitled *owner's draw* or *owner distributions* and offset it with retained earnings. Be sure to consult with your CPA or tax preparer if you are not familiar with this process.

To summarize what we have covered so far: many of the steps in the closing process are designed for you to review the transactions that have been recorded throughout the fiscal year, as well as make adjustments as needed for accruals such as wages, depreciation of fixed assets, and retained earnings of owner/partner distributions. The primary way these closing adjustments are recorded is through journal entries. We will take a brief break from going through the checklist now so that we can discuss this next.

Chapter 9

7. Setting a closing date and password

In an effort to maintain the integrity of your data, you should set a closing date and password after you have entered all transactions for the closing period. By setting a closing date, users will receive a warning message if they attempt to enter transactions that affect the closing period. For example, if you set a closing date of **12/31/24**, users will receive a warning message if they attempt to enter any transactions dated **12/31/24** or earlier.

Follow these steps to set a closing date and password in QBO:

1. Click on the gear icon, and then select **Account and settings** in the **YOUR COMPANY** column, as indicated in *Figure 9.8*:

Figure 9.8: Selecting Account and settings in the YOUR COMPANY column

2. Click on the **Advanced** tab, as indicated in *Figure 9.9*:

Figure 9.9: Clicking the Advanced option

3. The **Accounting** preferences are located at the very top of the next screen, as indicated in *Figure 9.10*:

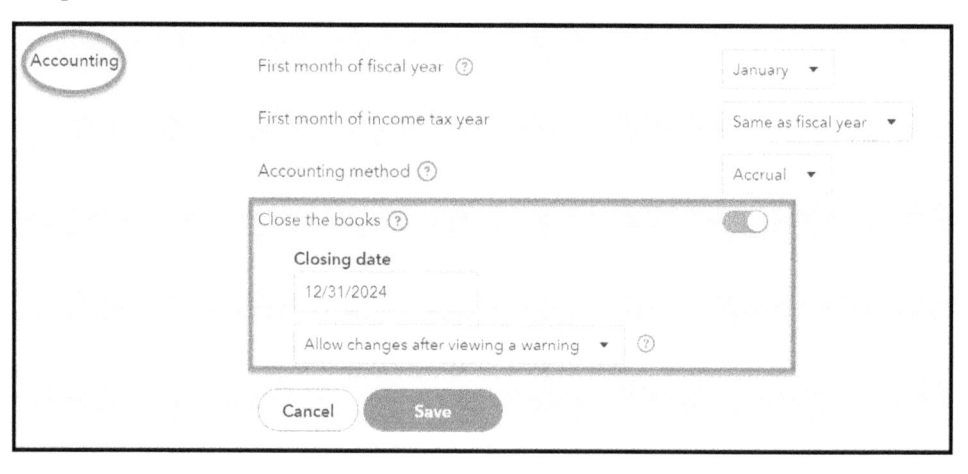

Figure 9.10: Reviewing the Accounting preferences

In the **Close the books** section, you can enter the closing date (that is, **12/31/2024**), which will give users a warning if they attempt to enter transactions dated on the closing date or prior to it. There are two types of warning messages. The first warning message is **Allow changes after viewing a warning**, as shown in *Figure 9.10*. This message will allow users to proceed with entering the transaction after they close the warning message. The second warning message is **Allow changes after viewing a warning and entering a password**. This message requires users to enter a password to proceed with entering transactions. To choose this option, select it from the drop-down field, as shown in *Figure 9.10*, and enter the password you would like to use.

> Since QuickBooks does not have a formal closing process, choosing the option that requires a password to make changes is highly recommended, keeping users from making changes to prior years where tax returns have already been filed. *Don't give the closing password to anyone who is not authorized to enter transactions after the closing date.* It is recommended that you set a closing date as of the last day of the tax year you are filing for. For example, if you are on a calendar year it would be December 31.

8. Preparing key financial reports

After you have completed the first seven steps in the closing checklist, you are ready to prepare financial statements. There are three primary financial statements you will need to prepare:

- **The trial balance**
- **The balance sheet**
- **The income statement (profit and loss report)**

In the online chapter, *Chapter 18, Business Overview and Cash Management Tools and Reports*, available online using this link: https://packt.link/supplementary-content-9781836649977 you can find out what the balance sheet and income statement reports are, how to interpret the data, and how to generate these reports in QuickBooks. Your accountant, or CPA, will also request a trial balance report. A trial balance report lists all of the debits and credits recorded in QuickBooks for the period. If everything has been recorded properly, debits will always equal credits on this report.

Follow these steps to run a trial balance report in QuickBooks:

1. Navigate to **Reports**, as indicated in *Figure 9.11*:

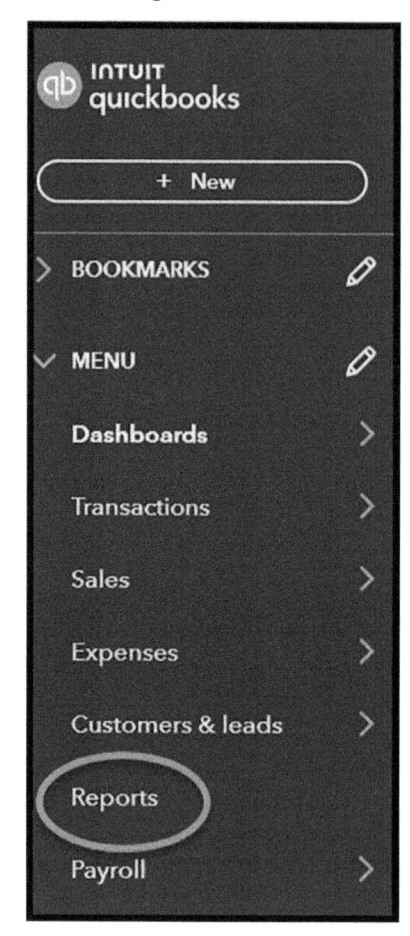

Figure 9.11: Clicking Reports to navigate to the Reports Center

Chapter 9 297

2. In the **For my accountant** section, click on **Trial Balance**, as indicated in *Figure 9.12*:

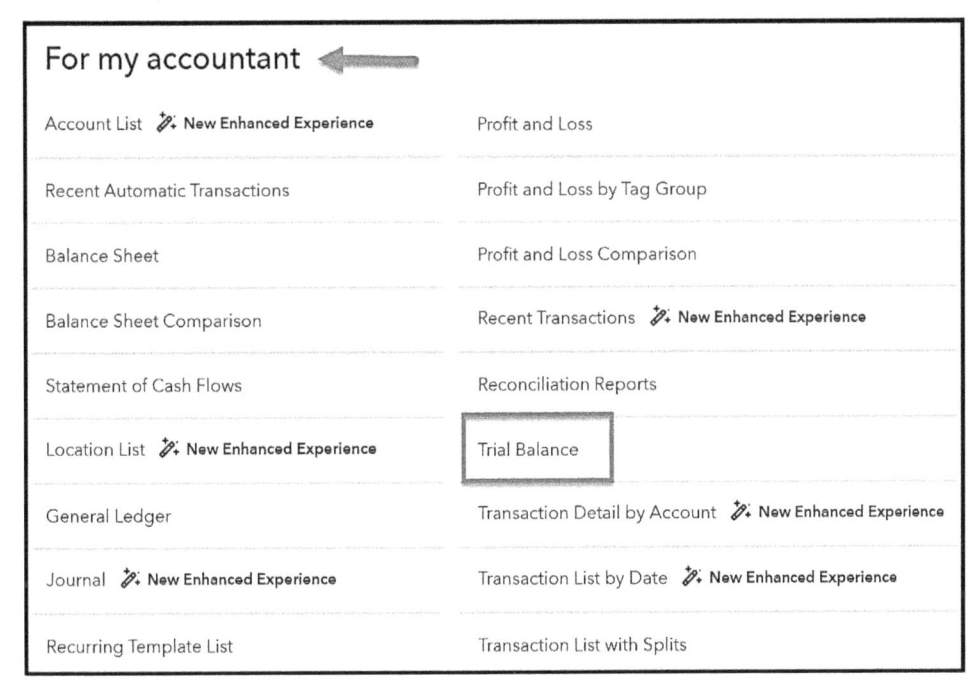

For my accountant	
Account List New Enhanced Experience	Profit and Loss
Recent Automatic Transactions	Profit and Loss by Tag Group
Balance Sheet	Profit and Loss Comparison
Balance Sheet Comparison	Recent Transactions New Enhanced Experience
Statement of Cash Flows	Reconciliation Reports
Location List New Enhanced Experience	Trial Balance
General Ledger	Transaction Detail by Account New Enhanced Experience
Journal New Enhanced Experience	Transaction List by Date New Enhanced Experience
Recurring Template List	Transaction List with Splits

Figure 9.12: Running the trial balance report

3. The trial balance report will appear. Click the **Customize** button:

Figure 9.13: Customizing the trial balance report (for better visualization, refer to https://packt.link/gbp/9781836649977)

The following report customization options will appear:

Customize report

▼ General

Report period

| This Month-to-date ▼ | 10/01/2024 | to | 10/09/2024 |

Accounting method

○ Cash ● Accrual

Number format
☐ Divide by 1000
☐ Without cents
☑ Except zero amount

Negative numbers
-100 ▼
☐ Show in red

▼ Rows/Columns

Columns
Total Only ▼

Show non-zero or active only
Active rows/active co ▼

▼ Header/Footer

Header

☐ Show logo

☑ Company name — Small Business Builders, LLC

☑ Report title — Trial Balance

☑ Report period

Footer

☑ Date prepared

☑ Time prepared

☑ Report basis (cash vs. accrual)

Alignment

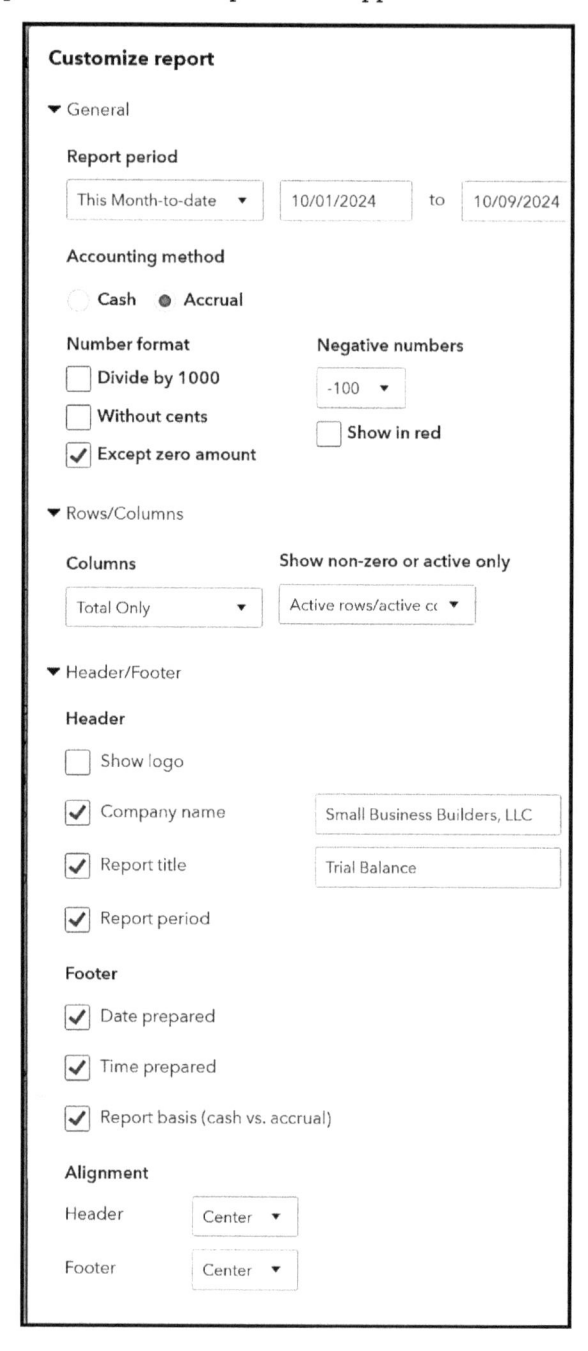

Header — Center ▼

Footer — Center ▼

Figure 9.14: Reviewing the report customization options

There are a number of options available to customize the trial balance report. The following is a brief description of some of the information that can be customized:

- **Report period**: You can select a preset report period such as **Last Year** from the drop-down menu, or type a date range in the fields to the right of the preset field.
- **Accounting method**: As previously introduced in this book, you can choose the accounting method you want to be applied to the report, **Cash** or **Accrual**.
- **Number format**: There are a variety of options to format the numbers on a report. Omitting the cents and excluding accounts with a zero balance are just a couple of the options shown in the preceding screenshot.
- **Rows/Columns**: Choose which rows/columns are visible on the report.
- **Header**: You can edit the company name and the title of the report in the header section.
- **Footer**: You can choose to show the date/time when the report was prepared.
- **Alignment**: You can decide how to best align the information that appears in the header and footer sections of the report.

4. When you are done with your customizations, click the **Run report** button.

A report similar to the one in *Figure 9.15* will appear:

Small Business Builders, LLC

Trial Balance

As of October 9, 2024

	DEBIT	CREDIT
Business Checking	4,975.00	
Accounts Receivable (A/R)	649.50	
Inventory Asset	165.00	
Accumulated depreciation		420.00
MacBook Air	2,100.00	
Accounts Payable (A/P)		0.00
Texas State Comptroller Payable		49.50
Opening balance equity		7,250.00
Sales of Product Income		600.00
Inventory Shrinkage	10.00	
Depreciation	420.00	
TOTAL	$8,319.50	$8,319.50

Figure 9.15: Example trial balance report

As discussed, the total debits column ($8,319.50) should always equal the total credits column ($8,319.50), as it does in the preceding report. If it does not, you will need to look into any discrepancies. The good news is, 99.99% of the time, this report will balance (debits equal credits) because QuickBooks does not allow you to post one-sided journals, which means that for every debit, there is always an offsetting credit to keep things in balance.

> If you do have a trial balance that does not balance (debits don't equal credits) as they do in *Figure 9.15*, you should calculate the difference between the debits and credits, and then look for that amount on the report. Most likely, there is an amount in one of the columns (debit or credit) that does not appear in the other column.

To summarize, you will need to review three key financial reports before closing your books: the balance sheet, the income statement, and the trial balance report. If you have a CPA or an accountant who reviews your financials and prepares your tax return, you can give that person access to your books so that they can run these reports without having to bother you. We will discuss giving your accountant access to your data next.

> Always review the information on your reports one last time before sharing them with any third party outside of your organization. You add these reports to a report group and send them out instead of running them individually. Refer to the online chapter, *Chapter 16, Reports Center Overview*, available online using this link: `https://packt.link/supplementary-content-9781836649977` for more information on this.

Giving your accountant access to your data

If you have an accountant or tax preparer to whom you need to grant access to your data, you can create a secure user ID and password for them. All you need to do is request their email address so that you can send them an invitation to access your data.

Follow these steps to invite an accountant to access your QuickBooks data:

1. Click on the gear icon and select **Manage users** in the **YOUR COMPANY** column, as indicated in *Figure 9.16*:

Figure 9.16: Selecting Manage users from the YOUR COMPANY column

2. On the **Manage users** page, click on **Accountants**, as indicated in *Figure 9.17*:

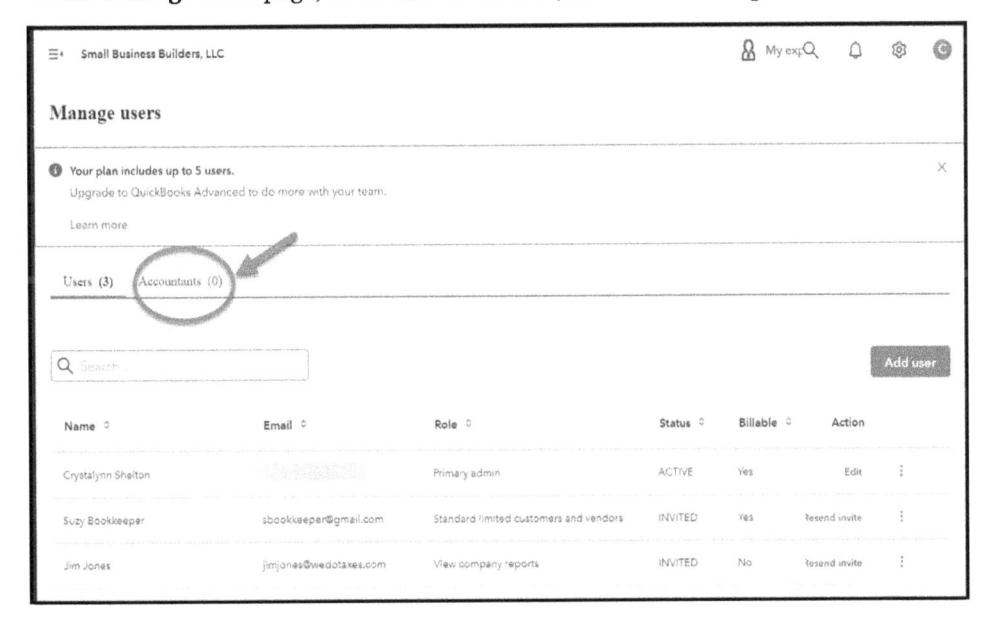

Figure 9.17: Clicking on Accountants (for better visualization, refer to https://packt.link/gbp/9781836649977)

3. Enter your accountant or tax professional's email address and click on **Invite**, as indicated in *Figure 9.18*, to invite your accountant to access your QuickBooks data:

An accountant can be your best business partner

Make it easy to work together. Invite yours to your QuickBooks.

mycpa@gmail.com   Invite

Your accountant and members of their firm will have admin access to your company data.

Figure 9.18: Clicking the Invite button

Your accountant will receive an email, inviting them to access your QBO account. They will need to accept the invitation and create a secure password. Their user ID will be the email address that you entered in the form (shown in *Figure 9.18*).

Once you have given your accountant access to your books, they can simply log in to QuickBooks to get the information they need to prepare your taxes. This is highly recommended if your accountant needs to make any year-end adjustments. You can add/remove permissions access as needed if you prefer them only to have access at tax time. To resend an invite or delete access, go back to the **Accountants** tab and tick the checkbox to the right of **Resend invite**:

Figure 9.19: Option to resend an invite from the accountant user page

Inviting your tax preparer or accountant to access your books is the last step on our closing-the-books checklist. Giving a user accountant access is equivalent to giving someone admin access. The accountant can do 95% of what the admin can do, except upgrade or cancel your QBO account. With that said, be thoughtful about whether someone needs this level of access. In most cases, you can give them access to view reports only and then consult you if there are any changes that they would recommend.

Summary

In this chapter, you have learned about the key tasks that need to be completed to close your books for the accounting period. As discussed, you need to reconcile all bank and credit card accounts, record year-end accrual adjustments (if your accounting is accrual-based), add fixed asset purchases, record depreciation expenses, take a physical inventory and make the necessary adjustments, adjust retained earnings for distributions made to the business owners, set a closing date and password, and prepare key financial statements. You can perform these tasks yourself, or you can give your accountant access to your QuickBooks data to take care of this for you.

This chapter is the last one that covers the QuickBooks features that most small businesses will use. Congratulations on successfully completing all of the chapters thus far! In the next chapter, we will cover some additional topics, such as adding apps to QBO, managing credit card payments, and recording bad debt expenses.

Join our community on Discord

Join our community's Discord space for discussions with the authors and other readers:

https://packt.link/powerusers

10
Handling Special Transactions in QuickBooks Online

So far, we have covered the most common transactions for which small businesses use QuickBooks. However, there are a few more topics that we would like to share with you. First, we will discuss how to properly set up a business loan or line of credit. If you have a business loan or line of credit, you need to keep track of payments and overall outstanding balances in QuickBooks. Then we will cover bad debt. While you always hope it doesn't happen to you, there may come a time when you are unable to collect payment from a customer. If this happens, you will need to record a bad debt, so I will show you how to properly record bad debt expenses. Let's say you provided a service to a customer but they were not completely satisfied with your work *or* you did not deliver a project by the agreed-upon due date; you can issue a credit memo that you can apply to a future invoice. This type of gesture can go a long way to ensure that you keep your client's business. Finally, I will show you how to record delayed charges. Delayed charges are used to keep track of the services you have provided to customers that you will invoice at a later date.

While some of these may not apply to your business when you are starting out, it's a good idea to be aware that they exist.

To sum up, in this chapter, we will cover the following topics:

- Setting up business loans and lines of credit
- Recording bad debt expense
- Creating a credit memo
- Applying credit memos to outstanding invoices
- Tracking delayed charges and credits

The US edition of QBO was used to create this book. If you are using a version that is outside the United States, results may differ.

Setting up business loans and lines of credit

If you secure a business loan or line of credit, you need to track the payments made, as well as the outstanding balance owed, in QuickBooks. This will ensure that your financial statements include the money that is owed to all creditors. If this information is not included in QuickBooks, it will not show up on your financial statements. If this information is not reported in your financial statements, you will have inaccurate reports and you could miss out on legitimate tax deductions.

In this section, we will cover how to set up a business loan or line of credit, how to track payments, and how to stay on top of the outstanding balances owed.

Adding a business loan or line of credit to the chart of accounts

The first step to properly tracking loans and lines of credit in QuickBooks is to set them up on the chart of accounts. We will do this next. Follow these steps:

1. Navigate to **Transactions** and select **Chart of accounts**, as shown in *Figure 10.1*:

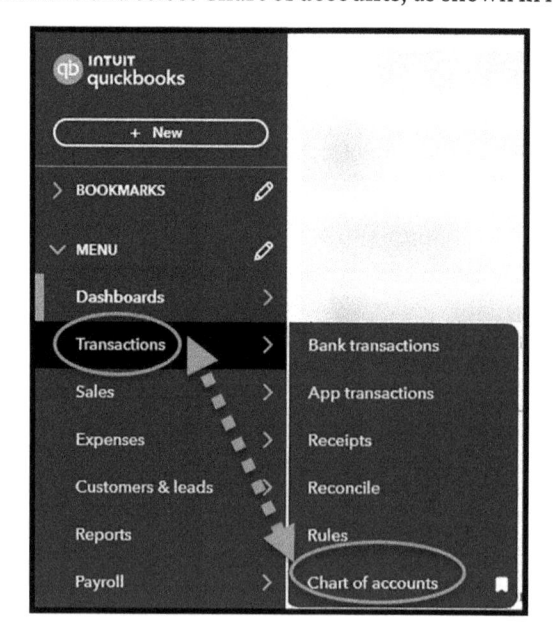

Figure 10.1: Navigating to Chart of accounts

Chapter 10

2. Click on the **New** button located to the right of **Run Report**, as shown in *Figure 10.2*:

Figure 10.2: Clicking the New button

3. Fill in the fields shown in the following screenshot to add a new business loan or line of credit account:

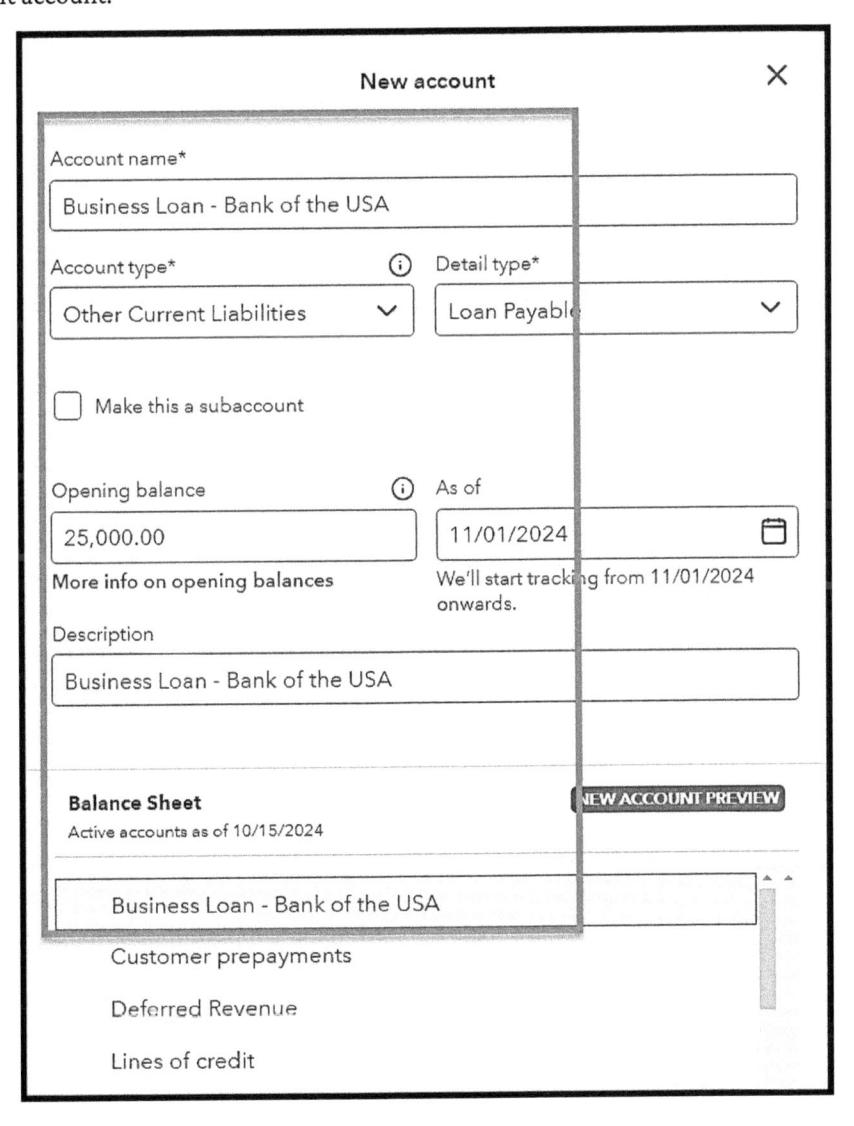

Figure 10.3: Adding a new business loan account

A brief description of the fields in the preceding screenshot is as follows:

- **Account name:** In this field, enter the name of the account. This will generally include the type of liability (loan or line of credit) and the name of the financial institution (`Business Loan - Bank of the USA`, in our case). If you have multiple loans at the same financial institution, be sure to include an account number or the last 4 digits of the account number so that you can easily identify each loan.
- **Account type:** Business loans and lines of credit are money that is owed to a creditor, also known as a liability.
- **Detail type:** From the drop-down menu, select the detail type that best describes the account you are setting up. In our example, the detail type is `Loan Payable`.
- **Opening balance:** Type the beginning balance of the principal portion of the loan as of the date you set this up in QBO. If you have not made any payments on the loan, this will be the amount that you borrowed (the principal portion of the loan). If you have made payments on the loan, you will need to refer to your most recent statement and enter the remaining balance of the loan.
- **As of:** Enter the date on the statement where you pulled the opening balance from. It should be the ending date on the statement, not the beginning date. For example, in the statement for the period `01/01/25 - 12/31/25`, the ending date is 12/31/25.
- **Description:** In this field, you can simply copy and paste the name or include a more detailed description, such as the account number of the loan or line of credit.
- **New Account Preview:** Directly below the description field is the new account preview. The new account preview shows you what financial statement the new account will appear on and in what order it will show up along with other accounts. In our example, the Business Loan – Bank of the USA account will appear on the Balance Sheet report right above the Customer prepayments account.

> Another way to record a beginning balance for a loan or line of credit) is by categorizing the transaction to the loan account (created above) when you receive the funds in your bank account or record a journal entry for a fixed asset purchased with a loan.

4. Click the **Save and Close** button to add the loan or line of credit account to your chart of accounts list.

If you haven't done so already, you will need to repeat these steps to add an interest paid or interest expense account to the chart of accounts list. You will track the interest portion of your payments in this account. Now, we'll cover how to make payments on a loan or line of credit.

> It is very important that you track the interest for loans and lines of credit in a separate expense account. The reason for doing this is that interest expense for most liabilities such as this is tax-deductible. If the amount is buried with the principal payments, it will be difficult to go back and calculate later on.
>
> Your financial institution should provide you with an amortization schedule that includes the breakdown of your payments between interest and principal. If they do not provide this schedule, you can google "amortization calculator" and create the schedule for yourself.

Making payments on a loan or line of credit

In general, you can make payments on a loan or line of credit in the same manner that you pay other creditors. You can write a check or have the funds automatically deducted from your bank account. Here, we will walk through how to record a payment.

Follow these steps to make payments on a loan or line of credit with a check:

1. Click on the **+ New** button and then select **Check** in the **Vendors** column, as shown in *Figure 10.4*:

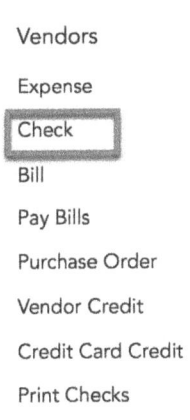

Vendors

Expense

Check

Bill

Pay Bills

Purchase Order

Vendor Credit

Credit Card Credit

Print Checks

Figure 10.4: Navigating to Check

2. Fill in the fields for the loan payment:

Check #1003

Payee	Bank Account	
Bank of the USA	Business Checking	Balance $6,525.00

Mailing address: Bank of the USA, 555 Banking Way, Dallas, TX 76063

Payment date: 10/15/2024

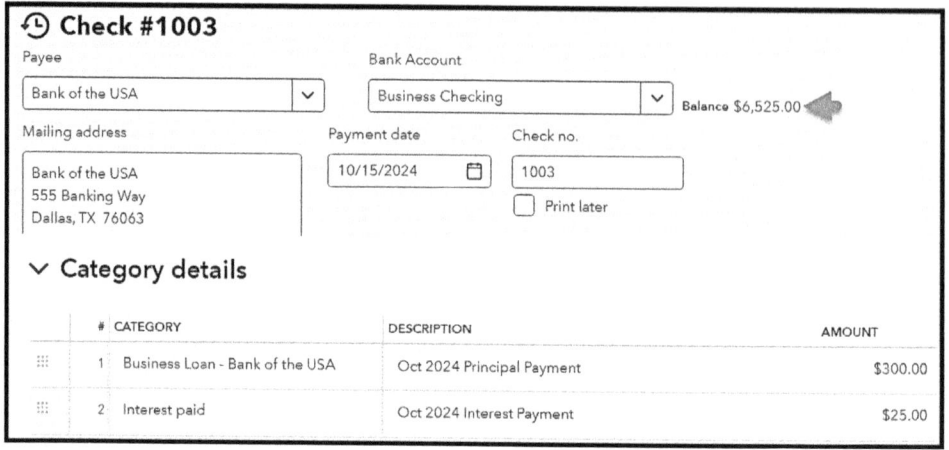

Check no.: 1003

☐ Print later

Category details

#	CATEGORY	DESCRIPTION	AMOUNT
1	Business Loan - Bank of the USA	Oct 2024 Principal Payment	$300.00
2	Interest paid	Oct 2024 Interest Payment	$25.00

Figure 10.5: Completing the Check form to record payment for the loan

A brief description of the fields you need to complete to record a payment for a loan or line of credit is as follows:

- **Payee:** From the drop-down menu, select the payee. If you haven't added the payee to QuickBooks, you can do so here by selecting **Add new** from the drop-down menu.

- **Bank Account:** If you have more than one bank account, you need to select the bank account that you want to write the check from in the drop-down menu. When you select the bank account, the current balance will appear to the right of the field, as indicated in the preceding screenshot.

- **Mailing address:** This field will automatically be populated with the address on file for the payee you've selected. If you don't have an address on file, you can type the information directly into this field. However, it's best to go to the vendor profile and add the address information there. If you type it in this field, the address will not be saved to the payee's profile.

- **Payment date:** Enter the check date or the date the payment was deducted from your bank account.

- **CATEGORY:** In this field, you need to select accounts that are affected by this payment. In general, that will be the loan payable account (principal) and an interest expense account. The portion of the payment that applies to the principal amount should be allocated to the loan payable account. The portion of the payment that applies to the interest should be allocated to the interest paid account.

- **DESCRIPTION**: Type a brief description of what the payment is for in this field.
- **AMOUNT**: Enter the amount you wish to pay in this field.

If your loan payments are automatically withdrawn from your bank account, you will enter these payments as an expense. You will repeat *step 1* but instead of selecting **Check**, you will select **Expense**. The fields you will complete are similar to the fields required on the **Check** form.

> In order to accurately record the proper amounts for the principal and interest accounts, you may need to refer to your loan statement to see how your payment was applied. Be sure to do this so that your books match up with those of the financial institutions.

One final step you should do to ensure that the business loans and lines of credit on your books match your statements is to reconcile these accounts on a monthly basis. The steps to reconcile business loans and lines of credit are identical to reconciling your bank accounts. Refer to the online chapter, *Chapter 15, Reconciling Uploaded Bank and Credit Card Transactions* at https://packt.link/supplementary-content-9781836649977, for step-by-step instructions on reconciling.

Remember, it's important for your financial statements to be as accurate as possible. This means including all of the money that is owed to creditors, such as loans and lines of credit. In addition, to deduct the interest expense, you need to keep track of it in QuickBooks.

Recording bad debt expenses

If you're in business long enough, there will come a time when a customer is unable or unwilling to pay you. If you use cash-based accounting, you don't need to record bad debt expenses because you don't have accounts receivable. However, if you do extend credit to your customers and, after attempting to collect the payment, you become aware that you will not be able to collect payment, you should write off the bad debt. This will ensure that your financial statements remain accurate and that revenue is not overstated.

There are three steps you need to follow in order to write off bad debt: first, you need to add a bad debt item to the products and services list; next, you need to create a credit memo; and finally, you need to apply the credit memo to the unpaid customer invoice. We will walk you through these steps in this section.

Creating a bad debt item

As established, the first step of recording bad debt expenses is to add an item to the products and services list for tracking. Follow these steps to create a bad debt item:

1. Click on the gear icon and select **Products and Services,** as shown in *Figure 10.6*:

Lists

All Lists

Products and Services

Recurring Transactions

Attachments

Figure 10.6: Completing the fields to add Bad Debt to the Products and Services list

As you can see in *Figure 10.7*, there are four item types to choose from. **Service** is the item type we will use for bad debt expenses:

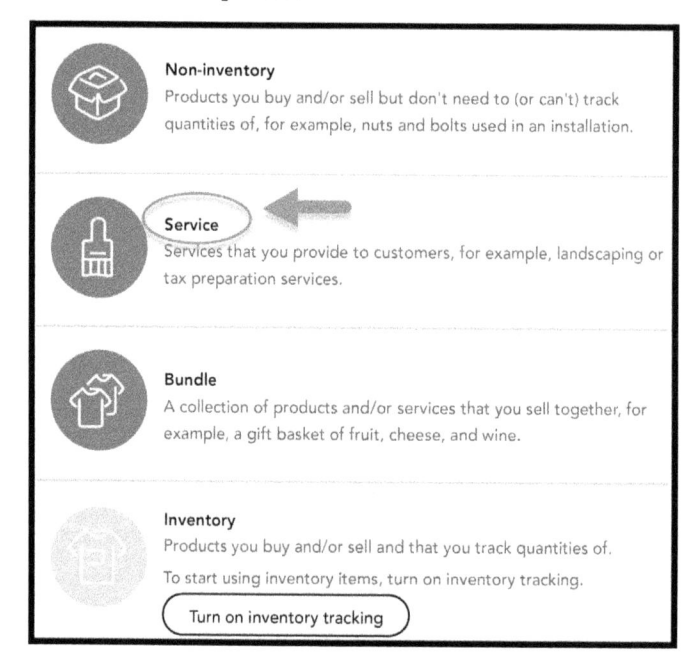

Non-inventory
Products you buy and/or sell but don't need to (or can't) track quantities of, for example, nuts and bolts used in an installation.

Service
Services that you provide to customers, for example, landscaping or tax preparation services.

Bundle
A collection of products and/or services that you sell together, for example, a gift basket of fruit, cheese, and wine.

Inventory
Products you buy and/or sell and that you track quantities of.
To start using inventory items, turn on inventory tracking.

(Turn on inventory tracking)

Figure 10.7: Selecting the item type

2. Fill in the following fields to add **Bad Debt Expense** to the items list:

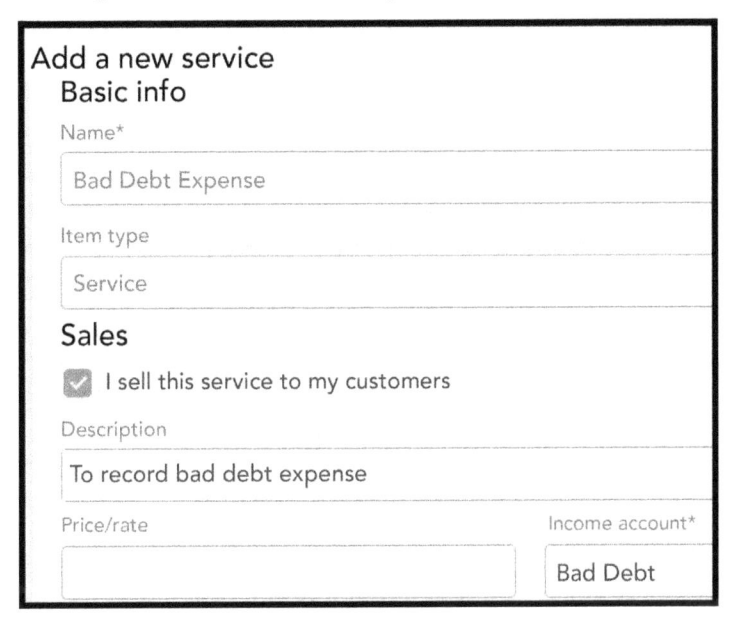

Figure 10.8: Complete the fields for adding a new service item

3. Brief descriptions of the fields to fill in are as follows:

- **Name**: Enter Bad Debt or Bad Debt Expense in the item's **Name** field.
- **Description**: Enter a brief description of the types of transactions that will be recorded using this item.
- **Price/rate**: You would normally enter the price/rate that you charge your customers for the service item that you are setting up. However, since this amount will vary, we will leave this field blank.
- **Income account**: From the drop-down menu, select **Bad Debt**. This should be an expense account on the chart of accounts list. If you did not create this account, click on the drop-down arrow, scroll up, and select **Add new** to create the bad debt expense account.

Now that you've set up the new **Bad Debt** expense item, you can use this item to record the bad debt on a credit memo form.

Creating a credit memo

In addition to recording bad debt, a credit memo is generally used to refund a customer for items purchased that were returned or services that were not rendered in full. After creating the credit memo, we can apply it to the unpaid customer invoice.

Follow these steps to create a credit memo:

1. Click on the **+ New** button and select **Credit Memo**, as shown in *Figure 10.9*:

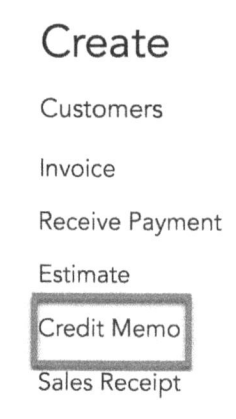

Figure 10.9: Navigating to Credit Memo

2. Fill in the fields shown in *Figure 10.10*:

Figure 10.10: Completing the fields in the Credit Memo form

Brief explanations of the fields to fill in to complete the credit memo are as follows:

- **Customer**: Select the customer from the drop-down menu.
- **Email**: The email address that you have on file will automatically populate this field. If you don't have an email address on file, you can type one in directly.
- **Billing address**: The billing address you have on file will automatically populate this field. If you don't have a billing address on file, you can enter one in this field.
- **Credit Memo Date**: Select the date you would like to record this credit memo.
- **PRODUCT/SERVICE**: Select the **Bad Debt Expense** item you created in the previous section from the drop-down menu.
- **DESCRIPTION**: The description field should automatically be populated with the description of the **Bad Debt** item.
- **QTY**: Select **1**.
- **RATE**: Enter the amount of the invoice that you want to write off in this field.
- **AMOUNT**: This field will automatically be populated with the amount you entered into the **RATE** field.
- **Message displayed on credit memo**: Provide a brief explanation for the bad debt to be written off in this field.

3. Once you've filled in all the fields in the credit memo, save it.

I will show you how QuickBooks applies the credit memo to the customer's open invoice next.

Applying a credit memo to an outstanding customer invoice

The final step in writing off bad debt is to remove the open invoice from accounts receivable. In most cases, QBO will automatically apply credits to open invoices if you have turned this feature on. In *Chapter 2, Company File Setup*, I showed you how to turn on the **Automatically apply credits** feature. If you choose not to use this feature, you can manually apply the credit memo to the open customer invoice.

Follow these steps to see how the credit memo shows up on the customer's account:

1. From the left menu, select **Sales**, as shown in *Figure 10.11*:

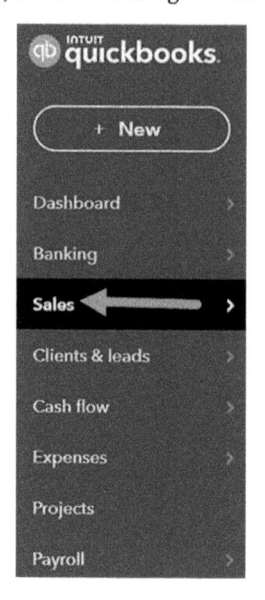

Figure 10.11: Navigating to Sales

2. On the next screen, click on the **All sales** tab, as shown below:

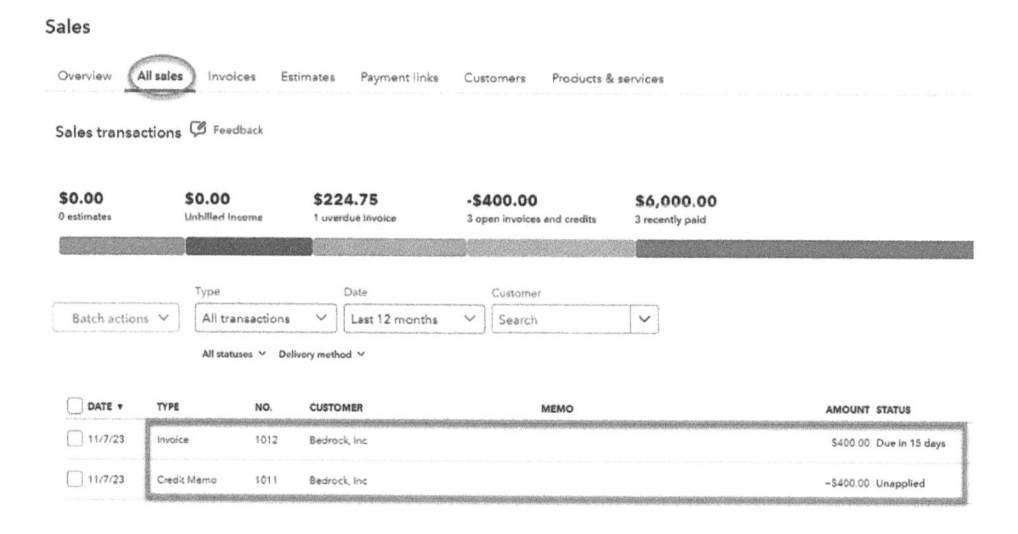

Figure 10.12: Selecting the invoices and/or credit memos to process (for better visualization, refer to https://packt.link/gbp/9781836649977)

Chapter 10

In *Figure 10.12*, you can see the invoice and the credit memo listed for **Bedrock, Inc**. However, the invoice remains open with a status of **Due in 15 days** and the credit memo has a status of **Unapplied**.

Now follow the steps below to apply the credit memo to the open invoice:

1. Click on **+New** and select **Receive payment**, as indicated in *Figure 10.13* below:

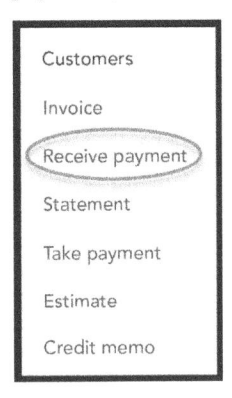

Figure 10.13: Selecting Receive payment

2. The **Receive Payment** window will be displayed, as shown in *Figure 10.14*:

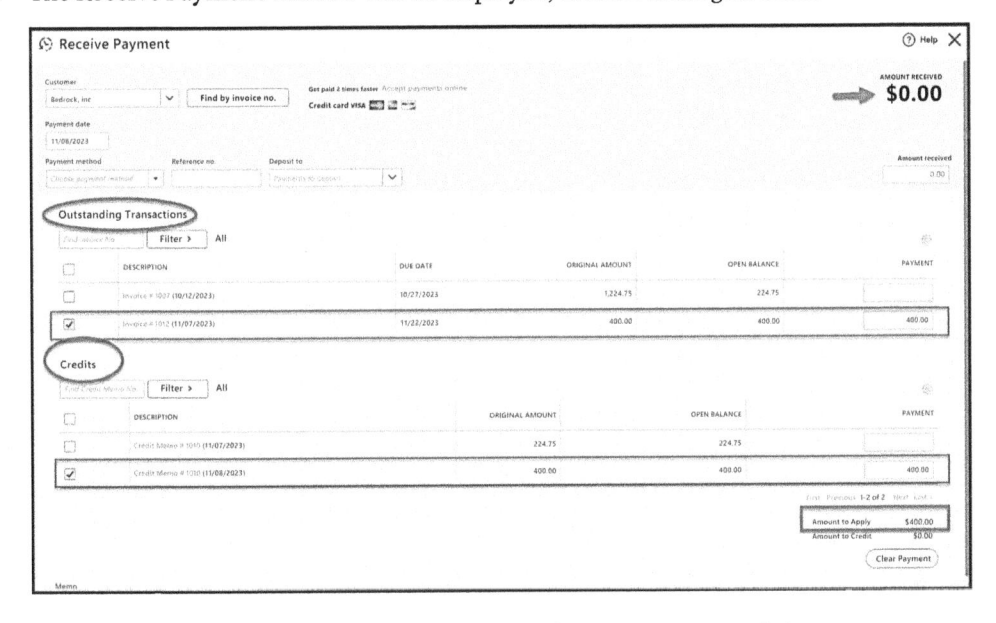

Figure 10.14: Completing the fields in the Receive Payment window

3. Select the invoice (**Invoice # 1012**) and the open credit (**Credit Memo # 1011**), as shown in *Figure 10.14*. The amount received should be **0.00** since they will offset each other.
4. After clicking on **Save and Close**, the following screen will be displayed:

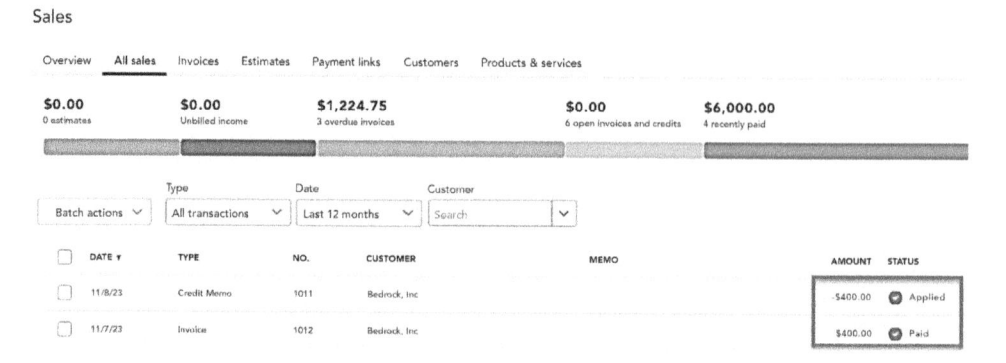

Figure 10.15: Reviewing the updated status for the invoice and credit memo

The status of the invoice is now **Paid** and the status of the credit memo is now **Applied**.

To summarize, it's important that you write off accounts as soon as they become uncollectible. This will ensure that the accounts receivable balance is not overstated. If you are an accrual basis taxpayer, you will not want to pay tax on income that you will never receive.

Issuing a customer refund

If the customer has already paid the invoice and you need to refund their money, you will not create a credit memo. Instead, create a refund receipt. To do this, click on the **+New** menu, select **Refund Receipt**, and complete the form as shown below:

Chapter 10   319

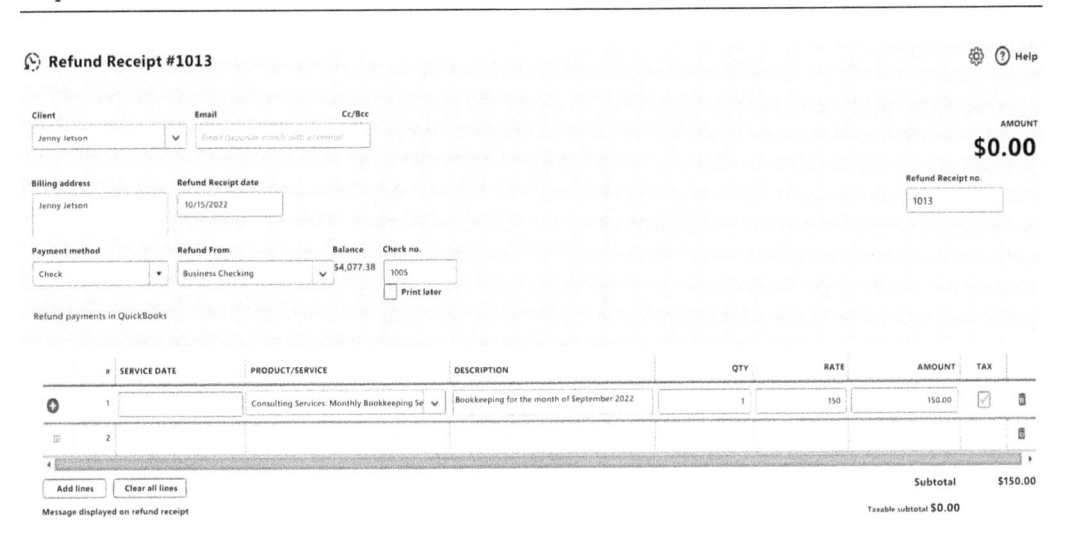

Figure 10.16: Creating a refund receipt

After saving the refund receipt, you will have the option to refund the customer's credit card on file **OR** issue a check.

If you provide ongoing services to customers on a weekly or bi-weekly basis but don't want to invoice customers that often, you should consider using delayed charges. Delayed charges allow you to accumulate charges in QuickBooks (without affecting the financial statements). Once you are ready to bill a customer, you can easily transfer the delayed charges to an invoice. We will discuss delayed charges and credits in detail next.

Tracking delayed charges and credits

Delayed charges and credits are used to keep track of services that are provided to customers so you can bill them sometime in the future. For example, if someone provides weekly pool maintenance or landscaping services to customers but does not want to bill them until the end of the month, delayed charges are ideal for keeping track of the services that are provided each week. These weekly services can easily be added to an invoice when it's time to bill the customer.

Follow these steps to record delayed charges:

1. Click on the **+ New** button and select **Delayed charge**, as shown in *Figure 10.17*:

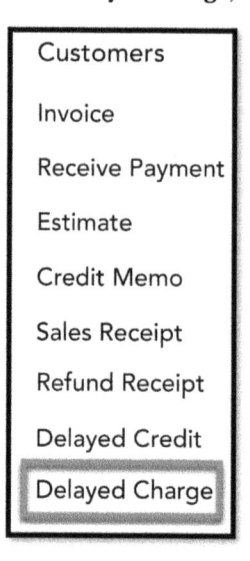

Figure 10.17: Navigating to Delayed charge

2. Fill in the necessary fields to record the delayed charge, as shown in *Figure 10.18*:

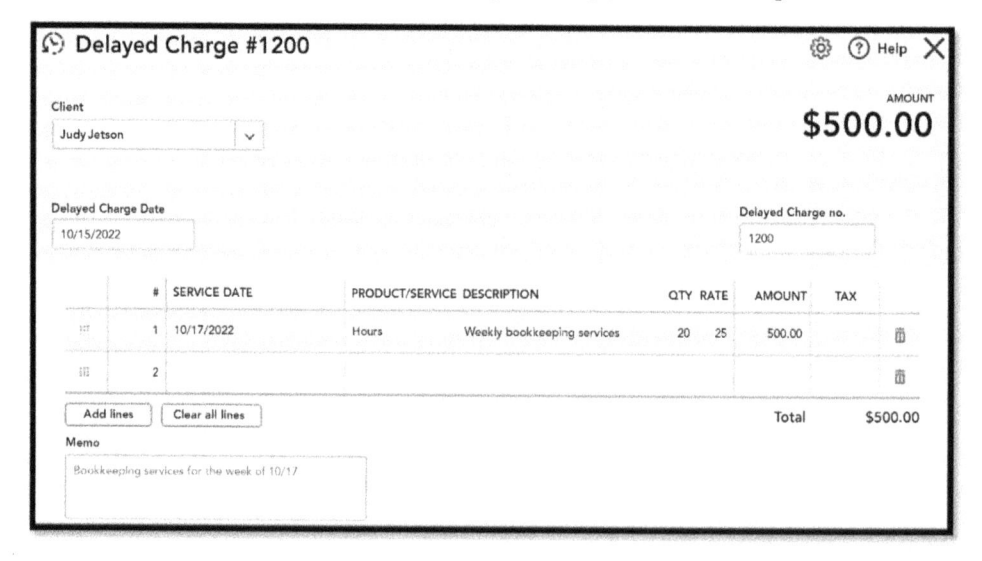

Figure 10.18: Completing the Delayed Charge form

Brief descriptions of the fields to fill in are as follows:

- **Customer/Client**: Select the customer from the drop-down menu.
- **Delayed Charge Date**: Select the date the services were provided.
- **PRODUCT/SERVICE**: Select the type of service that will be provided from the drop-down menu.
- **DESCRIPTION**: This field should automatically be populated with the description that was used to set up the product/service. However, you can also enter a description directly in this field.
- **QTY**: Type a quantity into this field, if applicable.
- **RATE**: Enter the total amount or the hourly rate for the service.
- **AMOUNT**: This field is automatically calculated by taking the quantity and multiplying it by the rate.
- **Memo**: Enter a brief description in this field.

> When you save a delayed charge, it is a non-posting transaction, which means it doesn't affect the financial statements.

Next, I will show you how to add delayed charges to an invoice:

1. From the **+New** menu, select **Invoice**. Select a customer from the drop-down menu and you will see a drawer open to the far right, listing the delayed charges that haven't been billed:

2. On this screen, click the **Add** button to add the charges to an invoice.

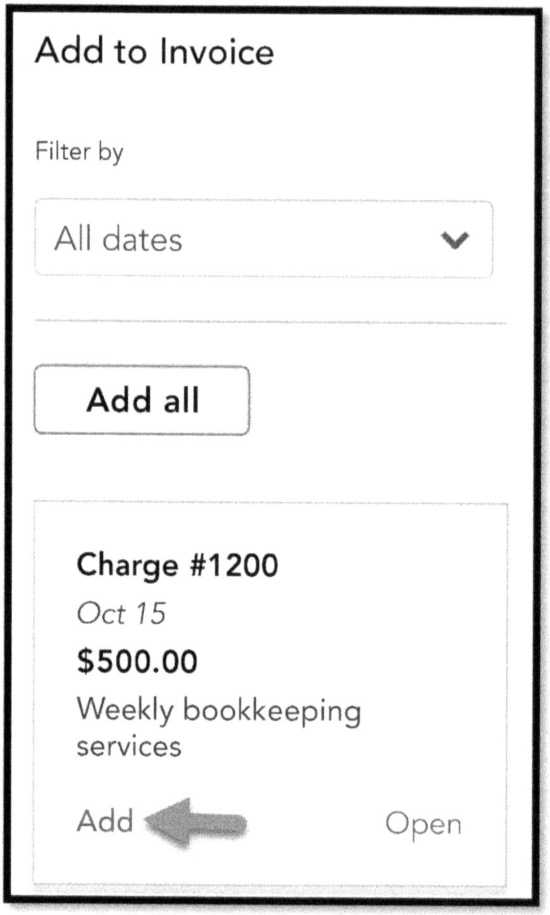

Figure 10.19: Selecting the delayed charges to bill the customer for

3. Save the invoice to record an increase in accounts receivable and income.

If you would like to review a list of unbilled charges before creating an invoice, you can do so by running an **Unbilled charges** report. I will show you how to generate this report next.

1. Click on **Reports**, scroll to the **Who owes you** section, and select **Unbilled charges**, as shown in *Figure 10.20*:

2. The **Unbilled Charges** report will appear:

Customer	Date	Transaction type	Num	Posting	Store full name	Memo/Description	Amount	Balance
∨ Astro Jetson (1)								
Astro Jetson	10/07/2024	Charge	100	No	-	Bookkeeping services	$100.00	$100.00
Total for Astro Jetson							$100.00	
∨ Bedrock, Inc (1)								
Bedrock, Inc	10/07/2024	Charge	101	No	-	Bookkeeping services	$200.00	$200.00
Total for Bedrock, Inc							$200.00	
∨ George Jetson (1)								
George Jetson	10/14/2024	Charge	102	No	-	Bookkeeping services	$100.00	$100.00
Total for George Jetson							$100.00	
							$400.00	

Figure 10.20: Sample Unbilled Charges report (for better visualization, refer to https://packt.link/gbp/9781836649977)

That's how delayed charges work. One last thing you need to know is that if you need to reverse a delayed charge, you can do so by recording a delayed credit. Similar to delayed charges, navigate to the **+New** menu and select **Delayed credit**. Follow the onscreen instructions to record the delayed credit.

Summary

In this chapter, you have learned how to handle many special transactions in QBO. You may be able to take advantage of a few of these now or keep them in your back pocket for later on when you need them. To recap, you now know how to set up and track payments for a business loan or line of credit. We also discussed the importance of recording bad debt expenses, which you now know how to record in QuickBooks to ensure that your financials are accurate. We covered how to issue a credit memo for products/services that did not meet the customer's expectations, as well as how to refund receipts for customers who don't have an invoice to apply a credit memo to. Finally, you learned how to record delayed charges and credits commonly used by landscaping and maintenance industries to track routine services provided to customers that will be billed monthly.

In the next chapter, we will cover the pros and cons of connecting your online store, like Shopify or etsy to QBO.

Join our community on Discord

Join our community's Discord space for discussions with the authors and other readers:

https://packt.link/powerusers

Part 5

Integrating E-Commerce Platforms and Advanced Inventory Management

If your business involves e-commerce or complex inventory needs, this next part is for you. We'll start by integrating your online store with QuickBooks Online, covering everything from connecting sales channels to evaluating the pros and cons of app integrations. Then, we'll dive into advanced inventory management—showing you how to track products, manage purchase orders, and generate reports to keep your business running smoothly.

This part comprises the following chapters:

- *Chapter 11, Integrating e-commerce platforms with QuickBooks Online*
- *Chapter 12, Advanced Inventory Management*

11
Integrating E-Commerce Platforms with QuickBooks Online

If you sell products on a sales channel like Etsy, Shopify, Amazon, or another online store, your business falls into the e-commerce industry. Like other small businesses, it's important that you stay on top of your bookkeeping. It doesn't take long before an e-commerce business owner realizes that putting their products on an e-commerce platform isn't enough. Why? Because most of these platforms only capture one aspect of your business – sales. They will typically keep track of customer orders, shipping, order fulfillment, and credit card processing. They do not keep track of indirect expenses like utilities, rent, monthly telephone bills, monthly internet bills, payroll, etc. In order to have a complete set of financial statements, all aspects of your business need to reside in one system – **QuickBooks Online (QBO)**.

In *Chapter 3, Customizing QuickBooks for Your Business*, we introduced you to the QuickBooks App Center. There are more than 40 sales channels that allow you to manage your e-commerce business. Some of the sales channels that seamlessly integrate with QBO are WooCommerce, Shopify, Etsy, Amazon, eBay, and Square, to name a few.

> Throughout this chapter, the terms e-commerce, sales channel, app, and online store are used interchangeably.

In this chapter, we will cover the following topics:

- Reviewing apps to decide if connecting them to QBO is right for you
- Pros of connecting a sales channel to QuickBooks
- Cons of connecting a sales channel to QuickBooks
- How to connect your sales channel to QuickBooks

To see the full list of e-commerce apps that integrate with QBO, navigate to the **Apps** (1) menu on the left navigation bar, click on the **Find Apps** (2) tab, click on **Browse Categories** (3), and select **e-commerce Management** (4) as shown below:

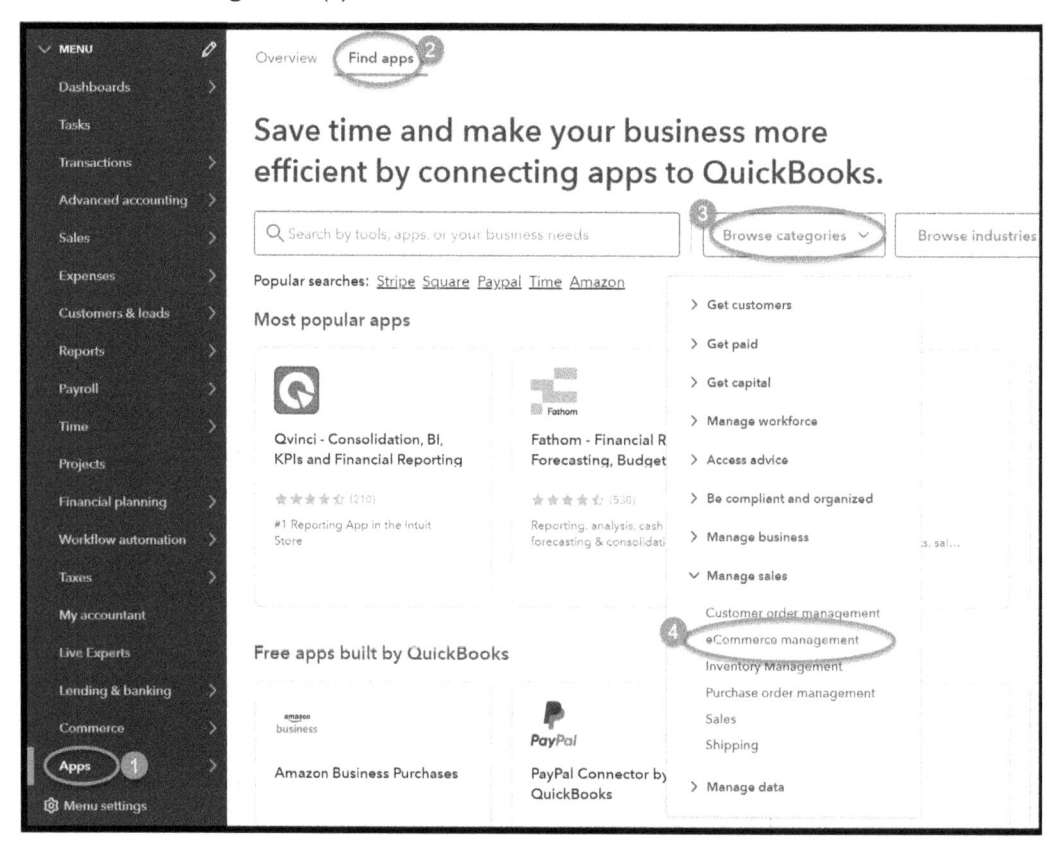

Figure 11.1: Finding eCommerce management

DO NOT proceed to connect to an app without fully understanding how the app works. You must find out how the app works and set up a few things before connecting it to QBO. Otherwise, you will run the risk of importing duplicate transactions that will cause your financial statements to be incorrect. There is no UNDO button.

Reviewing apps before connecting them to QBO

Intuit has done most of the legwork so that you don't have to start your research from scratch. For example, when you select an app from the App Center, you will find an overview of what the app does, how much it costs, customer reviews, apps similar to the one you have chosen, and FAQs, as shown here:

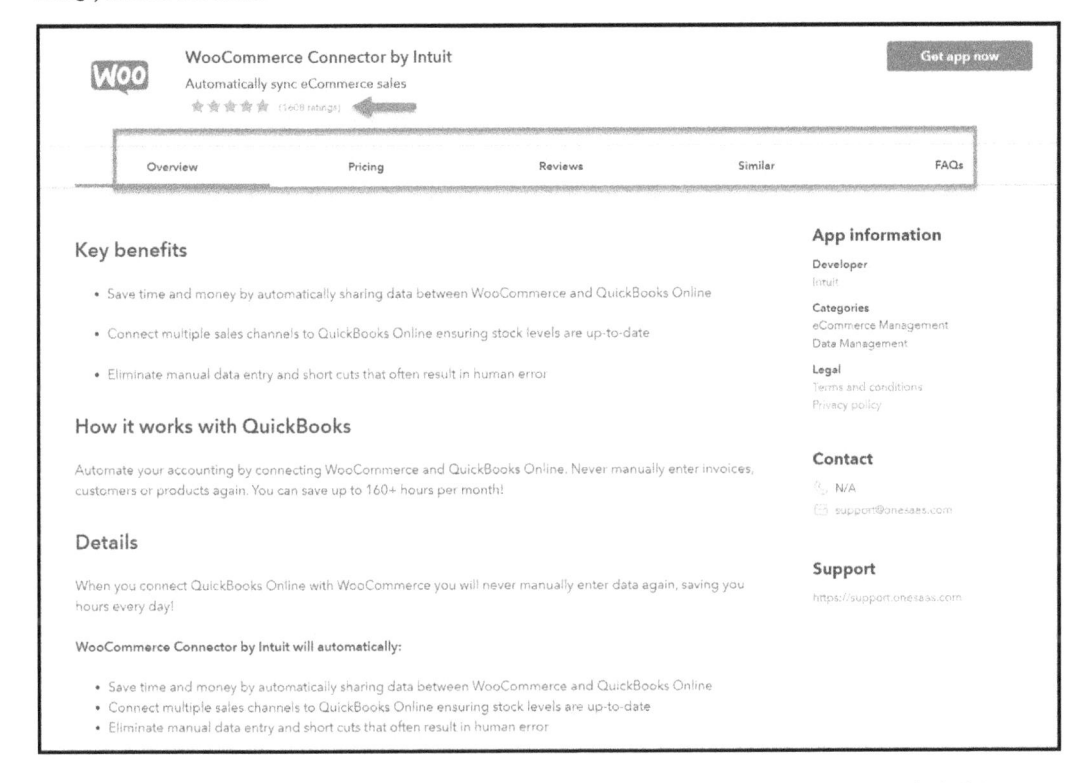

Figure 11.2: App overview in QBO (for better visualization, refer to https://packt.link/gbp/9781836649977)

Additional information you will find here are the key benefits of using the app, how it works with QBO, and the contact information for the company. Unfortunately, this information isn't going to be enough for you to make a decision. If the app sounds like it will work for you, contact the company to schedule a demo. Most of these companies will either point you to their website where they have a pre-recorded video you can watch, or they will contact you to schedule a live demo. I suggest you do both, if the option is available.

If you watch a pre-recorded demo, it will spark questions that are related to how things would work with your particular business; write these questions down. These questions can be answered during the live demonstration.

If you are not comfortable with making this decision on your own, be sure to have your accountant or bookkeeper attend the demo with you. They will know precisely what questions to ask.

There are both pros and cons to connecting a sales channel to QBO. We will cover the pros first.

Pros of connecting a sales channel to QuickBooks

There are several pros to integrating your e-commerce platform with QBO. Below is a list of pros that I've found invaluable when integrating e-commerce apps:

- **Access to complete financial statements**: When you integrate your e-commerce platform with QBO, all aspects of your business finances – the money coming in (sales) and the money going out (expenses) – are in one centralized location. This allows you to generate reports such as your profit and loss, balance sheet report, and statement of cash flows that include everything. Without this integration, you will need to generate reports from QBO and from your e-commerce system and then manually enter the numbers into an Excel spreadsheet to combine them.

- **Eliminates manual data entry**: E-commerce integration allows you to eliminate the need to manually record sales in QBO using an invoice or sales form. Instead, this data will automatically import from the e-commerce app into QBO on a daily or hourly basis and in some cases a few minutes!

- **Accurate and reliable data**: One of the benefits of eliminating manual data entry is you minimize errors that occur when data has to be entered manually. Importing the data takes the human element out of the equation, which improves the accuracy of the data, making it very reliable.

- **No expensive equipment or IT department required**: Like all the apps you will find in the Intuit App Center, e-commerce apps do not require you to purchase any expensive servers or IT personnel. The monthly cost of the app includes unlimited tech support. While the days/times when the support team is available might vary depending on the app, you can be assured that if you run into an issue, there will be a team that is available to assist you.

- **Access to new features/upgrades**: Similar to QBO, there are always improvements made to these apps as well as new features that you will gain access to as a subscriber.

- **Cloud-based**: All e-commerce apps that integrate with QBO are cloud-based. You can either access your information by logging into QBO or you can go directly to the app in most cases. For both, you just need a mobile device with an internet connection.

Cons of connecting a sales channel to QuickBooks

While there are many pros to integrating e-commerce platforms with QBO, there are a few cons that you need to be aware of too:

- **Additional costs**: The cost of the e-commerce apps is *not* included in your QBO subscription. You will have to pay a monthly fee that will typically be based on the number of users who need access to the app. As mentioned previously, pricing can be found in the Intuit App Center.

    > QuickBooks Certified ProAdvisors (like myself) may be able to get you a discount on the pricing of certain apps. If you need assistance with managing your books or researching apps, I recommend you check out the **Find A ProAdvisor** directory to locate a qualified QuickBooks Pro: `https://quickbooks.intuit.com/find-an-accountant/`.

- **Initial investment of time and/or money**: In my experience, many small business owners do not have the time or expertise to go about selecting the right app. This means you will need to hire an accounting professional who can do the research and manage the integration for you. Be sure to build this into your cost when considering integrating e-commerce apps.

- **Security risk**: One of the requirements of integrating QBO with any app is that you will have to agree to share information with the apps. This is part of having the ability for the data in both QBO and the e-commerce app to sync. There will always be a risk in doing this, but you can rest assured that Intuit has taken the steps to properly vet each product that has been granted access to the Intuit App Center. There are strict requirements that the apps must meet in order to be included. To learn more about this process and how Intuit protects your data, check out Intuit's privacy statement at `https://www.intuit.com/privacy/statement/`.

- **Email/chat support only**: To minimize costs, many of the customer service/support teams are only available via email or chat. It is rare that you will have access to a support person via telephone. Make sure that you read the reviews for the apps you are considering and find out what customers say about the quality of the support.

- **Access to support**: One other note regarding tech support for apps. Many of the support teams work overseas and may not offer 24/7/365 support. When reviewing apps to determine which will work best for you, find out the hours of operation for tech support. If they offer a subscription that includes 24/7/365 support, you may want to consider it.

How to connect a sales channel to QuickBooks

While I highly recommend you consult an accountant or QuickBooks Certified ProAdvisor to assist you with connecting your sales channels to QBO, you can do it yourself. Please note that the instructions in this section only apply to businesses that meet the following criteria:

- You sell only in the US and get paid in USD
- You don't need to bring in customers, products, or inventory from your sales channels

If you **DON'T** meet one or both criteria, consult with a QuickBooks Certified ProAdvisor who can assist you with other options. If you **DO** meet **BOTH** criteria, then follow the instructions below to connect your sales channel to QBO:

1. Sign in to QBO as the **company admin**. The only user who has the authority to connect sales channels is someone with **company admin** access. In *Chapter 3, Customizing QuickBooks for Your Business*, we covered how to give other users access to QBO.

2. On the left navigation bar, select **Commerce**, then select **Connect sales channel**, as shown here:

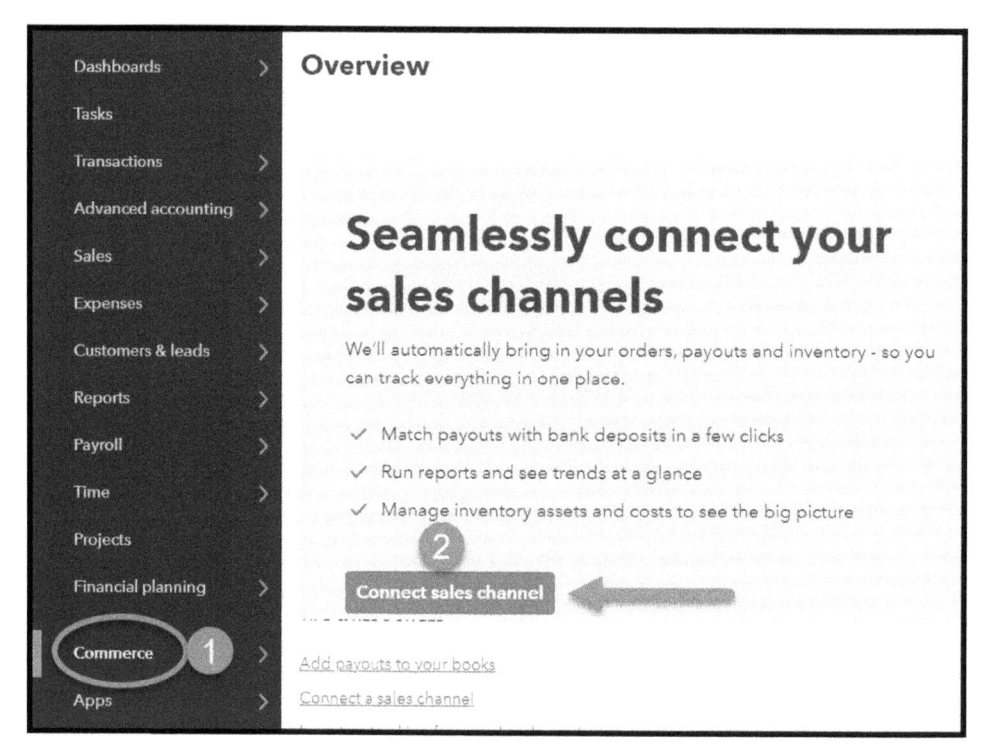

Figure 11.3: Navigate to Connect sales channel

Chapter 11 333

3. On the next screen, select the sales channel you want to connect and click on the **Next** button:

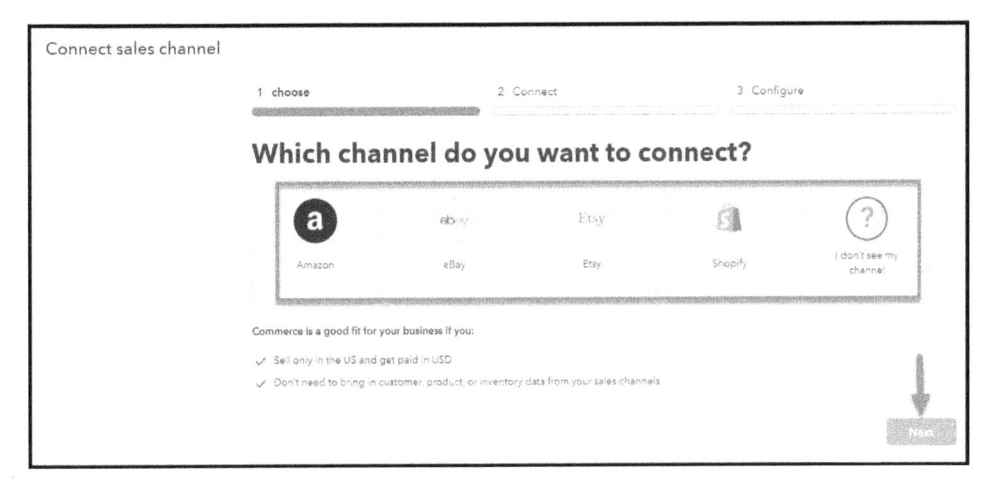

Figure 11.4: Select a sales channel to connect

If you don't see your sales channel listed, select the **I don't see my sales channel** option for a complete list of sales channels that integrate with QBO.

> For demonstration purposes, we are going to walk through how to connect to Shopify. Please keep in mind that the screenshots you see may differ if you are connecting to a different sales channel.

4. Select **Shopify** and you will see the following screen, where you'll be offered the option of turning on inventory tracking:

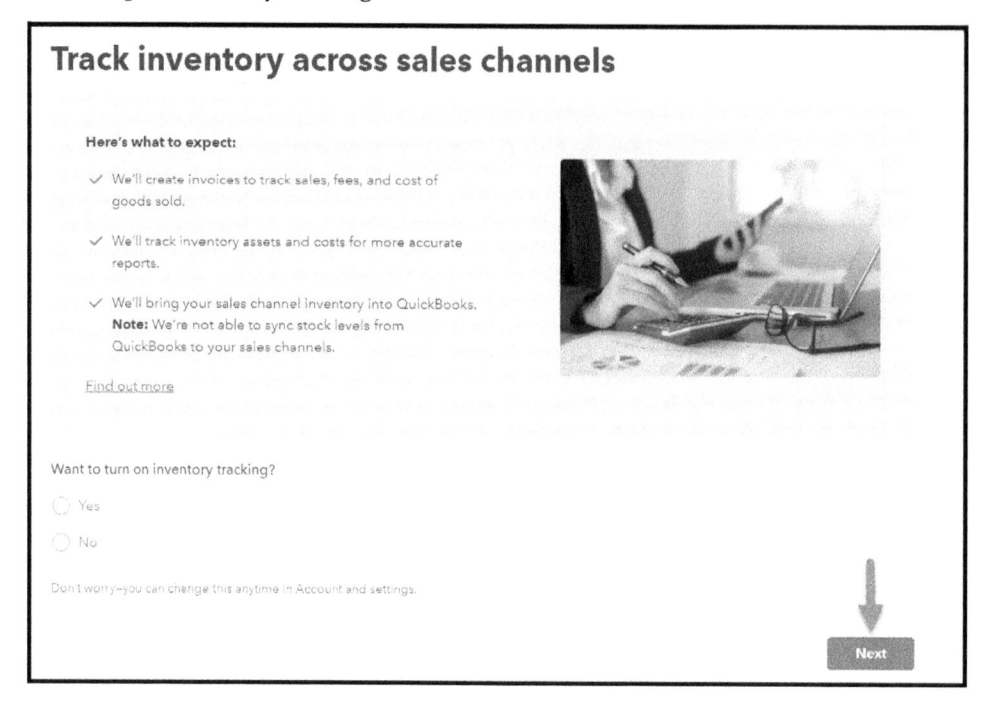

Figure 11.5: Determine whether to turn on inventory tracking

By turning on inventory tracking, you are enabling **Shopify** to do the following:

- Create invoices to track sales, fees, and cost of goods sold
- Track inventory products and costs
- Bring sales channel inventory into QBO

Shopify will not be able to sync stock levels from QBO to your sales channels.

Select **No** if you are not sure about inventory tracking. You can always turn it on later, if needed.

Chapter 11   335

5. Click the **Next** button and the following screen displays, where you'll observe two options for recording sales – **Individually** or **Summary**:

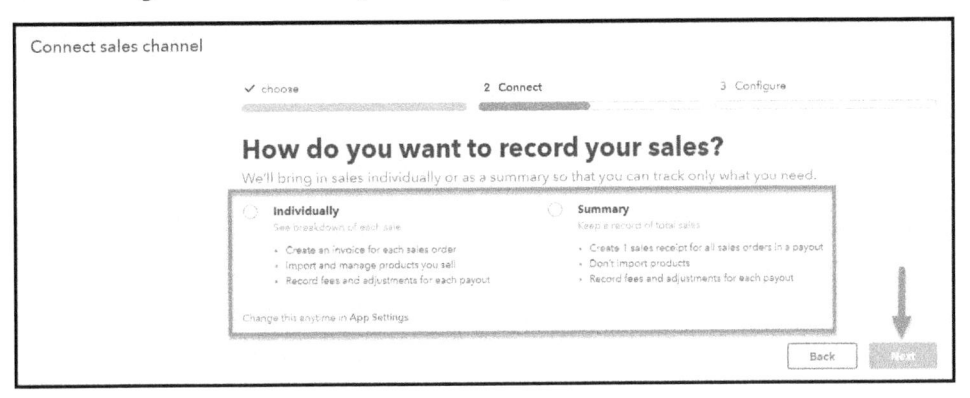

Figure 11.6: Individually or Summary

Below is a description of what each method entails:

- **Individually**: Sales will be recorded using an invoice for each sales order. Products will be imported from the sales channel into QBO. Fees and adjustments for each payout will be recorded. This method is ideal if you want the ability to track each item that you sell to a customer.

- **Summary**: Total sales will be recorded on a sales receipt for each payout. No products will be imported from the sales channel. Fees and adjustments will be recorded for each payout. This method is ideal if you *don't* need to record sales for each customer by product.

> In most cases, I recommend the **Summary** method because if you need individual sales data, you can always take a look at the e-commerce platform, which will have this information for you to refer to if needed.

6. Click **Next** and the following screen will display, where you can bring in historical sales data from your sales channel if you need to:

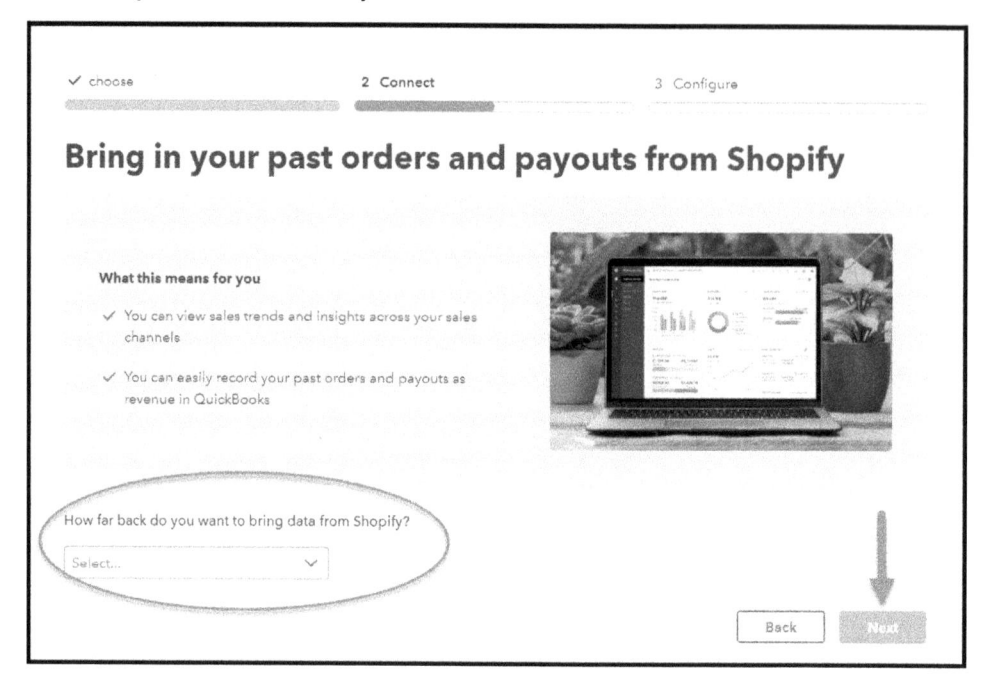

Figure 11.7: Bringing in historical sales data

Keep in mind that the time frame allowed will vary. In the case of Shopify, your options are as follows:

- Two years
- Beginning of the current year (January)
- Today
- Custom date

> **Caution**
>
> Be sure you select the correct date range. Once you click the **Next** button, you will not be able to change this. If you are not sure what date range to use, please consult with your CPA or ProAdvisor for assistance.

7. After making your selections, click **Next** and the following screen will display which is really just for informational purposes:

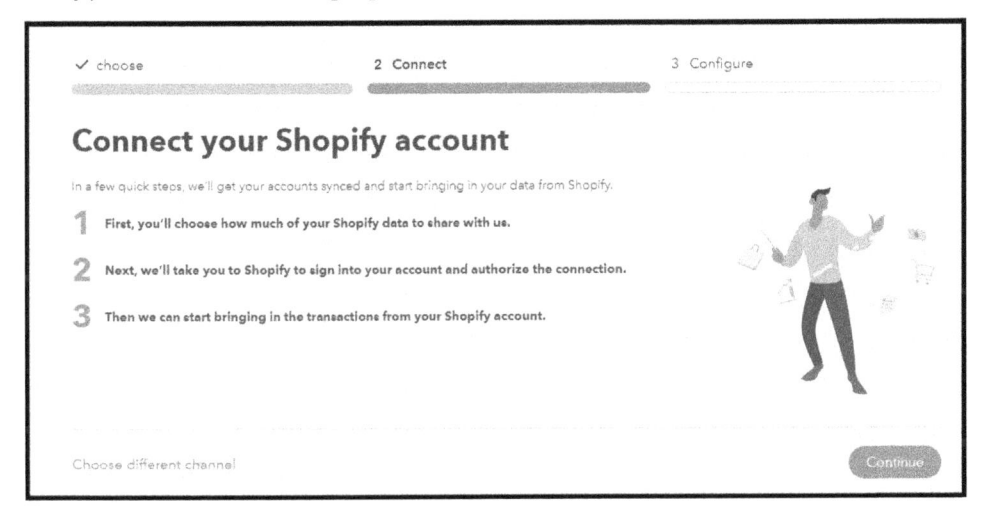

Figure 11.8: Connect your Shopify account (for better visualization, refer to https://packt.link/gbp/9781836649977)

This screen informs you that the next three steps will be as follows:

- You will verify how much data you would like to bring into QuickBooks
- You will sign in to your Shopify account and authorize the connection to QBO
- Your sales data will start importing from Shopify into QBO

8. Click **Continue** and the **Consent to Connect** screen displays:

Figure 11.9: Consent to connect QuickBooks to Sales channel account

In this screen, you will need to perform the following actions:

i. Confirm the start date that you want to bring sales data from Shopify into QBO for. Note that this will be your last opportunity to verify this date before the data imports; you cannot undo this action once it is complete.

ii. Click the **Agree** button to move to the next step.

iii. Enter your Shopify store address to get started as shown here:

Figure 11.10: Connecting your Shopify account

9. Select the **Connect** button and follow the on-screen instructions to sign in to your Shopify account and complete the integration.

> After you successfully connect your sales channel to QBO, you will need to ensure that payouts are mapped to the correct bank accounts. Be sure to consult your accountant or bookkeeper on the best way to do this.

Now that you have a better understanding of the importance of connecting your online store to QuickBooks Online, many of you may also need to know how to manage the complexities that often come with inventory. We will cover this topic in the next chapter.

Summary

In this chapter, we explained the importance of not only managing your sales for your online store but also having everything in one central location so that you can generate reports that include sales, expenses, assets, and liabilities for your business. We showed you how to navigate to the QBO Apps Center where you can find information on all the apps that help manage e-commerce businesses, such as pricing, demos, and customer reviews. Having this information at your fingertips will help you determine whether connecting the app to QBO is right for you. We covered several pros of connecting your sales channels to QBO as well as a few cons. Finally, we covered in detail the steps you would take to connect a sales channel, like Shopify, to QBO.

In the next chapter, we will cover how to properly manage the complexities that often come with purchasing and selling products.

Join our community on Discord

Join our community's Discord space for discussions with the authors and other readers:

`https://packt.link/powerusers`

12

Advanced Inventory Management

In the previous chapter, we discussed how Etsy, Square, Shopify, and other platforms allow you to easily manage sales and inventory for your online store but don't take into account all of the expenses that you incur, such as rent, payroll, and utilities. If you sell products in a brick-and-mortar store or out of your garage, you can easily keep track of these expenses as well as product orders, on-hand stock, and product sales to customers in QBO. While QBO is not ideal for the complex needs a manufacturing and wholesale business would require, it has the capability to manage simple, straightforward inventory.

In our *Small Business Bookkeeping* chapter, available as bonus content at https://packt.link/supplementary-content-9781836649977, we discuss three inventory methods: **LIFO (last-in, first-out)**, **FIFO (first-in, first-out)**, and average cost. QBO uses the FIFO method to track inventory. If you are not familiar with inventory methods, consult with an accountant to understand which method is right for your business. In this chapter, we will walk you through each step of the inventory management process, starting with turning on the inventory feature all the way to generating key reports that help you manage inventory. As discussed in *Chapter 1, Getting Started with QuickBooks Online*, the two plans that include inventory tracking are Plus and Advanced.

In this chapter, we will cover the following topics:

- Turning on inventory tracking in QuickBooks
- Adding products to QuickBooks
- Recording product sales in QuickBooks

- Ordering products from vendor suppliers
- Receiving products into inventory
- Generating inventory reports

Turning on inventory tracking in QuickBooks

If you have QBO Plus or Advanced, one of the questions you will encounter as you go through the initial setup is whether you need to track inventory. If you select *yes*, the inventory featured will automatically turn on for you. However, if you select *no*, you will need to go into the account settings to turn inventory tracking on before you can add your products to QBO.

Follow the steps below to turn on inventory tracking:

1. Click on the gear icon and select **Account and settings** as shown below:

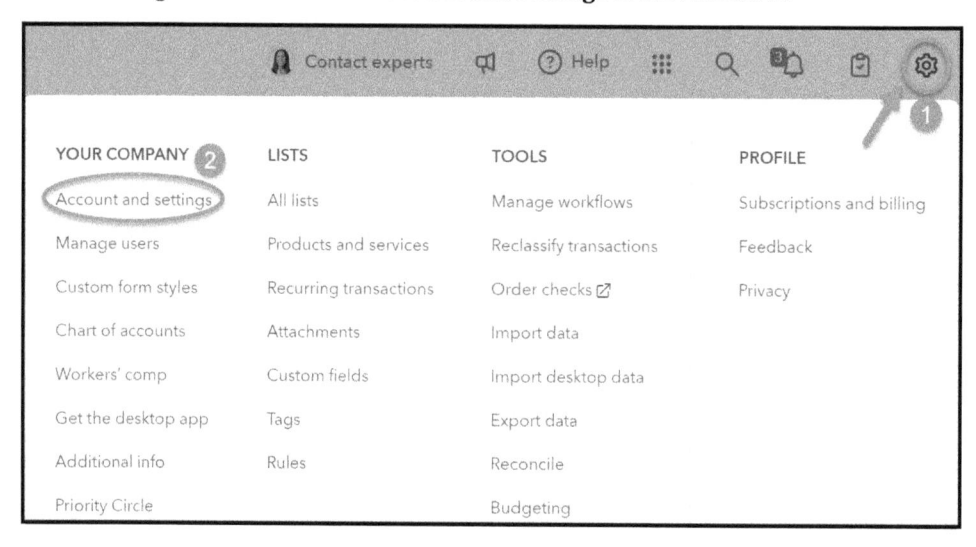

Figure 12.1: Navigating to Account and settings

Chapter 12 343

The following screen displays:

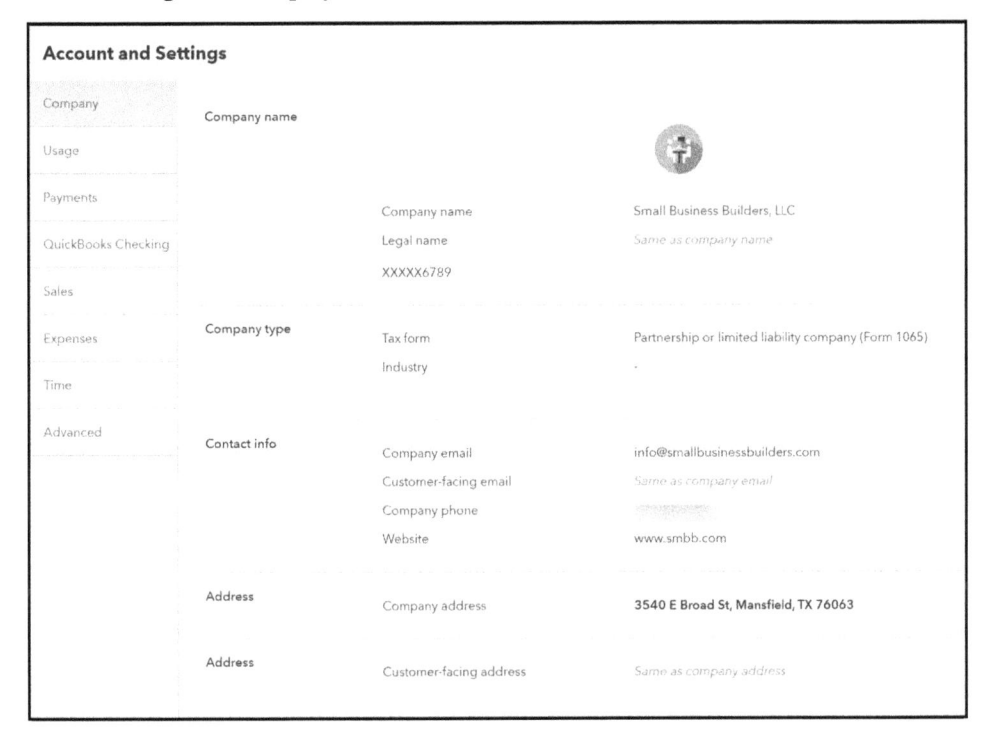

Account and Settings			
Company	Company name		
Usage			
Payments		Company name	Small Business Builders, LLC
QuickBooks Checking		Legal name	Same as company name
		XXXXX6789	
Sales			
Expenses	Company type	Tax form	Partnership or limited liability company (Form 1065)
		Industry	.
Time			
Advanced	Contact info	Company email	info@smallbusinessbuilders.com
		Customer-facing email	Same as company email
		Company phone	
		Website	www.smbb.com
	Address	Company address	3540 E Broad St, Mansfield, TX 76063
	Address	Customer-facing address	Same as company address

Figure 12.2: Displaying Account and Settings

2. Select **Sales** on the left menu bar. The **Products and services** section is where the inventory tracking options are:

Account and Settings			
Sales	Products and services	Show Product/Service column on sales forms	On
Expenses		Show SKU column	Off
		Turn on price rules BETA	Off
Time		Track quantity and price/rate	On
Advanced		Track inventory quantity on hand	On
		Track inventory for sales channels	Off
		Revenue recognition Learn more	Off

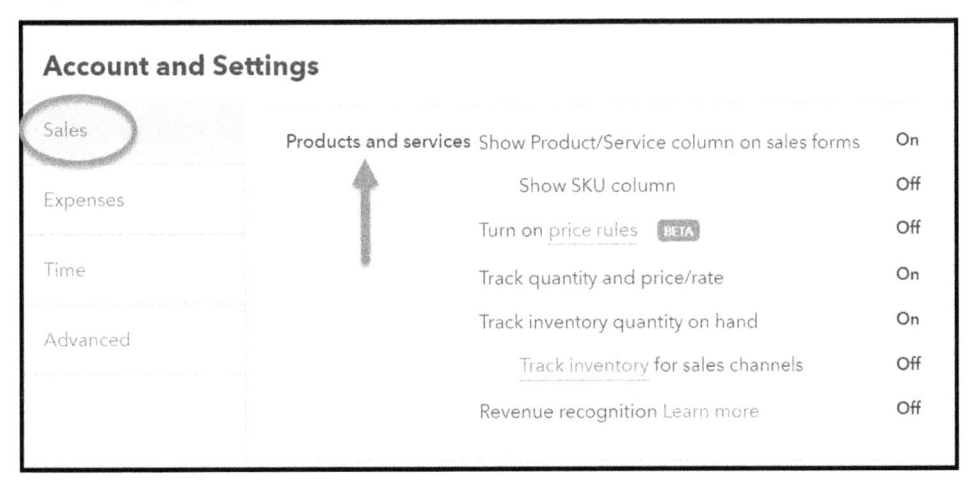

Figure 12.3: Reviewing inventory tracking options

Below is a brief description of the inventory tracking options available:

- **Show Product/Service column on sales forms:** This option is typically automatically turned on. It ensures that there is a column on your sales forms that shows what products the customer has purchased.

- **Show SKU column:** If you use an SKU to identify your products, turning this feature on ensures that there is a column on your sales forms that displays the SKU. An SKU is a unique number used to identify a retail product for inventory purposes. This option is normally turned off, so you will need to click on the radio button to turn it on.

- **Turn on price rules:** Price rules allow you to set up special pricing for specific customers for a specified timeframe. For example, you can create a price rule that allows for a 50% discount on all Christmas decorations that begins December 26th. By default, this feature is off so you will need to turn it on to start using it.

- **Track quantity and price/rate:** This option is typically automatically turned on. It ensures that there is a column on your sales forms that shows the quantity and price of products.

- **Track inventory quantity on hand:** This option allows you to track inventory quantities and cost. As mentioned previously, it will automatically turn on if you indicated that you need to track inventory during the setup process. If you did not, you will need to turn it on here.

- **Track inventory for sales channels:** If you have an online store, turning this feature on will automatically bring in your inventory from the sales channel you are using (e.g., Etsy, Shopify, etc.).

- **Revenue recognition:** This feature allows you to record a payment for a product or service you'll deliver in the future and recognize the revenue over time. This feature is only available in QBO Advanced subscriptions. It is recommended that you consult with an accounting professional before turning on this feature to ensure that you need it and that you understand how it works.

3. Turn on the following features for basic inventory tracking:

    - **Show Product/Service column on sales**
    - **Track quantity and price/rate**
    - **Track inventory quantity on hand**

4. Save your changes and click **Done** in the bottom-right corner of the screen to close the **Account and settings** window.

Adding products in QuickBooks Online

After you have turned on inventory tracking, you are ready to add the products that you sell in QuickBooks. You can choose to add products manually or import them from an Excel (.xls) or CSV (.csv) file. If you've got more than five products, I recommend using the *import* option. In this chapter, I will cover how to add products manually. To learn how to import from a spreadsheet, refer to *Chapter 4, Managing Customer, Vendor, and Products and Services Lists*, for step-by-step instructions.

Follow the steps below to add products to QuickBooks Online:

1. Click on the **Gear** icon and select **Products and services** below the **LISTS** column as shown here:

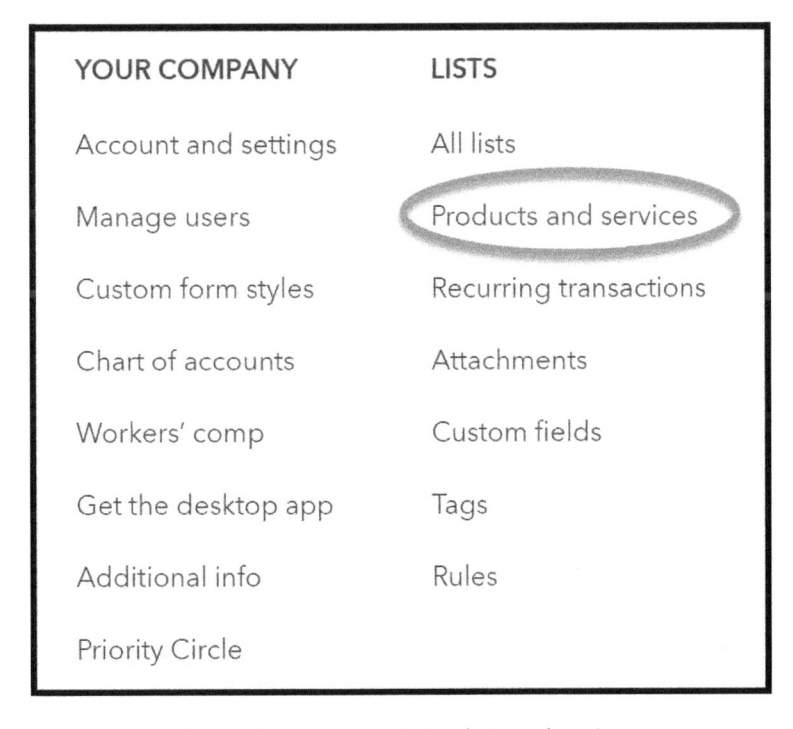

YOUR COMPANY	LISTS
Account and settings	All lists
Manage users	Products and services
Custom form styles	Recurring transactions
Chart of accounts	Attachments
Workers' comp	Custom fields
Get the desktop app	Tags
Additional info	Rules
Priority Circle	

Figure 12.4: Navigating to Products and services

The **Products & services** center displays:

Figure 12.5: Displaying the Products & services center

2. Click on the **New** button as shown in the preceding screenshot, and the item types display.

Figure 12.6: Selecting the Inventory item type

Chapter 12   347

3. Select **Inventory item** and complete the fields as shown below:

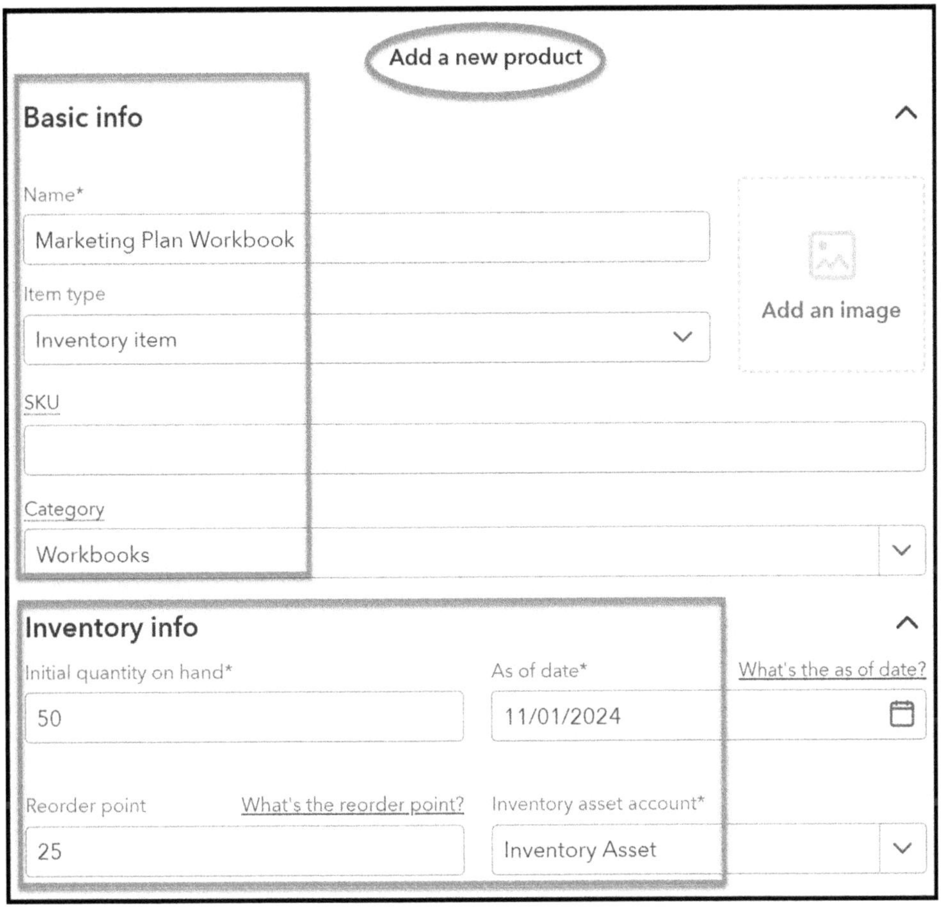

Add a new product

Basic info

Name*
Marketing Plan Workbook

Item type
Inventory item

SKU

Category
Workbooks

Add an image

Inventory info

Initial quantity on hand*
50

As of date*
11/01/2024

What's the as of date?

Reorder point   What's the reorder point?
25

Inventory asset account*
Inventory Asset

Figure 12.7: Completing the basic and inventory fields to add a new product to QBO

Below is a brief description of the fields to complete in the **Basic info** and **Inventory info** sections to add a new product.

- **Name:** Type the name of the product in this field (Marketing Plan Workbook).
- **Item type:** This field will automatically populate with the selection made in step 2 (**Inventory item**).
- **SKU:** Type the SKU in this field, if applicable.
- **Category:** Categories allow you to group products that are similar. For example, Small Business Builders has created a category for workbooks and one for the services that they sell. To create a new category, just click in the field and select **Add New** (Workbooks).
- **Initial quantity on hand:** You will need to know what your current inventory is for each product that you add to QBO. This is a required field so you will not be able to leave it blank (50).
- **As of date:** This is the date that you start tracking inventory in QBO; ideally, this will be the date that you set up the product in QBO (11/01/2024).
- **Reorder point:** A reorder point is the threshold when you should reorder more of a stock item. QuickBooks uses reorder points to let you know what's running low and what's out of stock (25).
- **Inventory asset account:** This field will automatically populate with **Inventory Asset**.

> Do not change **Inventory asset account** without consulting your accountant.

The following screenshot displays the sales and purchasing fields required when adding a new product:

Add a new product
Sales
Description
Marketing Plan Workbooks
Price/rate: 20	Income account*: Sales of Product Income
Sales tax category	What's a sales tax category?
Taxable–standard rate
Purchasing
Purchase description
Marketing Plan Workbooks
Purchase cost: 5	Expense account*: Cost of goods sold
Preferred vendor
A+ Printing

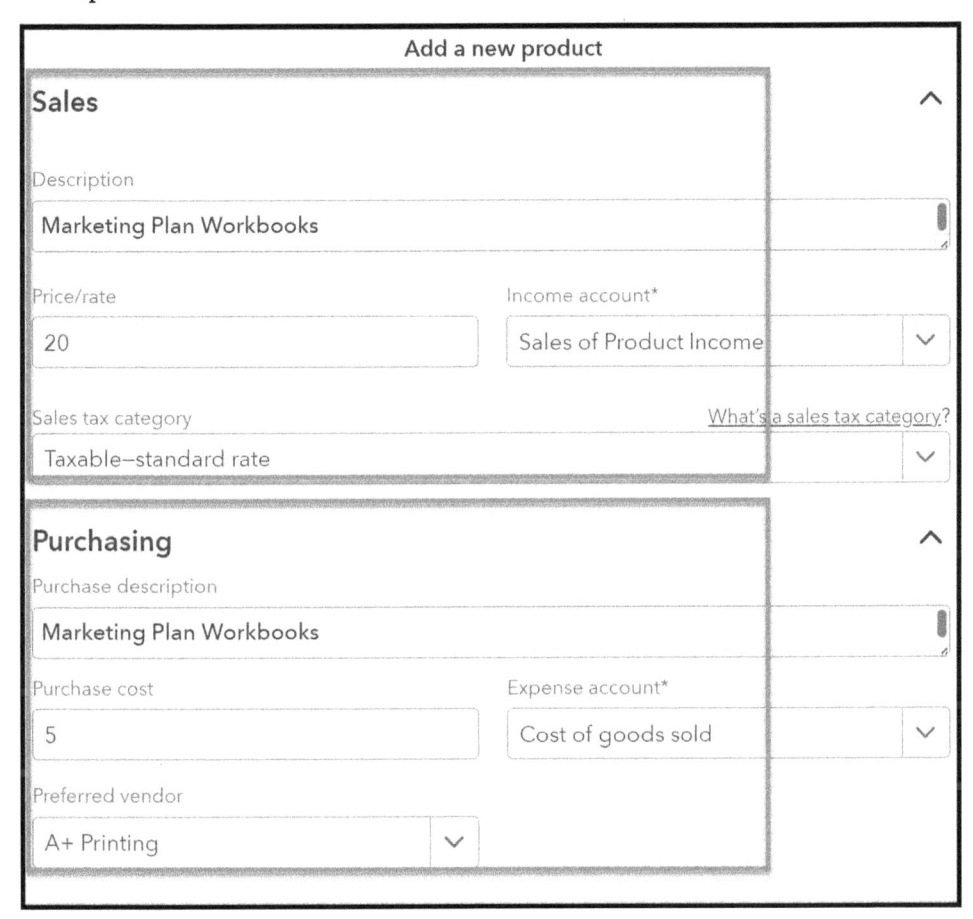

Figure 12.8: Completing the sales and purchasing fields to add a new product to QBO

The following sales fields will appear on sales forms such as invoices, sales receipts, and estimates:

- **Description**: Enter a brief description of the product for sale (Marketing Plan Workbooks).
- **Price/rate**: Enter the sales price per unit in this field (20).

- **Income account**: When setting up a product, this field will typically default to **Sales of Product Income**. However, if you would like to select a different account or set up a new account, you can do so. Simply click the drop-down menu and select the preferred account or choose **Add new** to create a new income account.
- **Sales tax category**: In most cases, products for resale are taxable. If you are not sure whether you should charge sales tax, please consult a tax professional or contact the state/local tax authority to find out (Taxable-standard rate).

The following purchasing fields will appear on forms such as purchase orders, bills, expenses, and checks:

- **Purchase description**: Enter a brief description of the product that you are purchasing from vendor suppliers. This description may vary from the sales description in *Figure 12.8* because you will need to use the description that your supplier has created to place your order (Marketing Plan Workbooks).
- **Purchase cost**: Enter what you pay your vendor/supplier for the product. Note that when calculating the cost of goods sold, QuickBooks will use what you actually paid to your vendor supplier.
- **Expense account**: This field will automatically populate with the account. (**Cost of goods sold**)

Similar to the inventory asset account, please do not change this account without consulting with an accountant. It could *significantly* affect your financial statements.

- **Preferred vendor**: The **Preferred vendor** field is *optional*. You can designate the vendor/supplier who you typically order this product from. If you cannot locate the vendor when you click the drop-down menu, choose **Add new** to add the vendor to QBO (**A+ Printing**).

Recording product sales in QuickBooks Online

After adding your products to QBO, you are ready to record sales to your customers. Recording sales for products is very similar to recording services. In *Chapter 6, Recording Sales Transactions in QuickBooks Online*, we covered how to record sales for services, and we touched on how this would work for product sales. In this section, we will cover how to record an invoice for product sales as well as the impact that would have on the financial statements.

Chapter 12

Follow the steps below to record product sales on an invoice:

1. Navigate to the **+New** button **(1)** and select **Invoice** **(2)** as indicated here:

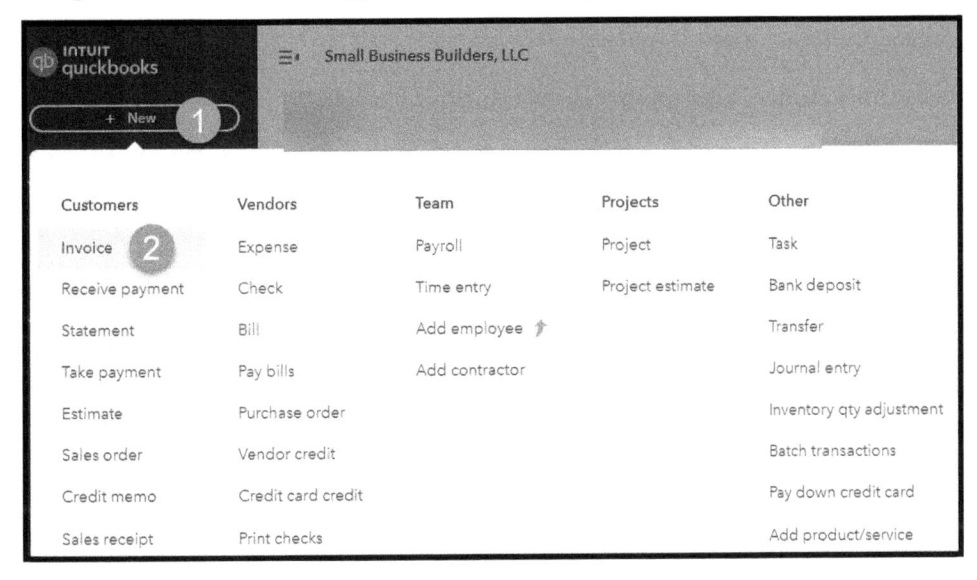

Figure 12.9: Navigating to the Invoice form

2. A blank invoice form will be displayed. Complete the form as shown:

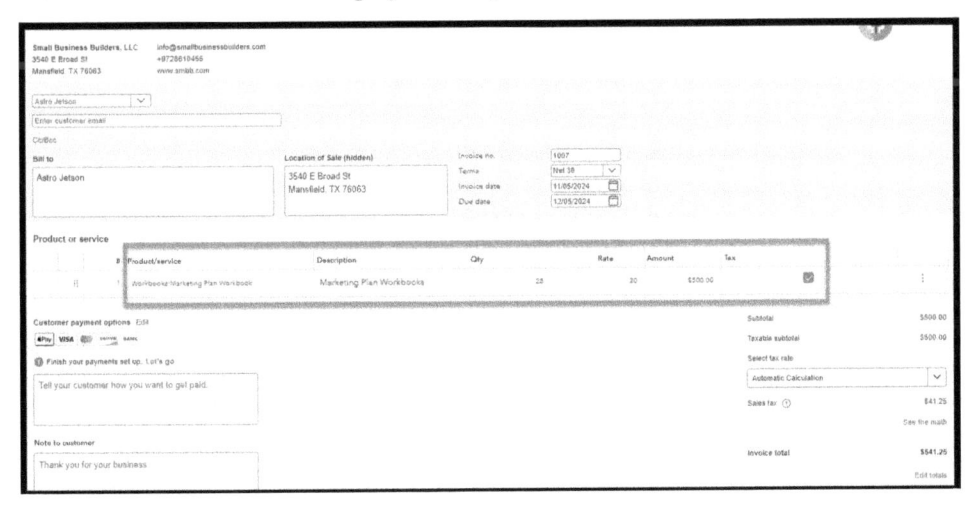

Figure 12.10: Completing an invoice form for a product sale

As you can observe, 25 marketing plan workbooks were sold to Astro Jetson. Since we added this product to QBO prior to creating the invoice, we simply selected **Marketing Plan Workbooks** from the drop-down menu below the **Product/service** column, and all of the other fields were automatically populated as follows:

- **Description: Marketing Plan Workbooks**
- **Qty: 25**
- **Rate: 20**
- **Amount: $500.00**
- **Tax**: Green checkmark indicates the item is taxable
- **Sales tax: $41.25**
- **Invoice total: $541.25**

When this invoice is saved, the following journal entry is recorded behind the scenes:

Transaction id	Date	Transaction type	Num	Name	Memo/Description	Account full name	Debit	Credit
27 (6)								
27	11/05/2024	Invoice	1007	Astro Jetson	-	Accounts Receivable (A/R)	$541.25	-
27	11/05/2024	Invoice	1007	Astro Jetson	Marketing Plan Workbooks	Sales of Product Income	-	$500.00
27	11/05/2024	Invoice	1007	Astro Jetson	Marketing Plan Workbooks	Inventory Asset	-	$125.00
27	11/05/2024	Invoice	1007	Astro Jetson	Marketing Plan Workbooks	Cost of goods sold	$125.00	-
27	11/05/2024	Invoice	1007	Astro Jetson	-	Texas State Comptroller Payable	-	$31.25
27	11/05/2024	Invoice	1007	Astro Jetson	-	Texas State Comptroller Payable	-	$10.00
Total for 27							$666.25	$666.25
							$666.25	$666.25

Figure 12.11: Transaction journal entry recorded on invoice for product sales

The **Balance Sheet** report was impacted by the increase of **$541.25** to the accounts receivable account, the decrease of **$125.00** to the **Inventory Asset** account, and the increase of the two **Texas State Comptroller Payable** accounts for **$31.25** and **$10.00** respectively for sales tax.

On the **Profit & loss** report, the **Sales of Product Income** account increased by **$500.00** and the **Cost of goods sold** account increased by **$125.00**.

> 💡 To see the transaction journal in QBO, display the invoice (after saving it), click on **More actions** located at the very bottom of the screen, and select **Transaction journal**.

Ordering products from vendor suppliers in QuickBooks

When you are running low on products and need to place an order with a vendor supplier, you should complete a purchase order form in QBO. The purchase order includes the contact details of the vendor supplier, a description of the product, the quantity, and the total amount. After completing this form, you can email it directly to your vendor supplier to place your order.

Follow the steps below to create a purchase order:

1. Click on the **+New** button and select **Purchase order** listed below the **Vendors** column, as shown below:

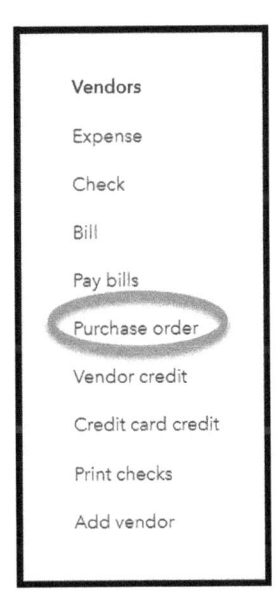

Figure 12.12: Navigate to Purchase order

2. A blank purchase order form displays. Complete the fields as follows:

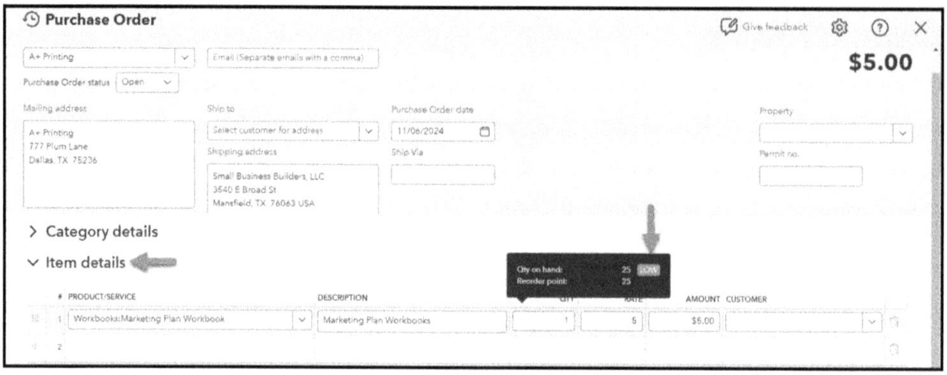

Figure 12.13: Complete purchase order form

- **Vendor name:** Select the vendor supplier from the drop-down menu.
- **Mailing address:** This field will automatically populate with the address you have on file.
- **Purchase Order date:** This field will default to today's date, but you can edit it if needed.
- **Shipping address:** This field will automatically populate with the address you have on file.
- **Ship Via:** Type the shipping method in this field (UPS, FedEx, USPS, etc.).
- **Category details:** This section is to be completed if you need to place an order for items that are not going into inventory (i.e., office supplies). This section is collapsed in *Figure 12.13*, but you can click the arrow to the left of **Category details** to display the fields to complete. Since we are ordering products that will be put into inventory, we will complete the **Item details** section.
- **Item details:** In this section, you will select the product/service from the drop-down menu and the **DESCRIPTION** field and the **RATE** field will automatically populate with the information you have on file for the product. You just need to type the quantity you would like to order and QBO will calculate the amount for you.

Hover your mouse over the **QTY** field and you will see a popup that shows the current quantity on hand and the reorder point as shown in *Figure 12.13*. Since the quantity on hand is the same as the reorder point, there is a **LOW** alert because once your inventory levels are less than or equal to the reorder point, it's time to place an order.

Chapter 12   355

After you complete the purchase order form, you can save it and print it out or email it directly from QBO to your vendor supplier. The purchase order does not have any financial impact on your books. It is simply a record of products ordered. Once you receive your products into inventory, that will create a financial record. We will cover receiving products into inventory next.

Receiving products into inventory

When your order arrives from your vendor supplier, you need to verify that everything you ordered has been received. If there are any discrepancies, you should notify your vendor supplier in writing immediately. To record the inventory received into QBO, you will complete a bill form. The vendor supplier might put your bill in the box with the products or they might send it to you via email or snail mail. Whether you have received the actual bill or not, you still want to record the inventory received.

Follow the steps below to record inventory received from a vendor supplier:

1. Click on the **+New** button and select **Bill**, which is listed below the **Vendors** column:

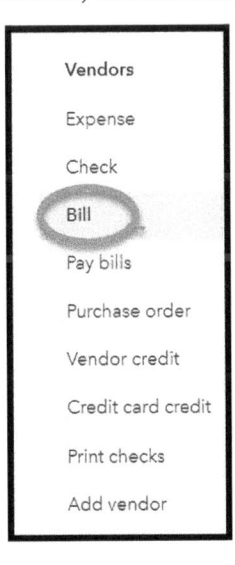

Figure 12.14: Navigating to the Bill form

2. A blank bill form displays as shown below:

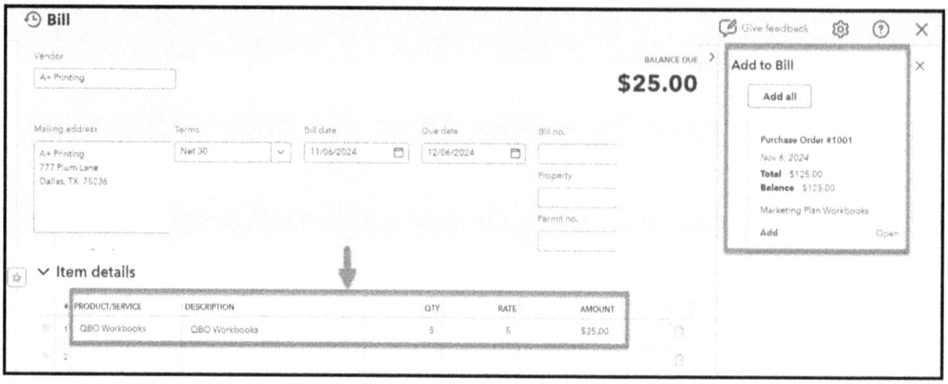

Figure 12.15: Completing the bill form

3. To the far right, you will see a window open and the option to add the items on the purchase order to the bill. Click the **Add all** button at the top of that window to confirm the transfer of the information on the purchase order to the bill form.

4. The purchase order information will appear in the **Item details** section. If all the items were received, you don't need to edit anything in this section. However, if you did not receive all the items, you will need to edit the **QTY** field to reflect the number of items that were received. For example, let's say that all five items were in the box, but two of them were damaged. You don't want to receive damaged items in your inventory because they are not sellable. In our example, you would change the quantity from 5 to 3 to accept the products that were not damaged.

> As mentioned previously, you would need to contact the vendor supplier to inform them of the issue so that they can either replace the damaged items or issue a credit memo to you. In *Chapter 10, Handling Special Transactions in QuickBooks Online*, we covered how to process a credit memo.

After completing the bills form, you can save it and pay it prior to the due date. To pay the bill, navigate to the **+New** button and select **Pay bills** located below the **Vendors** column. For step-by-step instructions on how to pay bills, refer to *Chapter 7, Recording Expenses in QuickBooks Online*.

So far, we have covered how to turn on inventory tracking, add your products to QBO, record product sales, order products from vendor suppliers, and receive those products into inventory. Now we will share key reports that will help you to stay on top of managing your inventory.

Generating inventory reports

As you know by now, the Reports Center in QBO includes several reports that you can generate with just a few clicks. While you can build your own reports, there is no need to. There are six reports that small businesses use regularly to manage their inventory: **Open Purchase Order List, Purchases by Product/Service Detail, Inventory Valuation Detail, Sales by Product/Service Detail, Purchases by Vendor Detail,** and **Physical Inventory Worksheet.** Each of these reports can be exported to Excel, PDF, or emailed directly out of QBO. Once you generate a report, the icons in the upper-right corner allow you to export the data into the format you need. For more information on reports, refer to *Chapter 16, Reports Center Overview*, available as bonus content at https://packt.link/supplementary-content-9781836649977.

Brief descriptions and screenshots of each report are included below.

Open Purchase Order List report

The **Open Purchase Order List** report is a standard report that you will find in the **Expenses and Vendors** report group. This report will show you a list of open purchase orders, grouped by vendor. You can use this report to determine which orders have not been received from vendor suppliers. In addition, if an order has been received but the purchase order form is listed on the report, the goods were not received against the purchase order. In that situation, you can simply click on the purchase order on the report to drill down to the purchase order and change the status to **Closed.**

Figure 12.16 is a screenshot of an **Open Purchase Order List** report:

Vendor	Date	Num	Memo/Description	Ship via	Amount	Open Balance
∨ A+ Printing (2)						
A+ Printing	11/06/2024	1002	-	-	$900.00	$900.00
A+ Printing	11/06/2024	1003	-	-	$50.00	$50.00
Total for A+ Printing					$950.00	$950.00
					$950.00	**$950.00**

Open Purchase Order List by Vendor
Small Business Builders, LLC
All Dates

Figure 12.16: Generating an Open Purchase Order List report

The **Open Purchase Order List** report includes the following information:

- Vendor name
- Purchase order date
- Purchase order number

358   Advanced Inventory Management

- Memo/description included on the purchase order
- Ship via method
- Purchase order amount
- Open balance

In our example, there are two open purchase orders for **A+ Printing**. Since the open balance for both purchase orders is the same as the total amount, that means that no items have been received for either order. To obtain additional details about these orders, hover your mouse over any field that has data (date, number, or amount) and double-click. The purchase order form will display with all of the details.

Purchases by Product/Service Detail report

The **Purchases by Product/Service Detail** report is a standard report that you will find in the **Expenses and Vendors** report group. This report includes a list of the purchases made for both products and services grouped by product or service. You can use this report to get an overall view of how much you have spent on all products/services or a specific product/service for the time period you specify.

Figure 12.17 shows a screenshot of a **Purchases by Product/Service Detail** report:

Product/Service	Date	Transaction type	Num	Vendor	Memo/Description	Qty	Rate	Amount	Balance
∨ QBO Workbooks (7)									
QBO Workbooks	10/06/2024	Bill	876543	A+ Printing	QBO Workbooks	5	$5.00	$25.00	$25.00
QBO Workbooks	10/06/2024	Inventory Starting Value	START	-	QBO Workbooks - Opening inv...	30	$5.00	$150.00	$175.00
QBO Workbooks	10/06/2024	Inventory Qty Adjust	2	-	Per physical inventory count on ...	-2	$0.00	-	$175.00
QBO Workbooks	10/06/2024	Inventory Qty Adjust	2	-	Per physical inventory count on ...	-2	$5.00	-$10.00	$165.00
QBO Workbooks	10/06/2024	Inventory Qty Adjust	2	-	Per physical inventory count on ...	2	$5.00	$10.00	$175.00
QBO Workbooks	10/15/2024	Vendor Credit	CM876543	A+ Printing	Order was short by 2 workbooks	-2	$5.00	-$10.00	$165.00
QBO Workbooks	11/06/2024	Bill	-	A+ Printing	QBO Workbooks	5	$5.00	$25.00	$190.00
Total for QBO Workbooks						36.00		$190.00	
∨ Workbooks (2)									
∨ Business Plan Workbooks (1)									
Business Plan Workbooks	11/01/2024	Inventory Starting Value	START	-	Business Plan Workbooks - Op...	0	$15.00	$0.00	$0.00
Total for Business Plan Wor...						0		$0.00	
∨ Marketing Plan Workbo... (2)									
Marketing Plan Workbook	11/01/2024	Inventory Starting Value	START	-	Marketing Plan Workbook - Op...	50	$5.00	$250.00	$250.00
Marketing Plan Workbook	11/06/2024	Bill	-	A+ Printing	Marketing Plan Workbooks	25	$5.00	$125.00	$375.00
Total for Marketing Plan W...						75.00		$375.00	
Total for Workbooks with su...						75.00		$375.00	
						111		$565.00	

Figure 12.17: Generating a Purchases by Product/Service Detail report (for better visualization, refer to https://packt.link/gbp/9781836649977)

The **Purchases by Product/Services Detail** report is grouped by product/service and includes the following information:

- Product/service
- Date of purchase
- Transaction type: bill, inventory adjustments, or vendor credit
- Reference number
- Vendor name
- Memo/description
- Quantity
- Rate/cost per unit
- Total amount of purchase
- Balance

In our example, there are three products that were purchased between January and December 2024. There were 36 QBO workbooks purchased for **$190.00**, no purchases were made for business plan workbooks, and 75 marketing plan workbooks were purchased for **$375.00**.

Inventory Valuation Detail report

The **Inventory Valuation Detail** report is a standard report that you will find in the **Sales and Customers** report group. This report shows the quantity on hand, the value of the inventory, and the average cost for each inventory item.

Figure 12.18 shows a screenshot of an **Inventory Valuation Detail** report:

DATE	TRANSACTION TYPE	NUM	NAME	QTY	RATE	FIFO COST	QTY ON HAND	ASSET VALUE
▼ QBO Workbooks								
10/06/2024	Bill	876543	A+ Printing	5.00	5.00	25.00	5.00	25.00
10/06/2024	Inventory Starting Value	START		30.00	5.00	150.00	35.00	175.00
10/06/2024	Inventory Qty Adjust	2		-2.00	5.00	-10.00	33.00	165.00
10/15/2024	Vendor Credit	CM876543	A+ Printing	-2.00	5.00	-10.00	31.00	155.00
11/06/2024	Bill		A+ Printing	5.00	5.00	25.00	36.00	180.00
Total for QBO Workbooks				36.00		$180.00	36.00	$180.00
▼ Workbooks								
▼ Business Plan Workbooks								
11/01/2024	Inventory Starting Value	START		0.00	15.00	0.00	0.00	0.00
Total for Business Plan Workbooks				0.00		$0.00	0.00	$0.00
▼ Marketing Plan Workbook								
11/01/2024	Inventory Starting Value	START		50.00	5.00	250.00	50.00	250.00
11/05/2024	Invoice	1007	Astro Jetson	-25.00	5.00	-125.00	25.00	125.00
11/06/2024	Bill		A+ Printing	25.00	5.00	125.00	50.00	250.00
Total for Marketing Plan Workbook				50.00		$250.00	50.00	$250.00
Total for Workbooks				50.00		$250.00	50.00	$250.00

Figure 12.18: Generating an Inventory Valuation Detail report (for better visualization, refer to https://packt.link/gbp/9781836649977)

The **Inventory Valuation Detail** report is grouped by product/service and includes the following information:

- Transaction date
- Transaction type: bill, inventory adjustment, or vendor credit
- Transaction number
- Vendor name
- Quantity
- Cost per unit
- FIFO cost
- On-hand quantity
- Asset value

There is also a summarized version of this report available within the **Sales and Customers** report group. In our example, there are three items: **QBO Workbooks, Business Plan Workbooks,** and **Marketing Plan Workbooks**. Both the QBO workbooks and the marketing plan workbooks have an on-hand inventory of 36 units and 50 units respectively. The FIFO cost is **$180.00** for the QBO workbooks and **$250.00** for the marketing plan workbooks. You can hover your mouse over any field on the report and double-click to drill down to additional details.

Sales by Product/Service Detail report

The **Sales by Product/Service Detail** report is a standard report you will find within the **Sales and Customers** report group. It includes a breakdown of all your sales for the time period specified.

Figure 12.19 shows a screenshot of a **Sales by Product/Service Detail** report:

Small Business Builders, LLC
Sales by Product/Service Detail
January - December 2024

DATE	TRANSACTION TYPE	NUM	CUSTOMER	MEMO/DESCRIPTION	QTY	SALES PRICE	AMOUNT
▼ Business Plan Workbook							
09/22/2024	Invoice	1001	Tina Turner	Business Plan Workbook	12.00	50.00	600.00
Total for Business Plan Workbook					12.00		$600.00
▼ Workbooks							
▼ Marketing Plan Workbook							
11/05/2024	Invoice	1007	Astro Jetson	Marketing Plan Workbooks	25.00	20.00	500.00
Total for Marketing Plan Workbook					25.00		$500.00
Total for Workbooks					25.00		$500.00
TOTAL					37.00		$1,100.00

Figure 12.19: Generating a Sales by Product/Service report

The **Sales by Product/Service Detail** report is grouped by product/service and includes the following information:

- Date of sale
- Transaction type (invoice, sales receipt, or credit memo)
- Transaction number
- Customer
- Memo/description of product sold
- Quantity sold
- Sales price per unit
- Total sales amount

Purchases by Vendor Detail report

The **Purchases by Vendor Detail** report is a standard report you will find within the **Expenses and Vendors** report group. It lists all the products you have purchased by vendor over the time period specified.

Figure 12.20 shows a screenshot of a **Purchases by Vendor Detail** report:

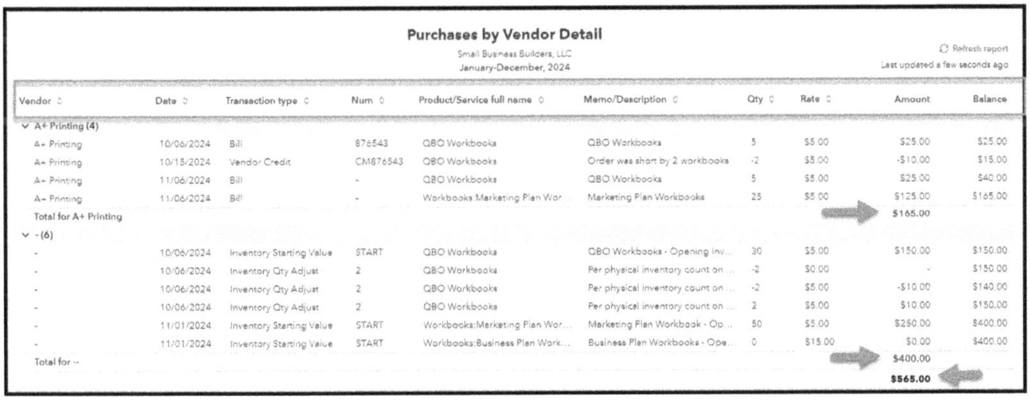

Purchases by Vendor Detail
Small Business Builders, LLC
January-December, 2024
Refresh report
Last updated a few seconds ago

Vendor	Date	Transaction type	Num	Product/Service full name	Memo/Description	Qty	Rate	Amount	Balance
A+ Printing (4)									
A+ Printing	10/06/2024	Bill	876543	QBO Workbooks	QBO Workbooks	5	$5.00	$25.00	$25.00
A+ Printing	10/15/2024	Vendor Credit	CM876543	QBO Workbooks	Order was short by 2 workbooks	-2	$5.00	-$10.00	$15.00
A+ Printing	11/06/2024	Bill	-	QBO Workbooks	QBO Workbooks	5	$5.00	$25.00	$40.00
A+ Printing	11/06/2024	Bill	-	Workbooks:Marketing Plan Wor...	Marketing Plan Workbooks	25	$5.00	$125.00	$165.00
Total for A+ Printing								$165.00	
- (6)									
-	10/06/2024	Inventory Starting Value	START	QBO Workbooks	QBO Workbooks - Opening inv...	30	$5.00	$150.00	$150.00
-	10/06/2024	Inventory Qty Adjust	2	QBO Workbooks	Per physical inventory count on ...	-2	$0.00	-	$150.00
-	10/06/2024	Inventory Qty Adjust	2	QBO Workbooks	Per physical inventory count on ...	-2	$5.00	-$10.00	$140.00
-	10/06/2024	Inventory Qty Adjust	2	QBO Workbooks	Per physical inventory count on ...	2	$5.00	$10.00	$150.00
-	11/01/2024	Inventory Starting Value	START	Workbooks:Marketing Plan Wor...	Marketing Plan Workbook - Op...	50	$5.00	$250.00	$400.00
-	11/01/2024	Inventory Starting Value	START	Workbooks:Business Plan Work...	Business Plan Workbooks - Ope...	0	$15.00	$0.00	$400.00
Total for --								$400.00	
								$565.00	

Figure 12.20: Generating a Purchases by Vendor Detail report

The **Purchases by Vendor Detail** report is grouped by vendor and includes the following information:

- Vendor
- Date of purchase
- Transaction type: bill, vendor credit, or inventory adjustment

- Transaction number
- Product/service purchased
- Memo/description
- Quantity purchased
- Cost per unit
- Total purchase amount

Physical Inventory Worksheet summary

In *Chapter 9, Closing the Books in QuickBooks Online*, we discussed the importance of taking an annual physical inventory count. We also covered how to record inventory adjustments. The **Physical Inventory Worksheet** summary provides you with the quantity on hand, the reorder point, and the quantity on order for all your products. You can also export this worksheet to Excel to facilitate the physical inventory count.

Figure 12.21 shows a screenshot of a **Physical Inventory Worksheet** summary:

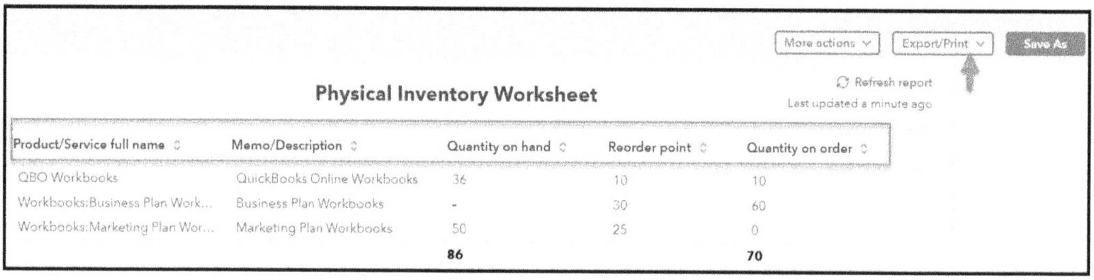

Figure 12.21: Generating a Physical Inventory Worksheet summary

The **Physical Inventory Worksheet** summary includes the following information:

- Product/service name
- Memo/description of the product
- Quantity on hand
- Reorder point
- Quantity on order, if any

You can export this report to Excel and use it for your physical inventory counts. Simply click on the **Export/Print** button shown earlier in *Figure 12.21* and follow the on-screen instructions to download the report, which should resemble the image below:

	A	B	C	D	E
1		**Physical Inventory Worksheet**			
2					
3	Product/Service full name	Memo/Description	Quantity on hand	Reorder point	Quantity on order
4	QBO Workbooks	QuickBooks Online Workbooks	36	10	10
5	Workbooks:Business Plan Workbooks	Business Plan Workbooks		30	60
6	Workbooks:Marketing Plan Workbook	Marketing Plan Workbooks	50	25	0
7			86		70

Figure 12.22: Downloading Physical Inventory Worksheet to Excel

After exporting the report to Excel, create a column next to the **Quantity on hand** column, label it **Inventory Count**, and hide the **Quantity on hand**, **Reorder point**, and **Quantity on order** columns. Print the worksheet with only the **Inventory Count** column showing and have the counters write in their counts. Plug the counts into the spreadsheet and create a column to calculate the difference. The variance calculated will be the inventory adjustments required to get your books to match what is on the shelf. As mentioned previously, please refer to *Chapter 9, Closing the Books in QuickBooks Online*, for instructions on how to record inventory adjustments.

Summary

In this chapter, we covered all aspects of managing inventory in QBO. First, we showed you how to ensure the inventory is turned on, and then we went through the process of adding products to QBO. After you have added products to QBO, you are ready to record product sales to your customers, so we showed you how to do that using an invoice. When you are running low on products and need to order, you will create a purchase order and email it to your vendor supplier. Once the products are received, you will record the inventory receipt on the bill form and pay your vendor supplier before the bill is due. Finally, we covered six reports that will help you stay on top of managing your inventory.

This is the last chapter in *Mastering QuickBooks® 2025*. It has been a pleasure to be your guide as you learn how to confidently manage your business finances. Congratulations on taking an important step in helping your business to be successful! Don't forget to head over to the online form at `https://packt.link/supplementary-content-9781836649977` where you can access the bonus/supplementary content for the following topics:

- Small business bookkeeping 101
- Business overview and cash flow reports
- Customer sales reports

- Reconciling uploaded bank and credit card transactions
- Reports Center overview
- Vendor & Expense reports
- QuickBooks Online Advanced
- QBO Shortcuts and Test Drive
- Intuit QuickBooks Certified User Exam

Join our community on Discord

Join our community's Discord space for discussions with the authors and other readers:

https://packt.link/powerusers

Part 6

Online Bonus Content

In this supplementary part of the book, we've expanded on some key topics and offered step-by-step video tutorials where I demonstrate the concepts taught in these chapters. Topics include bookkeeping fundamentals and navigating essential reports to track your business's financial health. You'll also explore advanced features, keyboard shortcuts, and tips to save time. Whether you're preparing for the QuickBooks Certified User Exam or simply looking to learn how to use new QBO tools, this online content is packed with practical insights. Access all this bonus material at https://packt.link/supplementary-content-9781836649977.

This part comprises the following chapters:

- *Chapter 13, Small-Business Bookkeeping 101*
- *Chapter 14, Customer Sales Reports in QuickBooks Online*
- *Chapter 15, Reconciling Uploaded Bank and Credit Card Transactions*
- *Chapter 16, Reports Center Overview*
- *Chapter 17, Vendor and Expenses Reports*
- *Chapter 18, Business Overview and Cash Management Tools and Reports*
- *Chapter 19, Shortcuts and Test Drive*
- *Chapter 20, Intuit QuickBooks Online Certified User Exam Objectives*
- *Chapter 21, QuickBooks Online Advanced*

‹packt›

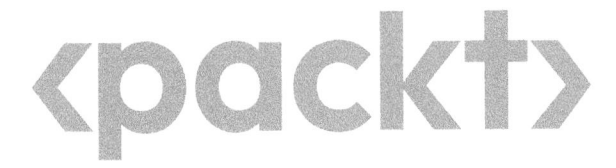

packt.com

Subscribe to our online digital library for full access to over 7,000 books and videos, as well as industry leading tools to help you plan your personal development and advance your career. For more information, please visit our website.

Why subscribe?

- Spend less time learning and more time coding with practical eBooks and Videos from over 4,000 industry professionals
- Improve your learning with Skill Plans built especially for you
- Get a free eBook or video every month
- Fully searchable for easy access to vital information
- Copy and paste, print, and bookmark content

At www.packt.com, you can also read a collection of free technical articles, sign up for a range of free newsletters, and receive exclusive discounts and offers on Packt books and eBooks.

Other Books You May Enjoy

If you enjoyed this book, you may be interested in these other books by Packt:

Learn Microsoft Power Apps

Matthew Weston, Elisa Bárcena Martín

ISBN: 9781801070645

- Understand the Power Apps ecosystem and licensing
- Take your first steps building canvas apps
- Develop apps using intermediate techniques such as the barcode scanner and GPS controls
- Explore new connectors to integrate tools across the Power Platform
- Store data in Dataverse using model-driven apps
- Discover the best practices for building apps cleanly and effectively
- Use AI for app development with AI Builder and Copilot

Mastering Microsoft Dynamics 365 Business Central

Stefano Demiliani, None Tacconi

ISBN: 9781837630646

- Developing a customized solution for Dynamics 365 Business Central
- Writing performant code following extensibility patterns
- Handling reporting, files, and printing on a cloud environment
- Handling Business Central telemetries with Azure
- Writing APIs and integrations for Dynamics 365 Business Central
- Applying DevOps and CI/CD to development projects by using GitHub
- Integrating Business Central with Power Platform
- Publishing your solutions to AppSource marketplace
- Manage Copilot capabilities and create your own generative AI copilot

Microsoft Power Apps Cookbook

Eickhel Mendoza

ISBN: 9781835465158

- Develop responsive apps with Canvas and Model-Driven frameworks
- Leverage AI-powered Copilot to accelerate your app development
- Automate business processes with Power Automate cloud flows
- Build custom UI components with the Power Apps Component Framework
- Implement data integration strategies using Dataverse
- Optimize your app for performance and smooth user experiences
- Integrate Robotic Process Automation (RPA) and Desktop flows
- Build secure, scalable, external-facing websites using Microsoft Power Pages

Packt is searching for authors like you

If you're interested in becoming an author for Packt, please visit authors.packtpub.com and apply today. We have worked with thousands of developers and tech professionals, just like you, to help them share their insight with the global tech community. You can make a general application, apply for a specific hot topic that we are recruiting an author for, or submit your own idea.

Share your thoughts

Thank you for purchasing this book from Packt Publishing—we hope you enjoyed it! Your feedback is invaluable and helps us improve and grow. Please take a moment to leave an Amazon review; it will only take a minute, but it makes a big difference for readers like you.

https://packt.link/r/1836649975

Index

Symbols

1099 contractors 262
  managing 262
  paying 265-268
  setting up 262-265
  tracking 265

1099 year-end reporting 268-274

A

accountant
  data access, providing 300-303

accountant user 103-105

accounts payable (A/P) 8, 218

Accounts payable manager role 101

apps
  benefits 107
  finding, for business 112-114
  reviewing, before connection 329
  risks 108
  using 107

B

bad debt expenses
  bad debt item, creating 312, 313
  credit memo, applying to outstanding customer invoice 315-318
  credit memo, creating 314, 315
  customer refund, issuing 318, 319
  recording 311

bank accounts
  banking transactions, importing automatically 73-77
  banking transactions, uploading from Excel or CSV file 77-85
  connecting, to QBO 73

billable roles 97
  Accounts payable manager 101
  Accounts receivable manager 100
  company administrator 102
  In house accountant 101, 102
  primary administrator 102
  reports-only user 103
  standard all access user 98-100
  standard limited customers and vendors 101
  standard no access user 100

bills
  adding 218
  capturing 243-246
  categorizing 243-246
  entering, into QBO 218-222

paying 218
paying, in QBO 225-229
uploading, to QBO 222-225
vendor credits, entering into QBO 230-233

bundle type 153

business loan
adding, to chart of accounts 306-309
payments, recording 309-311
setting up 306

C

Certified Public Accountant (CPA) 6, 103, 252

chart of accounts list
account, inactivating 67-69
account, reactivating 69
accounts, editing 64-67
accounts, merging 70-73
customizing 58
importing 62-64
new account, adding 58-62

checklist, for closing books
bank and credit card accounts, reconciling 285
closing date and password, setting 293-295
depreciation journal entries 289, 290
fixed asset purchases, adding to chart of accounts 286-289
fixed asset purchases, reviewing 286
inventory adjustments, recording 290-292
key financial reports, preparing 295-300
physical inventory 290
retained earnings, adjusting for owner/partner distributions 292
reviewing 285
year-end accrual adjustments 286

checks
printing 240-242
writing 237-239

company administrator role 102

company preferences, in QBO
advanced settings 52-54
company settings 38-40
expense settings 48-50
key information and documents 36, 37
payments settings 43
QuickBooks Checking settings 44
sale settings 44-48
setting up 38
time settings 51
usage settings 40-42

Contractor labor expense 265

credit card accounts
connecting, to QBO 85
credit card transactions, importing automatically 86-88
credit card transactions, uploading from Excel or CSV file 88-96

credit card payments
managing 206-209

credit memo
applying, to open invoice 214
creating 211-213
issuing 211
refunds, issuing to customers 211

customer lists
customers, adding manually 118-127
customers, importing 127, 128
customers, inactivating 131, 132
customers, merging 132-135
existing customers, modifying 129, 130
managing, in QBO 118

Index

customer payments
  recording 203-205

D

data access
  to accountant 300-303
delayed charges 319
  adding, to invoice 321-323
  tracking 319-321
deposit 186, 191
  for recording income 192, 193

E

electronic fund transfer (EFT) 262
Elite 256, 257
employer identification number (EIN) 38
entity types
  C-Corp 39
  Limited Liability Company (LLC) 39
  partnership 39
  S-Corp 39
  sole proprietor 38
expenses
  deleting 243
  editing 242
  voiding 243

F

federal employer identification number (FEIN) 252

I

In house accountant 101, 102
Internal Revenue Service (IRS) 251
Intuit payroll subscription
  signing up 254-258
inventory reports
  generating 357
  Inventory Valuation Detail report 359, 360
  Open Purchase Order List report 357, 358
  Physical Inventory Worksheet summary 362, 363
  Purchases by Product/Service Detail report 358
  Purchases by Vendor Detail report 361
  Sales by Product/Service Detail report 360
inventory tracking
  enabling 342-344
Inventory type 152
Inventory Valuation Detail report 359
  generating 360

J

journal entry 282
  recording 282-284
  template 284

L

line of credit
  adding, to chart of accounts 306-309
  payments, recording 309-311
  setting up 306

M

money-out transactions 217
MoneyThumb 89

N

non-billable roles 97
   accountant user 103-105
   time tracking user 103
Non-inventory type 153

O

Open Purchase Order List report 357
   generating 357

P

payments to deposit account
   payments, recording 209-211
payroll reports
   generating 258-261
   payroll tax forms and payments, filing 261
payroll setup 250
   checklist and key documents 251-253
   Intuit payroll subscription,
      signing up 254-258
Payroll Tax and Wage Summary report 261
Payroll Tax Liability report 261
Payroll Tax Payments report 261
Physical Inventory Worksheet
      summary 362, 363
point of sale (POS) system 186
products
   adding, to QBO 345-350
   ordering, from vendor suppliers 353, 354
   receiving, into inventory 355, 356

product sales
   recording, in QBO 350-352
products and services lists
   adding manually 150-157
   existing products and services,
      modifying 159
   importing 157, 158
   inactivating 160
   managing, in QuickBooks Online (QBO) 150
   merging 161-164
Purchases by Product/Service Detail
      report 358
   generating 358
Purchases by Vendor Detail report 361
   generating 361

Q

QBO account
   creating 10-21
QBO editions
   Advanced plan 9, 10
   Essentials plan 8
   exploring 4-6
   features 6, 7
   Plus plan 8
   selecting 7, 8
   Simple Start plan 8
QBO Mobile app
   downloading 107
QBO user interface
   navigation 21
   dashboards 22-28
   icons 29, 30
   left navigation menu 22-28
   menus 30-33

Index

QuickBooks 4
QuickBooks App Center 108
  key areas 112
  overview 108-110
QuickBooks Online (QBO) 3, 107, 117, 218
  used, for managing customer lists 118
  used, for managing products and services lists 150
  vendor lists, managing 135
  vendors, adding manually 138
QuickBooks Time (QB Time) 275
  Elite plan 276
  features 276
  Premium plan 276

R

receipts
  capturing 243-246
  categorizing 243-246
recurring expenses
  managing 233-237
reports only role 103

S

Sales by Product/Service Detail report 360
  generating 361
sales channel connection
  advantages 330
  disadvantages 331
  performing 332-339
sales forms 186
  income, recording with deposit 191-194
  income, recording with sales invoice 194-198
  income, recording with sales receipt 186-190

sales invoice 186, 194
  Intuit video tutorial 198
  recording 195-198
sales receipt 186
  Intuit video tutorial 190
  journal entry, recording 190
  recording 186-189
sales tax
  charging 170
  invoice, creating 177-180
  reports 180-182
  setting up 170-176
sales templates
  customizing 198-202
  Intuit video tutorial 202
service type 153
standard all access role 98-100
standard limited customers and vendors role 101
standard no access role 100, 101
stock-keeping unit (SKU) 154

T

track time only role 103
trial balance report 296

U

users
  billable roles 97
  non-billable roles 97
users access 97
  user privileges, editing 106

V

vendor lists
 adding manually 136-142
 existing vendors, modifying 143-145
 managing, in QBO 135
 vendors, importing 142, 143
 vendors, inactivating 145, 146
 vendors, merging 146-150

W

Wage and Tax Statement 269

Download the free PDF and supplementary content

Thanks for purchasing this book!

Do you like to read on the go but are unable to carry your print books everywhere?

Is your eBook purchase not compatible with the device of your choice?

Don't worry, now with every Packt book you get a DRM-free PDF version of that book at no cost.

Read anywhere, any place, on any device. Search, copy, and paste code from your favorite technical books directly into your application.

Additionally, with this book you get access to supplementary/bonus content for you to learn more about QuickBooks. You can use this to add on to your learning journey on top of what you have in the book.

The perks don't stop there, you can get exclusive access to discounts, newsletters, and great free content in your inbox daily.

Follow these simple steps to get the benefits:

1. Scan the QR code or visit the link below:

   https://packt.link/supplementary-content-9781836649977

2. Submit your proof of purchase.
3. Submit your book code. You can find the code on page no. 102 of the book.
4. That's it! We'll send your free PDF, supplementary content, and other benefits to your email directly.